W9-DBI-905

WITHDRAWN

ROGER QUILTER

His Life and Music

Quilter, portrait by Gabelli (by courtesy of the Grainger Museum, University of Melbourne)

ROGER QUILTER

His Life and Music

Valerie Langfield

THE BOYDELL PRESS

First published 2002
The Boydell Press, Woodbridge
Reprinted 2002

ISBN 0 85115 871 4

The Boydell Press is an imprint of Boydell & Brewer Ltd
PO Box 9, Woodbridge, Suffolk IP12 3DF, UK
and of Boydell & Brewer Inc.
PO Box 41026, Rochester, NY 14604–4126, USA
website: www.boydell.co.uk

A catalogue record for this book is available
from the British Library

Library of Congress Cataloging-in-Publication Data
Langfield, Valerie, 1951–
   Roger Quilter: his life and music/Valerie Langfield.
      p. cm.
'Catalogue of works': p.
Includes discography (p.), bibliographical references (p.),
and index.
   ISBN 0–85115–871–4 (alk. paper)
   1. Quilter, Roger, 1877–1953.   2. Composers – England – Biography.
I. Title.
   ML410.Q5 L36 2002
782.4′3′092 – dc21   2002008052

Typeset by Joshua Associates Ltd, Oxford
Printed in Great Britain by
St Edmundsbury Press Ltd, Bury St Edmunds, Suffolk

To my family
and the memory of my mother

Contents

Preface

The name of Roger Quilter is one I have known since my childhood; I first came across his music when I heard his *Children's Overture* at a Robert Mayer concert, at the Royal Festival Hall in London. I was so taken with it that I persuaded my father to buy me the record, which I still have, but it was rather later that I came to know the songs, when as a singing student at the Guildhall School of Music and Drama, I was introduced to them in the English Song class of Michael Pilkington. So when, one day in May 1996, John Turner, recorder-player extraordinaire, happened to say to me, 'And of course, you realise there's no biography of Roger Quilter, don't you?', he started me on a splendid adventure, during the course of which I have met many wonderful people, and have been much enriched by their friendship and kindness.

Quilter was a shy man, perpetually ill, plagued by his wealth, generous, humanitarian and a loyal friend. His taste in all things was exquisite. In comfortable company, he could relax, and he had a quirky sense of humour – he professed to dislike train journeys in Germany, on account of being afraid of the 'Night Rouchers', an allusion to the signs on the windows prohibiting smoking: 'Nicht Rauchen'. In his days as a student at the Frankfurt Conservatory, he would recite the Bible to his friend Percy Grainger, and on one occasion as he was about to go on stage to accompany a singer, he said to her, quoting from *As You Like It*, 'Let us clap into it roundly without any hawking and spitting!', expecting her to maintain some sort of dignity as she continued on to the platform. He was apparently rather a good mimic, too.

He had a superb lyrical gift – his songs are amongst the finest anywhere – but he has been belittled both for writing only miniatures, and also for writing light music. However, he knew where his strengths lay, and he put equal effort into all his work; his light music is as perfect in its theatre and concert environment as his songs are perfect in the drawing room. Those songs have remained firmly in the repertoire for decades, and rightly so. Some are showpieces, some are much more intimate; he knew what he wanted to say, how best to say it, and he did so with complete integrity. Pervading them all is a delicate wistfulness, that continues to haunt long after the song itself is ended.

Quilter's last years were marred by tragedies, and at the time of his death it was felt that the final details of his life were best left to settle. Fifty years later, it is possible to put those years, and the rest of his life, into perspective. The freedom to do so has given me an extraordinary task: those who knew him wanted to talk about him, and blind alleys of the 1950s were now avenues of exploration. As a result I have been able to uncover things that were simply not accessible before. I have on the one hand been constantly amazed at the generosity of people who knew him, and on the other, intrigued that in their voices, even their written voices, there is a smile at the memory of a man whom they loved. They have all been delighted that someone was telling his story. I have tried to make that story a fair one, and I have tried to do him justice.

Illustrations

Acknowledgements

First, a brief comment to explain how I have approached discussion of the songs; the reader may find their order a little unexpected. They are not in compositional order, but begin with the early songs, in which Quilter established his song-style, and then go on to the songs he wrote to texts by Elizabethan, Jacobean and Cavalier poets, and Blake. In the second song chapter, I discuss songs with words by poets from later times. On the whole, the poets are thus in their own date order, but I have adjusted this where it seemed to make more sense to keep the songs of a set together, rather than determinedly keep to the chronological poet date and split them. The various choruses are included amongst the solo songs, since it enables a more coherent approach to Quilter's settings of poets.

Many people have contributed to making this book possible. Some, in particular, have given me help over and above any conceivable call of duty, and I am especially delighted to acknowledge the continuous and uncomplaining help from Leslie East, who from the start was extraordinarily generous in allowing me access to manuscripts and papers from the archive of his uncle, Leslie Woodgate, Quilter's personal secretary in the 1920s. The book would have been utterly impossible without his support. I am extremely grateful to Stephen Banfield, Elgar Professor at the University of Birmingham, who was similarly generous in giving me access to all his earlier research on Quilter; his supervision of my Ph.D. studies has been critically invaluable. My thanks to Dr Trevor Hold, who wrote the excellent monograph on Quilter's songs, for his help and unwavering interest; to Stephen Lloyd who, when I telephoned him out of the blue one Sunday afternoon, was full of vital knowledge on where to seek further sources of information; and to Roger Raphael, son of Mark Raphael, Quilter's main singer after the death of Gervase Elwes. Roger Raphael's personal knowledge of Quilter was crucial and I am deeply saddened that he died before he was able to see the book. At a very late stage in my research, I was very fortunate to be able to have full access to the research on Quilter, undertaken some years ago by a former pupil of Mark Raphael, Jerry Laurie, who had essential and extensive information for which I am inestimably grateful.

Alessandro Servadei, formerly Deputy Curator of the Grainger Museum, University of Melbourne, enabled access to the substantial archive of letters between Quilter and his friend Percy Grainger; to him my grateful thanks. Stephen Gard, Australian writer and composer, made invaluable, detailed, apposite and very necessary comments on much of the manuscript; we are still friends, despite, or because of, his Antipodean frankness. My thanks to Bruce Phillips, my editor at Boydell and Brewer, who has consistently made the right comments and given the right encouragement at exactly the right time, and to Ruth Conti and Professor James Thayne Covert, who began as colleagues from whom I sought information and who have become dear friends, and encouraged me throughout. My thanks to Robert S. Clarke, Literary Executor of the Quilter Estate, who has been helpful and supportive throughout, and finally my thanks to John Turner, who started it all off.

If I were to describe how each of the people named below has helped me, it would double the size of the book. All have contributed to the jigsaw; those who have been of special help know who they are, and I have been able to elaborate a little in various footnotes. I offer my apologies to any whom I have omitted.

David Ades (Robert Farnon Society), Martin Anderson, Robert Anderson, Frank Andrews, E. V. Bailey (Cousans Organ Builders), Tessa Ballard, Elizabeth Bankes-Jones, Philip Barker, Rob Barnett (British Music Society), Mrs Patrick Barr, Bernard Barrell, Valerie Baulard, Gordon Beavington, Robert Beckhard, Harriet Bennett, Sir Richard Rodney Bennett, the late Christine Bernard, Roger Bevington, Doris Bevington, John Bird, the late John Bishop (Thames Publishing), the late James Blades, Dr Brian Blood, Anthony Boden, Lord Brabourne and Countess Mountbatten of Burma, John Brackenbury, Malcolm Brackenbury, Martin Brackenbury, Diana Brett, Gordon Brookes, Dr Roger Buckley, Professor Dr Peter Cahn, Professor Sir Frank Callaway, John Cameron, Dr Lionel Carley, George Carr, David Cheshire (Theatre Trust), Alan Clegg, Patricia Cleveland-Peck, Tamara Coates, Frank Colleran (Areen Design Services), John Coulter, Caroline Crawshaw (Royal Northern College of Music), Mrs Hugh Creighton, Anne-Cécile de Bruyne, Sheila Dodwell, Marguerite Dolmetsch, Brian Doyle, Gervase Elwes, the late Captain Jeremy Elwes, Professor William Everett, Christopher Fifield, Carl Flesch, Lewis Foreman, Rocky Frisco, Roger Frith, Edith Froebel, Mary Froebel, Rev. John Gates, Jean Geil, Valerie Gifford, Brian Glanvill, Mark Glanville, Jo Gosney, Jeffrey Green, Professor David Greer, the late Crystal Hale, George Hammond, Graham Hatton, Anne Hay, Afrika Hayes, Sarah Hewitt, Joseph Horovitz, Stephen Hough, Basil Howitt, Dr David Russell Hulme, Michael Hurd, Michael Imison, Stuart Jenkins, Katherine Jessel, Ewald Junge, Ernest Kaye, Pamela Kingsford, Florence Woodgate Konczewska, Dr Tony Kushner, Ian Lace, Erika Lambe, Nick Landau, Jerry Laurie, Martin Lee-Browne, Maria Lidka, Davidia Ling, Stephen Lloyd, Jeffrey Lockett, Derek and Christina Lockwood, Dr Louise London, Richard Macnutt, Bill Marsh (Delius Society of America), Andrew Mayes, Paddy McGuigan, Peter Melville-Smith (Eton College), Michael Meredith (Eton College), David Messum, Robin Miller, John Mitchell, Dr William Mitchell, Professor Michael Musgrave, Robin Nash, Charles Notcutt, Felicity Oglethorpe, Arthur Oldham, Beth Olsen (Boston Ballet), Leo Ornstein, Severo Ornstein, Barry Ould (Grainger Society), David Paramor, Jeremy Park, Dr Lynn Parker, Brian Parkhurst, Professor Ian Parrott, Sir Philip Pauncefort-

Duncombe, Dr Lynda Payne, Meg Peacocke, Bruce Phillips, Cindy Phillips, Professor Henry Phillips, the late Thomas Pitfield, Andrew Plant, Dr Steven Plunkett, Irene Porter, Alan Quilter, Sir Anthony Quilter, Graham Quilter, Margery, Lady Quilter, David Tudway Quilter, Susan Radovsky (University of Harvard), Onyx and Dennis Ralph, Irene Raphael, Dr Barbara Reynolds, Howard Rogerson, Suzanne da Rosa, Carole Rosen, Gordon Rumson, Desmond Scott, Philip Scowcroft, Dinah Sheridan, Stephen Shutt, Gail Sieveking, Nora Sirbaugh, Professor Barry Smith, Dr David Steel, Sue Stewart, Tessa Sutcliffe, Wendy Symington, Jane Szilvassy, Diana Tennant, Daniel Thiery, Professor R. K. R. Thornton, Candida Tobin, Niels Toettcher and Ann Alexander (Bawdsey College), Claire Tomalin, Ernest Tomlinson (The Light Music Society, and the Library of Light Orchestral Music), Fred Tomlinson (Peter Warlock Society), Hilary Tunbridge, Professor David Tunley, Richard Valentine (Warlock Society), Hugo Vickers, Percy Vickery, Laura Wakinshaw, Jacy Wall, Jack Watling, Allen Williams, John Wilson, Peter Wilton, Harry Winstanley, Rupert Withers, Laura Wortley, Dr Percy Young, Philip Ziegler.

It is a pleasure to acknowledge the libraries and archives whose resources I have used (again, with apologies to any I have omitted): Allerton Park Conference Center, University of Illinois at Urbana-Champaign; Archives of American Art, Smithsonian Institution (Judy Throm, Head of Reference); Belstead House, Ipswich; The Bodleian Library, University of Oxford; Boosey & Hawkes (Ian Julier, Bruce Macrae, Colin Dunn); BBC Written Archives Centre, Caversham Park, Reading (Susan Knowles); The British Library (Chris Banks, Roger Evans, Robert Parker); Britten-Pears Library, Aldeburgh (Helen Risdon, Readers' Assistant); Brookens Library, University of Illinois at Springfield (Thomas J. Wood); Center for Black Music Research, Columbia College Chicago (Suzanne Flandreau); Cheadle Hulme Public Library, Stockport Library and Information Service; Christ Church, University of Oxford (Judith Curthoys, Archivist); Church of Latter Day Saints, Wythenshawe; The Court of Protection (Master Denzil Lush); Derbyshire Record Offices, Buxton and Matlock; Eton College, Windsor; Samuel French, London; Grainger Museum Collection, University of Melbourne, Australia (Amelia Peachment); Grenadier Guards, Regimental Headquarters (Captain Mason); Hampshire County Archives; Imperial War Museum (Colin Bruce); Institute of Chartered Accountants (Vivienne Court); Archive Centre, King's College, Cambridge (Dr Rosalind Moad); Lancashire County Library, Preston; Lewes Public Library, Sussex; Lincolnshire County Archives; Manchester Central Library (Henry Watson and Social Sciences Libraries); Mander and Mitchenson Theatre Collection (Donna Percival); Musicians' Benevolent Fund (Helen Faulkner); The Trustees of the National Library of Scotland (Kenneth Dunn, Manuscripts Division); National Portrait Gallery; National Sound Archive (Timothy Day); National Tropical Gardens, Hawaii (Rick Hanna); Northampton County Archives; Rare Book & Manuscript Library, University of Pennsylvania (Dr Nancy M. Shawcross); Royal Academy of Music, London (Kathryn Adamson); Royal College of Music, London (Paul Collen, Oliver Davies, Dr Peter Horton);

Royal Military School of Music, Kneller Hall (James Meikle); Royal Philharmonic Society (Arthur Searle, Honorary Librarian); St Andrew's Hospital, Northampton (Sandra Neale); St Paul's Cathedral Library (Jo Wisdom); Savile Club, London (Tia O'Rourke); Simon Wiesenthal Centre, Paris; The Sorabji Archive (Alistair Hinton); Stainer & Bell (Carol Wakefield); Suffolk County Archives, Ipswich; Sussex County Archives (Brighton Record Office); Theatre Collection, University of Bristol (Sarah Cuthill); The Theatre Museum, Victoria and Albert Museum (Dr Janet Birkett); University Library, Cambridge (Godfrey Waller, Superintendent, Music Manuscripts Collection); W.A.T.C.H. (Writers Artists & Their Copyright Holders) and Location Register, Research Projects Office, University of Reading Library (Dr David Sutton, Director of Research Projects); Wakefield Deeds Registry; Wellcome Library for the History & Understanding of Medicine, London (Sue Gold); Wigmore Hall, London (Paula Best); The William Ready Division of Archives and Research Collections, McMaster University Library, Hamilton, Canada (Dr Kathleen Garay, Professor Paul Rapoport); Yad Vashem, Jerusalem.

I descended upon many friends, demanding food, lodging and good company and was not left wanting: the Caswells, Felicity Clark, Peter and Mary Davies, Sheila Dodwell, Duncan and Glenda Gillies, Jen Jousiffe and Ray Sidaway, Davidia Ling, Tony and Deborah Milledge, and Ruth and John-David Yule. They tolerated totally one-sided conversations: may they remain my friends.

I acknowledge with frank gratitude the financial assistance given to me by the Hinrichsen Foundation, the Ida Carroll Trust and the Vaughan Williams Trust.

I am grateful to the following for allowing the use of literary copyright material: the Archives of American Art, the BBC Written Archives Centre, the Grainger Museum Collection (University of Melbourne), the Quilter Estate and other private archives. I have been unable to trace the copyright owners of the estates of A. C. Landsberg, Edward Dent and John Irvine.

The music samples are reproduced by kind permission of the following publishers (the music is by Quilter except where otherwise indicated):

Boosey and Hawkes Music Publishers Ltd: 7.12 ('At Close of Day'), 7.13 ('The Answer'), 7.14 ('Come Away, Death'), 7.15 and 7.16 ('O Mistress Mine'), 7.17 ('It was a Lover and His Lass'), 7.19 ('What Shall He Have that Killed the Deer?'), 7.20 ('Orpheus with His Lute'), 7.21a ('Amaryllis at the Fountain'), 7.21b, 7.42 and 7.43 (*To Julia*, Prelude), 7.22 ('The Fuchsia Tree'), 7.25 ('Weep You No More'), 7.26 ('My Life's Delight'), 7.27a and 7.27b ('The Faithless Shepherdess'), 7.28 and 7.29 ('Brown is My Love'), 7.30 and 7.31 ('By a Fountainside'), 7.33 ('Fair House of Joy'), 7.36 ('To Daffodils'), 7.37 ('To the Virgins'), 7.41a ('I Dare Not Ask a Kiss'), 7.41b ('Take, O Take'), 7.44 and 7.45 (*To Julia*, 'The Night Piece'), 7.46 (*To Julia*, 'Julia's Hair'), 7.48a ('Dream Valley'), 7.49 ('The Wild Flower's Song'), 8.1 ('Arab Love Song'), 8.2b, 8.2c and 8.3 ('I Arise'), 8.7 ('Now Sleeps the Crimson Petal'), 8.9 ('Fill a Glass'), 8.10 and 11.5a ('A Last Year's Rose'), 8.11a, 8.11b and 8.17b ('Autumn Evening'), 8.16 ('A Coronal'), 8.17a ('Passing Dreams'), 8.19a (Gurney, 'I Will Go with My Father'), 8.20, 8.21 and 9.4c ('Freedom'), 8.22 and 8.23d ('L'Amour de Moy'),

8.24a, 8.24b, 8.24c, 8.25a, 8.25b and 8.25c ('Drink to Me Only'), 8.26 ('Charlie is My Darling'), 8.27 ('The Passing Bell'), 9.4b ('Non Nobis, Domine'), 10.2a (Study, Op. 4, no. 2), 10.3a ('Summer Evening', Op. 16, no. 2), 10.4 and 10.5b ('At a Country Fair', Op. 16, no. 3), 10.6 ('In a Gondola', Op. 19, no. 1), 10.7 ('Goblins', Op. 27, no. 2), 10.13a (*As You Like It*, 'Shepherd's Holiday'), 10.13b ('Blow, Blow, Thou Winter Wind'), 10.14 (*As You Like It*, 'Evening in the Forest'), 10.15 (*As You Like It*, 'Country Dance')

J. Curwen & Sons Ltd., 8/9 Frith Street, London W1D 3JB, England: 8.5 ('Music')

Éditions Salabert: 8.31 (Poulenc, 'C.')

Elkin & Co. Ltd., 8/9 Frith Street, London W1D 3JB, England: 7.4b ('Come Back!'), 7.5b ('A Secret'), 7.6a ('Lean Opening Blossom'), 7.6b ('Come Tender Bud'), 7.7a ('Where'er the Sun Doth Glow'), 7.7b ('The Glow of Summer Sun'), 7.8a and 7.9a ('The Dazzling Sun is Glistening'), 7.8b and 7.9b ('The Golden Sunlight's Glory'), 7.10b and 7.11b ('My Heart Adorned With Thee'), 8.14 ('Through the Sunny Garden'), 8.19b ('I Will Go with My Father')

Copyright for *Where the Rainbow Ends* is held by Elkin & Co. Ltd., and administered jointly by Music Sales, London W1D 3JB and EMI Music Publishing, London WC2 0QY: 9.1 and 11.4b (*Rainbow*, 'Rosamund'), 9.2 (*Rainbow*, 'Slumber Song'), 9.3 (*Rainbow*, Genie Music'), 9.4a (*Rainbow*, 'St. George'), 9.5 (*Rainbow*, 'Dragon King's motif'), 9.6b and 9.7a (*Rainbow*, 'Fairy Ballet'), 9.8 (*Rainbow*, 'Will-o'-the-Wisp'), 9.9 (*Rainbow*, 'Dance of the Mischievous Elves'), 9.10b (*Rainbow*, 'Dance of the Spirit of the Lake'), 9.11 (*Rainbow*, 'Dance of the Moon Fairies'), 9.12 (*Rainbow*, 'Fairy Frolic'), 9.13a (*Rainbow*, 'Entry of the Dragons')

Forsyth Brothers Ltd, 126 Deansgate, Manchester M3 2GR: 7.1a and 7.1b ('The Sea-Bird'), 7.2a and 7.2b ('Moonlight'), 7.3a and 7.3b ('By the Sea'), 7.38 ('Cupid'), 7.39 and 7.40 ('A Dirge')

International Music Publications Ltd: 7.24 ('The Pretty Birds Do Sing'), 7.35 and 11.7a ('Go, Lovely Rose'), 7.47a ('Tulips', solo song), 7.47b ('Tulips', partsong), 8.12 ('Foreign Children'), 8.13 ('Windy Nights'), 8.18 ('Dancing on the Green'), 8.20b (Coates, 'Dam Busters March'), 8.28a and 8.28b ('Daisies after Rain'), 8.30a, 8.30b, 8.30c, 8.30d, 8.30e and 8.30f ('Drooping Wings'), 10.16 (*The Rake*, 'Dance at the Feast'), 10.17 (*The Rake*, 'The Frolicsome Friend'), 10.18a and 10.18b (*The Rake*, 'Allurement'), 11.1a (*Love at the Inn*, 'Love Calls'), 11.1b (German, *Tom Jones*, 'Waltz Song'), 11.2b (*Love at the Inn*, 'Happy Birthday'), 11.3 and 11.4a (*Love at the Inn*, 'If Love Should Pass Me By'), 11.5b (*Love at the Inn*, 'Little Moth'), 11.7b (*Love at the Inn*, 'The Patch'), 11.8 (*Love at the Inn*, 'What Can Compare'), 11.9 (*Love at the Inn*, 'Mademoiselles and English Maids'), 11.10 (*Love at the Inn*, 'When Love is Ended'), 11.11a (*Love at the Inn*, Act 2 Finale)

Oxford University Press: 7.48b (Vaughan Williams, 'Infant Joy')

The Trustee of the Roger Quilter Estate: 7.5a ('A Secret'), 7.10a and 7.11a ('My Heart Adorned with Thee'), 7.23 ('Good Morrow, 'tis St Valentine's Day'), 8.2a ('I Arise'), 8.4 ('Music and Moonlight'), 8.6 ('Far, Far Away'), 8.8 ('Omar

Khayām'), 8.15 ('You've Money to Spend'), 8.23a, 8.23b and 8.23c ('L'Amour de Moy', various versions), 8.29 ('I Got a Robe'), 9.14 (*Rainbow* ('Fight'), 10.1a and 10.1b (Study, Op. 4, no. 1), 10.5a ('At a Country Fair', Op. 16, no. 3), 10.8, 10.9 and 10.10 (*Serenade*, first movement), 10.11 (*Serenade*, second movement), 10.12 (*Serenade*, third movement), 11.6a and 11.6b (*Julia*, 'A Ribbon Here')

The illustrations are reproduced by courtesy of John Brackenbury, Mrs Hugh Creighton, Leslie East, Roger Frith, the Grainger Museum Collection (University of Melbourne), Jenny Letton (administered by Composer Prints Ltd.), Robin Miller, the National Portrait Gallery (London), Dr Steven Plunkett, David Tudway Quilter, Mrs Irene Raphael, Mrs Jane Szilvassy, the Tate Gallery (London) and Percy Vickery.

My apologies to any people or bodies – literary, musical or illustrative – whose copyright I may have inadvertently infringed; I shall endeavour to rectify that situation in any future editions.

Finally, heartfelt thanks are due to my family: to my father, Frank Langfield, who – amongst other things – transcribed most of the Grainger correspondence for me, and was always interested when I wanted to talk about the research, and to my husband Dave, and sons Roland and Erik Le Good, who put up with my physical presence but my spiritual absence for so long, and hardly complained at all.

Valerie Langfield
Stockport, August 2001

Abbreviations

AAA   Archives of American Art, Smithsonian Institution
BL   British Library, London
GM   Grainger Museum Collection, University of Melbourne
NLS   National Library of Scotland, Edinburgh
RCM   Royal College of Music, London
WAC BBC Written Archives Centre, Caversham Park, Reading

1

Family Background and Frankfurt, to 1901

At the end of the road, beyond Felixstowe in Suffolk, is Felixstowe Ferry, a picturesque collection of houses and boats. A ferry still runs from there to the other side of the river Deben, and the twisting road leads back to the village of Bawdsey, then Alderton and eventually back to Woodbridge. Close to the jetty on the Bawdsey side of the ferry is a large entrance; as one looks up, mature trees obscure the view, but behind them is Bawdsey Manor, the magnificently absurd mansion built by William Cuthbert Quilter, Roger Quilter's father, in a breathtakingly unmatched mixture of styles.

The paternal side of the Quilter family was of Suffolk stock, going back possibly to Huguenot times, and William Cuthbert Quilter returned to those haunts when he bought the Bawdsey estate, around the little village of Bawdsey on the other side of the river Deben from Felixstowe, in July 1883. The purchase of the land brought with it a lay rectorship and lordship of the manor, which added to the charms of the area.[1]

The original manor house lay north-west of Bawdsey village; he ignored that, demolished the seventy-year-old Martello tower and battery on the high ground by the river mouth, and in their place built a holiday home at a cost of £4,000. The public road ran past the tower, and thus close to his new home, so he blithely rerouted it by the marshy ground alongside the river. But it was to be another ten years before Bawdsey Manor became the main family home.

William Cuthbert's father, William Quilter, was an accountant; he was born in 1808, the fourth and youngest son of Samuel Sacker Quilter, of Walton, Felixstowe. For about twenty-five years in the mid-nineteenth century he lived in Knight's Hill, Lower Norwood, two miles or so from Sydenham, to the south-east of London, and he had a house in Norfolk Street, Park Lane, London.

In Sydenham itself lived John Wheeley Bevington, born in 1816. He described himself as a gentleman and came of a wealthy Quaker family, tradesmen who had made their money with a successful leather business in Bermondsey; his father, Henry Bevington, left an estate of £18,000 in 1850. John Wheeley Bevington lived in Worcester in the 1840s, where he and his wife Eliza produced three children, Eliza Jane, Mary Ann and Timothy; they were comfortably

---

[1] William Cuthbert Quilter took advantage of the low land prices of the 1880s – a period of great agricultural depression – to buy the estate (of nearly 491 acres) at auction. He paid £22,600. So *The Times* reports, on 18 July 1883. The estate may have been previously owned by the late J. G. Sheppard, of Campsea Ashe.

well-off, with a moderately military background, though probably no more than was usual for the time. For a time, John Bevington's daughter Mary Ann was romantically linked with an unidentified European Jew, and she stayed in contact with him for many years. She did not marry him, however; on 7 May 1867, at St Bartholomew's Church, Westwood Hill, Sydenham, she married William Cuthbert Quilter.[2]

Sydenham was a sought-after area, but it was sparsely populated until the Crystal Palace was rebuilt there during 1852–4. The Palace had first been erected in Hyde Park for the Great Exhibition of 1851 and one of the reasons for the choice of permanent site was the excellent railway access. It became home to innumerable concerts: choirs, orchestras and audiences massed there in their thousands for the Triennial Handel Festivals and a significant musical culture grew up around it, bringing an enormous quantity of music to ordinary working people and centring particularly upon the Saturday Concerts (logically called so because they were held on Saturdays).[3] These were conducted by Sir August Manns who premièred a number of major works there; they were a vital part of the Crystal Palace scene for several decades and were absorbed into the local fabric.[4] It all came to a spectacular end when the Palace burnt down in 1936.

A stratum of society with money and a strong interest in the musical and literary arts was attracted to the area and lived largely in Sydenham and Norwood: George Grove, the first editor of the *Dictionary of Music and Musicians*, and Secretary to the Crystal Palace Society from May 1852, lived there until his death in 1900, first at 1 Church Meadow (now 14 Westwood Hill) and then at a house in Sydenham Road, Lower Sydenham. The renowned engineer John Scott Russell lived at Westwood Lodge; his daughters Louise and Rachel became known later for their liaisons with Sir Arthur Sullivan who was a frequent visitor both to the Scott Russells and also to George Grove. The von Glehn family lived at Peak Hill Lodge, half a mile away from Grove's home; Grove was devoted to one of the von Glehn daughters, Mary Emilie, called Mimi, and he used to call on the family regularly on his way home from the Crystal Palace.

The Quilters were part of this circle and in 1881 Grove travelled to Italy on holiday with one of them.[5] It is by no means certain which Quilter this was, though it is likely to have been either William Quilter, or his youngest son Harry. Harry, born in 1851, would have been a young companion for Grove,

---

[2] Her second name is spelt variously with or without an 'e'. Her wedding certificate, Roger's birth certificate and the 1881 census spell it without, but her tombstone shows it with, as does her husband's will. Her birth year is shown on the tombstone as 1843, although she was born in 1842.

[3] See Michael Musgrave, *The Musical Life of the Crystal Palace* (Cambridge, 1995), and H. Saxe Wyndham, *August Manns and the Saturday Concerts* (London, 1909).

[4] A story by Alec Nelson called 'The Deaf Musician', published in Volume 1 of the New Series of the *Strand Musical Magazine* in around 1898, was set in the environs of a Saturday Concert and noted that the concerts started at 3 o'clock, 'as everyone knows'.

[5] Charles L. Graves, *The Life and Letters of Sir George Grove* (London, 1903), p. 264.

but he had travelled widely, especially in Italy, and though in 1881 he was busy working in London, he had contributed pieces for *Macmillan's Magazine*, and was certainly well acquainted with Grove. William Quilter the father, for his part, was only twelve years older than Grove; he had retired from accountancy and had the leisure and money to travel. Over many years he had built up a substantial art collection, he had a reputation as a pleasant and genial man, and living so near, he had had ample opportunity to strike up a long and close acquaintance with Grove.

William Cuthbert Quilter's first family home was in Beddington Lane, Beddington, in Surrey. His first two children were born here: Maude Marian on 18 February 1868 and Norah Blanche in July 1870; his third child Evelyn, who died on 5 September 1872 aged ten months, may have been born there too. He had ambitions to improve his position in society, and when his father-in-law moved down to Brunswick Terrace in Hove in the fashionable part of Brighton, Sussex, he and his wife followed him, probably in 1873,[6] a little while after the birth of their first son, William Eley Cuthbert (known in the family as Eley, and named after his uncle Charles Eley, of the family of gun cartridge makers), on 17 July, in Streatham.

The house at 4 Brunswick Square was large.[7] William Cuthbert kept a full complement of servants[8] and the last four children were born there: John Arnold Cuthbert (called Arnie) on 29 January 1875, Roger Cuthbert on 1 November 1877 (his mother was dilatory about registering his existence, not doing so until the following March), Percival Cuthbert (called Percy) on 5 February 1879, and finally Eustace Cuthbert on 15 February 1881.

Mary always said she wanted six sons all over six feet tall. She nearly made it: she produced five and they were all tall, with Arnie in the lead at six feet seven inches. The whole family turned out to be hale and hearty, except for Roger, who was quiet and rather delicate; consequently, his mother was always very protective of him. All his life, Roger Quilter retained a love for the southern parts of England, stemming from his early years there.

In 1882 the family moved to Suffolk. For a season, they leased Broke Hall, near the river Orwell, and then moved into Hintlesham Hall, which they leased from Colonel Anstruther for the next ten years. It still stands, a beautiful Elizabethan house, with a Georgian façade and a splendid pond. Hintlesham served as an extremely useful base from which William Cuthbert could conduct his successful campaign to become a Member of Parliament: he stood as a

---

[6] At this point William Cuthbert Quilter left the 4th Surrey Rifles, which he had commanded, having been an active volunteer in the home counties for some years (*Suffolk County Handbook*, 1912, p. 462).

[7] Edward Carpenter, the writer, and pioneer in the campaign for equal rights for homosexuals, was born at 45 Brunswick Square in 1844, and his mother died there on 25 January 1881; for what it is worth, there is no evidence of any contact between the families, though there was clearly an overlap of residency, at least between the Quilters and Edward Carpenter's mother.

[8] Butler, footman, nurse, cook, lady's maid, under-nurse, housemaid, kitchen maid and under-housemaid (1881 census).

Liberal for the Sudbury division of Suffolk and was elected in December 1885 by a substantial majority; he was re-elected as a Liberal Unionist in July 1886 and held the seat until the general Unionist downfall of 1906. He spoke seldom in the House of Commons, perhaps because he had a slight speech impediment,[9] and when he did speak it was, endearingly, almost always as a proponent of the merits of pure beer. He established a local brewery, at Melton, to support the cause.

In 1885, he founded the stockbroking firm of Quilter, Balfour and Co.; he was in at the beginning of the development of the telephone, and as one of the founders of the National Telephone Company, registered four years before in 1881, made a fortune to add to the useful financial start given him by his father William. During his lifetime, William gave him over £28,000, and on his death in 1888 bequeathed him a further amount to make it up to a round £100,000; the estate was valued at nearly £600,000. When William Cuthbert died in 1911, he owned 8,000 acres of land in Suffolk and his estate was valued at just under a million and a quarter pounds – about seventy million pounds in today's prices – more than enough to provide adequately for his widow and children.

He cultivated a reputation as a patriarch of local society. As well as brewing beer, he bred Suffolk heavy horses: the Bawdsey stud was renowned, winning hundreds of prizes, and he was life-president of the Suffolk Horse Society. His other main interest was yachting. He was Vice-Commodore of the Harwich Yacht Club from 1875 to 1909 and owned a number of boats over the years.[10] House guests to Bawdsey Manor would usually travel by train to Woodbridge, at the head of the river Deben, where they would be met with the family yacht and ferried down river. One of his chief moments of glory in the yachting field was when he organised the Bremerhaven to Felixstowe race under the patronage of the German Emperor in 1908.[11] The Kaiser stayed at Bawdsey Manor on at least one occasion, supporting assertions that William Cuthbert had strong links with Germany.

The sea made valiant attempts to encroach upon William Cuthbert Quilter's land, but like some latter-day but more effective Canute, he commanded it to go back by building sea defences, at a cost of £25,000. He installed a ferry[12] and

---

[9] A. T. C. Pratt, *People of the Period* (1897).

[10] Amongst them were two steam yachts, the *Firefly* and the 43-ton *Peridot*. He bought the *Peridot* in 1894 and often moored it near the Houses of Parliament, for use as and when required. His first boat was a schooner, formerly owned by Edward Fitzgerald who famously translated the *Rubaiyat of Omar Khayyam*; at that time it was named *Scandal*, though Fitzgerald nicknamed her *Gossip*, apparently after the staple product of Woodbridge. Quilter renamed her *Sapphire*, and sailed her over many years. Other boats followed, including the 165-ton schooner *Zoe* which he made his temporary home while racing the 40-ton cutter *Britannia* around the coast.

[11] Another moment of glory was when *Britannia* came out as champion of her class.

[12] A report in an unidentified newspaper of 10 May 1793 refers to the ferry as an existing facility, and the *East Anglian Daily Times* of 28 December 1978 mentions its long existence. Indeed, there had been a ferry across the river mouth since around the year 1200, only being closed (not unreasonably) in times of piracy, plague and war. His new ferry was powered by steam and ran on chains. Three boats were used, first an unnamed one, and later the *Lady Quilter*, for use in

built 'model cottages' for his employees, and retirement homes. He became a magistrate, an Alderman, Deputy Lieutenant for the area, was associated with various local agricultural societies, thoroughly integrated and ingratiated himself into the local life, and was held in considerable esteem amongst the locals, not least because he gave employment to so many people.

His wife Mary supported him and performed the correct county duties, though local goodwill towards her may have been dented when, if she wanted a place on an already full ferry, someone had to be evicted to make room for her; the ferry would if necessary return for her, too. On one occasion, when she was waiting for her carriage to be rushed up the shingle ramp to the ferry, there chanced to be a young man paddling in the water, and having seen where she had come from, he asked her courteously about the 'man who built that monstrosity of a house'. She replied that she knew him quite well, but – tapping her head – 'to be honest he is a little peculiar up here'.[13]

Bawdsey Manor was recorded in the 1891 census as 'Mr Quilter's Mansion'. It is the statement of a successful man, assured of his position, lord indeed of his manor, summoning family to gatherings at Christmas and in the summer, holding shoots (and the Bawdsey shoot was considered a very fine one), organising, controlling, commanding, dominating. His study encapsulates the essence of the man: linenfold oaken panelling covers the walls to shoulder height; from there to the high ceiling red leather panels are decorated with golden-tooled lions and fleurs-de-lys; the wooden ceiling is panelled with the portcullis emblem derived from that of the Houses of Parliament. Everything in sections, in compartments, with boundaries, heavy, solid, unyielding, and durable. A sense of vision – but one with limits.

If William Cuthbert Quilter's sense of vision was bounded, his geographical sense however was not. He was a noted traveller, and spent time in South America, the southern United States, the West Indies (the intention of this trip was 'to promote the prosperity of the sugar planters, and to foster closer relations with Great Britain'[14]), South Africa and the Middle East. He also toured parts of India, including Delhi, Peshawar and the Khyber Pass.

His London house of that time confirms the picture of a man who set great store by a solid display of taste (good or otherwise, and there were many who thought it the latter); here was a man of means, one who claimed to appreciate fine things, who understood the requirements of a position in society. 74 South Audley Street was a very substantial property in Mayfair dating from the

---

summer, and the *Lady Beatrice*, smaller, for the winter; he opened the ferry in August 1894, to coincide approximately with his eldest son's coming of age. The steam chain ferry was in use until October 1975, run first by Charles Brinkley (known as 'One-Arm Brinkley' after he lost an arm in an unequal fight with an old muzzle-loader when out on a 'shiny night') until his death in 1931, and then by his son, also Charles, born in one of William Cuthbert Quilter's cottages. Charles Brinkley junior was ferryman and harbourmaster of Woodbridge Haven.

[13] Major Eustace Miller, 'Those were the Days My Friend, We Thought They'd Never End', *Suffolk Fair*, October 1981 and January 1982.

[14] From the *Suffolk County Handbook*, 1912, obituary of Sir William Cuthbert Quilter.

1720s[15] and William Cuthbert took pains to retain its decoration and preserve its architectural atmosphere; here he entertained lavishly and here too he built up a major art collection.

William Cuthbert's appreciation for the past, and his wish to preserve it and to stake his claim to it, was even more obviously manifest in his purchase and restoration in 1887 of the Guildhall in the mediaeval market town of Lavenham, in Suffolk. It was a way of preserving a little part of England, a little part of his heritage.[16] The Quilter family was one of substance, and of justly proud Victorian values, with a belief in the immutability of the past, bolstered by considerable financial help from the present. Amidst the celebrations for Queen Victoria's Diamond Jubilee in September 1897, it was no surprise that William Cuthbert became a baronet, known as Sir Cuthbert Quilter.[17]

Lady Quilter did not stand idly by. She accompanied Sir Cuthbert on his travels, but this was not much to her liking; she preferred to be at home, with her growing family, developing the gardens at Bawdsey. She presented prizes at Bawdsey Village School over many years, visiting sometimes with her daughter-in-law Lady Gwynedd, Eley's wife, and sometimes with her adored son Roger. She lent the school a harmonium, and in a special treat in July 1905, gave tea in the gardens of the Manor to all the schoolchildren; there were rides in motor cars, races, games, a cricket match, and gifts.

This was a family used to comforts, money and servants; a family that felt it had a reputation to maintain and develop. It was, above all, William Cuthbert Quilter's autocratic outlook and philosophy that dominated the family; it was from this background that Roger Quilter sprang, and against this background that his music is set.

Of the rest of Roger's immediate family, his uncle Edward Frederick Quilter was a rather less flamboyant character than either of his brothers. He was a businessman, though without the flair – or drive – of his elder brother. His London address was Savile Row, and his house in Suffolk was Belstead, known variously as Belstead House, or Hill House at Belstead. It was in a particularly beautiful setting, across low sweeping hills.[18] Edward Frederick was a popular

---

[15] The various ornamentations in the interior decoration included two relief-heads – still there – of the king and queen of Portugal, dating from the reign of George II when the house was occupied by the Portuguese ambassador (*Suffolk County Handbook*, 1912, p. 465).

[16] His heir, William Eley Cuthbert, continued that tradition, and restored the Guildhall even more thoroughly in 1939. In 1946, he gave it to the Lavenham Preservation Society, with its adjoining cottages, 'to be held in trust for the people of Lavenham for ever'. In 1951 it was handed over to the National Trust (F. Lingard Ranson, *Lavenham, Suffolk*, 1988, p. 55).

[17] William Eley Cuthbert, though called Eley within the family, was known in his turn as Sir Cuthbert. Eley's elder son, George Eley Cuthbert, died in 1919 before he could inherit the title; he too would have been known as Sir Cuthbert. But George's brother Raymond refused to be called Sir Cuthbert, on the grounds that only eldest sons were so known, and since he was not an eldest son, he would be called by his own name.

[18] It was a Tudor house originally, though there had been a house on that site since before that time. In the nineteenth century, it was a girls' school, and had links with Westfield College, the college of further education for women. Edward Quilter leased it, and though passed around as needed by three generations of Quilters, it did not come into their ownership until 1919.

landlord, a keen sportsman and, like his elder brother, bred Suffolk horses. He was generous but shrewd, and his early death in 1905 was much lamented. He never married.

Where Edward was unassuming, Harry the youngest son was the opposite. He was primarily an art critic, and because some of his relations considered this to be extraordinary behaviour – a different and not quite proper way of life – entire swathes of nieces and nephews were forbidden to meet him and his family.[19] His wife was Mary Constance Hall; in spite of the English-sounding name, she is alleged to have been foreign, perhaps Hungarian, and one of their daughters, Gwendolen, married Alan P. Herbert, the author, playwright and independent Member of Parliament. Harry was educated privately, went up to Trinity College, Cambridge in the autumn of 1870 to read moral sciences and took a third in 1874, having become rather too accomplished in playing billiards and racquets in the meantime. From 1876 to 1887 he was an art critic and journalist and from 1880 to 1881, he succeeded Tom Taylor as art critic for *The Times*, during which time his opinions upset the artist James McNeill Whistler (an easy thing to do). When Whistler was forced to sell the White House in Tite Street in September 1879 after filing for bankruptcy following the famous libel case against Ruskin, it was Harry Quilter who bought it; on Whistler's return after recovering his financial equilibrium, he refused to sell it him back, and Harry Quilter occupied it from 1879 to 1888.[20]

For all his dilettante and priggish perversity, and his voluminous but sometimes careless writing, Harry Quilter was a fine draughtsman, and his work was hung at several significant venues from 1884 onwards; he usually worked in oils, or watercolour on vellum, and favoured landscapes. He knew a decent painting when he saw it, even if he was not necessarily effective in writing about it.[21] His *Life of Giotto*, 1880, was reviewed thus: 'It is doubtful whether there is much left to be said respecting Giotto, . . . but, whatever the *residuum* may be, Mr Harry Quilter has not said it, nor, from what we can gather of his powers in this volume, is he likely to say it in the future.'[22] Nevertheless, it was reprinted in various editions for several years, and in fact he wrote extremely vividly; the book is something of a travelogue, based upon his own travels in Italy in the mid 1870s.

In the mid-1880s, Roger Quilter was sent away to prep school. Pinewood

---

Latterly it was occupied by Eustace, the youngest of William Cuthbert's five sons, and there are many photographs of Eustace's two sons growing up there; if it has ghosts, they are friendly ones. The house is now used for teachers' residential courses; the setting is not so attractive as it must once have been, since the view is marred by the noisy A12.

[19] Interview with Mrs Diana Tennant, Percy Quilter's daughter and Harry's great-niece, February 1997.

[20] Harry Quilter also had addresses in Mitcham, Surrey (not far from his brother's early home in Beddington, Surrey) and London (variously in Bryanston Square, Tite Street and Queen's Gate Gardens).

[21] The sale of most of his art collection in the year before his death in 1907 fetched over £14,000 – well over three-quarters of a million pounds in today's prices.

[22] *The Academy*, vol. xviii, p. 207.

School in Farnborough, Hampshire, was run by the Reverend Fabian Brackenbury. It was a new school and as was the usual practice, it prepared boys for the
Public Schools; it may also have offered preparation for the Royal Naval
College. The school building was a long, low, two-storey, late Victorian affair,
quite possibly purpose-built. It lay on high, well-drained ground – a good
healthy climate – and soon had Virginia creeper smothering the entrance porch.
Forty or fifty years on Quilter spoke of it with great fondness – here his interest
in music, drama and poetry was encouraged and nurtured.[23] He had a good
voice and sang in the school chapel choir, and was taught music by Fabian
Brackenbury's wife, Edith. Although it is not clear whether he could already play
the piano and violin before he went to Pinewood, he was certainly an
accomplished player on both instruments by the time he left.

Fabian Brackenbury was born in 1853 and so was in his early thirties by the
time Quilter knew him. There was a family atmosphere to the place –
Brackenbury had seven children, spread out over twelve years, the eldest of
whom, Dora, known as Do, was three years younger than Roger.[24] He was a
better teacher than a businessman: in 1899 he was declared bankrupt and he
moved away from Farnborough to Monkton Thanet, though the school
continued.[25]

Roger's father and uncle Harry had both been taught by private tutors, but
Roger's eldest brother, Eley, went to Harrow and then, as uncle Harry had done,
went on to Trinity College, Cambridge. The rest of the boys – Arnie, Roger,
Percy and Eustace – were sent to Eton. The eldest, Arnie, began in January 1889
and Roger joined him in January 1892.

Arnie flourished in Eton's hearty sporting atmosphere; he was athletic and
popular and was frequently mentioned in the various sports reports in the Eton
Chronicles. When he left, a special commendation was made, referring to 'the
captainship of Quilter which had a great deal to do with our success, and the
smartness and excellence of our fielding [which] was mainly due to his energy'.[26]
He went on to Trinity Hall, Cambridge, and then joined the Grenadier Guards.

At that time, Eton placed great emphasis on physical ability, and the highest
acclaim went to those who would be capable of joining the army. This was
disastrous for a delicate and sensitive boy such as Roger. He was shy, he

[23] Donald Brook, *Composers' Gallery* (London, 1946), p. 86.
[24] Many of Brackenbury's descendants followed in the family footsteps and maintained his
educational ethos, amongst them his youngest daughter, Biddy, who ran a girls' boarding
and day school, Copplestone House, in Budleigh Salterton, Devon, and a generation later his
grandson Tony Brackenbury, who became the first head of the Yehudi Menuhin School in
Cobham, Surrey. Tony's brother John was Warden of Impington Village College, Cambridgeshire, and later Chair of the Cambridgeshire Education Committee. (Family history information
given to the author via correspondence and interview with John Brackenbury, to whom warmest
thanks. Thanks too to Mrs Jo Gosney, local historian, for information on Pinewood and
Brackenbury's bankruptcy.)
[25] It moved to the West Country some time during the Second World War, and the Farnborough
building was then used as a furniture repository until its demolition.
[26] *Eton Chronicles*, July 1893.

stammered, he was never quite well, never really healthy. Because of his general physical weakness, he was excused sports – though he did occasionally play a little cricket, usually being put in to bat late – and instead was permitted to study music.[27] This departure from the norm, while it may not have alienated him from his fellows, certainly reinforced the difference. Quilter minor benefited from being Quilter major's brother, but he was nevertheless a fish out of water.

Solace came in the form of his walks up the hill to St George's Chapel, Windsor, to listen to the chapel choir, conducted by the great organist Sir Walter Parratt.[28] Parratt performed an eclectic choice of works ranging from Tallis to S. S. Wesley; it was a broad education and Roger Quilter's anthems, notably 'Non Nobis, Domine', benefited from it.

The system at Eton allocated the boys to 'houses', the house acting as a surrogate family; Arnie and Roger were in the Reverend T. Dalton's house. Roger was accepted as a member of the house debating society in July 1893 at the end of Arnie's tenure as its president,[29] and the journal of the society shows Roger's humanitarian outlook: in a debate about the national mining strike of 1893, where other society members considered the miners a spendthrift and ungrateful lot, Roger thought it 'a wonderful and at the same time an awful thing that these coal miners *can* go on in the mad and useless way – while their wives and children suffer starvation and are obliged to seek refuge in the work-house . . . as long as they work at the risk of their lives – their pay should be considerably high'. A debate about prize-fighting elicited the comment that 'prize-fighting . . . is not at all in my line'.[30]

The Eton College Musical Society had been founded by some of the boys in 1862. It was in a perpetual state of struggle for existence, for Etonians were musically apathetic.[31] Roger took no part in the administration of the Society, being neither president, treasurer, nor secretary, but he did play the violin in some of the Society's concerts. He kept up his piano study too, although it seems that he did not play the piano in public.[32] In a concert in December 1892, Quilter played Raff's *Cavatina* 'with considerable skill'.[33] The following March, he played a duet, Spohr's *Larghetto in B flat*, with T. H. Kelly (the father of the composer F. S. Kelly, who was killed in the Great War), and this performance 'shewed that classical concerted music, when carefully rendered, is bound to be appreciated'.[34] In May 1893 he was deemed to 'have a very fair mastery of the technique' when he played Mozart's *Adagio in D*;[35] but he was unable to play in

---

[27] Reminiscence by Mrs Diana Tennant.
[28] Brook (1946), p. 86.
[29] Eton College Archives.
[30] Debating record book, Eton College, 1893–94.
[31] *Eton Chronicles*, September 1892.
[32] Archives held by Leslie East.
[33] *Eton Chronicles*, December 15, 1892.
[34] *Eton Chronicles*, March 29, 1893.
[35] *Eton Chronicles*, May 31, 1893.

the December concert because he went down before the end of term suffering from various minor ailments.

Roger's next youngest brother, Percy, went up to Eton in January 1893, only a year after Roger; Arnie left in the July, and in September 1893 Roger's youngest brother Eustace came up. At last, Roger was no longer in the shadow of his popular elder brother. Percy, it would seem, took no part in the concerts, but Eustace did, singing to some acclaim. The following year, in the concert in December 1894, it was reported that, in singing Horn's *Cherry Ripe!*, 'he has a rich voice and ought to do well'. The previous June, Roger and T. H. Kelly had given an undistinguished performance of Kotek's *Duo d'Amour*, and Roger's final concert was in June 1895 when he and Wyndham performed a *Sonata for Two Violins* by Handel. Eustace, more robust physically as well as temperamentally, was better suited to the Eton milieu. In due course, his sons Ronald and John, and grandsons William and Thomas, also went to Eton; William and Thomas, like Eustace and their father Ronald, showed signs of being musical, Thomas especially: he played the bugle and studied at the Royal College of Music[36] though he was rather a dilettante in his studies. William played the clarinet.[37] Ronald, Eustace's elder son, showed an individuality of taste in choosing to play the banjo.[38]

Just before Easter 1892, not long after he went up, Roger Quilter won a Task Prize, but there is no record of his ever having won anything again and his school career was not notable. Having been overshadowed by his elder brother Arnie, he was now eclipsed by his youngest brother. Years later he told Mark Raphael, his protégé, that he had hated his time there. He left Eton in July 1895 and went back home to Bawdsey.

The question was what to do now. His brothers would go into business or the army, but he was clearly unsuited to those careers. He was six foot three inches tall, slim, hated being photographed (for formal photographs at least), had a predilection for lounging around in boating whites if the time of year was right, had an eye for objets d'art, was 'always ill or about to be ill',[39] was diffident, and had a droll sense of humour, much commented upon, but rarely reported. He was also musical, and at this point, his mother's Jewish friend suggested that he should continue his musical studies, at the conservatory at Frankfurt-am-Main.

Despite the foundation of the Royal Academy of Music in 1822 and the Royal College in 1883 (its predecessor, the National Training School for Music, was founded in 1873) musical education was perceived as being on the whole better if it was obtained on the Continent. In Germany alone, there were many

---

[36] Debrett's Peerage and Baronettage 1970.

[37] Reminiscence by Mrs Diana Tennant, January 1997.

[38] Ipswich Record Office. Tucked in one of the photograph albums that they hold is a banjo skin, signed by various friends and members of the family, including: Cecil Quilter (Ronnie's mother), John A. Denny (cousin: Aunt Maude's son), Eileen Denny (John's wife), Inez Quilter (cousin: Uncle Eley's daughter), Raymond Quilter (cousin: Uncle Eley's son), Eustace Quilter (Ronnie's father), Robert Laycock, Anthony Mildmay.

[39] Ruth Conti to Langfield, 14 January 1998.

eminent establishments, with honourable musical traditions: Munich had the Stadtische Singschule and the Königliche Musikschule, Dresden had a choir school, and Cologne had a conservatory. Berlin boasted several, including the Königliches Akademisches Institut für Kirchenmusik, the Hochschule für Musik, and the Berliner Musikschule. Leipzig was famous for its Conservatoire and had had many pupils – not only composers – who became well known, including Sir Adrian Boult, Frederick Delius, Carl Rosa, Ethel Smyth and Sir Arthur Sullivan. The Conservatory at Frankfurt dates from 1878, when it was endowed by J. Hoch, a businessman. Its director during Quilter's studies there was Bernhard Scholz, who presided from 1883 to 1908. Many years earlier, in 1860, Brahms, deeply distressed at the direction in which Liszt's musical developments seemed to be going, and concerned for the future of music, had attempted to organise a petition, a protest to Liszt and his 'Musicians of the Future' but it misfired, having been leaked to the press prematurely, and there were in the end only four signatories, one of whom was Scholz. Scholz's predecessor as Director of the Conservatory was Joachim Raff, a pro-Lisztian, and with Scholz's investiture came a decisive change of musical direction for the Conservatory: all those staff who had served under Joachim Raff's directorship until his death in 1882 and who sat on the Liszt-Wagner side of the fence had left, to found the Raff Conservatoire, leaving the Brahms-Schumann coterie in place.

Scholz brought order out of chaos. He ruled with absolute authority, re-establishing credibility for the Conservatory and attracting new teachers to the institution. One teacher stayed when so many others were deserting: until her resignation in 1892 because of deafness and ill-health, Clara Schumann, Robert's widow, was head of the piano department and her pedagogical techniques held sway for many years after her departure, well into the next century. The teaching was traditional: classes in harmony and counterpoint, thorough-bass, form and history were a fundamental and mandatory part of the training.

Although it was young, the Conservatory had thus established itself firmly upon the European scene. Why exactly Quilter chose Frankfurt cannot be known for certain; it may have been because of its growing reputation, or perhaps Mary Ann Quilter's friend was himself from Frankfurt: many Jews had emigrated to England from that city during the latter part of the nineteenth century.

Throughout the 1890s, there were on average about 240 students per year at the Conservatory, of whom generally about a fifth were from English-speaking countries – England, America and Australia – and of these, most were English.[40]

Quilter spent four and a half years in Frankfurt but when exactly this period was is debatable. He is recorded as having spent four semesters at the Conservatory; there were two semesters per year, starting in September and April, with July and August as holidays, and his first semester was during the

[40] Peter Cahn, *Das Hoch'sche Konservatorium 1878–1978* (Frankfurt, 1979).

academic year 1896–7, when he studied the piano with Ernst Engesser.[41] Quilter wrote later that he began composing only after a few months; at the end of March 1897 he wrote a short song, a setting of two verses of Tennyson's poem 'Now Sleeps the Crimson Petal', which after some alterations was eventually published in 1904 and became one of his most famous songs; it seems likely therefore that he started in the September semester, 1896, and was absent during the second semester.

A setting of Christina Rossetti's poem 'Should One of Us Remember' is dated August 1897, and was not published, but two other songs, 'Come Spring! Sweet Spring!' and 'The Reign of the Stars' were. They were his first, and he dedicated them to his mother. He had not quite the courage to use his own name and used instead 'Ronald Quinton', transparently retaining his initials. It was an inauspicious start – the words, his own, are routine and so is the music – but it was at least a start.

He was at the Conservatory for the entire year 1897–8 during which time he wrote several other songs: the manuscript of 'Should One of Us Remember' is dated August 1897, that of 'A Secret' is dated 6 May 1898 and 'Come Spring! Sweet Spring!' and 'The Reign of the Stars' were published in 1897 under a pseudonym, Ronald Quinton; there were probably other songs. He was also at the Conservatory for one semester during the year 1898–9, probably the first, since otherwise there would have been two breaks in his studies, which may not have been acceptable to the Conservatory. On 27 October 1898 his *Three Dances for Violin and Piano* were performed, Schumannesque pieces, now lost. He was in England to accompany Denham Price singing his *Four Songs of the Sea* at the Crystal Palace on 11 March 1901, but he was probably back in Frankfurt on 4 June 1901, when his *Sonata for Oboe and Piano* (also lost) was performed.

The best fit for his four and a half year stay is thus September 1896 to June 1901, with the four Conservatory semesters spread out from September 1896 to March 1899. He had probably returned to England in March 1898, for the occasion of the marriage of his sister Norah to Willie Miller, and he was certainly in England in July 1899 to spend a few days with her, celebrating her birthday. In July 1900 he was at Bawdsey helping his mother visit the village school.

Piano was his only formal study at the Conservatory; like a number of other English-speaking students, he studied composition privately with Ivan Knorr. Knorr's gift as a teacher of composition was to nurture his students' individuality, rather than impose a common stamp, but though he was undoubtedly a very fine and highly esteemed teacher, he also had a vicious sense of so-called humour. On one occasion, Knorr, ostensibly impressed with a set of variations that Percy Grainger (another of his pupils, though only for a short time) had written for string quartet, arranged for their performance solely for the purpose of mocking them.[42] Knorr's and Grainger's dislike was mutual.

[41] Engesser taught at the Conservatory from 1884 to 1923.
[42] John Bird, *Percy Grainger*, 3rd edition (Oxford, 1999).

Knorr had trained at the Leipzig Conservatoire, and in 1883 Brahms recommended him to the Frankfurt Conservatory. At first Knorr taught piano, theory and music history; he began teaching composition there three years later, and eventually stopped teaching piano. He was himself a composer, German-born (in West Prussia in 1853) but with strong Russian sympathies, and a Russian wife; he was also a personal friend of Tchaikovsky. Cyril Scott, another of his composition pupils, described him as placid and never angry, though he attested to Knorr's sarcasm at the expense of some of his unfortunate pupils. Scott also reported on his extraordinary physical appearance: he wore 'a pork-pie hat without the customary indentation',[43] trousers of a nondescript brownish-yellow, their bagginess suggesting a distinct resemblance to the posterior of an elephant, and a cravat that looked as if it might be made partly from cardboard; he was slender, sallow and bearded – the beard being rather mangy – and had hair that seemed to stand straight up on end. Following Scholz's resignation in 1908, he acceded to the Directorship the following year, and from then on refused to allow any of his compositions to be performed in the Conservatory concerts, since he felt that to do so would be an abuse of privilege. He was highly self-critical, and his surviving compositions, which showed Brahmsian as well as Ukrainian folk-song influences, were few. He died in 1916.

Four of Knorr's other composition pupils were to become significant in Quilter's life: Percy Grainger, Cyril Scott, Balfour Gardiner and Norman O'Neill. These five (all English, except Grainger who was Australian) were much of an age, with O'Neill the oldest, born in 1875, then Quilter in 1877, then Gardiner, just six days younger, Scott, born in 1879, and Grainger the youngest, born in 1882. They were not all at Frankfurt at the same time: O'Neill was there from 1893 to the summer of 1897, and studied piano with Lazzaro Uzielli;[44] so did Gardiner, after a short period studying with Engesser. Gardiner was first at Frankfurt for four semesters from 1894 to 1896 (he studied organ and clarinet as well as piano and composition), and then again from the autumn of 1900 to the end of the year, the intervening time being spent – unsatisfactorily – at New College, Oxford, although he did get his degree, just, in the summer of 1900.[45]

Scott went to Frankfurt as a boy, in the winter of 1891, to study piano with Uzielli for four semesters, an eighteen-month period; he returned to Frankfurt in 1896 (thus missing Balfour Gardiner) for a further six semesters, leaving in the summer of 1899. During this second period, he continued his piano studies with Uzielli, and studied composition with Knorr officially, rather than privately.

Grainger went to Frankfurt early in the summer of 1895 but did not start at the Conservatory until the autumn. He studied piano with James Kwast until summer 1901, though he was dissatisfied with his teaching. He was dissatisfied

---

[43] Cyril Scott, *My Years of Indiscretion* (London, 1924), and quoted in *Bone of Contention* (London, 1969).

[44] Derek Hudson, *Norman O'Neill, A Life of Music* (London, 1945).

[45] Stephen Lloyd, *H. Balfour Gardiner* (Cambridge, 1984).

with Knorr's teaching too, and claimed he learned considerably more from his other composition teacher, Klimsch.

These were very different characters, highly individual, variously argumentative and opinionated, but united in a common dislike, hatred even, of Beethoven. Scott was arguably the most innovative, the most arrogant and also the most flamboyant in his dress and manner, as he himself admitted in later years. Gardiner, like Quilter, was extremely wealthy, and generously used his money to support and encourage other composers. He was also highly changeable in his opinions, as Grainger explained: at one stage he was very much in favour of Arnold Bax's music, but (much) later said he disliked it extremely; in around 1909 or 1910 he was singing the praises of Scott's music, yet by the time of his 1913 series of Balfour Gardiner concerts would not have anything of his on the programme. Despite his undoubted idiosyncrasies, however, his cherubic appearance and naïveté were endearing, and the others of the group were fond of him.

Grainger remained cool towards O'Neill, always alleging that musically speaking he had somehow let the side down; perhaps it made a difference that O'Neill was seven years older, and Grainger was still a boy when they had first met. But O'Neill, who came from a family that had always mixed in artistic circles, was a delightful man, easy-going, very good-looking and popular, and he established a highly successful career as a theatre composer. Scott also regarded him as not quite one of the group, but Quilter was fond enough of him, and kept in touch with him until his death. In July 1899, O'Neill married Adine Ruckert, a concert pianist whom he had met while she was in Frankfurt studying with Clara Schumann; Adine kept up a substantial correspondence with Clara's daughter Eugenie for years,[46] and Quilter too stayed in touch with Adine and her family.

Of all the various personalities, Grainger's was possibly the most extraordinary. He had a remarkable energy and a complete belief in himself and what he did; he was a superb concert pianist, unfussed about the niceties of accuracy, and infinitely preferring an exciting performance to a staid one. He fought musical battles on behalf his friends; he was loyal and devoted and wrote them all countless letters throughout his life, giving them the benefit of his opinions on many subjects, and stirring them – or trying to stir them – to greater things. Many of these letters were written on trains and he evidently developed a useful technique for writing legibly while on the move. He was an inveterate traveller, globe-trotting between Europe, the States and Australia; upheaval was part of his life. He was devoted to his mother even more than to his friends; she accompanied him everywhere, dictating his life to him, whom he should and should not cultivate, and choosing his friends. It is significant that he did not marry until after her death.

Quilter found Knorr a hard taskmaster; the strict requirements of fugues, formal structures and academic writing did not come easily to him and in the

---

[46] Now held by the British Library.

company of Grainger, Scott and Gardiner, he felt inferior;[47] he especially envied Scott who revelled in such musical puzzles. Knorr did not think that Quilter would be a great composer, but thought his music would be as charming as he was himself. Quilter was grateful for the discipline that Knorr instilled, but he regarded his own lack of ready facility as a lack of ability. It depressed him and he was never willing to risk composing large-scale works. The nearest he came was the *Serenade* of 1907, which he dedicated to Knorr 'in gratitude'.

Quilter had various landladies while studying at Frankfurt, all now un-identifiable except one, Frau Orth, and Grainger and his mother Rose stayed with him there towards the end of their time in Frankfurt. In a gentlemanly and amiable way, he managed to offend his landladies at every turn; when he bought a carefully chosen bowl in a new and expensive metal, as a Christmas present for his then landlady (whom Scott described as snobbish[48]), it did not meet with her approval, because it was not silver. He used to put out crumbs for the birds, until the landlady complained, saying it was 'most unrefined'; it had to be explained to him that it was not his kindly action, but the consequences of the birds staying so long on the windowsill that was unrefined.

In the spring of 1899, Scott took rooms in Cronberg, a beautiful village up in the mountains, staying at the Bathing Establishment, and travelling back to Frankfurt for lessons. Sometimes Grainger cycled out to see him there, and from time to time Quilter came too since he knew people who lived in some of the nearby villas. They visited some of these acquaintances, and Quilter was intensely embarrassed at the sycophantic change in his hostess after the arrival of further guests from the Empress Frederick's castle; such falseness disgusted him.[49]

The five students – Balfour Gardiner, Percy Grainger, Norman O'Neill, Roger Quilter and Cyril Scott – became known as the Frankfurt Group or the Frankfurt Five or sometimes, with a rather boy-scout connotation, the Frankfurt Gang. Grainger, ever hopeful, thought that they would change the world, but that was not to be. They were linked by friendship as much as

---

[47] Extracts from the diary of Professor Sir Frank Callaway, Callaway to Langfield, 18 March 1997. The diary records Quilter's reminiscences when Callaway met him on several occasions in 1948–9.

[48] Cyril Scott, trans. G. Marbach, 'Die "Frankforter Gruppe": Erinnerungen von Cyril Scott', *Neue Leipziger Zeitschrift für Musik*, vol. 119 (3 Feb 1958), pp. 81–3. 'Seine nächste Wirtin, eine snobistische Frau Doktor Soundso, beleidigte er auf andere Art. Es gab zu jener Zeit ein neues, ziemlich teures Metall, Kaiser-Zinn genannt, aus dem die verschiedensten eleganten Schmuck-gegenstände und Gefäß hergestellt wurden. Der freigiebige Quilter erstand zum Weihnachsfest für sie ein solches Schmuckstück, um ihr eine besondere Freude zu machen. Aber die Dame war nicht im geringsten entzückt, sondern fühlte sich zutiefst beleidigt, weil, sie sagte, es kein richtiges Silber sei.' ['His next landlady, a snobbish Mrs Soundso, he offended in a different way. There was at that time a new, quite expensive metal, called "Kaiser tin", out of which the most diverse and elegant ornaments and vessels were produced. The generous Quilter purchased an ornament of this sort as a Christmas present for her, to bring her especial delight. But the lady was not charmed in the least, but felt herself deeply insulted, because, she said, it was not proper silver.']

[49] Cyril Scott (1924).

by any musical factor;[50] there was no real unifying aim between them, and they remained non-conforming individuals. What common factor there was – and Grainger was vocal in talking and writing about this – was harmonic: he wrote of the importance to them of 'the chord' and their compositions tended to be 'vertical' rather than 'horizontal', and so the more telling on the rare occasions when contrapuntal techniques were used.

At Frankfurt's fine opera house, they heard – amongst others – Wagner operas, and Quilter presumably heard the *Ring* and *Tristan* there, if his quotations from them in later works are anything to go by. But the Great War left their music untouched. It was not for them to set the war poets; their roots lay further back, into the heart of the nineteenth century.

---

[50] Stephen Lloyd, 'Grainger and the "Frankfurt Group"', *Studies in Western Music* (University of Western Australia), vol. 16 (1982), pp. 111–18.

2

From the Crystal Palace to *Where the Rainbow Ends* (1901–1911)

In London in 1901, aged twenty-three, Quilter was quite unknown. He had no particular sense of direction; he simply wrote songs. This was not a daunting task, as writing a large-scale work would be, and this meant a great deal to someone who was seldom if ever content with what he wrote, and who reworked his material again and again. The words were at least as important to him as the setting; on many occasions he claimed to love poetry at least as much as music, if not more.[1] The work of composition was set against a background of visiting friends and relatives around England, moving between London and country residences, and travelling abroad; normal behaviour for a wealthy upper-middle-class young man.

His musical career started at the Crystal Palace. There were many concert series there besides the Saturday Concerts, and a second season of Chamber Music Concerts took place in the winter of 1900–1. Within this series, the third concert, on 11 March, featured two violinists, two violists, two cellists, the baritone Denham Price and accompanists Samuel Liddle and Roger Quilter. Denham Price appeared regularly on the London scene in those years; his name can be found in programmes for the Queen's Hall Promenade Concerts, for Vocal and Instrumental Concerts at the Crystal Palace, the Bechstein Hall and the St James's Hall Ballad Concerts, amongst others, and he shared the platform with Frederic Austin, John Coates, Gervase Elwes and the like, the major names of the time. Price's name is long forgotten, but in singing the *Four Songs of the Sea* that evening, he brought Quilter's songs to their earliest public. They were published later that year by Forsyth and republished ten years later in 1911 as *Three Songs of the Sea* (omitting the first song, and with some alterations to the words, not always for the better).

Quilter followed up the modest success of his Crystal Palace début with the *Four Songs of Mirza Schaffy*, Op. 2, to German texts but with a translation by his friend Walter Creighton; they were published late in 1903 and marked 'In remembrance of Frankfurt days' but he revised them in 1911, and rededicated them to his friends Walter and Marie English. 'Come Back!' and 'A Secret' were settings of his own texts, also published in 1903, though 'A Secret' was written

---

[1] One occasion was recorded by Astra Desmond in a radio programme on the Frankfurt Group, BBC Radio 3, *Music Weekly*, 23 October 1977.

in 1898, and 'Come Back!' probably was too; and in 1904, two Binyon settings, 'At Close of Day' and 'The Answer', and two partsongs for four-part chorus, 'To Daffodils' and 'To the Virgins', were published. These were his first settings of Robert Herrick, whose poetry, in its feelings of the transience of humanity, struck so resonantly with Quilter's own outlook.

In 1902, he made a short setting for men's voices of verses from *Omar Khayām*, to a translation by E. A. Johnson, father of a girl friend. For unknown reasons, it was never published, despite Grainger's constant urgings.

Quilter held a particularly high regard for the singer Gervase Elwes. Elwes came of a very long-established county family; he also knew the major musical figures of the day – performers, composers, academics and critics – and many of them visited him at his main estate, Billing Hall, near Northampton: Quilter of course, and musicians such as Cyril Scott, Irène Dean Paul (professionally known as Poldowski, the composer), John Fuller Maitland (notable as editor of the second edition of Grove's *Dictionary of Music and Musicians*), the conductor and composer Anthony Bernard, the American publisher Winthrop Rogers, the tenor Hubert Eisdell, the composer Maude Valérie White, Sir Henry Wood, Frank Bridge, Ralph Vaughan Williams, and Sir Edward Elgar. Quilter's friends Wilfrid and Jane von Glehn were frequent visitors too. Elwes's accompanist Frederick Kiddle came often, as did Elwes's teacher Victor Beigel and Percy Grainger and his mother Rose.[2]

Gervase Elwes was born in 1866, the eldest child of Valentine Cary-Elwes, and his education as a gentleman included a spell at the Oratory School at Edgbaston, Birmingham; this was conducted by Cardinal John Henry Newman, who encouraged Elwes's musical studies. In 1889 Elwes married Lady Winefride Feilding, daughter of the Earl of Denbigh, and they produced eight children (which Grainger thought an extravagance). Elwes tried to live the life he was born to, but eventually he capitulated to what he felt was his calling – he had a fine tenor voice and studied singing for many years – and became a professional singer. His father was utterly unable to understand why on earth his son would want to do such a thing; after all, he already had a career, to go shooting with the tenant farmers. For a long time he forbade Elwes to take up such a ridiculous occupation, but was in time won over by his son's perseverance and dedication.

Elwes's humanity and integrity endeared him to his friends and family; he was much loved, and as a singer much sought after. When and how he and Quilter met is difficult to determine, but it was probably before the 'Jamborees' held by Elwes's brother-in-law, Everard Feilding, the exuberant and informal evenings in the winter of 1904 where composers, performers and London society met together. Grainger, as the young golden-haired virtuoso pianist, had long since been introduced into the realms of the London salon, and others came too, including Cyril Scott, Balfour Gardiner, William Hurlstone and Ralph Vaughan Williams. It was a widely spread circle.

---

[2] The Visitors' Book is held at Elsham Hall, Brigg, North Lincolnshire. Further information about life at Billing comes from the author's interview with Captain Jeremy Elwes, May 1998.

Although Elwes's voice was not considered great, he brought an extraordinary artistry and personality to his singing. He championed English song composers by programming their work in his recitals and they responded by dedicating many of their songs to him – not, one suspects, merely in order to encourage a performance by him as was common practice, but because he regularly performed the songs while still unpublished, quite possibly enabling their publication as a result. He sang songs by famous and obscure alike, ranging from Ralph Vaughan Williams to St John Brougham.[3] He gave the first performances of many of Quilter's songs, and Quilter acknowledged his debt to him more than once: 'I am sure you know what I feel about your singing of my songs – it can't be put into words. It has been the greatest stimulus and happiness in my life's work'[4] and 'It is a sheer joy & inspiration hearing you sing and playing for you. I need not tell you what I feel about your singing of my music; you must know well by now what I feel.'[5] Quilter stated categorically that Elwes's 'perfect renderings did more than anything else to make the songs known and liked'.[6]

Quilter's life revolved around his friends, especially the von Glehns. In 1828, Robert von Glehn came to England for the first of several visits before he finally settled; he was a merchant from Tallinn (then called Reval), the capital of Estonia, but was of north German extraction. He married a Scotswoman, Agnes Duncan, in 1835 and for some years they lived in Harley Street, London, in a house that his wife had inherited, as well as at Peak Hill Lodge in Sydenham, then a small village just south-east of London.[7] They produced thirteen children, of whom eleven survived to adulthood. Amongst these were Alick, Louise and Mimi, who was beloved of Sir George Grove and who died of tuberculosis in 1886 aged forty-three. Louise married an academic from Merton College, Oxford, Mandell Creighton, who later became Bishop of London, but they produced a mere seven children; Walter was their second son and fourth child, and their youngest daughter, Gemma, was for a time a pupil of Percy Grainger. Alick, Louise's elder brother, married a Frenchwoman, Fanny Monod, and their children were Louis, Wilfrid, Rachel, Lilian and Rennie. Though the

---

[3] Programmes show that he sang songs by Frank Bridge, St John Brougham, Rebecca Clarke, Alison Crompton, Harold Darke, Malcolm Davidson, Walford Davies, Thomas Dunhill, Edward Elgar, Balfour Gardiner, Ivor Gurney, John Ireland, Henry J. Ley, Poldowski, Roger Quilter, Cyril Scott, Martin Shaw, Grace Street, Colin Taylor, Felix White, Percy Whitlock, Ralph Vaughan Williams, and Peter Warlock – and there were surely many others.

[4] Quilter to Gervase Elwes, 25 May 1917, Lincolnshire County Archives, 2 ELWES 1.13 L-Q.

[5] Quilter to Gervase Elwes, 3 April 1919, Lincolnshire County Archives, 2 ELWES 1.13 L-Q.

[6] Autobiographical notes, Leslie East archive.

[7] For the information on the von Glehn family, and the Creightons in particular, I am greatly indebted to Professor James Thayne Covert, *Memoir of a Victorian Woman, Reflections of Louise Creighton 1850–1936*, ed. J. T. Covert (Bloomington, 1994); *A Victorian Family, as Seen Through the Letters of Louise Creighton to Her Mother 1872–1880*, ed. J. T. Covert (New York, 1998); and *A Victorian Marriage, Mandell and Louise Creighton*, J. T. Covert (London, 2000). Some information is also taken from the author's interview with Mrs Hugh Creighton in February 1999.

various families were large, the fecundity lay in the female line, and after only three generations, the name 'von Glehn' (changed later to 'de Glehn') died out. The connection between the Quilters and the von Glehn family was of long standing, going back to the mid-1800s when the two families lived near each other, even though later generations were not necessarily born in the area.

Quilter was close to Wilfrid von Glehn, and especially close to Wilfrid's cousin, the tall and good-looking Walter Creighton. Creighton and Quilter certainly knew each other well by 1901, and probably earlier, although neither ever lived in Sydenham. Creighton was highly personable, a few months Quilter's junior, and almost certainly homosexual. He went up to Emmanuel College, Cambridge, with a view to becoming a doctor, but left at the end of the Lent Term 1898 without taking his degree.[8] He sought a career as a singer and toured South Africa during June and July 1905.[9] This gave him valuable experience, so much so that for a while he thought seriously of living and working there, but he lacked the confidence to make – for him – such a big step and ultimately he remained in Europe. He and his siblings were under considerable pressure to match the intellectual feats of their parents, an impossible demand, and he and Quilter shared a common sense of somehow having failed to meet parental expectations.

At the beginning of the twentieth century Louis von Glehn, Wilfrid's elder brother, was teaching French at the Perse School in Cambridge.[10] He had a George V beard, a deep voice, a preference for wearing plus fours, and a personality to match. Wilfrid was a fine artist who often accompanied John Singer Sargent on his Continental and American painting tours and in 1904, Wilfrid married an American from New York, Jane Emmet. Through her cousin, Ellen Emmet (known as Bay), Jane was distantly related to Henry James, and all the family were artistically talented: her sister Lydia Emmet was a well-known and extremely successful portrait painter. An Irish ancestor, Robert Emmet, was commemorated in a poem by Thomas Moore, 'Elegy on the Death of Robert Emmet', and further commemorated in the song by Henri Duparc, 'Élégie', a setting of a French translation of Moore's poem.

These years established the circles in which Quilter moved. Through Wilfrid, he mixed with artists. Through Jane and her relation Henry James, he knew writers. His parents entertained lavishly at their house in South Audley Street, Mayfair; he moved in moneyed, upper-class circles with ease, albeit unwillingly, for their philistine attitudes sickened him. He was happier by far amongst artists; nevertheless, as a tall (he was sometimes ironically nicknamed 'Quilterino'[11]), graceful and wealthy young man, he was welcome wherever he cared to go.

Thoughts about people occupied his mind greatly, and in particular, thoughts

---

[8] Information from Professor James T. Covert.

[9] Walter Creighton to Quilter, BL Add. MS 70596, ff. 3–31.

[10] S. J. D. Mitchell, *Perse, A History of the Perse School 1615–1976* (Cambridge, 1976).

[11] In the middle of July 1906, Elwes's singing teacher Victor Beigel wrote a wryly good-natured comment in Elwes's Visitors' Book: 'owing to Quilterino's absence I was rather well treated'.

about women: he did not dislike them, but it generally took time before he felt comfortable with them, and then only a certain kind of woman appealed – the kind with 'the boy' in her, as he wrote in letters to Rose Grainger on the subject.[12] Jane von Glehn, Wilfrid's wife, was one such; she had an uncloying warmth about her, too, beneath a reserved exterior, to which Quilter responded positively, and they remained close friends until his death. He also felt there was much of 'the boy' in Rose Grainger. She had a possessive and demanding relationship with him; not, however, as much as she had with her son Percy.

Although his parents had a London base, Quilter wanted some measure of independence and privacy, and in November 1903, he took rooms at 27 Welbeck Street, in London's West End, in premises occupied primarily by assorted medical practitioners. This was his London *pied à terre* until the autumn of 1907.

He spent the early part of 1904 in the Latin quarter in Paris, to the concern of his mother; perhaps she was concerned for his morals, or health, or both. In that spring, she was on holiday in Granada, with Sir Cuthbert. She found marriage to him rather trying: he disliked going anywhere without her, he was always 'wanting to eat meals', and though kind, he was always serious and unappreciative of her.[13] She was infinitely happier looking at the scenery and the flowers, reading, and not talking to people. The travelling, too, along poor roads, was tiring.

Two years later, she wrote of her sons (while visiting their second son, Arnie, in South Africa) that it would only be 'by their taking wives that she would be able to push them away from her'.[14] But she was aware that her third son was not like her other children. She was passionately devoted to all of them, but to him especially, possessively so, and she was very protective of him. That her marriage was not an especially happy one was obvious to him, and he devoted himself to her almost by way of consolation. She, for her part, seems to have shown a degree of acceptance of his homosexuality that was surprising for the time.

To be homosexual in recent centuries has usually been to be misunderstood, maligned, vilified, to have to deny one's own sexual fabric. The Labouchère amendment of 1885 to the Criminal Law Amendment Act made all homosexual activity illegal; this was the amendment which gave rise to the nickname 'the Blackmailer's Charter' and which destroyed Oscar Wilde, and to be homosexual at that particular time was to have to cope with even greater stresses than normal. Some areas of existence, of society, showed a greater understanding and tolerance, but the degree to which this was possible was affected by one's character.

When young, the Quilter children had made an alphabet book, which they called 'The Hintlesham Alphabet', named after the house that they lived in

---

[12] Quilter to Rose Grainger, 28 November 1907, GM.
[13] Lady Quilter to Roger Quilter, 19 March [1904], BL Add. MS 70595, ff. 1–6.
[14] Lady Quilter to Roger Quilter, 23 February 1906, BL Add. MS 70595, ff. 13–14.

during the 1880s. The entry for 'R' shows a child-drawn cartoon of a small boy sitting quietly on a cushion by the fire, a pack of cards on the floor by him. 'R is for Roger who loves a quiet game' runs the caption. Quilter's family knew that he was 'different'. To be 'musical' was a euphemism for being homosexual, and was thus doubly applicable in his case. The differences Quilter displayed as a child, when he was so often ill, and not bursting with the rude health and energy of all his brothers and sisters, the increasing sense of isolation as his artistic sensibilities developed, his strong emotional dependence on and bond with his possessive mother – all added bricks to the wall of depression that surrounded him throughout his life. His father all but disowned him for being artistic, on one occasion, when Quilter had had a good concert review, pointedly ignoring both it and him.[15] Quilter was forever ill and forever obsessed with health and ill-health, his own and that of his friends, and he was full of self-doubt.

But he continued to compose, painstakingly. On 2 June 1904, Ada Crossley (with whom Grainger toured in Australia) sang 'Now Sleeps the Crimson Petal' at a recital at St James's Hall, with Quilter accompanying. Back in April, Grainger had suggested that Quilter show Crossley some of his songs, that one in particular.[16] On the twenty-third of the same month, Gervase Elwes sang it, accompanied by Quilter, at a concert (shared with the pianist Ada Thomas) at the Bechstein Hall in London, and in a review of the concert in the *Globe*, Quilter was already being described as a 'well-known' composer. Elwes sang the song again at a concert at 8 Chesterfield Gardens on 30 June where he also sang songs by Maude Valérie White and Massenet, and shared the platform with Mrs Patrick Campbell, amongst others.

Elwes encouraged Quilter and persuaded Boosey, the publisher, to take the song, and so 'Now Sleeps the Crimson Petal' was published in that year, seven years after its beginnings at Frankfurt. Quilter dedicated it to Mrs E. P. Balmain, a relative or old family friend. After a concert on 13 September at which Elwes almost certainly sang it, he wrote to his wife, 'Roger Quilter's new song having a great success – he was there and delighted'.[17]

On 15 December 1904, Quilter accompanied Mrs Duncan Gregory at a 'Concert of English Music' held at 37 Cheyne Walk, Chelsea;[18] the programme

---

[15] Reported in an interview between Mark Raphael and Professor Stephen Banfield, 28 February 1974.

[16] Percy Grainger to Roger Quilter, 25 April 1904, published in *The Farthest North of Humanness*, ed. K. Dreyfus (Melbourne, 1985).

[17] Elwes to Lady Winefride Elwes, 14 September 1904, Lincolnshire County Archives, Elwes papers.

[18] The concert was held under the auspices of Madame Henriette Schmidt, and by 'kind permission of Mrs Ashbee'. Cheyne Walk boasted many artistic luminaries – patrons or practitioners – amongst its occupants at various times. Jane and Wilfrid von Glehn moved to number 73 in August 1904; Vaughan Williams came to live at no. 13, George Eliot had lived at no. 4, Hilaire Belloc at no. 104 and J. M. W. Turner at no. 119; Rossetti, Swinburne and George Meredith had shared no. 16, the Queen's House, and James Whistler had lived at no. 96 (though at the time it was known as 2 Lindsey Row) and at an earlier period, no. 101. Later Sir Edwin Lutyens, architect father of the composer Elizabeth, moved to Cheyne Walk, as did Laurence

included 'Now Sleeps the Crimson Petal' and early performances of three other songs, 'Amaryllis at the Fountain', 'Passing Dreams' and 'The Starlings'. The score of 'Amaryllis' is dated 1914, when it was published. 'Passing Dreams' was published in 1907; it became one of the four settings of Dowson poems, the *Songs of Sorrow*, Op. 10, and 'The Starlings' was not published until 1938, and then as a partsong.[19] Following these try-outs, he withdrew them until he had worked on them further.

His songs were being sung more and more often. Alys Bateman sang his setting of Binyon's 'At Close of Day' at the Bechstein Hall on 21 November 1904, along with another song of his, called 'A London Spring Song', to words by Julian Sturgis; it was published under the name C. Romney, in 1928.

The set of *Three Songs*, Op. 3, came out the following year, the ever-popular 'Love's Philosophy' placed first, dedicated to Elwes, and 'Now Sleeps' republished as the second song. 'Fill a Glass with Golden Wine' completed the set and was dedicated to Quilter's friend, the singer William Higley. In 1905, 'June' was published, a setting of a poem by Nora Hopper; her work also appeared in *The Yellow Book*, the quarterly publication of the circle of aesthetes that included Oscar Wilde.

Some of the songs of this period show Quilter well aware of his market – the accompaniments are straightforward, and the vocal lines end with high notes, pleasing for the singer if not necessarily for the singer's audience: the success of 'Now Sleeps' was the more remarkable for the absence of a rousing climax. Many of these songs were in the tradition of the royalty ballad, the quality-destroying practice of publicising songs by paying the singer a royalty for every performance, and these songs were often dedicated to the singers who were to be their prime income-generators. Even when the royalty practice died out, many composers continued to dedicate their work to the artists whom they hoped would perform them, though the plan did not always succeed. Quilter seems to have demonstrated both his understanding and his dislike of the system: he generally assigned opus numbers only to those songs that he took seriously.

Quilter spent most of July 1905 with the Elwes family at Billing, and most of August at Bawdsey Manor, and he followed this with a visit in September to his brother Percy in a little cottage that Percy had taken just by the golf links at Limpsfield in Surrey. Here he worked on an orchestration of the *Three Shakespeare Songs* in anticipation of Higley performing them at Bath at the end of October.[20] Quilter had been working on a Trio – of which no trace now

---

Olivier and Vivien Leigh. For these details, I am indebted to Ben Weinreb and Christopher Hibbert, *The London Encyclopedia* (London, 1983) and to Laura Wortley, *Wilfrid de Glehn RA*, The Studio Fine Art Publications (Marlow, n.d.); and for the details of James Whistler, to James Laver, *Whistler*, 2nd edn (London, 1951).

[19] Most of these programme details come from the programmes themselves, courtesy of the Royal College of Music; Bechstein Hall details are from programmes held at the Wigmore Hall archives.

[20] Quilter to Percy Grainger, 2 Oct [1905], GM.

remains – and here he also wrote the cycle of six songs, with two piano interludes, called *To Julia*, Op. 8; he said of it that he was

> going through a Herrick fever, and there was something about the very name of Julia that fascinated me. The lady of Herrick's dreams became, in a way, the lady of mine. I chose six of the most beautiful and singable lyrics, which seemed sufficiently varied in mood and shape to make a little garland of songs . . . I think, perhaps, Devotion is the keyword to the cycle.[21]

He performed it with Gervase Elwes on 31 October at the Aeolian Hall, London, one item in a recital by Elwes that included songs by Schubert, Schumann, Vaughan Williams, and Brahms; for these items Elwes was accompanied by his regular pianist, Frederick Kiddle. Quilter had been up to Billing the week before – along with Grainger and Kiddle[22] – to accompany Elwes when he sang a number of Quilter songs at his recital at Northampton Town Hall on 24 October; the programme there included the first set of *Shakespeare Songs*, Op. 6: 'Come Away, Death', 'O Mistress Mine', and 'Blow, Blow, Thou Winter Wind'; and also 'Fill a Glass with Golden Wine', the last of the Op. 3 set. The première of *To Julia* in the recital at the Aeolian Hall was successful and the reviews were generally warm, and perceptive. *The Chronicle* called the song cycle 'unconventional in character, bright and melodious', the third and fourth songs, 'To Daisies' and 'The Night Piece', pleased *The Times* and the *Morning Post* (and the audience encored them), the *Morning Post* describing them as having 'great originality and charm'. *The Standard* credited the whole cycle with 'imagination, melody and strength', though *The World* thought them a 'little unequal'.[23]

Quilter's Op. 5 was a collection of settings of four of R. L. Stevenson's poems, called *Four Child Songs*. The manuscript is dated 1914, like the date of publication, but it is clear from the opus number that they are from this time, preceding the Shakespeare songs, and the date reflects simply the date of tidying up and preparation for publication by Chappell. They are pretty, if lightweight, and the last one is spectacularly politically incorrect, though for the time – with the Empire still in full swing – such chauvinism would not have seemed out of place.[24]

For two years, Quilter had hawked the *Three Shakespeare Songs*, Op. 6, round publishers, but in vain: Shakespeare was deemed 'no good', and the dearth of English Lieder was a self-fulfilling prophecy – there were none, and so there was no market. The climate was changing, however, and once Boosey published them in 1905, they became three of his best-known songs.[25]

Spending Christmas at Bawdsey Manor with the family was a peculiar kind of

---

[21] Leslie East archive.
[22] Entry in Visitors' Book for Billing.
[23] *Morning Post*, November 1, 1905; *Chronicle*, November 1, 1905; *Standard*, November 1, 1905; *The Times*, November 2, 1905; *The World*, November 7, 1905.
[24] The first verse reads (and the last verse repeats): 'Little Indian, Sioux or Crow,/ Little frosty Eskimo,/ Little Turk or Japanee,/ O! don't you wish that you were me?'
[25] George A. Greenwood, 'A Composer of Quality', *Great Thoughts* (December 1936), pp. 122–3.

hell that Quilter was obliged to endure for many years, trying to avoid the heartiness of unmusical guests. Christmas 1905 was no exception, and he returned to London as soon as he could, to see Creighton who was about to go to Berlin to study singing; he would be there for about eighteen months.

It seems that Lady Quilter, despite her apparent acceptance of his sexual orientation, persuaded her son to become engaged, even though he told her that women usually bored him. It was an engagement – and the identity of the lady remains unknown – intended to maintain social appearances but the notion of marriage utterly repelled him, thanks at least in part to his parents' example, and for three months, Creighton tried hard to get him to come out to Berlin to give him a means of escape. Quilter told his mother he would be going and there seems no reason why he should not have done so. But in February he had been ill with influenza. It laid him low, and he prevaricated.

Creighton tried to distract him by arranging an introduction to a concert pianist, Buhlig, who was very interested in meeting him, and came to London especially to do so. The introduction was to take place after a symphony concert in London on 17 March 1906, but the attempt was disastrous. Creighton's mother and his sister Gemma were at the concert and noticed Quilter there, looking particularly superior, and commenting disparagingly on Buhlig's playing and appearance. Buhlig was not a little startled – and considerably put out – to find that on his approach, Quilter fled, long-legged, into the darkness.[26] What exactly was going on in Quilter's mind remained unknown, however.

Quilter resisted all Creighton's efforts to get him to Berlin and he was more depressed than ever. In March, on his parents' return from a tour of South Africa, he went to Bawdsey, and at some point the engagement – surely not a long one – was broken off. By the end of May, Quilter was finally getting over the influenza, and his recovery was helped by the stimulus of offering Grainger financial help in getting his music better known (though it was many years before the offer was finally taken up). A recuperative weekend at Elwes's Northampton home at Billing at the end of July helped too. The house party on that occasion included the von Glehns, a distant Elwes relation called Edward Ward, and Quilter, and was commemorated in a drawing by Jane von Glehn, called 'The Twins' and dated 31 July 1906, which shows Ward and Quilter seated at a piano, Quilter playing secondo to Ward's primo.[27]

The recovery was not complete; that spring had brought enormous physical and emotional strain, and over the next few months Quilter became more and more ill, with long periods at Bawdsey being looked after. He was greatly shaken by the death from enteric fever on 1 September of Willie Miller, husband of his sister Norah, and he tried to comfort her as best he could, though he felt his attempts were hopeless. The funeral on 4 September was a bizarre affair, a full military ceremony held at Singleton, not far from Blackpool. Willie Miller had

[26] BL Add. MS 70596.
[27] Billing Visitors' Book. The drawing hangs at Elsham Hall, Brigg.

been a senior captain in the 3rd Loyal North Lancashire Regiment, and thus there was a captain's escort and firing party of 120 officers and NCOs, with a supporting cast of regimental band and buglers. The newspaper reports scarcely mention the Miller side of the family, as if dazzled by the Quilter contingent who dominated the event, in numbers as well as in height: the entire family was present, Sir Cuthbert and Lady Quilter and all seven children, with Arnie in full Grenadier uniform and Eustace in the uniform of the Suffolk Hussars Imperial Yeomanry.[28] Maude's husband, Fred Denny, was also there to lend a hand, and the lion's share of coffin-bearing was inevitably taken by Willie's brothers-in-law, although his own brothers were allowed to make a contribution too. The contrast between the pageantry of the occasion and the genuine grief (Miller was very good-looking, only thirty-one at his death and a popular local squire[29]) was made the more poignant because his brother Ernest was also dangerously ill with enteric fever nearby (though he survived) and at that point knew nothing of his brother's death.

Quilter's condition worsened and by December 1906 he was in a nursing home (where he was gratified to find that his nurse, female, was good-looking) at 22 George Street, Hanover Square, and managed to avoid a Bawdsey Christmas by staying there instead. Jane von Glehn reported to her mother that he had 'ulceration of the bowel'[30] and Mark Raphael, Quilter's protégé, reported later that he had had a stomach ulcer,[31] but given Quilter's age, build and nature, it is much more likely to have been a duodenal ulcer. He had an operation, but years after, Quilter told Raphael that it was not a success; he had to eat carefully and sparingly for the rest of his life, and many of his subsequent health problems stemmed from that time.[32]

This period of physical ill-health was unquestionably the worst he had had so far; Jane was extremely worried about her friend, and she and Wilfrid wanted him to consult Wilfrid's brother-in-law, Edward Rist, a Parisian doctor, but as Jane said to her mother, 'it is rather difficult to recommend one's brother-in-law, especially to rich people who are supposed to have the best London [doctors]'.[33] After one visit to Quilter, Jane von Glehn reported disgustedly back to her mother that he was being fed meat and medicines and on that diet was apparently expected to heal.

Not to be outdone, his mother was ill too, though not too ill to arrange for

---

[28] *Westmorland Gazette*, 12 March 1898, p. 2.

[29] Jeremy Park, 'The Millers' Tale', unpublished biography of the Miller family (1998).

[30] Jane von Glehn to her mother, Mrs W. J. Emmet, undated and illegible postmark, but judging by the following letter, early 1907, AAA.

[31] Raphael also said that Quilter was in his thirties. He was however reporting this many years after the event (in conversation with Dr Trevor Hold on 25 May 1976), and not from direct knowledge, but from what Quilter had told him; it would be very understandable if details were not precisely accurate.

[32] This was possibly a vagotomy and pyloroplasty – division of the nerves to the stomach and refashioning of the opening of the stomach – and such an operation can cause many problems, including severe and ongoing diarrhoea.

[33] Jane von Glehn to her mother, Mrs W. J. Emmet, *c*.13 March 1907, AAA.

some pheasants from the Bawdsey estate to be sent to Rose Grainger. Bawdsey in January afforded some period of recovery for Quilter and a change of scene, but by February he was back in bed yet again, and this time being cared for at his parents' London home at 74 South Audley Street. In March 1907, Jane and Wilfrid dined with the Quilters there; Roger was carried down to the drawing room to see them, and Jane told her mother that the Quilters had 'beautiful pictures and no taste'.[34] He spent much of May at another nursing home, in Hampstead, which did little for him, and he was still unwell by the end of the month; in mid-June he was better – having moved out to Bawdsey for the sea air – and despite see-sawing between sickness and health, was able to work hard during that time.

His *Songs of Sorrow*, Op. 10, settings of poems by Dowson, and the only Dowson poems he ever set, were written as a consequence of his illness (except for his setting of *Passing Dreams* which existed at least by December 1904), and he dedicated them to Wilfrid and Jane von Glehn who had been so supportive of him through a frightening and difficult time. Rose Grainger was not impressed by the dedication and wrote pointedly to him asking him to dedicate something to Percy. 'The Von Glehns tell me you have dedicated yr new songs to them – be a darling & dedicate something to Percy – he wld be so pleased – that is, of course if you feel like it.'[35]

On 25 July, Grainger went to Norway to meet his idol Edvard Grieg again, this time at Grieg's summer home 'Troldhaugen', at Hop. At the end of the ten-day visit he also played and sang some of Quilter's songs – 'To Daisies' from *To Julia*, 'O Mistress Mine', 'Come Away, Death' and the partsong 'To the Virgins' – all of which pleased Grieg greatly, and he commented favourably on the 'sympathetic personality in them'.[36] Both Grainger and Quilter were delighted at his response, and at Grainger's suggestion, Quilter promised to send Grieg some of his music.

In the meantime, Quilter dedicated Op. 7, the set of *Five Lyrics of Robert Herrick*, partsongs, to Grainger. The offering appeased Rose, but she seemed unable to appreciate that Quilter's reluctance to dedicate anything to Grainger stemmed simply from the feeling that he wanted to offer only his best work to his dear friend of whom he thought so very highly, and he did not yet feel that he had composed anything worthy.

He was still struggling with his Trio, rewriting the first and fourth movements and renovating its slow movement, and finishing off the scoring of the *Three English Dances*.[37] He had been in touch with Balfour Gardiner, discussing a Suite, and at the end of April 1907, Henry Wood had written to ask for his latest scores.[38] Wood evidently thought a 'suite' meant a set of dances, but what

[34] Jane von Glehn to her mother, Mrs W. J. Emmet, AAA.
[35] Rose Grainger to Quilter, 17 July 1907, GM.
[36] Percy Grainger, *Doings and Sayings at the Griegs, Troldhaugen, 25.7.07–4.8.07.*
[37] Quilter to Percy Grainger, 3 August 1907, GM.
[38] Balfour Gardiner to Quilter, 24 April 1907, BL Add. MS 70602, f. 59.

he got was the *Serenade*, Op. 9, whose manuscript is marked 'finished May 1907'.[39]

Walter Creighton was going through a personal crisis, wondering whether to continue to try to be a singer and what to do with his life. He began writing plays and moved to a little cottage in Upton Grey, near Basingstoke in Hampshire, where he lived a rather meagre existence. In the midst of this, he fell in love with a young lady called Fanny and became engaged to her. The engagement was secret at first, but the news leaked out, and soon afterwards it was broken off, though the reasons are not known. His family, especially his mother Louise, deemed it a great escape, though he had mixed feelings. Creighton poured his heart and soul out to Quilter, and told him, 'I want badly to get away from women. I do dislike them so, and there are so few men in life and doing artist's work one never comes across them. I am so sick of emotion and beauty. I want guts, backbone, coarseness, virility'.[40] He eventually found it when he served in the First World War and was awarded the Military Cross. Throughout Creighton's soul-searchings, Quilter remained immensely supportive and sympathetic.

A new friend came into Quilter's life in the form of Major Benton Fletcher. Fletcher was a popular guest at dinner parties, interesting, witty, good-looking; he was a noted artist and author and much travelled. His varied and highly unusual career included periods of living in the slums of south London (at the end of the nineteenth century) and doing social work there; he saw military service in the Boer war from which he was invalided out; and he established the 1st Cadet Battalion (The Queen's), the first cadet battalion to be raised in the British Empire. He was also deeply fascinated by archaeology and spent every season from 1903 to 1914 working with Professor Sir Flinders Petrie on his archaeological digs in Egypt; he was no mere dabbler in this, since he was credited with the discovery of the Temple of Seti I.[41] For good measure Fletcher was a licensed peddler, a useful transferable skill for an itinerant such as he. He knew the Graingers, at one time sharing a house with them at 14 Upper Cheyne Row, and after the visit to Egypt that summer, 1907, was due to meet them when they went to Denmark en route to Norway. He fell extremely ill in Cairo however with blood poisoning and returned to Walton-on-Thames in England. From there Quilter retrieved him and brought him to Bawdsey to be looked after.[42] William Higley the singer had not been well for several weeks either; he came to stay nearby and both invalids gradually improved, to Quilter's delight.

Quilter's health, physical and mental, was improving too, and he told Percy Grainger 'I am bigger & fatter, and the life-force is beginning to make itself felt a little, so that a bit of neighbouring flesh & muscle in the bed betimes at night

[39] Archives held by Leslie East.
[40] Walter Creighton to Quilter, 9 August 1907, BL Add. MS 70596, f. 140.
[41] Now housed in the Metropolitan Museum, New York. For more details on Fletcher, see *Who was Who 1941–1950*, pp. 393–4 and his obituary in *The Times*, January 3 1945, p. 7 c. 5.
[42] Quilter to Rose Grainger, 14 August 1907, GM.

would be welcome – but, oh, but *marriage* is not for me – the greasy eye warns me off'.[43]

On 27 August 1907, Quilter was at the Queen's Hall for the Promenade Concert and the first performance of his *Serenade*, Op. 9, his first orchestral piece to be performed. At the rehearsal in the morning, Quilter stood by the conductor's desk making suggestions all the time: one can only wonder at Henry Wood's forbearance. The supportive audience included Quilter's mother, his brother Percy and sister Norah, Balfour Gardiner, Frederic Austin, Benton Fletcher, William Higley and Walter Creighton, but although the reviews were enthusiastic, and overall, Quilter was really quite pleased, he also felt that 'several bits [wanted] a lot of alteration'.[44]

Lady Quilter wanted her son to go to a health resort and take restorative waters. Quilter had no say in the matter: she considered variously Harrogate (which had the merit of being sufficiently close to Leeds to enable him to get to concerts), Strathpeffer in Scotland, and Buxton, Derbyshire, and she decided finally on Buxton. The two of them went there immediately after the première of the *Serenade*, Sir Cuthbert joined them within a few days and they all stayed for most of September. The visit was intended to complete his cure, but as far as he was concerned, it was a 'God-forsaken hole' and he freely cursed the baths and the water.[45] The Empire Hotel where he stayed was comfortable and fairly new, being one of several hotels built to help accommodate the influx of visitors wishing to be seen at the spa resort. Although the people there were of his class, they were not of his artistic inclination and the waters tasted disgusting, but he had a piano in the sitting-room and perhaps the spa music pleased him. The hotel itself was magnificent; only the gates and their twenty-foot Ozymandian arch remain now, however.

Quilter gave up his rooms in Welbeck Street and put his furniture into store.[46] In October he was ill again, and endured medical treatment administered by his mother night and morning: he was probably extremely thankful to be able to get to the rehearsal of Frederic Austin's new work, a Rhapsody.[47] He reported pessimistically that another performance of the *Serenade* was to be given, this time by the Amateur Orchestral Society, on 13 November,[48] and on 16 November, Edith Miller, recommended to Quilter by Victor Beigel, Elwes's teacher, gave the première of the Dowson songs, but the lack of critical acclaim was a bitter disappointment to him, happy though he was with her performance.

He withdrew the *Serenade* and it was never published, and never performed again. The ostensible reason was that he wanted to reorchestrate and alter it, but the reception of the Dowson songs may have been a factor, and the underlying

---

[43] Quilter to Percy Grainger, 3 August 1907, GM.
[44] Quilter to Percy Grainger, 31 August 1907, GM.
[45] Quilter to Percy Grainger, 31 August 1907, GM.
[46] Walter Creighton to Quilter, 23 October 1907, BL Add. MS 70596, f. 170.
[47] Quilter to Frederic Austin, 21 October [1907], private archive.
[48] Quilter to Percy Grainger, 27 October 1907, GM.

reason, above all, was that Quilter, self-doubting as ever, could not face the risk of this, his largest-scale work to date and so very different from anything he had so far composed, being weighed in the balance and found wanting. He never again put himself in such a position; although he wrote long works, they invariably consisted of many short items, joined as pearls on a string.

Some months earlier, feeling that his mother 'disapproves of everything I do and think', he had written to Rose Grainger of his belief that 'most women, particularly "good" women, are without *any* real sympathy with men's thoughts'.[49] Now he wrote excitedly to Percy and Rose Grainger about Otto Weininger's misogynistic treatise, *Sex and Character*, first published in Germany in 1903 and soon translated into English; Quilter asked his mother to give it to him as a birthday present, though she could not understand why he wanted to read it.[50] He wrote to Rose Grainger:

> Sex questions chiefly fill my mind just now & also the shortness of our little time on this earth – I want to do so much & I seem to do nothing – So much there is to read, so many people to know & like & so much in them, & such a lot to feel & enjoy – and every minute I am away from actual work seems a waste. It is all very disturbing. But *sex* is wildly interesting, & things are beginning to get clearer for me.[51]

An unexpected and very complimentary letter from Hamilton Harty at the end of November pleased him inordinately,[52] but at a time when his emotions were clearly unstable, he was disturbed again:

> We went to hear Tetrazzini at Covent Garden on Tuesday night – & the whole programme & the rich audience & everything made me so sick I had to come out. O dear! What a life – So one goes on living a lie till death comes & covers everything with a cloth.[53]

He was back at Bawdsey for another trying family Christmas. At one such Bawdsey Christmas, he found himself sitting next to a haughty lady whose entire conversation revolved around field sports; on hearing from him that he did not hunt, she exclaimed loudly, 'You don't *hunt*? But what on earth do you *do* in the winter?' to which no reply could ever be worth the effort.[54]

Nevertheless, his inner turmoil, both physical and mental, was beginning to settle down and he put on weight. He began reading Maeterlinck's *Life of the Bee* which Rose had given to him: it and Weininger's book were best-sellers of the time.

Early in the new year of 1908, he was finishing the *Seven Elizabethan Lyrics*. He was pleased with the first of the set, 'Weep You No More', but discarded two (their ultimate fate unknown) and replaced them with two others. The seven

[49] Quilter to Rose Grainger [16 July 1907?], GM.
[50] Quilter to Rose Grainger, 6 Nov 1907, GM.
[51] Quilter to Rose Grainger, 25 Nov 1907, GM.
[52] Quilter to Rose Grainger, 28 November 1907, GM.
[53] Quilter to Rose Grainger, [12 December 1907], GM.
[54] Anecdote via the family of Herbert Withers, cellist.

songs heralded a lean period of composition, however; he wrote nothing else for many months.

By the end of January, he was ill again, and had to miss a musical evening at the Graingers', attended by the artist John Singer Sargent (also a fine interpreter of French and Spanish piano music), Victor Beigel, the actor Ernest Thesiger, the von Glehns and Sibyl Colefax (later Lady Colefax).

March 1908 was spent at Castle Gyar at Marazion, in Cornwall, providing a change of scene and climate (not necessarily a welcome change: the weather was dreadful) but, forever chasing health, he went to Bad Kissingen in July, to Dr Dapper's Sanatorium for treatment, which he told Rose Grainger made him feel 'like a stuffed swine'.[55] Over the summer, he shared a place near the Thames for a few weeks with his younger brother Percy, a final fling before Percy became engaged, and the Elwes family paid a long and happy visit to Bawdsey.[56]

His short anthem for four-part chorus, tenor solo and organ, 'Lead Us, Heavenly Father', appears at this time, out of nowhere; the circumstances of its composition are not known, nor is there any evidence of its performance. It is dated 1908, although it was not published until 1924, and it was dedicated to Ida Legge (Robin Legge was music critic of the *Daily Telegraph*).

In November, Norman O'Neill had asked Quilter to join the London committee of the Musical League that was in the process of being founded, but Quilter was about to go on a long holiday with his parents and had to refuse. At the end of the month, they set off for Egypt, Lady Quilter because Sir Cuthbert desired her company, and Quilter because his mother desired his. His parents were both strong-willed people (Jane von Glehn once described Lady Quilter as 'awfully nice but a regular Spartan mother of men'[57]) and now that his father was no longer a Member of Parliament, Lady Quilter had to endure Sir Cuthbert's company more than before. She did not enjoy it and so her son's company helped her cope with her husband's. They travelled first to Cairo and Luxor, celebrated Christmas abroad and by early January 1909 they were in Taormina, Sicily. Quilter returned to Cairo in February and stayed with Benton Fletcher in a small hotel in the shadow of the Pyramids.

He and Fletcher met Sir Cuthbert and Lady Quilter in Naples and they all returned to Taormina in April, where he caught influenza but still managed to work on some of his piano music: the manuscript of the second study of the set of *Three Studies for Piano*, Op. 4, is marked 'Taormina 1909', and the whole set is marked 1909, although the first was written in 1901. The studies were dedicated to Madame Pura Heierhoff-de Castelaro, a friend from Frankfurt times, and were published by Winthrop Rogers. Some time in 1909, he also began writing a lightweight but charming characteristic piece for piano 'Dance in the Twilight', which ended up as the first in the set of *Three Pieces for Pianoforte*, Op. 16 (which Rogers also published).

[55] Quilter to Rose Grainger 17 June [1909], GM.
[56] Winefride and Richard Elwes, *Gervase Elwes* (London, 1935), p. 185.
[57] Jane von Glehn to Mrs W. J. Emmet, [15 March 1907], AAA.

At this time too his interest in the theatre began to take a more practical form. Cyril Maude was preparing a production of Fagan's *A Merry Devil*, and Quilter had been asked to provide some incidental music, in the form of songs. Their identities are unknown and were probably written especially, though one – 'I Love Thee' – was unsatisfactory and Cyril Maude returned it 'as I am afraid you are right in saying it is too modern'.[58] The play (it was described as a sixteenth-century Florentine farce, written by the late nineteenth-century James Bernard Fagan[59]) opened at the Playhouse, London, on 3 June and ran till the end of July; the songs were for the character Cherubino, though with no apparent Mozartian connection.[60]

In June, Quilter returned to Bad Kissingen with Lady Quilter for another course of health treatment with Dr Dapper. The visit reminded him how much he liked Germany and he resolved to spend the autumn in Frankfurt, renewing old acquaintances, but he was unable to put his plan into practice until the following year. Percy Grainger visited him at Bawdsey at the end of July, enjoying the pleasures of Sir Cuthbert's steam yacht *Peridot* and swimming in the sea in the company of Bertram Binyon, the tenor.

Sir Cuthbert closed down 74 South Audley Street, transferred the London household to his elder daughter Maude's home at 28 South Street, round the corner from South Audley Street, and in July 1909 put much of his art collection up for sale at Christie's.[61] He was convinced he was ruined financially – or would be – when supertax was introduced in Lloyd George's famous People's Budget of 1909,[62] though once he realised that the situation was not after all so desperate, he began collecting again. He still had Bawdsey Manor, of course, and Quilter spent another awful Christmas there, trying desperately to avoid the seasonal shoots, which appalled him.

In 1910, Boosey published his set of *Four Songs*, Op. 14, containing 'Autumn Evening', 'April', 'A Last Year's Rose' and 'Song of the Blackbird'; the opening notes of the last song were taken from those of a real blackbird that Quilter had heard. Just after finishing the manuscripts of 'Autumn Evening' and 'Song of the Blackbird', he left them in a taxi. They were never found, and he 'had to think and write them all over again'.[63]

---

[58] Cyril Maude to Quilter, 2 April 1909, BL Add. MS 70602, f. 71.

[59] James Bernard Fagan, actor and playwright, 1873–1933.

[60] These details are from the programme.

[61] It was considered a major collection and included paintings by Reynolds ('Venus and Piping Boy'), Turner, Millais, Holman Hunt, Leighton, Landseer, Romney, Rossetti, Constable, Corot, Velasquez, Zoffany, Hals, Lely, Millet, Murillo, Steen, Veronese, and many others. The sale fetched £87,780 10s. He didn't have things all his own way, however – not all the paintings in the sale sold: for example, Holman Hunt's *The Scapegoat* of 1854–5 which he had bought from Sir Thomas Fairbairn at a sale at Christie's in 1887, at £2,800, failed to reach its reserve of £2,940. It remained in the family until 1923, when it was sold at Christie's to Lord Leverhulme; it is now part of the major pre-Raphaelite collection at the Lady Lever Art Gallery, Merseyside, Liverpool. The sale details were published in *The Times*, 10 July 1909.

[62] Interview with Margery, Lady Quilter, December 1996.

[63] Autobiographical notes in the archives held by Leslie East.

He was one of several to provide music for a production of *The Merchant of Venice* at His Majesty's Theatre at the end of April 1910, with a song to Portia, now lost; his music was in the company of Bruch, Sullivan and Humperdinck, although not all the music was composed especially for the occasion: Bruch's *Kol Nidrei* was included, for example, as the Entr'acte following Act 1. He never saw the production since by mid-April he was again in Taormina, after a 'very trying March'. He had been 'hors de combat for a long time' with what he described as rheumatics trouble,[64] but by May he was looking well for once, and in July played in a piano trio at Grainger's home at 31A King's Road, as part of a birthday present to Rose.

On 26 June 1910, Quilter paid a visit to Eton, for a concert in the School Hall at which he accompanied Christopher Stone in his first set of Shakespeare songs, Op. 6: 'Come Away, Death', 'O Mistress Mine', and 'Blow, Blow, Thou Winter Wind'. In the audience was a fifteen-year-old Etonian, Philip Heseltine, who was a devotee of Delius's music, and who was bowled over by Quilter's songs, especially 'O Mistress Mine'. Heseltine became better known by the pseudonym Peter Warlock; he admired Quilter enormously and famously wrote on a copy of one of his songs that he sent to Quilter 'To R.Q. without whom there could have been no P.W.'

A few days later, on 30 June, Henry Wood gave the first performance of Quilter's *Three English Dances*, at a Promenade concert at the Queen's Hall; Quilter had been working on them since at least 1907 and had scored them 'very small' in October of that year, as a discipline and in the hope of having a performance in Bath.[65] It became better known in its small band arrangement, by Percy Fletcher, and was published by Boosey in 1912.

In October he was able to get to Frankfurt at last, old haunts, staying at the Imperial Hotel until early December. He admired the poetry and tenderness of Delius's music immensely and while at Frankfurt, heard a performance of *Brigg Fair*; shortly afterwards Delius himself arrived to hear *Sea Drift*. Quilter had known Delius since before November 1908 and Grainger had met him in April 1907 at John Singer Sargent's.[66]

Christmas at Bawdsey in 1910 left him feeling negative in musical terms, but with a resigned determination to do something useful. He wrote to Rose 'I've given up hoping ever to be an artist myself – I have the English rich upper-middle class blood in my veins too much, I'm not strong enough to fight it',[67] but again repeated his offer – last voiced in the November a few weeks previously – to pay for publishing something of Grainger's: if he was a useless artist, at least let his money be of use. January was spent at 28 South Street, talking to Willi Strecker of Schott's the publishers, but Lady Quilter was anxious to get away again and, leaving negotiations to continue in his absence, Quilter

[64] Quilter to Rose Grainger, 17 April 1910, GM.
[65] Quilter to Percy Grainger, 27 October 1907, GM.
[66] Frederick Delius to Jelka Delius, 21 April 1907, GM.
[67] Quilter to Rose Grainger, 6 January 1911, GM.

left England with his mother on 9 February, for Marseilles en route to Egypt – Luxor again, Cairo and Assouan – and they were back in London by the end of March.

A glimpse of his parents' married life is given in a rare outburst: '[My mother] has been quite happy, but begins to feel wretched already at the idea of meeting Father. Sweet, *beautiful*, married life! – made in Heaven & all the rest of it, sanctified by Holy Church. What B. rot it all is, the whole bally thing!'[68] Quilter sided with his mother and he seldom mentioned his father.

Shortly before the holiday, Quilter had begun planning a Chinese opera. Amidst the general interest at the time in things oriental, he had, along with half the world, been reading Cranmer-Byng's translation of Chinese poems, *A Lute of Jade*, first published in 1909 and reprinted many times over the next twenty years; his particular copy had been lent to him by Edith Sitwell as a result of conversations they had had in September 1910. Amongst the collection was a translation of 'The Never-Ending Wrong' by Po Chü-I, a poet of the T'ang dynasty. Its coupling of idealised love and honour with a strong, dramatic and tragic story appealed to Quilter and he set to work to write a libretto. He discussed it with Edith Sitwell; at twenty-three, she was ten years younger than he and wrote to him respectfully, although her comments were authoritative, with constructive suggestions on how to introduce the characters and give information to the audience.[69]

He wrote excitedly to Rose about it; but there is a sense that he was playing rather than working at it. 'I think it will be rather pretty. . . . It will . . . give me something to do & I have been writing hard ever since being on this deadly boat.'[70] It was a very different project from anything he had attempted before; Edith Sitwell wrote encouragingly, well aware of the difficulties involved in balancing words against music: 'I envy you, having it to write, for it is a subject of endless possibilities. If there is anything I can do, in the way of looking out things for you, please let me know, as I should be delighted.'[71] But to produce such a work on his own, with no external librettist to sustain him, was a substantial undertaking, even though he proposed keeping it on a small scale, with only two singers and a great quantity of peach blossom.

In the meantime, another friend had come into Quilter's life, a young American called Robert Allerton. He knew Jane von Glehn's American family and also knew Victor Beigel, Gervase Elwes's singing teacher,[72] and was the son

---

[68] Quilter to Percy Grainger, 5 March 1911, GM.

[69] The first of these (there are but two extant) is Edith Sitwell to Quilter, 16 September 1910, BL Add. MS 70602, f. 77.

[70] Quilter to Rose Grainger, 12 February 1911, GM.

[71] Edith Sitwell to Quilter, 16 May 1911, BL Add. MS 70602, f. 91.

[72] Sources of information about Samuel and Robert Allerton are varied. Samuel Allerton has entries in the *Dictionary of American Biography* and in *Who was Who in America*, vol. 1, 1897–1947, and Robert Allerton's obituary appeared in the *New York Times* on December 23, 1964, p. 27 c. 4. Other information is to be found through the Robert Allerton Park and Conference Center, University of Illinois at Urbana-Champaign.

and heir of the Chicago businessman Samuel Allerton. Samuel Allerton, a man of strong character and sturdy appearance, who was proud to trace his ancestry back to the Mayflower Pilgrims, had made much of his money in meat-marketing – specifically, pork – and was one of the founding directors of the Chicago First National Bank; his phenomenal wealth made Sir Cuthbert look a pauper in comparison. He owned about 40,000 acres of land, 19,000 acres of it near Monticello, in Illinois, and made over to his son Robert a 6,000 acre part of it known as 'The Farms'.

Robert's cosmopolitan and eclectic outlook had developed through his studies over four years at the Royal Academy in Munich and the Academy Julien in Paris, and he was now in Europe extending his extremely well-informed interest in architecture by studying various styles, with a view to building something of suitable stature back home. A highly personable and spirited young man, four years older than Quilter, and devoted to him, he urged him to come out to the United States and looked forward with great excitement to Quilter's visit, and to all the music that he would compose while there. Quilter himself was rather taken with the idea and wrote to Grainger, 'I want to go very much & yet I hate the idea of the journey – & I don't want to be away from you for very long but also, I fear, I *do* want to be away from family etc (nice as they are)'.[73]

He claimed he had all but decided to go, but set himself up with a reason not to, by determining to hear Grainger's orchestral rehearsal; its scheduling, if too late, would have prevented him from travelling to the United States with Allerton. But in any case, he was ill again in April, and now his father was not well either; in a letter that is undated but clearly from this period, he said he had 'practically given up composing, it is impossible to live two lives', and that he was 'not physically strong enough to withstand claims of family etc'.[74] So the visit to Robert Allerton never happened, and none of the plans to visit the United States ever came to fruition.

There was always a reason, on the face of it fully justified and sensible, why he should not go, but the reality was that crossing the ocean meant leaving behind all that was familiar. To travel to and from Europe took only a few days and could be undertaken with minimal fuss, but the journey to the United States was far more complicated: there were too many unknown quantities and it was too terrifying. What if he should fall seriously ill again? He knew nothing of the medical facilities there. He would be dependent on his hosts, no matter how close to them he was, no matter how fond of them. He was trapped by his fear of the unknown and the unpredictable.

During winter 1913–14 Allerton was travelling around the world again, but his apparently dilettante air belied his purpose. He was seeking works of art of all kinds, to bring back to the States for his house; there was an underlying seriousness to him and when news reached him in Tahiti early in February 1914

[73] Quilter to Percy Grainger, 25 February 1911, GM.
[74] Quilter to Percy Grainger, Friday, GM. Its subject matter dates it to this time.

that his father was ill,[75] he returned to Chicago as quickly as he could: his letter to Quilter written at this time is turbulent and immediate. His homeward route was circuitous, since he mentions Pekin, Paris and the Atlantic, and somewhere on the way it would seem that he heard that his father had died.[76] His new responsibilities following his father's death curtailed his European travels and he devoted the rest of his life to philanthropic activities. His name appears briefly as dedicatee of Quilter's song 'I Arise from Dreams of Thee';[77] although short-lived, the relationship was very important and the only homosexual one that Quilter admitted to.

In May, Quilter visited one of his brothers at Kimbers House, Maidenhead, but pressure was on him to be at Bawdsey: his father, who had never given him any encouragement, was now demanding his presence, and was '*very* feeble and nervous'.[78] Quilter hated the heavy atmosphere there and by July was saying to Grainger, 'It is perfectly *bloody* here & I'ld [sic] give my soul (if I've got one) to go away & never come back'.[79] He escaped for occasional days out – to his sister Norah's house at Foxboro', a few miles beyond Woodbridge, and there was a memorable day at the Mill House, Wormingford near Colchester, which Jane and Wilfrid von Glehn had taken for the summer; the day is captured in a painting by Wilfrid called *The Picnic* which shows Quilter – grey suit, bow tie, white shoes – lying languorously by a white table cloth spread out on the ground, untouched fruit in a bowl by him, a few books strewn around him.[80]

By 1911, he had a well-established reputation as a song-composer; he had drifted from one doctor to another in search of health, and survived a serious illness, he had fought off an engagement and had moved into and out of the first of his London bases. He had already met many of the people who would have the greatest significance in the rest of his life. Yet despite the success of his songs, he had no confidence in himself as an artist. He felt handicapped by his social background and thought his only path was to help others. His musical style was set, and so was his way of working – he composed very slowly and was easily distracted if conditions were not exactly amenable.

His world was dramatically altered by two events. The first was that he was approached by an actor he knew, Reginald Owen, to provide the incidental music for a children's fairy play, *Where the Rainbow Ends*, a story written by Emlie Clifford.[81] It was to be produced for Christmas 1911 by the great actor-manager Charles Hawtrey, with Italia Conti in charge of the children. The second event was that his father, unwell since April, died on 18 November. In

[75] Memoir by his adopted son, John Gregg Allerton, Brookens Library, University of Illinois at Springfield, Illinois 62794–9243.

[76] Samuel Allerton died on 22 February 1914.

[77] There is an oil portrait of Allerton by Glyn Warren Philpot (1884–1937) at the Tate Gallery, London. It is called 'The Man in Black' and dates from 1913.

[78] Quilter to Rose Grainger, 8 June [1911], GM.

[79] Quilter to Percy Grainger, 4 July [1911], GM.

[80] The picture is shown on the cover of Laura Wortley's excellent book *Wilfrid de Glehn RA* (n.d.).

[81] George A. Greenwood (December 1936), p. 122.

the will, Quilter was left £25,000, with a further £10,000 to come in ten years' time, and another £25,000 on the death of Lady Quilter, although these later amounts were dependent upon intervening circumstances. The title naturally went to his eldest brother Eley, and his mother was given a life interest in Bawdsey Manor, if she wanted it, with money for its upkeep. She was also offered the use of one of Sir Cuthbert's many properties, Wood Hall, a few miles from Bawdsey Manor, and she took up that option a few years later.[82] In the meantime, Bawdsey Manor continued to be his Suffolk base, and he brought all his friends there to meet her.

---

[82] It is an attractive Elizabethan country house; parts of it date from 1566 and it was restored by Sir Cuthbert in 1906.

3

Inheritance, Montagu Street and the First World War
(1911–1919)

Quilter had not fully anticipated the effects of the independence that such a substantial inheritance would give him. He and his mother had talked about what would happen after his father's death, and were looking forward to being able to spend more time together. Now that she was a widow, Lady Quilter wanted, hoped and expected that Roger would live with her in the London house, albeit with his own key and entrance. But with the reality upon him, he realised that what he wanted, and indeed needed, was a greater freedom than his own key to his mother's house could possibly give him, and he stammered to her that he would be moving into 'his own house, [with] his own servants'.[1]

It was easier said than achieved. Lady Quilter felt betrayed and deceived at her son's decision and expressed her feelings strongly to Rose Grainger. But he managed to appease her a little with his choice of accommodation, 7 Montagu Street, only half a mile away from South Street; it had 'a lovely quiet room over looking trees and grass'.[2]

Over the previous months and years, Quilter had offered financial help to get Grainger's music published. The details are confused: he had offered some degree of help in April 1906,[3] and again in January 1911,[4] and he and Rose Grainger discussed possibilities with Willi Strecker of Schott's. According to Grainger,[5] after Sir Cuthbert's death, Quilter kept making so many excuses to Rose as to why he could not help yet, and so exasperated her, that she burst out with 'It's all right. Nobody wants you to publish Percy's music. But don't make a song about it',[6] at which he took offence. He wrote an indignant letter to her in marked contrast to his usual civilised manner.[7]

The backdrop to all Quilter's theatrical excursions – and indeed to his life from this time on – was the children's fairy play *Where the Rainbow Ends* which ran annually at Christmas for nearly five decades, from 1911 until 1959, with

[1] Grainger's 'Anecdotes', an assortment of memories written down in the 1950s, GM, 423–86.
[2] Quilter to Rose Grainger, 23 Feb 1912, GM.
[3] Quilter to Percy Grainger, 13 April 1906, GM.
[4] Quilter to Percy Grainger, 2 January 1911; Rose Grainger, 6 January 1911; Percy Grainger, 16 January 1911, GM.
[5] Grainger's 'Anecdotes', GM, 423–86.
[6] Grainger's 'Anecdotes', GM, 423–86.
[7] Quilter to Rose Grainger, [3 February 1912], GM.

only two seasons missed. It vied in popularity with *Peter Pan*, and hundreds of children – all trained by Italia Conti – passed through its stage doors; such names as Noël Coward, Clive Dunn, Hermione Gingold, George Hammond, Jack Hawkins, Millicent Martin, Graham Payn, Leslie Phillips, Dinah Sheridan, Richard Todd, Jack Watling and Esmé Wynne were all Conti children. *Rainbow* linked performers and audience across three generations.

It began in about 1902, in Chatham, Kent, when a small girl called Evelyn Clifford cried herself to sleep because 'while St Andrew and St Patrick were duly celebrated, St George was left out in the cold'. With a child's sense of justice, she thought this very unfair, she wrote a poem about it, screwed it up into a ball and threw it on the bedroom floor, and while she was asleep, her mother found it.

> Alas for St George of England,
> The valiant knight of old,
> Who slew the fiery dragon,
> And of whom many tales are told.
> For though he is our patron saint
> We think nought of his day,
> And there is silence everywhere,
> Where there ought to be grand display.[8]

Her mother, Emlie Clifford, wrote short stories. For a long time she had tried to get them published under her own name, but they were invariably rejected. When a friend suggested she write under a man's name, she at first dismissed the notion, but when she took elements of her husband's name, Harold Mills Clifford, and called herself Clifford Mills, she was appalled to find that her work was now accepted for publication.

She wrote a story to alleviate her daughter's distress and called it *Where the Rainbow Ends*. At one level, its patriotism is from a lost world, too fervent for modern times, though entirely reasonable for the Edwardian period, and in keeping with the pre-war mood. At another level, it is simply an exciting adventure story, with a hero and a dragon, children and half-mythical creatures, and hope and magic; a story that remains hugely enjoyable by children to this day.

Clifford Mills – from this point on, Emlie Clifford wrote under this name – had a talent for telling stories with good twists in the plot. Of the plays she wrote, the best known was *The Basker*, a comedy mounted at St James's Theatre in January 1916; another was a spy story, *The Luck of the Navy*. After *Where the Rainbow Ends* was first staged, she quickly turned it into a novel, which saw a number of editions.

She and her husband lived in India, and when in England, she and her husband used to stay in Richmond, Surrey, and it was here that they met

---

[8] Reprinted in 'Women Who Have Made Good, VI: A Woman Playwright: Mrs Clifford Mills', *Lady's Pictorial* (13 March 1920), p. 338.

Reginald Owen and his wife. Owen, the English actor and dramatist,[9] made no
contribution to the content of *Rainbow*, but Clifford Mills sought his help with
the technical aspects of writing a play, and so the agreement was made by which
Owen appeared as co-author, though under the name John Ramsey (or
Ramsay). Owen then took it to Charles Hawtrey, who was most certainly
interested in putting on the play; possibly his very considerable admiration for
Owen's particularly beautiful wife Lydia Bilbrooke was a factor in his decision.[10]

A number of children were needed, and having been impressed by Italia
Conti's handling of children in the fairy scenes in a play called *The Two
Hunchbacks*, Hawtrey approached her to acquire and produce them, while
Owen approached Quilter to write some music. Hawtrey left Conti to her own
devices, and she drew more and more music from Quilter for the children to
dance and play to, until, when all came together at rehearsal for the first time,
Hawtrey exclaimed, 'I thought it was a play but I can see it's an opera!'[11]
Reginald Owen played St George, and Lydia Bilbrooke played the children's
mother, Mrs Carey.[12] It is a substantial play, four acts (for a time rearranged
into three without losing any of the material), with a substantial quantity of
music. Sometimes this is used simply to punctuate the text, but much is
extended music, supporting the stage action.

Italia Conti was a tremendous driving force. She was steeped in a musical and
theatrical background: her father Luigi was a nephew (or a great-nephew) of the
singer Angelica Catalani and was himself a singer.[13] Italia had been on the stage
from the age of eighteen. After the success of *Rainbow*, the children themselves
wanted her to continue to work with them, and so the Italia Conti School was
born; with only the very occasional exception, she gave up her acting career for
it.

She was passionately devoted to *Where the Rainbow Ends*, its production, its
story, the whole package. Although they were never especially close, she held a
great affection and liking for Quilter, and never felt quite the same empathy
with Clifford Mills, much though she appreciated her talents.

The Prelude to *Rainbow* started out as a short patchwork of children's nursery
rhymes, inspired by Walter Crane's book of old rhymes, *The Baby's Opera*,
which was first published in 1877. This delightful book contains numerous
colour illustrations of well-known nursery rhymes, with simple but not
simplistic piano arrangements of the tunes. Crane's illustrative style was in

[9] Reginald Owen was probably best known for his part in the film *Mary Poppins* in which he
played Admiral Boom.

[10] He had performed with her in Gladys Unger's *Inconstant George* at the Prince of Wales's theatre
in October 1910.

[11] R. Conti to Langfield, 30 January 1998.

[12] She was the first of Reginald Owen's three wives; their marriage was dissolved in 1923.

[13] Angelica Catalani was the first to sing Mozart's Susanna in English in London: one of Luigi
Conti's given names was Catalani, although he never used it. He had a singing studio in
Brighton, and he was accustomed to give recitals with his pupils at the Royal Pavilion (family
details: Ruth Conti to Langfield, 14 April 1998).

the same vein as Caldicott, Folkard, Frank Adams, and Kate Greenaway: strong black outlines, the physical exaggerations associated with cartoons, bold colours, images of rosy-faced, well plumped-out children with smooth skins and golden curls, and considerable detail, especially in the showing of folds of clothes.

Having intended to use Crane's work as the basis for the Prelude, Quilter was then 'tempted to use more of these charming and "workable" tunes, [and] decided to make the overture into a concert piece by itself'.[14] This project languished until later in the decade, but the result then was his Op. 17, *A Children's Overture*, which was therefore not used for *Rainbow*, and he wrote instead a completely new prelude.

However, Quilter was not convinced he should be writing the music. This was summer 1911: his father was still alive though very weak and near to death, and Quilter's mother needed his support.[15] Quilter was depressed and thought perhaps he ought 'to chuck this play-music & go to Switzerland for a cure'.[16] Fortunately he did not do so, and he completed the score remarkably quickly, working at high pressure for about two months and wondering later how he had ever managed to do so.[17] It was originally intended that the play should be put on at the Prince of Wales Theatre,[18] but this fell through and the first performance of *Where the Rainbow Ends* took place at 8 o'clock on 21 December 1911 at the Savoy Theatre, London. The two principal rôles were taken by Philip Tonge (Crispian) and Esmé Wynne (Rosamund) with the minor rôle of William being taken by Noël Coward. He nicknamed Wynne 'Stoj' and they were close friends for many years.

The reviews were enthusiastic, praising variously the story, staging, music, acting, dancing, children, the entire *mise en scène*, and Esmé Wynne in particular. It was extraordinarily successful: a little while before it even opened, Quilter agreed a contract with Elkin for the music and soon began arranging an orchestral suite from it. Henry Wood wanted to perform it at a Promenade concert though he was anxious that it should not be too long.[19]

Rainbow closed on 27 January 1912 having had sixty-nine performances. Quilter's name was already familiar; this set the seal on the popularity of his music.

At the end of February, Quilter made one of many visits to Hill Hall in Essex, home of Mr and Mrs Charles Hunter. Mrs Hunter, the sister of Ethel Smyth the

[14] Archives held by Leslie East; undated autobiographical notes.

[15] Quilter to Rose Grainger, June 8 [1911], GM.

[16] Quilter to Rose Grainger, no date, but since it was written from the Mill House, Wormingford, it must date from the summer of 1911, when the von Glehns stayed there; letter held at the GM.

[17] George A. Greenwood, 'A Composer of Quality, A Talk with Roger Quilter', *Great Thoughts* (December 1936), pp. 122–3.

[18] According to the Register of Lord Chamberlain's Plays, vol. IX (1910–14), the licence was dated 26 June 1911, and showed that the play was scheduled for the Prince of Wales's Theatre. BL Add. MS 61953.

[19] Henry Wood to Quilter, 21 February 1912 to Quilter, BL Add. MS 70602, f. 98.

composer, had a loud personality and artists were liable to be in and out of favour with her. Henry James was a regular visitor, and so was John Singer Sargent, who, when staying there, would take the opportunity to practise the suite of pieces *Iberia* by Albeniz: Grainger said 'he played them stunningly'.[20] In 1922, Jane de Glehn reported to Quilter the sale of the contents of Hill Hall. The Hall itself had been sold to 'Lady Northcliff that was', Mrs Hunter having acquired a house in London. 'So *that* chapter is over.'[21]

Quilter's friend Balfour Gardiner was in full swing organising his substantial and remarkable series of concerts. There were eight, four each in 1912 and 1913; they were held at the Queen's Hall and were known as the Balfour Gardiner Concerts. The first series ran between 13 March and 1 May 1912, and the second between 11 February and 18 March 1913. Small scale concerts, such as those held at the Bechstein Hall, were reasonably straightforward to arrange and finance, and were fairly numerous, but larger orchestral concerts, especially those with a strong British content, needed strong backing. When Vaughan Williams said, 'The English composer is not and for many generations will not be anything like so good as the great Masters',[22] he was simply being realistic. He understood that having lost the tradition, the contemporary British composers needed to learn to draw upon their national resources and not falsely imitate composers whose roots lay elsewhere.

After colourful vicissitudes, Gardiner's concerts were mounted and proved critical successes. However, the levels of exasperation generated in the process were so high that Gardiner said, 'Never again' and never did.[23] Nearly every concert included at least one item by Grainger, and indeed almost all the items were by contemporary composers: Austin, Bantock, Bax, Delius, Elgar, Holst, Parry, Poldowski, Stanford, and Vaughan Williams were represented and so were all the members of the Frankfurt group, though Quilter only made one appearance, in the second season, 25 February 1913, with two songs from *To Julia*: 'To Daisies' and 'The Night Piece'.

These were extraordinary concerts. The musicologist Edward Dent, later professor of music at the University of Cambridge, was present at some of them. His comments in his diary are idiosyncratic but generally very perceptive: he liked Grainger's 'Green Bushes' from the concert on 11 February 1913 and of Vaughan Williams's *Tallis Variations* wrote that they were 'rather long & hard to follow, as he never states his Theme: but with great beauty & poetry'. He found Grainger's *Hill Song* (25 February 1913) for wind

> interesting, & the 'Colonial Song' though very sentimental & colonial quite took one by storm with its sincerity & directness: it is set for soprano & tenor, singing

---

[20] Grainger, 'Anecdotes', GM, 423–62.

[21] Jane de Glehn to Quilter, 22 September 1922, BL Add. MS 70597, f 131.

[22] Ralph Vaughan Williams, 'Who wants the English Composer?', *R.C.M. Magazine*, vol. IX, no. 1 (Christmas Term 1912), reprinted in Hubert Foss, *Ralph Vaughan Williams* (London, 1950).

[23] See Stephen Lloyd, *H. Balfour Gardiner* (Cambridge, 1984) and Arnold Bax, *Farewell My Youth* (London, 1943).

no words, but just a tune to ah – w^h is overwhelmingly beautiful. If there had been words it w^d have been a failure – either they w^d have been bad & disgusted one, or good & then the music w^d have spoilt them.

Of the concert on 4 March 1913, the seventh of the series, he found:

Bax's 'Christmas eve on the mountains' [which was] said to be very mystical seemed . . . sheer nonsense: & the same more or less of McEwen's 'Grey Galloway'. Von Holst's long Sanskrit poem about Clouds and Rain was serious music – but straggling & formless: also I cannot do with this sham orientalism. Vaughan Williams & Grainger were again the best of the lot.

And of the final concert on 18 March 1913, he wrote:

Bantock's 'Fifine at the Fair' was vulgar and stupid, with extremely well-managed orchestration. Bax's Faery Hills had some poetry, but was wandering and over-scored: Austin's new symphony was good virile stuff, but rather dry, though not at all a conventional symphony: all very 'strenuous' i.e. noisy. Delius' concerto – indifferently played by Evelyn Suart was vague & wandering, but with a good sense of beauty & a curious loveableness. . . . The concert ended with Gardiner's popular 'Shepherd Fennel's Dance' w^h I find . . . vulgar.[24]

Dent was amused by Grainger's style of conducting which resembled 'the Lion fighting the Unicorn'.

A few weeks later, from 20 to 22 May 1912, there were four performances of *The Merchant of Venice* at His Majesty's Theatre, with Sir Herbert Beerbohm Tree playing Shylock (as he had in 1910), and using Quilter's music. There is no indication of what music was played, however, nor whether it was composed especially. Nor is there anything to show whether or not Quilter attended any of the performances. If he did, it would have extended his experience in writing theatre music, if only by a little, but it is much more likely that he was involved in preparations for Grainger's major concert of compositions and folksong settings at the Aeolian Hall. It took place on 21 May and Quilter played the guitar and the xylophone.[25]

A few days later, he began his Visitors' Book for his new home at 7 Montagu Street where, over the next twenty-five years, he entertained countless artists, musicians and writers; one of his first guests was Henry James, who dined with him on 5 June 1912.

With no Sir Cuthbert to drag or drive her away from home, Lady Quilter was happy to stay in England, dividing her time between London, Suffolk and later Bath. Quilter was left free to travel abroad at will. In September 1912 he went to Paris to stay with the American playwright Edward Knoblauch. He was better known as Edward Knoblock and in 1911 had written a highly successful play called *Kismet*;[26] it was immortalised when it was later turned into a musical of

---

[24] All quotes are from the Dent Diaries, 11 and 25 February, 4 and 18 March 1913, King's College Archives, Cambridge

[25] Concert programme (held by the RCM).

[26] It ran at the Garrick from 19 April 1911 until 27 January 1912, and the incidental music was by Norman O'Neill.

the same name, using the music of Borodin. From Paris, Quilter went on to Frankfurt, stayed there for a fortnight and returned to London in mid-October.

He became incorporated into another circle of friends, of whom the core was the expatriate American jeweller and painter Florence Koehler who lived in London. As did so many of Quilter's acquaintance, she played the piano more than usually competently; she and Quilter often played duets and attended concerts together. Mrs Koehler was usually referred to as Mrs K, perhaps as Mrs Koehler, but never as Florence, although she signed herself thus occasionally. Rather reclusive, she visited Paris occasionally to see her select group of friends; she moved there early in 1914 and stayed there throughout the war, sometimes under great personal difficulties. She was well acquainted with Quilter's Chicago friend, Robert Allerton, with the Graingers, and also with Paul Rodocanachi and Bertie Landsberg, a homosexual couple.

Rodocanachi was a 'critic who wrote for numerous journals'[27] and who lectured on the music of Leo Ornstein at the Sorbonne, and Albert Clinton Landsberg – Bertie – was a dilettante, a poet, and the despair of his father, a Jewish Brazilian banker. Full of the future and never worrying about achieving anything in the present, Bertie Landsberg was totally exasperating, utterly irresponsible, but adorable, and his younger sister could not abide him. He was also extremely knowledgeable about art, despite the dilettantism, and he was known to Edward Dent, who 'found him very gentle and pleasant, though very shy' and 'liked his naturalness and freedom from affectation, though by way of being an aesthete'.[28] One morning he called on Dent to apologise for his non-appearance at a dinner to which Dent had invited him. His father had forbidden him to go out after discovering that at a dinner party he had held at home, one of the male guests had 'appeared in female costume'.[29] This was only fourteen years after the Wilde trials and he seemed worryingly unaware of the consequences of his sometimes rash and impulsive behaviour.

Others in the coterie were Oxford undergraduates, all old Etonians. Norman Romanes was the son of the biologist, Professor Romanes, and was fifteen years Quilter's junior. He was at Christ Church, and with his academic career disrupted by the war was unable to take his degree until 1918. He seemed to have caused some shock waves throughout the group when he married. Robin Hollway was a high-flying classicist from Balliol, Mrs Koehler's favourite. He was born in 1894, also served in the war, and went into the diplomatic service. Willie King – W. A. H. King – was a Balliol man too. He collaborated with Colin Taylor, Philip Heseltine's mentor at Eton College, on some sentimental ballads; neither was prepared to put his own name to the work, and Taylor wrote under the name Cecil Trent, while King took the name Elizabeth Stokes.[30] Like the

[27] Severo Ornstein (Leo's son) to Langfield, 21 October 1999.
[28] Dent Diaries, 1 February 1910, King's College Archives, Cambridge.
[29] Dent Diaries, 24 May 1910, King's College Archives, Cambridge.
[30] Colin Taylor's Diaries, vol. IIA, 12 October 1915, University of Cape Town Library, MS and Archives, BC 76. I am indebted to Professor Barry Smith for alerting me to this source.

others, King served during the war, and was Colin Taylor's senior officer at one point, a turnaround after having been his pupil at Eton. In after years he became a ceramics expert – he was the Assistant Keeper in the Department of Ceramics and Ethnography at the British Museum – but he always retained his intense interest in music. His book, *English Porcelain Figures of the Eighteenth Century*, published in 1925, is dedicated 'in affectionate homage to Poldowski', which was the pseudonym of the composer Irène Dean Paul.[31]

Perhaps the liveliest character was the extrovert and amusing Luigi Franchetti, known as Luigino. Born around 1891, he was the son of the Baron and Baroness Franchetti, went up to New College, Oxford, in October 1910 and took a first in modern languages in 1913. He was a pianist, and nephew to the Italian composer Alberto Franchetti. Luigino joined the Italian Artillery Officers' Training Corps in 1915, and in August 1917 chanced to meet Wilfrid and Jane de Glehn in France, at a dinner at which he was playing, a happy and serendipitous meeting, even if he did break one of the notes of the piano.

Many of these friends were undoubtedly homosexual, but it seems not to have been a specifically gay circle. They shared a common sensibility and Quilter adored the youthful enthusiasm and vitality of the young men.

One other of the circle, though very much on the fringes, was Mrs A. S. Green. She was born Alice Stopford and married the historian John Richard Green in 1877. Both were very well known to Walter Creighton's father, Mandell; J. R. Green was a frequent visitor to Peak Hill Lodge in Sydenham, the Glehn family home, and was particularly fond of Louise von Glehn, transferring his affections to Olga when Louise married Mandell Creighton in 1872.

At the end of the year, *Rainbow* had its second season, this time at the Garrick Theatre, where it was conducted by W. Jackson Byles. Many of the cast were the same as had been in the opening season – Noël Coward again played William, Esmé Wynne played Rosamund, Mavis Yorke played Will-o'-the-Wisp, Reginald Owen played St George, and Lydia Bilbrooke played Mrs Carey. Quilter found time to dine with Wilfrid and Jane von Glehn at Henry James's on 21 December and he held his end-of-season party for the *Rainbow* cast on 25 January 1913.

Leo Ornstein was the twenty-one-year-old Russian[32] who was making a formidable reputation for himself as a virtuoso pianist and a composer, though his work was in many quarters held to be rather impenetrable. Ornstein was keen, anxious even, to make his name, and while living in Paris had met Paul Rodocanachi, who was very enthusiastic about his music. He in turn introduced Ornstein to Mrs Landsberg, Bertie's mother. She 'liked to sing and had [Ornstein] accompany her and also had him give small recitals in their

---

home';[33] he recalled playing Bach at these events. Landsberg responded as enthusiastically as his mother to this fascinating emigré and was eager to introduce him to Quilter as a fellow composer, though their musical inclinations were very different. Thus when Willie King invited Ornstein to Oxford[34] to give a concert, Quilter came. So did King's friend Philip Heseltine – they had met the previous November, almost certainly in Oxford, and Quilter had played some songs to the young man[35] – and Heseltine reported delightedly: 'These developments of "music" (?) are truly fearful and wonderful: we are all old academics now!!'[36]

While in Oxford, Ornstein met Robert Bridges, Balfour Gardiner and Ernest Walker, and renewed acquaintance with some of the people whom he had already met in Paris. Following their meeting, Quilter insisted on his coming to London[37] and staying with him.[38] Quilter gave a dinner for him, and also introduced him to his mother, to Cyril Scott, to Robin Legge (music critic of the *Daily Telegraph*), and to the American publisher Winthrop Rogers. A recital was arranged to which Quilter again came. Ornstein was delighted, and so apparently was Quilter, though given Ornstein's reputation as a composer for outdoing Schönberg in complexity, there may have been an element of puzzlement as well as delight.[39]

At the time, Ornstein's pleasure was genuine – he returned to Paris 'bubbling over with praise and gratitude',[40] took surprisingly meekly some programming advice that Quilter proffered,[41] wrote to him 'you are the kindest soul'[42] and of his songs wrote that 'Some of them are splendid indeed'[43] – but changed his mind over the years and several decades later said, 'I didn't think too much of Roger Quilter's music', which presents a rather different viewpoint.[44]

One summer – probably that of 1912 or 1913 – the members of a Scout trip to Bawdsey Manor had included a young man called Arthur Frith. Musical, and owning a voice of some potential, he soon caught Quilter's attention.[45] Frith joined the London Rifle Brigade, which was quartered in Ipswich and

[33] Severo Ornstein to Langfield, 21 October 1999.
[34] Philip Heseltine to Colin Taylor, 1 February 1914.
[35] Heseltine to Olivia Smith, 20 November 1913, BL Add. MS 58127, f. 48.
[36] Heseltine to Colin Taylor, 4 February 1914; my thanks to Professor Barry Smith for bringing this letter to my attention.
[37] Frederick H. Martens, *Leo Ornstein, The Man – His Ideas – His Work* (New York, 1918).
[38] Leo Ornstein to Langfield, written interview. Ornstein's nurse noted down his answers to written questions, January 1998.
[39] This recital cannot now be specifically identified – Ornstein gave two in London at that time, one on 27 March, and one on 7 April 1914.
[40] Landsberg to Quilter, 5 February 1913, BL Add. MS 70599, f. 151.
[41] Leo Ornstein to Quilter, 14 February 1914, BL Add. MS 70602, f. 143.
[42] Leo Ornstein to Quilter, 14 February 1914, BL Add. MS 70602, f. 143.
[43] Leo Ornstein to Quilter, 18 May [1914], BL Add. MS 70602, f. 156.
[44] Leo Ornstein to Langfield, January 1998.
[45] Interviews with Arthur Frith's son, Roger, between December 1996 and February 2000. Other sources are shown as relevant.

Bawdsey,[46] and he served in France during the First World War. At Montagu Street one evening shortly before he went, he met Elwes who sang 'The Temple was Rent in Vain' to him, and Quilter gave him a copy of one of his favourite books, Whitman's *Leaves of Grass*. After the war, he lived briefly with Quilter who apparently would have liked a rather closer relationship, but Frith 'wasn't that way inclined'. Quilter bore no grudge. He wrote a letter to the Port of London Authority dated 23 January 1919 to try to speed up his demobilisation and successfully persuaded Winthrop Rogers to give him a job. Frith recalled Peter Warlock's occasional appearance at the publisher's offices, dressed all in black and looking distinctly sinister. On 25 January 1920, St Paul's Day, Frith became a chorister in St Paul's Cathedral Choir, London, but like countless others, he was deeply and permanently scarred by his war experiences; he drowned the memories in alcohol and in 1933 finally lost his job.[47] Quilter was best man at Frith's marriage to a singer, Gladys Peer (née Goose), in 1922, and later he was godfather to their son Roger Crispian, named after Quilter and after one of the heroes of *Where the Rainbow Ends*. Having Quilter as a godfather ensured continuity of contact, of course, and Frith was not averse to dropping a heavy hint that a little financial help would not come amiss.[48] Quilter was not susceptible to hints, however: he helped those whom he felt needed help and he seemed to think that he had done enough.

Quilter's visit to Venice in September 1913 was probably his first. He stayed at the Casa Biondetta, San Via, on the Grand Canal – Wilfrid and Jane von Glehn had stayed there for part of their painting tour in Italy in 1909[49] – where he found that his next-door neighbour was the Marchesa Casati, a remarkable woman, second to none in her sense of the dramatic and display of eccentricity. Quilter was in the company of Edward Knoblock and Wilfrid and Jane, and one evening they did the equivalent of looking over the garden wall to spy in neighbourly fashion on a party; they had not been invited since they had not yet been introduced to her.

From Quilter's balcony, they saw La Casati greeting her guests, and they also saw a cheetah, sitting peacefully next to her, her latest favourite. In the early hours of the next morning, Quilter was woken 'by a heavy thud on his balcony. Then he heard the scraping of claws and a mysterious strange patter'.[50] He lay there for hours, petrified, imagining the cheetah there. At length, hearing other people moving about, he grew brave enough to seek help, got up very softly and gently, and saw that he had been imprisoned by 'a huge, magnificent peacock, another of La Casati's pets'.[51]

[46] Quilter to Percy Grainger, 9 November 1915, GM.

[47] Frith continued to sing at St Paul's occasionally until November 1934; details from St Paul's Cathedral Library.

[48] Arthur Frith to Quilter, [28 Dec 1925], BL Add. MS 70604, f. 65.

[49] Indicated by a letter sent from Lydia Emmet to her sister Jane, 28–30 August [1909], AAA.

[50] Edward Knoblock, *Round the Room* (London, 1939), p. 183. In a later recollection of the same incident, Knoblock identifies the cat as a leopard, Knoblock to Quilter, BL Add. MS 70598, f. 154.

[51] Edward Knoblock (1939).

Venice was wonderful. He enjoyed 'all the marvellous art works there, as well as . . . the sun & the places'[52] and from there he moved on to the Villa Bellosguardo, near Florence, to stay with Luigi and his mother the Baroness Franchetti.[53] The Italian tour revitalised him, yet family pressures retained their tight grip: Quilter felt he had to attend the wedding of Willie Miller's brother at the end of October 1913. Willie Miller was Norah Quilter's first husband; he had died in 1906 and she had married again, this time to Guy Noel Vivian. But the Millers were family now and so Quilter told Grainger 'I have to go down to the country for the wedding of my sister's brother-in-law, Miller – I simply must go'.[54]

The poet Alfred Williams (1877–1930) was known as the 'Hammerman Poet': he was a railway worker, a man of toil, and his humane love for his fellow-worker imbued his poetry with an appealing simplicity and directness, some-what Whitmanesque in outlook. Grainger had introduced Quilter to Walt Whitman's work many years before, but though Quilter loved his poetry, he never set any. Williams was an English equivalent – a kind of working man's poet with a rough-hewn quality – that he felt he could work with, and in July 1913, he finished his 'Cuckoo Song', from Williams's 1909 collection *Songs in Wiltshire*.[55] The market for books of poetry was such that, though his books received good reviews, Williams had perforce to sell many of them himself: he was fortunate that Quilter came across them. In 1921 Quilter set another poem from *Songs in Wiltshire*, 'The Brook', renaming it the 'Song of the Stream'. Quilter had probably come across Williams's book on its publication and set to work on 'Cuckoo Song' straight away.

In November 1913, 'Cuckoo Song', dedicated to Dame Nellie Melba, and 'Amaryllis at the Fountain', which had first seen the light of day back in 1904, were about to be published and Quilter offered to dedicate 'Amaryllis' to Rose; he described it to her as his 'most sincere of any' and there is a sense that this was a peace offering.[56] She was very pleased with it but the rift, caused by her sharp words to him over his delays in fulfilling his promise of financial help to Grainger, was never fully healed, and there is a marked reduction in the frequency of their correspondence from this time on. The two songs were published by Boosey in November, together with a third song, 'Blossom-Time' (the words by Nora Hopper again), to make a set of *Three Songs*, Op. 15.

This year, Quilter finished three of the Op. 18 set of songs, 'To Wine and Beauty', 'Where Be You Going?', and the first of his Blake settings, 'The Jocund Dance',[57] with three more being added over the next three years, to bring the set

---

[52] Quilter to Rose Grainger, 29 October 1913, GM.

[53] Florence Koehler to Quilter, 24 September 1913, BL Add. MS 70599, f. 6.

[54] Quilter to Percy Grainger, 22 October [1913], GM.

[55] In the biography of Williams by Henry Byett (1933), it was reported as being mentioned in the *Daily Telegraph* of 1 November 1912, but no such entry has been found.

[56] Quilter to Rose Grainger, [late November 1913], GM.

[57] The contractual details for these three songs are dated 1913.

to six songs. The first of these extra three was 'Spring is at the Door', to words by Nora Hopper, and published in 1914.[58] The remaining songs (*Two September Songs*) came later, in January 1916.

For Quilter, the years between Sir Cuthbert's death and the start of the First World War were lively and, for him, happy. He no longer had his father's overbearing presence hanging over him disapprovingly and he felt an unfamiliar sense of release and well-being. Nevertheless, he still felt a need to justify his existence and when, at the end of 1913, he was invited to be a signatory and backer to the National Appeal for funds for Rutland Boughton's English Arthurian Music Drama at Glastonbury, he accepted. It was a way of using his money to help others, and was one of several such appeals to which he contributed. It was only a pity that Boughton's dream, to establish English music drama, ultimately came to nothing.

During 1914, the *Four Child Songs*, Op. 5, written in 1905, were published. Quilter began working on a piano piece that he called 'Barcarole' [sic], but when he returned to Venice in May 1914, this time to stay with Theodore Byard at the Ponte Gazziola, he renamed it 'In a Gondola' and it became one of the *Two Impressions*;[59] one of the Oxford contingent, the brilliant and mercurial Robin Hollway, pictured him 'floating in a gondola in [his] white clothes'.[60]

Quilter and Ornstein were on friendly terms and Ornstein was interested in seeing the piano pieces in the hope of including some of them in his tour to Norway, which was scheduled for autumn 1914; they almost certainly discussed 'In a Gondola'. Quilter may also have begun 'At a Country Fair' at this time since he dedicated it to Ornstein. It became the third of the *Three Pieces for Pianoforte*, Op. 16,[61] but Ornstein never played it.[62]

The declaration of war tore all plans to shreds. Percy Grainger decided that his first duty was to his music and he decamped to the States with Rose on 1 September, though Quilter managed to play 'In a Gondola' to him before he left. Ornstein also returned to the States, and established himself there, though opinions of him were rather mixed: the travel writer Lucian Swift Kirtland observed that 'Ornstein is apparently a fad. Articles appear in the ultra fashionable magazines . . . about him'.[63]

The following year Quilter completed a piano piece, 'Dance in the Twilight', begun some six years before, in 1909; it became the first of the set of *Three Pieces*, and achieved a fame in its day that doubtless pleased its dedicatee, Luigino Franchetti, who adored Quilter's music and was more than able – and willing – to play it.

The pencil sketch of 'Summer Evening' is dated 5 May 1915. This became the

[58] The contract is dated April 1914.
[59] The MSS of 'In a Gondola' and 'Lanterns' (the other *Impression*) are held by Leslie East; that of 'In a Gondola' shows 'Barcarole' rubbed out and renamed.
[60] Robin Hollway to Quilter, 25 May 1914, BL Add. MS 70598, f. 53.
[61] The MSS of the *Three Pieces* are held by Leslie East.
[62] Leo Ornstein to Langfield, January 1998.
[63] Lucian Kirtland to Quilter, 24 April 1917, BL Add. MS 70598, f. 128.

second of the set and is dedicated to the memory of Charlotte Emelia Bellot; she was an old friend and teacher who had died in 1903. It is an evocative piece, with a serenity that Quilter was perhaps in need of at the time he finished it: at least three of his brothers were serving in the army and inevitably giving cause for concern.

Of all his brothers, Quilter was perhaps closest to Arnold. He was a career army man through and through; he had been a second-lieutenant in the Grenadier Guards, and during his service in the second Boer War, risked his life at one point by entering an area of burning veld in order to rescue some of his men, while under attack; the event was commemorated in a dramatic painting. His height alone – six feet seven – gave him a natural authority, but he was clearly much respected, and popular. He was promoted Brevet-Major, and served as Military Secretary, first in the Northern Command and then to the Governor-General of Australia, Lord Denman. Now he was a Lieutenant-Colonel in the Hood Battalion of the Royal Naval Division. On 22 April 1915, he threw an olive wreath into Rupert Brooke's grave as he helped to bury him on the island of Skyros, and a fortnight later, on May 6, he too was dead, killed at Gallipoli with thousands of others.

Their sister Norah gave birth to a son fifteen days after, and she named him Arnold Guy: Guy after her husband, and Arnold surely after her brother.

Lady Quilter spent more and more time at Wood Hall, though she kept her hold on Bawdsey Manor for a few years further. She and Quilter both stayed at Hill House, Belstead, in July and August to sort out Arnold's affairs; Bertie Landsberg might have had no sense of responsibility, but learning of their task, showed a surprising sensitivity and sympathy. Landsberg was now busily writing poems with a view to publishing a selection of them: he hoped to convince his father that he was not the wastrel he thought him, and he sought Quilter's help to choose the best and put them in a suitable order.[64] This was not an easy task: Quilter was pleased to be of use, but must surely have had difficulty with some of the poems:

> *The Stone*
> Like a stone
> Alone,
> I roll
> In a hole.
>
> Such is life
> And its strife,
> And rest
> At its best.
>
> All champagne
> Is vain –
> All drink
> Makes breath stink.

---

[64] Bertie Landsberg to Quilter, 2 August 1915, BL Add. MS 70599, f. 168.

In a hole
I roll
Alone
Like a stone.

One can only wonder what the rejects were like. A poem Quilter particularly liked, however, which he considered setting, was called 'Morning and Willows' of which the second verse reads:

Weeping willows
Piled up to a height
Trembling with tears of dew!
Drooping billows
In the morning light
Tangled with beauty new!

It was in keeping with the type of poem and 'nature' subject matter that Quilter favoured.[65] Their mutual friend, Robin Hollway, described some of them as 'marvellous';[66] he was presumably the 'R. H.' of one of the later (and slightly less pretentious) poems, called 'To R. H., 1916'. It was not until 1923 that the book – *Tumult and Order*, with a frontispiece portrait of Landsberg by Picasso – saw the light of day, and then not until Quilter had been saddled with finding a publisher for him (Elkin and Mathews). He was rewarded by being one of the dedicatees, the others being Landsberg's mother, and Paul Rodocanachi.

Landsberg lived in Neuilly for most of the war. The artist Henri Matisse spent the winters of the war in France too, at his studio in Paris, and his close colleague Matthew Prichard – a friend of Willie King – introduced him to Landsberg.[67] The Matisse family became 'very friendly'[68] and the well-known portrait of Landsberg's younger sister Yvonne dates from 1914,[69] though Matisse's plan to do an etching of Landsberg does not seem to have materialised. Landsberg's father was causing some concern to the rest of the family – his health was deteriorating, and his finances were insecure, embarrassing for a banker, and embarrassing too for a son who had no desire to bother his head about money or the lack of it.

In the meantime, sorting out Landsberg's poems helped to distract Quilter from the immediate horrors. He was unable to concentrate on any music and undertook some routine writing work for the War Office,[70] but it made him feel ill and by November he had given it up.[71] He now felt able to compose again, though he still found it all but impossible to focus his mind on the task. It was probably around this time that he wrote the gentle and rather poignant *Two*

---

[65] Bertie Landsberg to Quilter, 23 July 1915, BL Add. MS 70599, f. 161.
[66] Robin Hollway to Quilter, [16 July 1916], BL Add. MS 70598, f. 56.
[67] Alfred H. Barr, *Matisse, His Art and His Public* (New York, 1951), p. 184.
[68] Bertie Landsberg to Quilter, 23 July 1915, BL Add. MS 70599, f. 161.
[69] The portrait is in the collection of the Philadelphia Museum.
[70] Quilter to Rose Grainger, 4 August 1915, GM.
[71] Bertie Landsberg to Quilter, 1 October 1915, BL Add. MS 70599, f. 173.

September Songs to words by Mary Coleridge, 'Through the Sunny Garden' and 'The Valley and the Hill'.[72]

In October he withdrew two of his earliest songs, 'Come Back!' and 'A Secret', paying Elkin (who had published them in 1903) £10 for the plates to be destroyed.[73] They had never been graced with an opus number, and he probably felt that though they had fulfilled a need at the time of publication, they were simply not up to standard.[74]

In April 1916 he was called up for service but '[l]uckily for me, the military doctor would not pass me, so I need not be a soldier – much to my relief, as you can imagine', he wrote to Rose Grainger.[75] A year later the authorities, being desperate for men, had another attempt and called him for re-examination, but the result was the same.

The tercentenary of Shakespeare's death was celebrated on 2 May 1916 at Drury Lane with a six-hour extravaganza, starting with a complete performance of *Julius Caesar*,[76] in the presence of King George V and Queen Mary.[77] The Prelude and incidental music for the play was composed and conducted by Raymond Roze, who had provided some of the music for *The Merchant of Venice* a few years earlier.

Preceding *Julius Caesar* was a curtain-raising programme of music arranged by Sir Hubert Parry, Director of the Royal College of Music, and Sir Alexander Mackenzie, Principal of the Royal Academy of Music, with contributions from Norman O'Neill, who conducted his own *Hamlet* Overture; from Hamilton Harty, who conducted music by Frederick Corder and Sir Arthur Sullivan; from Sir Alexander Mackenzie, who conducted his own music; and Edward German, who conducted his *Three Dances from 'Henry VIII'*, which had been written for Sir Henry Irving's production of *Henry VIII* in 1892. Quilter's contribution was his song 'Blow, Blow, Thou Winter Wind', sung by Robert Radford, which had been published several years earlier, in 1905. Sir Henry Wood was also billed as one of the conductors, though it is not clear what he conducted – possibly Quilter's song, and two songs by Eric Coates.

This was not all. After *Julius Caesar* there was an interval, with music, and the afternoon's entertainment continued with the Pageant. This consisted of short

---

[72] The contract for these is dated 28 January 1916.

[73] Quilter to Elkin, 28 October 1915, Novello archives.

[74] Falling sales may also have been a contributory factor: sale of the songs had initially generated a royalty of 2d to Quilter, and under the royalty ballad arrangement with the designated singer Suzanne Adams, 2d to her too. This arrangement was to have stood for five years, but after only two years, the royalty to Quilter was reduced to 1d. (Contract between Quilter and Elkin, dated 24 September 1903; contract between Suzanne Adams and Elkin, dated 9 November 1903; letter, Quilter to Elkin, 7 November 1905; all in Novello archives.)

[75] Quilter to Rose Grainger, 2 May 1916, GM.

[76] Frank Benson played the title rôle, and H. B. Irving, Sir Henry's son, played Cassius. Gerald du Maurier also put in an appearance as First Citizen.

[77] The event raised money for charity, more than £3,000 for the Joint Fund of the Red Cross and the Order of St John. It also provided a splendidly theatrical opportunity to knight Frank Benson, while he was still in full Roman costume.

arranged scenes from eight plays, intended to depict their essence and main characters. Each scene had its own incidental music, by Edward German (who provided music for the scenes from *Romeo and Juliet, Much Ado about Nothing, As You Like It,* and *Coriolanus*), Sullivan (*The Merchant of Venice*), Elgar (*The Merry Wives of Windsor, Twelfth Night*), and lastly, Quilter (*The Winter's Tale*).[78]

Nothing is now known of Quilter's contribution, and he probably knew little or nothing about it either, since in a letter to Rose Grainger dated the day of the Pageant, he made no mention of it whatsoever.[79] The only song from *The Winter's Tale* that Quilter is known to have written is 'When Daffodils Begin to Peer', from the set of *Four Shakespeare Songs*; but the composition date on the score is much later, 1933, and it can only be a matter of guesswork whether or not there was any kind of version used previously.

By 1916, then, he had been involved in some way in four productions, *A Merry Devil, Where the Rainbow Ends, The Merchant of Venice,* and *Julius Caesar,* with music being especially written for at least the first three, and he had the continuing experience of *Where the Rainbow Ends* to draw upon.

His efforts at composition (he was working on a piano piece called 'Carnival', which became 'Lanterns', the second of the *Two Impressions*)[80] were more than matched by his involvement in organising concerts, his contribution to the war effort. At about this time, he came to know the remarkable Harrison family, presided over by Mrs Harrison. She was a strong-minded woman with a Celtic streak of unconventionality, whose husband had given up a successful career in India in the Royal Engineers to return to England, because his wife hated India so much. He re-established himself in the Royal Engineers in Kent, but eventually gave even that up, in order to concentrate entirely on his daughters' musical careers.[81] May was the eldest, then Beatrice, Monica, and last, Margaret;[82] Beatrice was famous for her broadcasts of alfresco cello playing while accompanied by nightingales. At a soldiers' concert in September 1916, she, May (on violin) and Quilter played an arrangement of Grainger's 'Handel in the Strand'[83] and since playing in a variety of venues meant playing on a variety of pianos, playing the vigorous 'Handel in the Strand' on a cottage piano was a memorable experience for all. Quilter – in spite of his nervousness when performing[84] – gave several concerts in military hospitals, making use of his numerous musical friends including the Harrison sisters and the cellist Herbert Withers, and these proved so popular that a 'chamber-music club was founded

---

[78] For the sake of completeness: Landon Ronald directed all the music, and it was arranged by Henry Geehl. The Pageant alone was played again at Covent Garden a few weeks later, on 7 June.

[79] Quilter to Rose Grainger, 2 May 1916, GM.

[80] Quilter to Percy Grainger, 13 September 1916, GM.

[81] See Beatrice Harrison, ed. Patricia Cleveland-Peck, *The Cello and the Nightingales* (London, 1985).

[82] May was born in 1890, Beatrice in 1892, Monica in 1897 and Margaret in 1899.

[83] Quilter to Percy Grainger, 13 September [1916], GM.

[84] Leo Ornstein to Quilter, 14 February 1914, BL Add. MS 70602, f. 143.

. . . that functioned for a few years after that war in the Lindsey Hall, Notting Hill Gate';[85] the concerts continued at least until late 1924.

Wilfrid and Jane von Glehn were involved in the war more directly: they worked in the hospital at Arc-en-Barrois as medical orderlies. Quilter was horrified on their behalf, well aware that he had no stomach for such a task as theirs.[86] In the meantime, the firm of Alexander von Glehn was having business problems involving exports reaching enemy territory, and though the family was British (and Robert von Glehn had become a naturalised British subject), Wilfrid and Jane began calling themselves 'de Glehn' rather than 'von Glehn'. On 17 May 1917, the entire British contingent of the von Glehn family officially changed the name to 'de Glehn', and were all evermore known thus.[87]

Like many others at such a time, Quilter was unable to allow himself displays of emotion, an unhealthy repression, and he was ill for the whole of the winter, from early December until the late spring. His latest doctor gave him renewed faith – at any rate he said of him, 'I am under a doctor whom I really believe in, and who says in time, some months, he swears I ought to be *quite* a *healthy man*. This of course fills me with hope and gratitude'.[88] His illnesses varied in how much they prevented him from working; during this latest one he was unable to write anything, though by May 1917 he was looking forward to the publication of the Blake songs, Op. 20. The first, 'Dream Valley', dated from September 1916 and the other two, 'The Wild Flower's Song' and 'Daybreak', dated from 1917, though given how little work he had done in the previous few months and that these two songs have consecutive dates (3 and 4 March 1917), this is probably the date they were finished, with most of the work done substantially earlier.

A few months before, he had decided to take up the violin again, and even to start learning the cello. This was no doubt inspired by the Harrisons, although it was Beatrice Langley who gave him violin lessons, and he did not acquire a cello until around May 1918. Beatrice Langley had cause to be grateful to Quilter: on learning of her financial difficulties which had arisen because of a long illness – and her husband had just been wounded which exacerbated things – Quilter enlisted the help of Gervase Elwes and Kirkby Lunn, with May Harrison playing the violin, for a benefit concert in late May 1917. On hearing about it, Percy and Rose Grainger contributed £5 too. Beatrice Langley was touched at the very real help she received, and the event gave Quilter an opportunity to express his appreciation to Elwes: 'I am sure you know what I feel about your singing of my songs – it can't be put into words.'[89] A few days later, on 5 June, Quilter was at

[85] Leslie Woodgate, 'Roger Quilter', *The Musical Times*, XCIV (November 1953), pp. 503–5.
[86] Their lot was made less uncongenial by the presence of the poet John Masefield (Constance Babington Smith, *John Masefield, A Life* (Oxford, 1978)).
[87] The date of the deed poll was 17 May 1917: information from Laura Wortley, author of *Wilfrid de Glehn, RA, John Singer Sargent's Painting Companion* (Marlow, n.d.).
[88] Quilter to Percy Grainger, 4 May 1917, GM.
[89] Quilter to Gervase Elwes, 25 May 1917, Lincoln County Archives, 2 ELWES 1.13 L-Q.

the Wigmore Hall, helping to raise money for the '"Khaki" Prisoners of War Fund'. He accompanied May Harrison in Rachmaninov's 'Romance' and in 'Dream Valley' and 'Cherry Ripe', arrangements he made especially for her. These were well in advance of publication of the Blake Songs which included 'Dream Valley'; the manuscript for 'Cherry Ripe' is dated 1918 by which time Quilter had renamed it 'Love Song to Julia' and it was published in 1919. Quilter also played for Hilda Wynne in 'A Last Year's Rose'. He amused himself with a 'frivolous fiddle piece', an arrangement of 'Three Poor Mariners',[90] which Winthrop Rogers published that year as one of *Two Old English Tunes*; the other tune was 'Drink to Me Only', and he arranged the pair both for violin and piano, and for violin, cello and piano.

'At a Country Fair', the last of the *Three Pieces for Pianoforte*, was published late in 1916, and he began on some incidental music – unidentified except that it seems to have been intended for a production at the Ambassador's theatre. Nothing came of it: he may have abandoned it because of illness, but he may have recycled it later for Lilian Baylis's production of *As You Like It* at the Old Vic.

The Blake songs were finally published in late November or early December, which cheered him, and they were performed at the Wigmore Hall by Muriel Foster on 14 December, with Quilter accompanying.

He made an arrangement of Rosamund's theme from *Where the Rainbow Ends* for violin and piano (the publishing contract was dated 17 June 1918) and he still talked to the Graingers about going to America: 'I wish I could come to America! perhaps *if* the war is ever over, I may be able to.'[91] There were always plausible reasons for being unable to go, consciously or unconsciously disguising his fear of such a major undertaking.

Although Quilter was devoted to Wilfrid de Glehn, and especially to Jane, he was also fond of Louis de Glehn, Wilfrid's elder brother, who lived at Grantchester, near Cambridge, in a house called Byron's Lodge. As a linguist, de Glehn sometimes took in paying guests for intensive language coaching, and in the summer of 1918 one such was Marc Allégret, an eighteen-year-old protégé of the French writer André Gide.[92] Giving a rare glimpse of Quilter's behaviour with young men, Allégret wrote in his diary that Quilter was rather free with his hands, 'un peu peloteur'.[93]

In the autumn, he unknowingly came into contact again with Philip Heseltine. Heseltine, through Colin Taylor, had sent the publisher Winthrop

[90] Quilter to Percy Grainger, 4 May 1917, GM.

[91] Quilter to Rose Grainger, 20 May 1918, GM.

[92] Allégret later became a noted film director. Gide also spent that summer at Grantchester, as a paying guest a little way away. In later years, Jean Cocteau also came to visit, bringing a young male companion with him; Louis's Scottish wife Dinah, reportedly shocked at their behaviour, insisted they sleep in the garden. But Dinah thought well of Quilter; he was probably more discreet.

[93] Marc Allégret, 'Notes prises en courant sur le voyage en Angleterre' ed. Daniel Durosay, *Bulletin des amis d'André Gide*, no. 125, vol. XXVIII (Janvier 2000), pp. 87–131.

Rogers some songs by his friend Bernard van Dieren, with a view to having him publish them. Rogers showed them to various colleagues – John Ireland, Frank Bridge, Anthony Bernard and Quilter – and the consensus, reached independently, was that the songs were very poor. Heseltine was bitterly disappointed that Quilter, whom he admired so much, should have been amongst the number, but he was utterly furious with Rogers. He took revenge by playing a joke on him: he sent him some of his own songs but under an assumed name, Peter Warlock, and then, when Rogers showed great interest (and Quilter 'expressed great admiration and a desire to meet the interesting new composer!!!'[94]) he visited him, so disguised that Rogers did not recognise him, they talked for an hour and a half, and Rogers offered to publish the songs. Heseltine forgave Quilter, for in 1926 Heseltine gave him a copy of his scholarly work *The English Ayre*, and inscribed it 'To Roger Quilter, who has maintained so well the true tradition of the English Ayre. With all good wishes from Peter Warlock. Eynsford. September 1926'.[95] In a collection of ribald rhymes in which no one was safe from Warlock's acid tongue, Quilter is conspicuously absent, as if Warlock – having scarcely any respect for anyone – could not quite bear to lampoon the composer who had sparked his own vitality.[96]

As far as Quilter was concerned, the war drifted to an end. He never appeared to become deeply involved in anything – he had escaped raids whenever he could, and he had continued to visit friends and family – but this, a measure of self-protection, was needed precisely because he was so appalled by the events of the war, and did feel the horrors so keenly, even if at a distance. Jane and Wilfrid de Glehn had certainly been in a position to tell him the truth of matters at the front, and the death of his brother and of a young cousin, as well as others whom he knew, made the war all too real to him.[97] Though his medical record exempted him from war service, he did what he could, particularly in arranging and giving concerts, but it was a mixed period with compositions started, set aside, other music resumed, and arrangements of music made; sustained creative effort, difficult enough at the best of times, was all but impossible now.

---

[94] Philip Heseltine to Colin Taylor, 29 October 1918; reproduced in Barry Smith, *Peter Warlock, The Life of Philip Heseltine* (Oxford, 1994).

[95] Ernest Kaye, 'Hermann Baron, An Appreciation', *Peter Warlock Society Newsletter*, no. 44 (April 1990), p. 8.

[96] Peter Warlock, *Cursory Rhymes, Limericks and Other Poems in the Best Interests of Morality* (London, 2000).

[97] The young cousin was Ralph Upton, his mother's sister's grandson. He was killed in May 1917, aged 19. A few years previously, he had visited Quilter at 7 Montagu Street and had signed in the Visitors' Book.

4

Friends and Relations (1919–1929)

The war had appalled him. It had also officially endorsed his state of ill-health, and in financial terms, had left him considerably less well-off, his income being less than half its pre-war level.[1] He had 'many extra expenses, having several stranded people entirely on [his] hands' though they are not identified. The situation was so bad that he seriously considered letting the house in Montagu Street and renting somewhere cheaper for himself – Kew was a possible area – but in the event he was able to put himself back on an even financial keel, and apart from the usual rounds of visiting friends, he was firmly London-based for the next few years, years which would be marred by the deaths of several friends and relatives.

He continued to add to his tally of illnesses: in November 1918, he fell foul of the influenza epidemic, but on recovery, he determined to 'do all [he could] to make some money, by urging on the publishers, and also . . . by the theatre'.[2]

He buried himself in work but also continued his regular attendance at concerts, especially at the Wigmore Hall, where he heard Beatrice Harrison play Delius's cello sonata on 31 October 1918 and May Harrison, Delius's violin sonata on 11 November; in the same concert May played 'Dream Valley' again, in the arrangement he had made for her the previous year. Margaret Harrison gave the first performance of Quilter's violin and piano arrangement of 'Rosamund', from *Where the Rainbow Ends*, at the Wigmore Hall on 4 December 1918.[3] Quilter himself played there on 1 April 1919, when he accompanied Beatrice Langley on the violin, and Cedric Sharpe (of the Philharmonic String Quartet) on the cello, in his arrangement for piano trio of *Two Old English Tunes*, 'Drink to Me Only' and 'Three Poor Mariners'.

When Frederick Delius came over to England from his retreat at Grez-sur-Loing, near Paris, in early December, they renewed acquaintance and Quilter also met Delius's wife Jelka who was '*awfully* nice'.[4] Quilter loved the 'rich, lovely, melting flow of gliding harmonies'[5] of Delius's music and after the

[1] Quilter to Percy Grainger, 9 February 1919, GM.
[2] Quilter to Percy Grainger, 9 February 1919, GM.
[3] She also gave the first performance of Stanford's *Irish Concertino in D minor*, Op. 161.
[4] Quilter to Percy Grainger, 12 December [1918], GM.
[5] Quilter to Rose Grainger, 3 March 1920, GM.

rehearsal of the violin concerto, at the Queen's Hall in January 1919, remarked that he thought it 'very beautiful & tender'.[6]

He began to write some incidental music for *As You Like It*. Lilian Baylis had put on an Old Vic production of *As You Like It* at the Royal Victoria Hall every season from 1914; Sybil Thorndike played Rosalind until 1917. In these productions, unidentified music had been used, but Quilter provided the music for the production of the 1921–2 season. It was claimed a few years later that he offered to write it,[7] though some of his comments in letters to Grainger suggest that it may have been a combination of speculative writing and commission.

Quilter first mentioned providing music in a letter to Grainger dated 12 December 1918,[8] when he wrote that he was 'just going to do incidental music to "As you like it" – after Christmas, I suppose, for end of Feb or some such time. Blow, blow will come in'. He mentioned it again the following February;[9] and a production was indeed mounted during that winter's season, lasting through until May 1919, and also in the following season, from October 1919 until May 1920.

Although Quilter's music was all ready a good time in advance – the songs were available in 1919, and the autograph orchestral score for the suite (arranged from the incidental music) is dated 1920 (and performed in September 1920, apparently with five movements, not the final four) – it was not premièred in the theatre until 17 October 1921.[10] The music was scored for thirteen-piece chamber ensemble,[11] he 'brought a Male Quartette from St Paul's Cathedral to sing the ballads and Concerted Music'[12] – the 1921 programme lists six singers, including Arthur Frith, Quilter's protégé, and Leslie Woodgate, who was Quilter's personal secretary at that time and later became Chorus-master for the BBC – and he conducted on each occasion. There were three songs: 'Under the Greenwood Tree'; 'Blow, Blow, Thou Winter Wind'; and the duet version of 'It was a Lover and His Lass'. 'Under the Greenwood Tree' and the solo version of 'It was a Lover and His Lass' were included in the Op. 23 set of *Five Shakespeare Songs* of 1921; 'Blow, Blow' had first been published back in 1905. In addition to the songs, his partsong 'What Shall He Have that Killed the Deer?' for men's voices (tenor, baritone and two basses) was written for this occasion, though it was not published until 1924. A few years later when Italia

---

[6] Quilter to Percy Grainger, 9 February [1919], GM.

[7] Royal Victoria Hall – Old Vic: Annual Report 1921–22 season, p. 11.

[8] Quilter to Percy Grainger, 12 December [1918], GM. Amongst other points in this letter, he mentions hoping to hear Delius's violin concerto soon after the New Year; Albert Sammons gave it its first performance on 30 January 1919 at the Queen's Hall, with Boult conducting.

[9] Quilter to Percy Grainger, 9 February [1919], GM.

[10] The reason can only be a matter for conjecture now; in Harcourt Williams's history of the Old Vic, he makes no mention of music at all, nor sufficient hint of differences between productions to give any clue (Williams, *Old Vic Saga* (London, 1949)).

[11] Quilter to Percy Grainger, 9 February [1919], GM.

[12] Royal Victoria Hall – Old Vic: Annual Report 1921–22 season, p. 11.

Conti mounted a production of it at an unidentified venue, he provided some further music.[13]

The original incidental music was not used again until the 1928 season, despite further performances of the play (under Lilian Baylis's management) in 1923, 1924 and 1926, and it is now lost. However, Quilter fashioned a suite from it, which he dedicated to Balfour Gardiner. On 26 December 1921, Gardiner wrote appreciatively to him: 'It was a charming thought of yours to dedicate "As you like it" to me. I *do* like it, as I like all your simple and honest music, and I hope it will not be long before I hear it performed.'[14]

In late November 1918, he assembled an album of dances from *Where the Rainbow Ends*, for piano, which Elkin agreed to publish, and he also promised to arrange the Fairy Frolic for trio; the album was published a year later, but the piano trio was not published until 1929. The orchestral suite – first performed at a Promenade concert in 1912 – he arranged so as to be 'practicable for most smallish orchestras';[15] it was finished by July 1919 and Elkin published it in 1920. The Chinese opera had faded out of sight, but he began talking about a 'little ballet' and he planned to begin work on a light opera in the summer of 1919; it was to be a fairy opera, and a friend of Louis de Glehn, called Richmond, was helping him with the libretto.[16]

Music from *Where the Rainbow Ends* continued to be popular. Grainger played his own version of the music for the lake scene, 'Moonlight on the Lake', and it also turned up as background music to a love scene in a film.[17]

He returned to the overture he had originally intended for *Rainbow* and by February 1919, he had reworked it and renamed it *A Children's Overture*, Op. 17; its opus number clearly dates it from much earlier in the decade. He dedicated it to his brother Percy and Sir Henry Wood conducted it at a Promenade concert on 18 September 1919. Quilter was typically nervous about it, but justifiably: it was under-rehearsed, and Wood seemed to be out of sympathy with it. Overall, though, Quilter was moderately pleased. It said what he wanted to say, it had 'a *genuinely* warm reception'[18] and reviews were encouraging.

It has retained its freshness and appeal over many years; it has been many times arranged so as to be playable by whatever resources are available – from ten-piece spa band to full symphony orchestra – and it has always survived the experience. It has been recorded many times too, and Alick Maclean's recording for Columbia was the first, recorded on three sides of a two-record set; Quilter 'had to cut out the introduction and a lot of the middle' to enable it to fit.[19] Maclean was conductor of the New Queen's Hall Light Orchestra from its

[13] George A. Greenwood, 'A Composer of Quality', *Great Thoughts* (December 1936), pp. 122–3.
[14] H. B. Gardiner to Quilter, 16 December 1921, BL Add. MS 70603, f. 130.
[15] Quilter to Percy Grainger, 15 July 1919, GM.
[16] Quilter to Percy Grainger, 15 July 1919, GM.
[17] Quilter to Percy Grainger, 12 July 1920, GM.
[18] Quilter to Percy Grainger, 1 November 1919, GM.
[19] Quilter to Percy Grainger, 1 November 1919, GM.

inception in 1916 and he conducted some of the Chappell Ballad concerts, but he was best known as musical director of the Spa Orchestra in Scarborough, a post he held from 1912 until his death in 1936. Seeing the worth of the Overture, he performed it on a number of occasions.

By the following June the Overture had already been performed frequently, and Winthrop Rogers published it as a piano solo. It was too expensive to publish as an orchestral score in the original version: Rogers complained to Quilter that the 'high cost of production, coupled with persistent slump everywhere [make it] impossible for us to proceed with the idea'[20] and when it was sent to the States, it was a manuscript score and parts that were sent. The orchestral score was finally published in 1921 by Chappell's in association with Winthrop Rogers, in a 'Popular Orchestral Arrangement by the Composer'. It is indicative of its popularity that it was included in the first orchestral concert broadcast by the BBC, on Saturday 23 December 1922.

Quilter performed regularly on radio, particularly during the 1920s, and his music was often broadcast – even as late as 1949, there were over 170 performances of his songs in that one year, and nearly double that in 1948.[21]

Quilter's nephew, George Eley Cuthbert, Eley's elder son and thus heir to the Bawdsey estate, had been ill with kidney disease and died in March 1919, aged eighteen. That autumn, Quilter's mother, Lady Quilter, finally relinquished her hold on Bawdsey Manor and moved to the smaller property of Wood Hall, only a few miles away, with a winter home at Bath. Eley, known as Sir Cuthbert Quilter, installed himself in the family seat and lived there until the house became too much of a white elephant; it was sold to the Royal Air Force in the mid-1930s and, because of its isolation combined with its proximity to Europe, proved an ideal place from which to develop radar. The emblem of RAF Bawdsey, a watchdog with a chain around its neck, was taken directly from the mosaic floor in the porch of the Manor.

Early in 1920, Quilter sent copies to Grainger of the newly published piano pieces *Two Impressions*, containing 'In a Gondola' and 'Lanterns'. Grainger was delighted with them, 'particularly the gondola one'.[22] He encouraged Quilter to make arrangements of his pieces, especially those already published, for use by Carolyn Beebe's chamber group (flute, oboe, clarinet, bassoon, horn, strings and piano): during her tours of the States the pieces would get a wide coverage. Grainger made specific recommendations on how to orchestrate them for her combination, and suggested arranging 'Lanterns', 'Rosamund', 'St George', 'Fairy Frolic', 'Moonlight on the Lake' and the third of the *Three English Dances*, though he probably wanted a denser orchestration than Quilter would care for. He urged him – not for the first nor the last time – to develop his short pieces, wanting 'freer delivery and less concentrated, less formal, expression' with a 'longer warmer treatment' and complaining that Quilter '[stopped] as soon as

[20] Winthrop Rogers to Quilter, 3 May 1921, BL Add. MS 70603, f. 110.
[21] BBC WAC, transmission listings.
[22] Grainger to Quilter, 6 June 1920, GM.

the bare idea is spat out'.[23] He reminded Quilter of the richness of such choral pieces as his 'Omar Khayām' partsong, he criticised the polite formal divisions of Quilter's lighter music, and encouraged him to write something more passionate, more in keeping with what he felt in Quilter's songs. Quilter liked the idea of arranging for the 'Beebe forces',[24] but never actually did so, being too busy with other matters, and a 'free, thick, self-unburdening orchestral . . . work' such as would please Grainger would have required a lack of restraint that was foreign to his nature.[25]

During the summer of 1920, Quilter spent a few weeks at Wood Hall. He would probably have done so anyway, but his mother was ill with some kind of 'flu and he wanted to be with her to help her recuperate: he had always been concerned for her health, as she had been for his. The visit also more or less coincided with the marriage of Louis de Glehn to Dinah Cassels, who had met both Louis and Quilter as a result of her serving in France alongside Wilfrid and Jane de Glehn, during the First World War.

The Gramophone Company, later HMV, published a monthly magazine *The Voice* and on 30 July 1920, the editor, Arthur Russell, wrote to Quilter to ask for his views on 'the future of the Gramophone', the contribution to be published in a symposium in the next edition of the magazine. Quilter's reply was thoughtful, and unusual in that he rarely set down his thoughts in such detail:

> I think there is a very great future for the gramophone. In the first place it will be invaluable to young students of singing – listening to the rendering of songs and arias by first rate artists, is the best lesson for a young singer, and with the gramophone they can hear the same song again and again till they have every shade and nuance by heart.
>
> I think there is a greater future for records of orchestral pieces and compositions for strings – quartets etc. The string quartet records are, at present, more satisfactory than orchestral records, the string instruments having the same quality of sound and so combining better. But I think, with continual experimenting with the orchestra, there might be very great improvements, and by careful rearrangement of the instruments very good records could be made of the best known orchestral works. I also think there might be more records of part songs and unaccompanied chorus singing, which can be very effective. Composers of today might with advantage learn more about the making of records so as to know how best to arrange the instruments of the orchestra, how to make any particular passages 'tell', and so forth: in fact, I do not see why they should not orchestrate especially for the gramophone, when records are to be made; it would be far more satisfactory.
>
> When all these improvements have been made, the gramophone will become more and more valuable for teaching purposes, for illustrating lectures, etc, as well as for the enjoyment and education of people who do not live in large towns and are unable to hear good orchestras or chamber music. Eventually most interesting

---

[23] Grainger to Quilter, 6 June 1920, GM.
[24] Quilter to Grainger, 12 July 1920, GM.
[25] Grainger to Quilter, 6 June 1920, GM.

and instructive concerts might be arranged in every school and even villages and small towns.[26]

The educative value of records clearly appealed to Quilter, and his view of exact imitation as a means of learning was a commonly held one (and is still endorsed).

Towards the end of the year, Wilfrid de Glehn began painting a portrait of Quilter in oils. It was finished the following year, and Wilfrid included it in his show when he and Jane went to America: it was '*vastly* admired'.[27] It brings out an aloofness and an aristocratic air that was not Quilter's by blood, though friends often spoke of the sense that he was out of his period, as if he was a gentleman of an earlier time. Many years later, Wilfrid offered it to the National Portrait Gallery, London, but because of the Gallery's policy of not accepting portraits of living subjects, it was refused. So in the December after Quilter's death, Jane approached the Gallery again. This time, and with the support of Sir Arthur Bliss, Sir Malcolm Sargent and Ralph Vaughan Williams, who co-signed a letter of emphatic recommendation on the grounds of Quilter's distinguished place in English music and the permanent contribution of his songs to the national heritage, it was accepted.[28]

Gervase Elwes sailed to America on 24 November 1920 for his third tour there, and Lady Winefride accompanied him, largely because of a curious presentiment on his part that their time together might not be for much longer.[29] The tour was extremely successful, and he was in excellent voice, as usual introducing his audiences to new songs. Part of the way through the tour, on 12 January 1921, the morning after his recital at Princeton University, Elwes and his wife were at the railway station at Boston, Massachusetts. Elwes suddenly realised that in leaving the train he had acquired someone else's coat by mistake. He ran to the conductor of the train to hand it back, but in a moment, slipped over and fell between the track and the train just as it was moving off. Lady Winefride tried to pull him out but she was struck on the head and knocked unconscious. Elwes died of his injuries some hours later.

The suddenness of the tragedy was shattering to everyone who knew him, and Lady Winefride received hundreds of letters of condolence. Newspaper obituaries from all over the world were unanimous in acknowledging his fine musicianship and interpretative skills: it was fully realised that the musical world had lost a great English singer of notable artistry. Quilter's letter to Lady Winefride reveals his appreciation of the man and the singer:

---

[26] Leslie East archive.

[27] Jane de Glehn to Quilter, 18 November [1921], BL Add. MS 70597, f. 116.

[28] The portrait was accepted on 9 April 1954; the decision had had to be postponed from the initial February meeting while the Board considered the matter – in other words, while they made enquiries about the suitability of the subject. Jane, in a letter of thanks to the Gallery (held in the Gallery's archives), made it very clear that she had had nothing to do with the letter from the 'eminent musicians'.

[29] Lady Winefride and Richard Elwes, *Gervase Elwes* (London, 1935), p. 264.

What can I say? but tell you how my heart simply aches for you and how I long & pray that you may find comfort. . . . The dear man will be missed so tremendously by *countless* people . . . the world of art has suffered a loss that is irreparable. No one can ever take his place. I think you know what *I* thought of him. I feel as if a part of me had been taken away – He was the *greatest inspiration* to me always, as well as being a splendid friend whom I could always look up to and love and reverence. . . . Dear friend – I know you will understand a good deal of what I feel, and will read into these stupid words something of what I long to express. God protect you and comfort you. . . . I feel now that whatever I write in music will be somehow influenced by him . . . I feel I owe him so much; I can never repay him but I shall try to honour his beloved memory in the way I can.[30]

There were others who recognised the significance of Elwes to Quilter and his work, and Vaughan Williams wrote to Quilter to say that he 'always loved to hear [Elwes] sing such songs as Julia especially and also Blow Blow'.[31] Edward Knoblock, the playwright, added his sympathy: 'I knew what a friend of yours he was – & what a noble one. It seems a brutal death for one so much loved and needed in this raw world of [ours].'[32] Both Rose and Percy Grainger wrote to Quilter too, appreciating the loss to him of a singer who understood his songs so well. But perhaps the letter to Lady Winefride from Elwes's accompanist, the faithful Frederick Kiddle, is the most moving and wholly grief-stricken:

To me he was the finest man I ever knew. . . . You know what I thought of him as a musician and an artist. No man ever gave me as much pleasure to accompany as Gervase or ever will do and I do hope you will allow me to accompany him for the last time when he is laid to rest at Billing. . . . That God has Gervase's soul in His keeping and that he will always bless you and all your family is the sincere hope of Gervase's old heart-broken accompanist.[33]

Elwes's teacher, Victor Beigel, set up a Memorial Fund in his memory which later became the Musicians' Benevolent Fund. The first meeting of the Executive Committee was on 9 February 1921 and Quilter was a founder member, staying on its council and attending meetings faithfully, until his death; some of the early meetings were held at his home in Montagu Street.[34] This was a substantial testament to Elwes, since Quilter was not a committee person as a rule: to put himself in the position of having to attend meetings regularly was too much of a commitment and he always refused invitations to join committees.[35]

[30] 16 January 1921, Lincoln County Archives, 2 Elwes 1.13 L-Q.
[31] Vaughan Williams to Quilter, 13 February 1921, BL Add. MS 70603, f. 103.
[32] Knoblock to Quilter, 19 February 1921, BL Add. MS 70598, f. 161.
[33] 18 February 1921, Lincoln County Archives, 2 Elwes 1.13 F-K.
[34] Mark Raphael, from the text prepared for the centenary broadcast, BBC Third Network 1 Nov 1977.
[35] G. Herbert Thring, of the Society of Authors, invited him to allow his name to be nominated to fill a vacancy on the Society's Composers' Committee, but he refused, although later in the decade he contributed to their 'fighting fund', set up to help the members. (Thring to Quilter, 26 October 1921, BL Add. MS 63318, f. 84; Quilter to Thring, 28 October 1921, BL Add. MS 63318, f. 85; Secretary to Quilter, 10 May 1929, BL Add. MS 63318, f. 86 and Quilter to Secretary, 24 May 1930, BL Add. MS 63318, f. 87).

That did not prevent him joining clubs and societies, however: he was a member of the Society of Authors, and in September 1923, he became a full member of the Royal Philharmonic Society.[36] For a few years he was also a member of the Savile Club, noted for its largely 'artistic' membership; he joined it in 1906, though he ceased membership in the year of Elwes's death. Perhaps visiting the Club reminded him too much of Elwes, who had proposed him in the first place.[37]

Another sudden death rocked his equilibrium. Robin Hollway, one of the Oxford circle, committed suicide on 7 March 1921. Florence Koehler (writing from New York) wrote impassioned letters to Quilter, expressing her grief and anger, and perhaps helping him through his loss too. The reasons for Hollway's suicide were never clear; the strain of working in hospitals during the war might have caught up with him, his acute sensitivities too much battered. Koehler had always thought that Hollway's temperament was diametrically unsuited to a career in the diplomatic service and she mourned the loss of a 'fine flower of civilisation'.[38] Hollway's father founded the Robin Hollway Scholarship from Eton to Balliol in his memory,[39] and Quilter dedicated his Shakespeare setting 'Fear No More the Heat of the Sun' to his memory as well.

Wilfrid de Glehn's sister Rachel had married Frank Marsh, who was several years older than she. When Marsh died prematurely in 1921 – another death for Quilter to cope with – Wilfrid undertook to provide for Rachel and her four children. He helped them to procure a house in Cornwall to live in, and arranged holidays for them. One such holiday venue was at Mudeford, Christchurch, in Hampshire. Quilter stayed with Wilfrid and Jane there in September 1921, and returned to London afterwards to be involved with *As You Like It*.

Rose, deeply distressed over accusations of incest between her and Grainger, committed suicide on 30 April 1922 by jumping from a window in the Aeolian Building in New York (where Antonia Sawyer, Grainger's agent, had her offices). Her death, and its manner, shocked Quilter, though according to Grainger, he did not mourn adequately for her: Grainger wrote (in what he termed 'blue-eyed English', avoiding words of Latin and Greek origin – 'self-kill-ment' means suicide), 'If I was not to find comfort, after mother's self-kill-ment, from dearest friends such as Roger Quilter, Cyril Scott, where was I to look for comfort?'[40] Perhaps Quilter was too numb from so many unexpected, and in some cases violent, deaths. The relationship between Quilter and Rose

[36] He had been elected an Associate in October 1918, proposed by the composer Thomas Dunhill and seconded by Norman O'Neill, then treasurer of the Society, and by Waddington Cooke. The RPS archives are on loan to the British Library, Loan 48.2/13 and 48.22/2.
[37] The other proposers and supporters included Robin Legge, C. V. Stanford, Harry Plunket Greene, C. H. Lloyd and Bertram Binyon (Savile Club archives).
[38] Florence Koehler to Quilter, 31 March 1921, BL Add. MS 70599, f. 115.
[39] Sir Ivo Elliott, Bart, ICS (Retd), ed., *Balliol College Register, 1900–1950*, 2nd edn, printed for private circulation by Charles Batey at the University Press (Oxford, 1953).
[40] Grainger's 'Anecdotes', 423–87, GM.

Grainger had been a strange one, and their friendship had cooled many years before, when Quilter had offered Grainger financial help to get his music published, while at the same time appearing dilatory in carrying out his promise. Nevertheless, he had written a cordial letter to her only a few weeks before her death,[41] and had had a letter from her, in connection with his portrait by Wilfrid de Glehn which she had just seen. In the letter she said, prophetically, 'in case I should not recover – I want you to know this, dear friend . . . I hope to see you again some day – but we never can tell, can we'.[42]

Grainger had simply been informed of his mother's death, and learned the details from a newspaper report. He aged rapidly, and grieved for her as passionately as he had loved her while she was alive; to compensate, he took on a massive workload, and on 10 August 1922, left the States to begin a long European tour. He started in Denmark, and moved on to Norway where he met Balfour Gardiner who had arranged to spend a few days with him there; back to Denmark, then the Netherlands – after much prevarication, Quilter went to Amsterdam to visit him in the last few days of October[43] – reaching Frankfurt in December and staying there for several months. In the midst of his sojourn in Germany, Grainger made a flying visit to London to hear Delius's *Song of the High Hills*, with Quilter, on 7 December in a Royal Philharmonic Society performance, though he was tired and poor company.[44] Later, he returned to Dordrecht in the Netherlands, then to Norway and he was back in the States by the middle of August.

While he was in Germany, Grainger had long talks with Willi Strecker, who had enabled the publication of Grainger's music back in the first decade of the century. Strecker, now head of Schott's, was pessimistic about the German market for songs but considered Quilter to be the 'finest song composer in English' and 'if *any foreign* songs are worth tackling . . . [his] should be the first, or amongst the very first'.[45] It was deemed essential to publish them in German translation, and during the summer of 1924, this was undertaken by an old friend of Quilter's, Ida Goldschmidt-Livingston, who lived in Frankfurt.[46] 'Dream Valley' was a possibility at one stage but the final selection was: 'Now Sleeps the Crimson Petal', 'Love's Philosophy', 'To Daisies' (from *To Julia*), 'Weep You No More' and 'It was a Lover and His Lass', the last three of which were Grainger's suggestions, and Schott published them in 1924. Schott also published the first set of Shakespeare songs: Goldschmidt-Livingston made translations of all three, although only her version of 'O Mistress Mine' was used; the other songs were translated by Schlegel.

A very young man called Leslie Woodgate, who was born in 1902, was one of

---

[41] Quilter to Rose Grainger, 22 March 1922, GM.
[42] Rose Grainger to Quilter, 11 April 1922, GM.
[43] Percy Grainger to Quilter, 9 November 1922, GM. On 27 October, they evidently had some photographs taken, by a photographer called Merkelbach.
[44] Percy Grainger to Quilter, 10 December 1922, GM.
[45] Percy Grainger to Quilter, 5 June 1923, GM.
[46] Ida Goldschmidt-Livingston to Quilter, 1910–1925, BL Add. MS 70598.

the children in *Rainbow* one year and met Quilter 'on the stairs leading to the dressing rooms in the Victoria Palace Theatre'.[47] Woodgate claimed this to be in December 1916, but the production was at the Globe that season, and was not mounted at the Victoria Palace until the seasons of 1918 and 1919. Woodgate went to work for the publisher Winthrop Rogers in 1918, became Quilter's musical secretary in 1919 and remained in that rôle until his appointment as Assistant Chorusmaster to the BBC in 1928; he became Chorusmaster in 1934. Woodgate was a fine musician, though not universally liked, and in 1931 became the first conductor of the BBC Theatre Orchestra, which he had also founded.[48]

During the first few years that he worked for Quilter, he was also a student at the Royal College of Music. This was possible because his job for Quilter was not an onerous one: it was primarily to write out fair copies of songs from Quilter's sketches; it only occupied him in the mornings and so his afternoons were free. He became engaged to another College student, Lena Mason, in early September 1925, and Quilter was a witness at their wedding in Marylebone on 28 July 1926; his present to them (belated and dated October 1926) was an elegant leather-bound three-volume miniature full-score edition of Wagner's *Die Meistersinger*.

Woodgate's help was invaluable, and this was a productive time. Five of the folk-song arrangements that would later find their way into *The Arnold Book of Old Songs* were published in 1921: 'Drink to Me Only', 'Over the Mountains', 'The Jolly Miller', 'Barbara Allen' and 'Three Poor Mariners'. The second set of Shakespeare songs was published in 1922: Grainger particularly liked the first of these, 'Fear No More the Heat of the Sun',[49] written in 1921, which both he and Quilter thought of as a requiem to Robin Hollway.

Three of the *Five English Love Lyrics*, Op. 24, date from the same year: 'There be None of Beauty's Daughters', 'Morning Song' and 'Go, Lovely Rose'. 'There be None' was given its first performance at a Promenade concert on 22 August 1922, sung by Tudor Davies (though dedicated to the black tenor Roland Hayes) with Frederick Kiddle playing and 'Morning Song' was premièred at another Promenade concert on 4 October 1922, sung by Hilda Blake (though dedicated to John Coates), and accompanied by Kiddle. 'Go, Lovely Rose' was not heard until 17 August 1923, at another Promenade concert, with Hubert Eisdell singing, and Kiddle, as resident accompanist, playing again.

Three songs from the Op. 25 set of *Six Songs* date from the early part of the decade: the 'Song of the Stream' is dated 6 November 1921, 'The Fuchsia Tree' is dated 18 February 1923 and 'An Old Carol' dates from 1923.

Two Songs, Op. 26, settings of words by R. L. Stevenson and containing 'In the Highlands' and 'Over the Land is April', date from June 1922; these were

[47] Leslie Woodgate, 'Roger Quilter', *The Musical Times*, XCIV (1953), pp. 503–5.
[48] From the career details contained in the application by Leslie Woodgate for the post of President, Guildhall School of Music, dated 11 March 1938.
[49] Percy Grainger to Quilter, 9 November 1922, GM.

dedicated to Louis and Dinah de Glehn. His four *Country Pieces*, Op. 27, for piano were published in the first part of 1923 and dedicated to his old teacher at his preparatory school, Pinewood in Farnborough. Edith Brackenbury wrote back a very nostalgic and wistful letter, in which she said:

> For myself I shall always keep a most happy remembrance of our music lessons together. It was very little I did, after all only getting the soil ready for the sowing. Your letter has given me the greatest pleasure all the same, as well as the dedicated music, and I thank you very much for both which I shall treasure.[50]

In the early 1920s, Quilter made the acquaintance of a young composer called Muriel Herbert. She was twenty when she went to study composition at the Royal College of Music in 1917, with Sir Charles Stanford. She may have met Quilter through Leslie Woodgate, a fellow student there, or possibly through the Duchess of Wellington, a musical patroness who had asked the College to suggest and supply a young musician as a sort of musical companion, someone to help her with her music.

Quilter was kind to the budding composer, as was his wont with young musicians; throughout his life, he was discreetly generous to 'poor and struggling' artists.[51] Quilter helped her to find a publisher – Augener – for her songs in 1923, and he witnessed the contract. The first song to be published was a powerful setting of a poem by Alice Meynell, 'Renouncement', which she dedicated to Quilter in gratitude.[52] Unfortunately for them both, she, with the naïveté of a young woman in a post-war world with too few young men, fell in love with him. Quilter never realised, but when the Duchess told him, he backed away and the relationship ended, to Muriel Herbert's great distress. Later, she married Emile Delavenay, but was divorced, and in later years told her daughter that Quilter remained the love of her life.[53]

A mention of another fiancée occurred in December 1922 (the last mention being in 1906) when Bertie Landsberg described how 'your fiancée . . . goes on beautifully being her beautiful self'.[54] He may have been referring – rather sarcastically – to one of his own sisters, since he was almost certainly writing from France.

At a concert of 'Pops' at the Wigmore Hall on 10 February 1923, promoting the Guild of Singers and Players, Quilter accompanied Norman Notley in four of his songs. Easter was spent in company with Eric Coates and the singer Carrie Tubb in Bournemouth, to watch Dan Godfrey and the Bournemouth Municipal Orchestra in action for the second Bournemouth Musical Festival. Both *A Children's Overture* and the music from *As You Like It* were performed and Eric Coates was there to conduct some of his own works in the five-week festival.

[50] Edith Fabian Brackenbury to Quilter, 19 July 1923, BL Add. MS 70603, f. 160.
[51] Sir Quintin Hill, 'Roger Quilter: 1877–1953', *Music and Letters*, XXXV (1954), pp. 15–16.
[52] Muriel Herbert to Quilter, 24 March 1923, BL Add. MS 70603, f. 158.
[53] Conversations with Muriel Herbert's daughter Claire Tomalin, April 1999 – June 2000.
[54] Landsberg to Quilter, 1 Dec 1922, BL Add. MS 70599, f. 211. He was probably writing from Neuilly.

Quilter spent the summer at his mother's at Wood Hall, followed by a few days in September at Eastbourne, and he also went to Paris for a week.

Since he loathed having his photograph taken, formal portrait pictures of Quilter are rare (though there are plenty of informal photographs), but in June 1923, F. and B. Goodwin published a book by the photographer Herbert Lambert, a collection of portraits of seventeen contemporary composers, from Elgar to Eugène Goossens, and including one of Quilter[55] which has become his most familiar image. Goossens wrote a short prefatory note for the book, in which he acknowledged his own debt to his 'elder contemporaries' and provided thumbnail sketches of the subjects from a musical angle. He touched on various aspects of English music and took the view that 'the moment arrives when the composer with something to say becomes impervious to outside influences, and there emerges an idiom which in itself constitutes a basis for the foundation of an entirely new speech'. He commented favourably on Quilter's ability to '[convey] the national spirit in his music', and on 'the delicacy and refinement of his settings'.[56]

1923 was a relatively quiet year, but a concert on 30 June 1923 initiated a musical partnership that lasted for the rest of Quilter's life. He attended a Wigmore Hall recital given by a young Jewish baritone from London's East End, Mark Raphael. Raphael was accompanied by Lawrence Brown, a black pianist whom Quilter knew very well, in a programme ranging from Bassani and Handel to Schubert, Debussy and Negro spirituals.[57]

> After the recital [at which I had sung two of Quilter's *Blake Songs*, 'Dream Valley' and 'Daybreak'], [Quilter] came around to the artists' room, and was most appreciative of my singing of his songs. A few days later, he asked me to call and see him at his home in Montagu Street, and there on the piano was a new song he'd written specially for me, 'The Jealous Lover', one of a set dedicated to me, called Jacobean Lyrics. From this time on, a friendship and professional partnership grew.[58]

Quilter and Raphael had met some months earlier at Wilfrid de Glehn's studio in Cheyne Walk; the manuscript of 'The Fuchsia Tree' is dated 18 February 1923 and Raphael gave the first performance of it there. On 8 December 1923 Raphael gave 'The Jealous Lover' one of its earliest performances – again at the Wigmore Hall, which was perfect for such programmes – and Quilter accompanied. The recital saw too the first performance of Quilter's artless and extremely effective song 'An Old Carol'.

Quilter maintained a steady stream of appearances at concerts, giving or attending them. In January 1920, he had been involved in a series of three

[55] The others were Smyth, Bantock, Vaughan Williams, Holst, Boughton, Holbrooke, Bridge, Scott, Ireland, Lord Berners, Bax, Gibbs, Bliss, Howells and Quilter. Delius would have been included but was too ill.
[56] Herbert Lambert, *Modern British Composers, Seventeen Portraits* (London, 1923).
[57] There were also songs by Hubert, Santoliquido, Wolf-Ferrari and Leo Holt.
[58] Mark Raphael, *Roger Quilter*, broadcast on BBC Radio 3, 1 November 1977.

concerts at Leighton House given primarily by the cellist Herbert Withers, whom he had known for several years. Their professional relationship was maintained well into the decade with the continuation of the concerts begun during the war at the Lindsey Hall, Notting Hill Gate. At one of these, on 16 December 1924, Quilter accompanied Mark Raphael in a group of five of his own songs, flanked by works by Chausson and Brahms (the *Horn Trio*, with Aubrey Brain playing horn). This was an especially felicitous combination, given the Brahmsian touch as well as the French lyricism in Quilter's style.

Quilter remained very unsure of his abilities as an orchestrator, despite the clarity of *A Children's Overture*. He used this as his excuse for not writing longer orchestral pieces, something that Grainger was forever nagging him to do – he felt that he still needed to gain experience and that he was still, in his forties, developing his technique. But sustained musical thought, of the German organic kind, was not his métier (nor was it Grainger's); his strengths lay in writing finely detailed miniatures. He wrote too of the 'sheer labour and agony to get anything done at all',[59] partly because of continuous ill-health, and partly because of lack of confidence, which resulted in his continually working and reworking the music. Mark Raphael described arriving at Montagu Street for a rehearsal too soon one day, and hearing him 'working at a phrase over and over again'.[60] Quilter also claimed that writing short pieces was a reaction against the, to him, stultifying effect of 'the long English Straussian compositions [he had] listened to in the last ten or fifteen years'.[61] He complained that 'length and mass and elaborated orchestration, when there is no real live stuff to lengthen, enlarge or elaborate, does rather sicken one', and explained that the 'effect that hearing such works have upon me, is to make me either give up trying to write music, or at least to try & make something short, pleasing, light and clear'.[62]

Quilter had been intrigued by Negroes and 'nigger music' for many years – in 1907 he wrote to Grainger about a tune that his singer friend, Higley, had given him:

> I don't know what it's called, no more does he – what heart-rendingly lovely things they are!; do niggers write them, and is all that tenderness out of their funny black bodies? I think we must go among the niggers sometime & get to know something of them.[63]

A few months after Grainger went to the United States at the start of the First World War, Quilter wrote to Rose Grainger:

> I do hope Percy will be able to see a lot of the negroes and that he will write to me some time about them. They thrill me. I went to a night-club one day a few

[59] Quilter to Percy Grainger, 12 July 1920, GM.
[60] Quoted in Stephen Banfield, 'Roger Quilter, A Centenary Note', *The Musical Times*, CXVIII (1977), pp. 903–6; it refers to the text of the Radio 3 broadcast by Raphael on 1 November 1977; this particular quote was not in fact broadcast, but is in Raphael's notes for it.
[61] Quilter to Percy Grainger, 12 July 1920, GM.
[62] Quilter to Percy Grainger, 12 July 1920, GM.
[63] Quilter to Percy Grainger, 14 June 1907, GM.

months ago to hear 4 niggers play & sing, it was the most inspiring and exhilarating thing I've heard for a long time.[64]

The black composer Samuel Coleridge-Taylor, born two years before Quilter, had blazed a trail that many sought to follow, and Edmund Jenkins, the jazz clarinettist and saxophonist, came to England in 1914 and trained at the Royal Academy of Music, later teaching the clarinet there.[65]

The black singer Roland Hayes came to England from the States in April 1920 to study and to make a name for himself.[66] He gave several recitals over a few months, including a well-reported one in November 1920,[67] but it was the recital on 21 April 1921 at the Wigmore Hall that attracted significant notices, even though Hayes was extremely ill with pneumonia; Quilter was to have accompanied a group of his own songs, but was ill as well.[68] Hayes was overshadowed later in the decade by his younger compatriot, Paul Robeson, and is now largely forgotten. He was, however, one of the earlier black singers to establish a career, his fine tenor voice characterised by a careful, trained way of singing that contrasted strongly with Robeson's simpler, more direct manner, and Quilter was a significant factor in his success.

Hayes regularly included groups of Negro spirituals in his recitals, but sang songs from the standard repertoire as well. His career made headway gradually, and throughout these years, Quilter gave him food, money and encouragement.[69] Lady Quilter invited Hayes and Brown to Wood Hall and made them welcome, a contrast with the treatment they sometimes received in other quarters: Hayes's landlady in Maida Vale, London, was boycotted by her neighbours because she took him as a lodger.[70]

Hayes claimed that one of the Shakespeare settings, 'Take, O Take Those Lips Away', was written for him, though it was dedicated to Bertie Landsberg,[71] and he may have been confusing it with 'There be None of Beauty's Daughters' which was dedicated to him. On the recommendation of King George V and Queen Mary – Hayes had been invited to sing to them, following his Wigmore Hall recital – Quilter took him to meet Dame Nellie Melba, and Hayes recalled how 'she and Quilter shouted ribald stories at each other, down the length of the luncheon table'[72] – plainly Quilter in an unusually relaxed mood. Later that

[64] Quilter to Rose Grainger, 4 August 1915, GM.
[65] Howard Rye and Jeffrey Green, 'Black Musical Internationalism in England in the 1920s', *Black Music Research Journal*, vol. 15, no. 1 (Spring 1995), pp. 93–108.
[66] Quilter to Rose Grainger, 21 or 24 April 1921, GM. Further information on Hayes is to be found in: Jeffrey P. Green, 'Roland Hayes in London, 1921', *The Black Perspective in Music*, vol. 10, no. 1 (Spring 1982), pp. 29–42.
[67] Jeffrey P. Green, 'The Negro Renaissance and England', Chapter 10 in *Black Music in the Harlem Renaissance*, ed. Samuel A. Floyd Jr. (Knoxville, 1993).
[68] *Daily Telegraph*, 23 April 1921, 5c.
[69] Roland Hayes to Quilter, 23 July [1922], BL Add. MS 70603, f. 141. Also MacKinley Helm, *Angel Mo' and Her Son, Roland Hayes* (Boston, 1943), p. 130.
[70] Roland Hayes to Quilter, 25 November 1921, BL Add. MS 70603, f. 122.
[71] MacKinley Helm (1943), p. 150. Norman O'Neill wrote some songs for Hayes too.
[72] MacKinley Helm (1943), p. 141.

year, Hayes sang at Norman O'Neill's house and was astonished that the audience was so silent when he had finished singing; Quilter whispered to him, 'They are in the dark corners, hiding behind their handkerchieves. The English are ashamed to show their emotions, you know'.[73]

In the spring of 1922, Hayes went to Paris and sang in many salons, and while in France he met Delius and Fauré. He gave a recital at the Wigmore Hall on 19 October 1922, accompanied throughout by Quilter, unusual since Quilter generally only accompanied his own songs. It was an eclectic programme, with works by Handel, Mozart, Caccini, Paradies, Fauré, Moreau, Brahms, Schumann, Quilter of course ('Fair House of Joy' was arranged for voice, piano and cello), and an obscure composer called Jean Ten Have. In a joint recital given by Hayes and the Philharmonic String Quartet on 22 May 1924 at the Queen's Hall, Hayes sang two of the *Three Pastoral Songs*: 'I Will Go with My Father A-Ploughing' and 'Cherry Valley'; and also 'Blow, Blow, Thou Winter Wind' and 'It was a Lover and His Lass' with Quilter playing.

Hayes's accompanist was Lawrence Brown, an extremely skilful arranger of spirituals, and later in the decade, Paul Robeson's accompanist. Music theory was sometimes rather a puzzle to Brown, however, and for a time, he took theory lessons with Leslie Woodgate, reporting to Quilter that he had been 'to Leslie's Monday and escaped with my life, things are becoming easier now tho one time I lost myself in a maze of first inversions and second inversions'.[74] Brown's father had been a slave and Brown himself was in consequence often uncomfortable in white company; he was also homosexual and was especially wary with some white homosexuals.[75] He was very comfortable with Quilter, however, and though it is a matter of conjecture, it is possible that they had a brief relationship.

Brown already knew Paul Robeson well, and was keen that when Robeson came to England, to play the lead in *The Emperor Jones* at the Ambassador's Theatre, he and Quilter should meet. After the play closed on 17 October 1925, Robeson and his wife Essie stayed in England for a further two weeks. During that time, they dined with Quilter, but it was probably a rather one-sided relationship: Quilter was very interested in Robeson's career, he was keen to help, and wrote to him several times, but there was little help needed.

Quilter offered generous help to the American black contralto Marian Anderson, although their relationship got off to a shaky start. She came over to England in late 1927 to train, to broaden her experience vocally and musically, and to further her career. She had first written to Quilter in 1922 to express her admiration for his songs (addressing him as 'Sir Roger Quilter'), and others now wrote to him to ask for his help on her behalf: Anderson's teacher in the States, Giuseppe Boghetti, asked him to coach her on her singing of his songs, and to look after her artistically.[76] Her accompanist Billy King, who

[73] As quoted in MacKinley Helm (1943), p. 150.
[74] Lawrence Brown to Quilter, 1 September 1921, BL Add. MS 70603, f. 112.
[75] Martin Bauml Duberman, *Paul Robeson* (London, 1989), p. 78.
[76] Giuseppe Boghetti to Quilter, 20 October 1927, BL Add. MS 70604, f. 108.

had toured the States with Roland Hayes, probably wrote too. Anderson was instructed to telephone Quilter when she landed, and she arrived, a black woman in a white man's world, the first time she had been out of her own country, in an unfamiliar culture, and dealing with an unfamiliar telephone system.

She rang Quilter, only to find herself talking to Quilter's manservant: Quilter was ill in a nursing home and had left no instructions for her. She was alone in a strange country with nowhere to stay, but fortunately she had another friend in London, the black singer Johnny Payne. He rescued her from her predicament and she stayed with him at his home at 17 Regents Park Road.[77]

Mark Raphael's teacher, the renowned Raimund von zur Mühlen, agreed to take Anderson as a pupil, but she only had a few lessons before he had to stop all teaching through ill-health.[78] She studied vocal technique with Amanda Ira Aldridge, who also taught Roland Hayes, and took lessons with Mark Raphael who had been a pupil of Mühlen, but though happy with his teaching, she felt disappointed since she had come primarily to study with the teacher, rather than the former pupil. She was befriended by all, and in particular by Eva Raphael, Mark's wife, who took her under her wing and used to go shopping with her. Eva's presence was essential at times: on the first occasion that Anderson went to Harrod's of Knightsbridge, the famous department store, she was refused entrance because of her colour, but was graciously allowed in on a second visit when Eva accompanied her to vouch for her good character.

Anderson was a regular visitor to Quilter's home at 7 Montagu Street, and 'sang for the gatherings in his spacious music room' frequently.[79] On 16 June 1928, she gave a recital at the Wigmore Hall.[80] For most of the songs, she was accompanied by Joan Singleton, but Quilter himself accompanied her in a group of his own songs. He made a new arrangement especially for her of the Negro spiritual 'Heav'n, Heav'n', first arranged by Harry Burleigh, retitling it 'I Got a Robe'. She included it in a group of five spirituals, and remained ever grateful for his kindness.[81]

There is scant evidence of Quilter's income from royalties, but in a letter to Elkin, who published all the *Rainbow* music and *Three Pastoral Songs* amongst

---

[77] Payne was an extremely interesting character in his own right: on 13 October 1923, he had given a 'Programme of Negro Music' at the Wigmore Hall, with Lawrence Brown accompanying (the programme contained Negro folk-songs and spirituals) and in some circles at least, he was considered the unofficial black US ambassador. (Jeffrey Green to Langfield, 10 June 2000, referring to statements about Payne by the Jamaican Leslie Thompson, who settled in London in 1929.)

[78] Marian Anderson, *My Lord, What a Morning* (New York, 1956), p. 107.

[79] Marian Anderson (1956), p. 108.

[80] The programme demonstrates a broad repertoire: she sang songs by Caldara and Martini, Purcell (*Dido's Lament*), and Debussy (*Air de Lia*, from *L'Enfant Prodigue*). The *Times* review mentions Schubert's *Wiegenlied*, which is not shown on the programme, and was perhaps an encore.

[81] Allan Keiler, *Marian Anderson, A Singer's Journey* (New York, 2000), p. 79.

others, he thanks him for his royalty cheque of £23–0–8d for the year 1923.[82] This was a substantial sum and certainly gives credence to Quilter's comment that there was a time when he could have lived off composing – 'paying grocers' bills by music'.[83] The *Rainbow* music was available in many forms: for piano, there was the *Music from 'Where the Rainbow Ends'* and a *Suite from 'Where the Rainbow Ends'* as well as *Two Dances*, which were included in the selection of *Four Dances*; there was the orchestral suite, a different group of items from the piano suite; the 'Slumber Song' had been published separately, and there were arrangements for piano and strings of 'Moonlight on the Lake' and 'Water Nymph'. The popularity of the music was such that there was still a call for arrangements of it in 1937, when these two items were published in orchestral versions.

Quilter regularly accompanied Mark Raphael in recitals. When Raphael went to Vienna in the autumn of 1924 on what was basically a self-promotional tour, Quilter came for part of the trip, and they performed ten of his songs to an excellent reception, with a still warmer reception after a concert in Frankfurt. Over the next few years, Raphael, seen primarily as a Lieder singer, did much to promote the European view of Quilter as an English Lied-composer.

A new manservant, Watkins, began service with Quilter. Quilter was completely dependent upon his various servants; he could not so much as boil the proverbial egg, and from the references to him in later correspondence, Watkins was clearly well known to Quilter's friends and visitors. He was an occasional subject for a photograph, too, and appears as a lean, pleasing-looking man. Quilter's domestic staff impinge upon the scene from time to time, usually anonymously; he had a maid, a cook and a chauffeur in varying combinations at varying times, as a well as a manservant.

Quilter's frequent visits to the Continent were often in search of warmth; he went as frequently to visit his mother, reporting all his latest activities. His visits now were also out of concern for her: she was 82 and frail. Sometimes, however, he went in order to introduce his friends to her. They were all invited, whether it be for her approval or to have an opportunity to express their admiration of her; at any rate, Wood Hall provided a peaceful environment.

Grainger had been trying very hard to persuade Quilter to visit the States, being sure he would do well there. He wanted him to come in March 1925 to take part in the second of his planned series of chamber concerts, and offered him accommodation at Grainger's home in White Plains if he wanted. He stressed the desirability of the artistic collaboration, as well as the importance of personal appearances in order to promote his music.[84] But, according to Quilter, this was a dangerous time to cross the Atlantic and change climate, and he used his ill-health to make his excuses. Writing in November 1924, he

---

[82] Quilter to Elkin, 24 January 1924, Elkin archives.
[83] This comment is quoted in some of Quilter's obituaries (*Evening Standard*, 21 September 1953; *Daily Mail* and *Daily Mirror*, both 22 September 1953), but the original source has remained elusive.
[84] Grainger to Quilter, 26 November 1923, GM.

suggested the comfortably distant autumn of 1925 as a better time, though a convenient visit to Germany was to prevent it.

Early in 1925, the impresario Charles B. Cochran was recovering from financial disaster, which had largely been the result of the failure of his Wembley rodeo spectacle in 1924; his association with Noël Coward was more fortunate, if not always smooth. Soon after the play *The Vortex*, which Coward wrote and starred in, opened in December 1924, he began work on a revue for Cochran. After a hiatus while the pair of them argued over whether Coward was to provide the music as well as the book, both Coward and Philip Braham (Cochran's original choice) contributed. Although Coward wrote most of the music, to his utter fury his name was on none of the billing; as soon as he realised, he burst into Cochran's room at the theatre and remonstrated with him, but Cochran, just out of the bath, was unperturbed, even though he was dressed in only a towel which showed every sign of being about to slip. The argument was eventually settled over several glasses of sherry.[85] On 17 March 1925, St Patrick's Day, after a formidable twenty-seven-hour-long dress rehearsal, the revue *On with the Dance* opened at the Palace Theatre, Manchester, and transferred to the London Pavilion on 30 April, where it ran for 229 performances until the following November.

With nonchalant egocentricity, Coward, in his autobiography *Present Indicative*, made no mention of the other providers of the music for the evening's programme, though he referred to the two ballets choreographed and danced by Massine. One of these was called *Crescendo* and the other was called *The Rake*, subtitled *A Hogarth Impression*, for which Quilter wrote the music. A brief description given in the programme ran: 'Massine has taken a number of Hogarth's characters – symbolic and realistic. William Nicholson [who designed the scenery and costumes] has given them a characteristic environment for a Hogarthian Orgy.' 'The Rake' lolls drunkenly in a chair while his wanton companions disport around him. The Negro Cupid is busy with bow and arrows, plumbing the hearts of his victims; and the worship of women and wine whips itself up into a passionate whirl. And while the revellers seek their pleasure, the sages are wrapt in contemplation of their globe, and a window frames the faces of a curious crowd, who see, and are silent.[86]

The programme shows a Trio, a Solo and a Duo followed by the 'entrance of grotesques' but there is no real clue as to how these might have matched the five movements: Dance at the Feast, The Light-hearted Lady, The Frolicsome Friend, Allurement, and Midnight Revels, though the Light-hearted Lady might have been the Solo dance, and Allurement, the Duo. The music lasts no more than ten minutes.

Early on in the run, the sketch followed Hermione Baddeley, Alice Delysia and others in 'Poor Little Rich Girl' (a hard act to follow), but over the months

[85] For which details, see Philip Hoare, *Noël Coward, A Biography* (London, 1996), p. 143; or James Harding, *Cochran, A Biography* (London, 1988), p. 118. The tale is told in many places.
[86] This description differs very slightly from that given in the published score.

the running order changed. It was a reasonably substantial sketch, with twenty-two dancers taking part. Massine danced the rôle of the Beau, there was a group of 'musicians' – a Dog, a Bull, a Cat and a Cock – and the bizarre collection of grotesques also included a Posture Woman, a Corset Woman, a Woman with the Bound Hair, a Boot Man, a Giant, a Globe Man, and a Man with Compass and Cupid.

According to the unnamed *Times* reviewer, the evening's entertainment was a 'varied series of dances' with 'a brilliant succession of dancers', and the same reviewer thought that 'as a whole, with the dancing always preponderating, the revue [was] excellent'.[87] Other reviewers thought the whole show rather full of tricks, considerable acclaim apparently having been given by the audience to one dancer who walked across the stage on her hands. But it was generally well received, even if the *Sunday Times* reviewer sardonically wrote of the show that there was 'not a good tune in the whole piece' (including, by implication, Quilter's contribution), and that it 'braved the world without a comedian', with 'a curious mixture of perfect beauty and perfect drivel' without specifying which sketch fell into which category, or indeed whether any sketches contained aspects of both.[88] The revue amused, was generally frivolous, was not too silly, and it revived Cochran's fortunes.

Quilter thought his orchestration too thin.[89] Although there is nothing specific to indicate whether or not Quilter adjusted it, a comment on the extant score, in his writing, explains that it was rearranged from the original by Sydney Baynes; the score itself is not in Quilter's hand.[90] Nothing else is now known of the original version and the music as published is described as a 'Ballet Suite'.

At the Manchester rehearsals, Coward and Quilter renewed the acquaintance that had begun in 1911 with *Where the Rainbow Ends*, and the link between them continued sporadically for some years after: in June 1929 Coward sent Quilter a note expressing the hope that he would come to see *Bittersweet* and that he would 'tell me honestly what you think about the music as I've been working very hard at it'.[91] After the first night, Quilter wrote to congratulate him and Coward replied, addressing him as 'Roger': 'I was awfully pleased to get your really delightful letter about "Bittersweet".'[92] Whether Quilter actually commented upon the music is not known, but he never regarded himself as a teacher, he never took a teaching post, he worked with singers (they were not pupils as such) normally only on his own songs, and it seems very unlikely that Quilter would have offered any especially critical comment.

Quilter had always admired Fauré's music. In 1908, Grainger had made Quilter envious by describing meeting Fauré, and recalled

[87] *The Times*, 1 May 1925.
[88] *The Sunday Times*, 3 May 1925.
[89] Percy Grainger to Quilter, 3 October 1925, GM.
[90] This manuscript is held by Leslie East.
[91] Coward to Quilter, 4 June 1929, BL Add. MS 70604, f. 140.
[92] Coward to Quilter, 27 August 1929, BL Add. MS 70604, f. 151.

I can well remember your enthusiasm for the Fauré 4ets some years ago. . . . Last Saturday I played my English Dance, Wamphray Ballad, Died for Love, Irish F-S, Tiger Tiger, Morning Song, for Fauré and he was so kind and interested. It was at Sargent's, and only him, F, Rathbone and I were present. Fauré said, 'Il a beaucoup de flamme' and 'C'est un energie supreme' [sic], or something like that.[93]

Of Fauré's two piano quartets, Quilter wrote, 'I thought them both entrancing and have not had an opportunity of hearing either since [in the past two years] – Fauré you see is french, and therefore the sensual & passionate is handled very knowingly & lovingly'.[94]

Fauré died on 4 November 1924, and a Memorial Concert was held on 9 June 1925, at the Wigmore Hall. Quilter and Mark Raphael performed *En Sourdine*, *Le Voyageur* and *Nell* and the distinguished line-up of artists also included Albert Sammons, Lionel Tertis, Cedric Sharpe, William Murdoch, Olga Lynn, Eugène Goossens, Henry Wood, Alfred Cortot, Anne Thursfield, Daisy Bucktrout, Kirkby Lunn, and Landon Ronald.

Soon after, Raphael went to Wood Hall, a visit that Quilter anticipated with pleasure: 'It will be splendid to get Mother's mind away from the family even if only for an hour.'[95]

Raphael returned to Vienna for another tour and it was at this time that he met his future wife, Eva Taglicht. Her family was originally from Poland, but her parents now lived in Palestine and she had been sent to Germany to learn about gardening, her father having acquired a substantial plot of land.[96] Raphael bubbled with the excitement of new, young love, but Quilter was horrified. At the very least, Quilter wanted to be the important person in Raphael's life; he persistently sought a close relationship with him, which Raphael could accept while it remained broadly a father–son relationship, but not if it was to be anything more intimate; Quilter found this hard to believe and he saw Eva as the reason for Raphael's refusal. Quilter tried to use Raphael's ambitions to be a composer as a lever, telling him that he could not hope to be a composer unless he had some appreciation of the sensibilities that a homosexual relationship would bring, but Raphael remained unmoved.[97]

Quilter also saw Eva as an unwelcome distraction from Raphael's main task, to establish himself as a singer. She, for her part, was amazed that England seemed to be full of homosexuals, and wondered greatly that anyone ever managed to produce any children.[98] Quilter never had any long-term relationships but there was certainly a succession of young men – secretaries – over a long period and normally there was no difficulty in establishing at least short-

[93] Percy Grainger to Quilter, 25 March 1908, as published in *The Farthest North of Humanness*, ed. Kay Dreyfus (Melbourne, 1985).
[94] Quilter to Rose Grainger, 27 March 1908, GM.
[95] Quilter to Mark Raphael, 24 June 1925, BL Add. MS 70607, f. 26.
[96] Mark Raphael to Quilter, 15 February 1925, BL Add. MS 70600, f. 41.
[97] Interview with Mark and Eva Raphael's son, Roger, 29 June 1997.
[98] Interview with Roger Raphael, 29 June 1997.

term liaisons. Raphael was patient and probably obdurate; eventually Quilter was won round to Eva, and he moved on to other young men. She had a delightful personality, beautiful dark eyes, and was an accomplished linguist. Quilter shared her anguish and distress at events in Poland, and he became increasingly concerned about the anti-Jewish riots in Vienna. He was, in the meantime, funding Raphael – who was careful and concerned about his budgeting – and they had planned that Quilter should come out to Berlin for some concerts, but the music and rehearsals for *The Rake* took up too much time and energy,[99] and he was too unwell.

Jane de Glehn invited him to go abroad with them in September, but he was delayed correcting proofs of *The Rake*, being published by Ascherberg, Hopwood and Crew, and he was delayed still further because his 'internal arrangements [had] again been troubling [him]'.[100] His doctor at Wood Hall had wanted him to go to Harrogate again for another cure but he avoided that unpleasantness by making use of a 'wonderful American arrangement with which I can do the business myself at home, without any trouble or expense. I think it is answering quite well'.[101] This 'arrangement' was likely to have been an enema kit, though in writing to Raphael, he spared his feelings and did not elaborate.

The rest of 1925 was spent working on songs, almost certainly the rest of what was to become the set of *Five Jacobean Lyrics*, Op. 28, and Quilter wrote to Raphael to tell him how they were going. Raphael was in Palestine in December visiting Eva's parents, and planned to return via Territet, Montreux, in early January. He was due to meet Quilter there on 5 January and Maude Valérie White also intended to be there for two days.[102] For some reason Raphael changed his plans, making Quilter extremely cross and upset in the process, and in the event, Quilter left London for Rome – his first visit there – on 8 January 1926, travelling via Paris. Maude Valérie White was already in Rome and Quilter spent a stimulating ten days there. He saw Mrs Koehler while he was there, too – it was several years since they had last met. Suggestions of her caustic manner come through, though Quilter was never subjected to it since he was 'never . . . intellectual enough to have mental "situations" & "complications" with her' but they were simply 'very warm friends'; she appreciated his friendship and '[did] not mind [his] inferiority of mind and brilliance'.[103]

Quilter became more and more concerned about his mother, though the concern did not prevent him travelling abroad yet again, this time to Venice and Florence during September 1926 (his Florentine visit was to T'Emmie White, Maude Valérie White's sister, at the Villa Baldi, San Gervasio). But it was his last Continental jaunt for a year or more since most of 1927 was overshadowed by

[99] Mark Raphael to Quilter, various dates between 19 February and 14 March 1925, BL Add. MS 70600, ff. 47–72.
[100] Quilter to Mark Raphael, 22 August 1925, BL Add. MS 70607, f. 30.
[101] Quilter to Mark Raphael, 22 August 1925, BL Add. MS 70607, f. 30.
[102] Quilter to Raphael, 14 December 1925, BL Add. MS 70607, f. 41.
[103] Quilter to Percy Grainger, [22 February 1926], GM.

his mother's deterioration, as his life up to that point had been overshadowed by her.

Grainger had recently met Ella Ström, his future wife, and in the spring of 1927 he arranged for Ella to meet Quilter. Grainger – thanks to Ella – was coming out of his long dark time of the past five years since his mother's death, while Quilter was going into deeper shade than usual, and Grainger's happy letters strike discordantly with Quilter's. At the turn of the year, however, he sent Grainger a generous £50 for the Rose Grainger Fund that Grainger was setting up; Grainger thought this was too great a lump sum and suggested he pay in instalments instead.

By April 1927, Lady Quilter was 'very feeble and . . . very peculiar and confused in her speech', and she could do nothing for herself.[104] Quilter spent long periods at Wood Hall during that summer, and despite being so used to illness, he was depressed and exhausted by hers. The rest of the family wanted him to leave the Hall for a few days, since they were nearly at the point where he was the only one able to do anything with her.[105] She died peacefully on the morning of Monday 12 September 1927. The funeral took place three days later and Quilter returned to London the following Monday, going on to Bath to see to her affairs there. She was two months short of her eighty-fifth birthday, and dominated her son up to the very end of her life, even though it was, on the whole, a willingly accepted dominion.

He did not age in the way that Grainger had after Rose died, but after fitting in a concert in Cambridge in early October, he fell ill again.[106] He went into a nursing home – the one that left him unavailable when Marian Anderson came to England – and recuperated during November with his elder sister Maude at her home, Horwood House, near Winslow, Buckinghamshire, where he had a surprisingly merry time, considering he was none too fond of her hearty ways. He was back at 7 Montagu Street in early December, still a little shaky, and in need of Italian warmth and sunshine which he went to find in late January 1928.[107] In April he was to be found in Paris, outside the opera house, in the company of Roland Hayes, Lawrence Brown and Mark and Eva Raphael, and in July he went to the Grand Hotel at Harrogate, presumably for a cure – perhaps the American contraption had not been as satisfactory as he would have liked.

He learned of a large house, Buckhurst Cottage, in Withyham, Sussex, on the de la Warr estate, that was available for rent, and he spent the summers of 1928, 1929 and 1930 there. Many of his friends came to stay, just as they used to come to Wood Hall. It was an excellent replacement for the Hall, where he had gladly spent so many previous summers: it had lawns and woods and a tennis court. Roland Hayes stayed there, the Raphaels and their family, sundry nieces, the de

---

[104] Quilter to Mark Raphael, [early April 1927], BL Add. MS 70607, f. 51.
[105] Quilter to Mark Raphael, [April–July 1927], BL Add. MS 70607, f. 54.
[106] Jane de Glehn to Quilter, 18 October 1927, BL Add. MS 70597, f. 142.
[107] Quilter to Percy Grainger, 12 Dec 1927, GM.

Glehns and their family, Leslie Woodgate and his wife Lena, Evelyn Marthèze Conti – Italia's sister, who adored Quilter – and many others; picnics on sunny days, and peace.

September 1928 saw him in France, at Paris and Versailles, and from there he went on to Venice, and to Malcontenta, Palladio's great villa, at that time still looking rather dilapidated and unhappy, though in the process of being restored by Bertie Landsberg. The Baroness d'Erlanger was there, and the Baron, her composer husband, may have been there too,[108] and Quilter had word about his old friend Walter Creighton through Jane de Glehn, who had gone to visit Creighton in his 'rather queer little place' near Antibes to which he had moved. 'It is rather amusing & would be quite nice when open & cleaned up. Rather far from anything'.[109]

At some point – regrettably the date cannot be established – Quilter proposed marriage to Nora Forman, a very long-standing friend and extremely knowledgeable music-lover, daughter of a Scottish railway engineer.[110] Nora Forman was very wealthy, and was a discreet patroness of the arts, very much in sympathy with Quilter's own ethos. He may well have proposed to her as a means of social self-protection, but it is scarcely possible that she did not know of his disposition, and the liaison would have been a very positive one, with only artistic claims on either side. They were both well-off, they had similar sensibilities and a mutual understanding, and when he broke the engagement off, she was broken-hearted. Mark and Eva Raphael, who knew them both very well indeed, were disgusted with Quilter's cruel behaviour and told him so. Nevertheless, she remained friends with Quilter. She was great-hearted, with a very generous personality.

By late 1928, it was time to be ill again, and although he was meant to have played in a concert at Eton on 30 November, of works composed by old Etonians, he went down with 'flu and was unable to go. His violin and piano arrangement of 'Three Poor Mariners' was played by A. C. Bonvalot, and his brother-in-law, Guy Vivian, sang a group of his songs, 'To Daisies', 'O, the Month of May', 'O Mistress Mine' and 'Blow, Blow, Thou Winter Wind'.[111]

After such gadding about Europe, he decided that it was also time to set to work on his long-awaited venture into light opera, and he sought a collaboration with a suitable librettist and lyricist. In October 1928 Quilter had heard the BBC broadcast of a ballad opera, *Charming Chloë*, with words by Rodney Bennett, with music arranged and composed by Gerrard Williams, and he liked what he heard. For his part, Bennett, a popular writer of light poetry

---

[108] He was an obscure composer, whom Joseph Holbrooke described as 'a fine artist', with work 'full of good tunes and fluid inner counterpoint, and . . . devoid of pretension', high praise from Holbrooke. (Joseph Holbrooke, *Contemporary British Composers* (London, 1925), pp. 254–5.)

[109] Jane de Glehn to Quilter, 29 August 1928, BL Add. MS 70597, f. 154.

[110] Interview with Roger Raphael, 29 June 1997.

[111] *Eton Chronicles*, 19 December 1928.

and children's stories,[112] had been searching for a suitable composer to work with, and had earlier tried to interest Quilter, but unsuccessfully.

The time had not been right then, but now it was: by the end of December 1928 Quilter had written to Bennett to ask if he was interested.[113] Soon after, he sent him a synopsis and a copy of the rough sketch of Act 1: the work was inspired by an unnamed French story, and by a portrait by Boucher, *Madame de Pompadour*, and was set in the mid-eighteenth century.[114] It was to be called *The Blue Boar*, though soon nicknamed *The Blue Pig*, and the venture filled his life for the next eight years.

---

[112] They were pleasing little stories. *Widgery Winks in the Wide World* (Bickley, 1943) came later but was in the same mould as those which Quilter liked.

[113] Quilter to Bennett, 31 December 1928, Bennett archive.

[114] The primary source for information on the collaboration is a series of 115 letters from Quilter to Bennett, held in a private archive, covering the period 31 December 1928 to 11 August 1943. They are often not fully dated; in many cases dates can be deduced, but some remain intractable. Detailed citations are only made if pertinent.

5

Julia, Acacia Road and the Coming of War
(1929–1939)

Quilter planned to spend the rest of the winter, early in 1929, in Mentone, and he invited Bennett and his wife Joan to stay with him at the Hotel Cap-Martin there, partially at least at his own expense. The holiday began disastrously: Quilter's train arrived ten hours late at two o'clock in the morning; his manservant Watkins and chauffeur Twiner were both ill and so was Mrs Bennett, and they could not travel with Quilter, and so it was agreed that Twiner should drive the Bennetts down a few days later. By then the roads were too dangerous to travel and the constant changes of plan upset Quilter dreadfully.

He moved to somewhere less grand and expensive, the Riviera Palace Hotel, and about a fortnight after his arrival, Joan and Rodney Bennett arrived too.

It was an inauspicious start, but they settled down and Quilter and Bennett found that they could work hard and well together.[1] After a month, the Bennetts returned to England while Quilter stayed on and reported progress: a Gavotte from Act III and an item that he called 'tic-a-tec'.[2] He remained there a few more days, moved on to San Remo, and then to Avignon.

He returned to England at the beginning of May 1929. Grainger, together with Basil Cameron, conductor of the Harrogate Orchestra during its summer seasons, was planning a short festival of British music to be held at Harrogate: there were three concerts, on 24, 25 and 26 July, with works by living composers: the Frankfurt five (Gardiner, Grainger, O'Neill, Quilter and Scott), Austin, Bax, Bedford, Delius, German, Heward, Holbrooke, Milner and Warlock, and some dead ones: Arne and Purcell; scheduled pieces by Byrd and Gibbons were not, in the event, played. Generally, the modern composers conducted their own orchestral works; otherwise, Cameron conducted. Quilter conducted *A Children's Overture* and *Three English Dances* on the middle day, and on the first day, four of his songs were performed ('The Jealous Lover', 'It was a Lover and His Lass', 'Weep You No More' and 'To Althea from Prison') with Mark Raphael as soloist. This first concert was devoted to music by the Frankfurt Group, with a contribution from Delius. Grainger often spoke of the 'Frankfurt Group' as if it was of major importance, but it was never a force to be

---

[1] Rodney Bennett, 'How the Blue Boar Came to be Written', *Radio Times*, 20 October 1933.
[2] Quilter to Bennett, 9 April 1929, Bennett archive.

reckoned with, and anyway Grainger seems not quite to have thought of O'Neill as a member of the group. That is not to disparage the individual achievements, however: O'Neill's theatrical contribution was significant – the sound of his *Mary Rose* incidental music of 1920 may have had some influence on the soundtracks of films of the 1930s, and Scott's contribution to the harmonic world was well recognised, as was Gardiner's to the world of orchestration and of financial backing. The five were very different from each other, though united in distancing themselves from the late Victorian Parry and Stanford school – the unofficially named 'South Kensington' school of the Royal College of Music.

The Festival received a mixed reception, with the *Daily Telegraph* pleased that it was put on, but *The Times* disappointed with its content, protesting at 'the disservice . . . done to our native music by the performance of works which in the aggregate must give the uninitiated a very poor opinion of the abilities of contemporary composers in England',[3] and complaining that on the whole the programmes contained nothing that would 'advance the cause of British music'. The items by Delius were very well appreciated, but the *Nocturne* by Leslie Heward was not: with Beatrice Harrison present, Ferruccio Bonavia of the *Daily Telegraph* suggested that it must have been tempting to substitute Elgar's cello concerto for one of the items, and regretted that, in the case of the *Nocturne*, the temptation had not been irresistible.[4]

Another of Quilter's songs was given its first performance at the Festival, a setting of Shelley's 'Indian Serenade' known by its first line 'I Arise from Dreams of Thee', in a version for tenor and orchestra; Mark Raphael gave the first performance, though it was really too high for him: Quilter had wanted another singer, but Raphael pleaded with him to let him sing it. Quilter's correspond-ence makes no mention of this song before July 1929, but one of the manu-scripts – for voice and piano – is dated 1928;[5] Grainger mentions the song afterwards, congratulating Quilter on its beauty. It is not clear at what stage it became a song for voice and orchestra, and whether Quilter envisaged it that way from the outset: he regularly orchestrated songs, but this score is very detailed, far more complex than usual. Since he was so very much involved with the opera during the first half of 1929, it seems probable that once asked to provide something for the Festival, he only had time to take an existing but unpublished song and orchestrate it. After that, it took on a life of its own. In its voice and piano form, it was published and in its orchestral form it was performed around the world.

'I Arise' – subtitled 'Serenade for Voice and Orchestra' – is dedicated to Robert Allerton, his close friend from before the Great War. Allerton scarcely crossed his life now, although he was on the distant fringes: back in March 1921, Mrs Koehler told Quilter that Allerton was now in charge 'of American

---

[3] *The Times*, 29 July 1929, p. 10, c. 2.
[4] *Daily Telegraph*, 27 July 1929, p. 9, c. 2.
[5] Two versions of the voice and piano reduction are held by Boosey and Hawkes; they are in a copyist's hand, in low and high keys. The low key copy is dated 1928.

drawings and water-colours at the Chicago Art Institute', and that he had bought one of her paintings for it.[6] There are no records to show whether Allerton knew that the song had been dedicated to him, and it appears out of the blue, full-grown and remarkable. In 1932 Quilter and Grainger had much discussion about the orchestration and as a result Quilter reorchestrated it for lesser resources. In that form Grainger performed it, or had it performed, a number of times in the States and Canada, in the tenor or baritone version according to the singer available.[7]

A photograph of Quilter, flanked by Cyril Scott and Percy Grainger, and all three propped against a balustrade, was taken at the Festival, perhaps by Quilter himself; it is a photograph of which Grainger was particularly fond. Others show some of the musicians who took part in the Festival.

Grainger was especially grateful to Quilter for his contribution to the Festival, for 'yr lovely works, yr fine conducting, yr joy-giving nearness, yr give-willing lavish help in many ways. . . . If I seemed a little geisterabwesend [absent-minded] or worried or missing at rehearsals at Harrogate you must not take it ill'. This comment referred to an event that had rather frightened him, when on the second day of the concerts, he had received an anonymous postcard from someone accusing him of cowardice – a reference to his departure for the States at the outbreak of the First World War – and advising him to return there at once. Grainger tried to persuade Quilter to sit next to him in the concert, but would not tell him why, and Quilter sat with friends, elsewhere.[8] Anticlimactically, nothing happened.

Grainger continued his eulogy:

> I was very much impressed by yr conducting – steady, safe, nice to look at & getting ideal results. I am glad that you are one of the *practical* musicians, playing & singing & conducting in fine & helpful fitness as well as giving birth to new sound-beauties. "I arise" is *perfect* in every way, & *Children's Overture* is richer & more stalwart & better knit, under yr stick, than I have ever heard it. I worthprized [admired] all you did & was very thankful for your taking part & yr help.[9]

At the beginning of August, Quilter had a minor operation on his nose and he recuperated at Buckhurst Cottage, Withyham, but more frequent bouts of arthritis began to bother him too. Nevertheless, work on the light opera continued apace throughout the summer and in September, he and Bennett had an extended work session at the Cottage.

By December, Quilter was beginning to think about possible singers, and in January 1930 he was delighted to receive at last a neatly typed copy of the libretto. This was his cue to start trying to place the operetta. Quilter had kept in touch with C. B. Cochran, who had produced the revue *On with the Dance* in 1925, and he was the obvious person to approach first. But in the first part of

[6] Florence Koehler to Quilter, 27 March 1921, BL Add. MS 70599, f. 103.
[7] Quilter to Grainger, 15 and 16 June 1932 and 28 September 1932, GM.
[8] See John Bird, *Percy Grainger*, 3rd edn (Oxford, 1999), p. 236.
[9] Grainger to Quilter, 13 August 1929, GM.

1930, Cochran was occupied with his new revue. In June, he wrote to Bennett, 'No news for you yet about C.B.C. but I shall have another go when this German, French, Japanese stunt is off his mind!'[10] But on 16 July, he wrote to Bennett about a disastrous meeting during which Cochran obviously showed neither interest nor enthusiasm and was offhand and distrait. Quilter tried hard to persuade him but the encounter was totally unsuccessful and he found the whole experience highly distressing. Cochran's criticisms however were echoed some years later, in December 1936 in the wake of the disappointing reception of *Julia*, the reworking of *The Blue Boar*. Cochran found it conventional, and not what the public wanted at that time. He showed scarcely any interest in the libretto, and Quilter felt obliged to play some of the numbers through, rather hurriedly. At this point, Cochran seems to have brightened a little – 'he *said* the music was delightful – particularly the serenade & "Little Moth"' – but 'he took up a very hostile, or else a *very* guarded attitude'.[11] Quilter's letter is eloquent in its manner of writing; underlinings are applied liberally, the tone is defensive, anxious and worried, and unlike his normal style. He concluded:

> Of course the poor man has lost *heavily* lately & the theatre business has been awful – naturally he is frightened to do anything now which isn't a certainty. Suppose he decides against doing it – what do you advise as the best next step? – Can you see me when you are in London? & what sort of day & what sort of hour? I think if we can get hold of some person who really knows a lot about the theatre now, – it would be wise to ask his advice about the play etc. before another attack.[12]

He retained his faith in the piece, though his final comment, 'we must not be discouraged', seems to be aimed at himself as much as to Bennett. However, when he received Bennett's soothing response, he wrote again:

> I think I will wait 3 or 4 days – then I will write again to Cochran as you suggest. I shall wait till Monday, I think. I hope to see Creighton for a few minutes today & will see what he has to say. But I know he thinks Cochran much the best man![13]

Creighton was Walter, Quilter's dear friend from the first decade of the century. He had developed into a brilliant organiser; in 1924 he organised the Pageant of Empire, part of the Empire Exhibition, and had written to Edward Elgar to commission a work from him for it. In his letter he reminded him that when they both lived in Worcester – they overlapped from 1885 to 1889 – Elgar had taught him the violin.[14]

One summer – possibly that of 1930 – the Annual Dinner of the Musicians'

[10] Quilter to Bennett, 20 June 1930, Bennett archive.
[11] Quilter to Bennett, 16 July 1930, Bennett archive.
[12] Quilter to Bennett, 16 July 1930, Bennett archive.
[13] Quilter to Bennett, 18 July 1930, Bennett archive.
[14] Jerrold Northrop Moore, ed., *Edward Elgar, Letters of a Lifetime* (Oxford, 1990), p. 378. The work he commissioned in 1924 became the *Empire March*. At the time of his violin lessons, Creighton would have been aged between 7 and 11. Creighton's whereabouts are detailed in James Covert, *A Victorian Marriage, Mandell and Louise Creighton* (London, 2000).

Benevolent Fund was held at the Savoy Hotel, and was notable for its inclusion of fanfares by Granville Bantock, Arnold Bax, Arthur Bliss, Walford Davies, Eugène Goossens, Ethel Smyth and Quilter.[15] All seven fanfares were played by trumpeters from the Royal Military School of Music at Kneller Hall. Quilter's was called 'Fanfare for Children', based on 'A Frog He Would A-Wooing Go', from *A Children's Overture*. It was recorded but not published.

During July 1930, Quilter was having daily treatment for arthritis but *The Blue Boar* progressed and in mid-August, Quilter wrote from the Cottage to tell Bennett:

> Anthony Bernard is coming Tuesday for one night – he is being very jolly about the opera – & wants to interest money'd folk of whom he seems to know a fair supply (no fool, Mr Anthony!). Mark heard from Marguerita that Playfair is *very* keen![16]

Bernard and Quilter had been long acquainted; Bernard arranged *A Children's Overture* for piano duet, and his daughter Nicolette was one of Quilter's many godchildren. Playfair was Nigel Playfair, the director and theatre-manager.

Composer and librettist gave up on Cochran. In October of that year, 1930, Quilter suggested exploring further avenues, with Spencer Curtis Brown, and Barry Jackson, who was about to produce Somerset Maugham's *For Services Rendered*.[17] He was also in touch with Edward Knoblock. Quilter rather pinned his faith on Knoblock – 'he is an old hand at this game'.[18] Knoblock was indeed interested and keen to help in whatever way he could, but it came to nothing. Bennett's heart problems gave Quilter some cause for concern, but there was little to be done for the time being.

Quilter spent Christmas with his sister Maude again, at Horwood House, though he was glad to get back to Montagu Street where he could work properly, but in February Quilter was ill with sinus trouble and within a few weeks his arthritis was so much worse that for a time his letters were written by an amanuensis.[19]

He and Bennett were still trying to place the piece. Quilter talked over the orchestration with Alfred Reynolds, whose skills in that field he admired very much, but Reynolds, composer and orchestrator, and musical director of the Lyric Theatre, was too busy to help him much.[20]

Gervase Hughes (a man of many parts, mostly but not exclusively connected with the theatre) approached them, expressing an interest in seeing both script and music,[21] and in May, Hubert Foss, music editor at Oxford University Press,

[15] Eugène Goossens, *Overture and Beginners* (London, 1951), p. 282.

[16] Quilter to Bennett, 17 August [1930], Bennett archive.

[17] Quilter to Bennett, 28 October 1930, Bennett archive.

[18] Quilter to Bennett, a series of undated (and undatable) letters.

[19] Quilter to Bennett, 12 March 1931, Bennett archive..

[20] Dr Barbara Reynolds to Langfield, 27 July 1997. Quilter to Bennett, probably 9 February 1931, Bennett archive; also 17 June 1931.

[21] Quilter to Bennett, 12 March 1931, Bennett archive.

asked to see the libretto but returned it a month later, unable to 'do anything with the opera'.[22] In June, there is a mention of the London Play Company, but that idea too was abortive. In August, Quilter spent a few days at Pevensey Bay, with Percy and Ella Grainger, where they doubtless discussed the difficulties of getting works performed.

Life continued normally and matters drifted on for months. He tried a new doctor in May 1931 and visited friends and relations as usual. He went to Dartmouth in May 1932 to see his niece Norah Nichols's new play; he conducted *Where the Rainbow Ends* in Bournemouth in May. In the evenings he would often go to the theatre. He particularly favoured first and last nights, though he was such a frequent theatre-goer that this was largely inevitable; after a theatre evening, he would often stay up until one or two o'clock in the morning, talking to his servants, and then would make up for the late night by resting the following afternoon.

He went out to Suffolk regularly, sometimes to visit his sister Norah, but sometimes to fulfil his obligations with amateur music groups and associations there. His ties with local music-making were strong: he was Patron of the Woodbridge Music Festival from some time in the 1920s until around 1938, and regularly presented the certificates; occasionally he conducted particular items performed by the Woodbridge Choral Society and he became President of the Woodbridge Orchestral Society in 1932; he remained its president until his death, when his sister-in-law Lady Gwynedd, Eley's widow, took over; she was succeeded by Imogen Holst. He was greatly honoured and respected by the local amateur groups and the affection embraced his sister Norah Vivian, who was an enthusiastic violinist and also highly supportive of local amateur music.[23]

Quilter's wish to help others was one facet of a humanitarian ethos, which derived partly at least from his mother's example. Putting it into practice usually involved financial outlay, and he frequently complained that he was short of money '& so many friends have to be kept from starvation',[24] though this is tempered by the knowledge that his lifestyle was not an economical one. But he was undoubtedly generous to people whom he thought deserving and in need of help. Similarly he responded to Grainger's request for financial help for the Dolmetsch Fund and always showed an interest in what it was trying to achieve, even though he felt little affinity for the kind of music that it promoted.

Meanwhile, as far as *The Blue Boar* was concerned, in December 1932 Quilter and Bennett were still seeking backers. Various names cropped up in conversation – Cecil Paget, Barry Jackson again – but the same comments recurred: it did not have 'enough *meat*'. Quilter, for his part however, 'long[ed] for gaiety, & to get away from sentimentalism'.[25]

In February 1933, they tried a different tack. Quilter prepared two dances

---

[22] Quilter to Bennett, 17 June 1931, Bennett archive.
[23] Bernard Barrell to Langfield, 9 and 15 February 1997.
[24] Quilter to Grainger, 16 January 1933, GM.
[25] Quilter to Bennett, 19 December 1932, Bennett archive.

which he named *Pastoral Dance* and *Gavotte*, for a BBC programme on Quilter to be broadcast on Saturday 4 March, without, however, identifying them as being from *The Blue Boar*.[26] Leslie Woodgate conducted it, and Mark Raphael sang in other items in the programme which included the incidental music to *As You Like It*, some extracts from *Where the Rainbow Ends*, and sundry songs, including 'I Arise from Dreams of Thee'.[27]

This was an exceptionally frantic time, with Beatrice Harrison asking him in early February to orchestrate 'L'Amour de Moy' for HMV, on top of all his other commitments; it was a pity she took a month before sending him the copy she worked from.[28]

For Quilter and Bennett, their patience – and persistence – was at last paying off, though only just. The BBC were interested in broadcasting the work, in a music-only, hour-long concert version with linking narrative and on the last Friday in July, just before he went to his sister Maude for the weekend, Quilter sent the manuscript of *The Blue Boar* by hand to the conductor Stanford Robinson, at Robinson's request. The BBC were well aware of the difficulties that Quilter and Bennett had had in placing it, and they offered only £50 for the rights for two transmissions. Quilter felt this was too low, but Gordon McConnel, the producer, saw no reason to pay more, given that Quilter and Bennett were getting a chance for potential theatrical producers to hear a performance produced under excellent conditions.[29] Leslie Woodgate also advised them, very broadly, not to look a gift-horse in the mouth, and advised them also to let it be done as a concert performance, rather than by the production department, so as to preserve their rights. By this means, too, it would be performed in the Concert Hall of the BBC, with its pleasant ambience, rather than in the confines of a studio. But with some of the key BBC staff away on holiday, Quilter and Bennett decided to wait for their return before making a final decision. While waiting, they approached Sir Thomas Beecham, though this led nowhere.

On 31 August, the overture, billed simply as an 'Overture to a new Comic Opera', was broadcast in a concert of music played by the BBC Orchestra, and conducted by Alfred Reynolds. Quilter made it very clear that this was *light* opera, and that he had no interest in musical comedy.[30]

Quilter and Bennett decided to accept the BBC's offer. Quilter slipped in an appearance at the Wigmore Hall on 15 October, accompanying the black soprano Ruth Morris in a group of his songs, and Billy King accompanied her for the rest of the recital. As much as anything, this was a distraction, almost a relaxation, from the rigours of *The Blue Boar* which was finally broadcast, live as was usual, on two consecutive nights, Monday and Tuesday, 23 and 24 October.

[26] Quilter to Bennett, 10 February 1933, Bennett archive.
[27] *Pastoral* was billed as a first performance, though it is not clear why the *Gavotte* was not similarly billed; no other performance of it before 4 March is known.
[28] Quilter to Beatrice Harrison, 7 February and 3 March 1933, RCM.
[29] BBC WAC, Contributor file, 31 August 1933.
[30] Ralph Hill, 'Exquisite Miniaturist', *Radio Times*, 25 August 1933.

The synopsis published in the *Radio Times* for 20 October 1933 made it clear that this was a three-act light opera, being broadcast in a one-act form; it was produced by Gordon McConnel, with Stanford Robinson conducting, Raymond Newell singing the lead tenor rôle as the Marquis, and Ina Souez the lead soprano as Anne, Countess of Clovelly. Mark Raphael sang the rôle of Robert, the Marquis's manservant. The second performance was marred by technical difficulties in transmission, which caused some rumpus and much blaming of other people, and opinion was divided overall as to the quality of the music.

Rehearsals for the annual production of *Rainbow* took Quilter's mind off *The Blue Boar*, though he and Bennett gave much thought about what to do next. *The Blue Boar* always had an unsettled life. They sought to make the piece more appealing and saleable, but in a sense, it was out of date before it ever reached the audience.

1934 began badly with the sudden death on 21 January of Quilter's youngest brother Eustace, after a day's shooting; he was fifty-two. Three major composers died that year: Elgar on 23 February, Holst on 25 May and Delius on 10 June. On 12 February, Norman O'Neill, the oldest of the Frankfurt Group, was struck by a car and fell, hitting his head; blood poisoning set in and he died on 3 March. With his tremendous experience of writing music for the theatre, he had helped Quilter with orchestration and especially with his writing for theatre orchestra.

Walter Creighton came back into Quilter's life when he approached him to write a piece for the Pageant of Parliament, to be mounted at the Royal Albert Hall in the summer of 1934. Creighton wrote, devised and produced the celebration, and Quilter's contributions – those that can be positively identified – were a light song for chorus, 'You've Money to Spend', and an anthem, 'Non Nobis, Domine'. The words were by Rudyard Kipling, and they inspired a stirring, solidly patriotic piece. Malcolm Sargent thought it splendid: 'for years at almost all country festivals it has been the custom to end with Parry's *Jerusalem* & in many cases people are asking for a change but I have found no suitable tune. *I found it last night!*'[31] Kipling 'heard enthusiastic reports' of it, though he was unable to come.[32] The Pageant contained a mixture of choral items – hymns, songs, chorales – and illustrated a series of tableaux, including one of Queen Elizabeth as an old lady speaking to the House of Commons; the anthem's music was heard several times with different sets of words, not appearing in its official, complete, form until near the end.

The Pageant ran nightly from 29 June to 21 July, with matinées on Saturdays, and taking part were Yvonne Arnaud, Laura Cowie, Shayle Gardner and Donald Wolfit, together with two thousand other performers. It drained Creighton of all his mental and emotional resources, and the pressure nearly destroyed him. 'I am coming to from the nightmare of these past days, when inside I was longing to escape and wake up from the terror of it and could only

---

[31] Malcolm Sargent to Quilter, 10 July 1934, BL Add. MS 70605, f. 9.
[32] Rudyard Kipling to Quilter, 21 September 1934, BL Add. MS 70605, f. 2.

pray for courage', he wrote afterwards. 'But it is lovely Roger that our long friendship should have led to work together which has really perfected itself into something worthwhile.'[33] He loved the music that Quilter had written, and so did others – 'Non Nobis, Domine' was used the following year in the Empire Day celebrations, and was also used as the Olympic Hymn in the XIV Olympiad of 1948, in London, and again for the Winter Olympic Games of 1952, in Oslo.[34]

In the autumn of 1934, Quilter and Mark Raphael began planning a set of recordings of seventeen Quilter songs, to be issued privately for the Roger Quilter Society (about which no further information can be found), and Quilter was kept busy making lists of potential subscribers. The result was a group of definitive performances, produced as a presentation set of six records, with a small paper insert on which Quilter signed his name; the recordings were made in November and December 1934 and the set appeared at the beginning of 1935.[35] The records were then taken by Columbia and issued individually at bi-monthly intervals, starting in autumn 1935, and going through to summer 1936. Three of the songs were accompanied by piano quartet, with Frederick Grinke on violin, Max Gilbert on viola, Herbert Withers on cello, and Quilter: 'Come Away, Death', 'I Dare Not Ask a Kiss' and 'Take, O Take Those Lips Away'; and 'Cherry Valley' was accompanied by piano trio. The rest were for voice and piano alone.

In 1935, Curwen published 'Music and Moonlight' and Goodwin and Tabb published a curious and uncharacteristic piece by Quilter called 'Gipsy Life', one in the English String Series, which was a 'Collection of music for string orchestra' selected by Alec Rowley. It was dedicated to Leslie Bridgewater of the BBC; he was also leader of a quintet bearing his name.

The following summer, Grainger succeeded in persuading Quilter to attend the Dolmetsch Festival. It ran from 20 July to 1 August and Grainger was there for the whole period though Quilter was there only for a few days. Grainger's interest in early music and the early music movement went back many years, and he had attended the 1931 Festival; following that, he had met Dom Anselm Hughes and they embarked on an ambitious and long-running project. Quilter's interest was but slight; he preferred the literature of the time to its music.

On 4 August, Grainger went to the BBC with Quilter for a joint programme of their music. Grainger was very moved by the occasion, at the opportunity to 'enter the BBC at [Quilter's] side with [his] music alongside [Quilter's]'.[36] The programme included Grainger's 'Shepherd's

---

[33] Walter Creighton to Quilter, summer 1934, BL Add. 70596, f. 200.

[34] Coming so soon after the end of the war, there was neither time nor money to commission, prepare parts for and rehearse a new work, but 'Non Nobis' was felt to be 'eminently suitable' (Official Report, 1948).

[35] Recording details from the National Sound Archive. Quilter refers to sending out the records: Quilter to Alec Plumpton, 8 January 1935, BL Add. MS 70605, f. 21.

[36] Percy Grainger to Quilter, 7 August 1936, GM.

Hey', played by the Bernard Crook piano quintet, and Quilter's *To Julia*, also for piano quintet. At the end of the month, Quilter in his turn was excited and unusually enthusiastic at the prospect of a Prom concert that was to include some of Grainger's music. Although Grainger's works had been broadcast before, this was the first that Grainger was to conduct; Quilter offered whatever help was in his power, to provide a meal before the broadcast and a meeting-place afterwards.[37] In November, Grainger's 'The Bride's Tragedy' was broadcast, conducted by Leslie Woodgate. Grainger was at the rehearsal and despite being extraordinarily busy on what was to become *Julia*, Quilter came too, much to Grainger's joy; the music seemed to him to sound better, and more expressive, because of Quilter's presence.[38] This was a very striking thing for him to say, and even allowing for Grainger's usual exuberance, shows how much he valued and appreciated Quilter. Though they undoubtedly had considerable mutual respect, for each other and for each other's work, it is curiously difficult to extract exactly what Quilter and Grainger meant to each other; Grainger wrote so copiously to everyone, that the fact of the voluminous correspondence with Quilter is not of itself significant. There is almost no extant correspondence between Quilter and the rest of the Frankfurt group, and it is hard to escape the conclusion that those relationships must have been less important than that between Quilter and Grainger – but Quilter stayed in touch with O'Neill's family for many years, and Scott certainly thought of Quilter in the warmest terms. What is clear is that the impact he had on his friends was always a positive one, and that the relationships – inevitably – varied, depending on the nature of the other person. It is not surprising that Grainger's vigorous and energetic personality should engender a particular response from Quilter, and that Quilter's gentleness should be a source of wonder to Grainger.

In December 1936 *Julia* emerged from the ashes of *The Blue Boar*. There is no precise running order of the songs of *The Blue Boar* but there is enough indication in the letters that Quilter wrote to Rodney Bennett to show that the songs in *Julia* were broadly the same songs, reused, reordered, and of a similar atmosphere to the original version.

It was performed at the Royal Opera House, Covent Garden, London, by the British Music Drama Opera Company, the creation of the Russian tenor Vladimir Rosing. Rosing was the producer-in-chief, and the brilliant conductor-composer Albert Coates was the chief conductor. Rosing had a long-established career in England and firm ideas on the dramatic nature of operatic productions; he felt that opera had a tendency for artificiality and convention, and tried to stress the importance of the dramatic aspects of opera. But the company name was ungainly and unmemorable, even if it was precise: amidst the 'moribund and renascent institution, British opera', it employed 'British artists and [set] out to produce operas as music

[37] Quilter to Percy Grainger, 7 August 1936, GM.
[38] Percy Grainger to Quilter, 12 November 1936, GM.

dramas'.[39] Though the company ran regular short, annual, seasons at Covent Garden, newspaper reviews were generally dismissive and it sank with very little trace.

The three-week season of 1936 ran from 18 November to 8 December, and six operas were staged, all of them conducted by Coates: as well as Quilter's *Julia*, audiences could choose from Moussorgsky's *Boris Godounov* and *The Fair of Sorochinsk*, Puccini's *Madame Butterfly*, Leoncavallo's *Pagliacci*, and the first performance of Albert Coates's *Pickwick*. *Pickwick* made history when it became the first opera to be broadcast, in the form of excerpts, on the new television service in November 1936.

Julia, initially billed as *The Wild Boar*, seemed to be rather the poor relation, with ticket prices cheaper than those of the other performances, though this may simply have reflected a lesser cost of production. Rosing was one of the librettists, Caswell Garth the other, and the producer was Henry Cass. The première was to have been on Wednesday 2 December, but was altered[40] and so the first night was on Thursday 3 December 1936, at 8pm, with the remaining scheduled performances on 4, 5, 7 and 8 December, and matinées on Saturday 5 December and Tuesday 8 December at 2.30pm; the BBC broadcast Act 1 on the Monday evening.

Right up until the first night, Quilter was working phenomenally hard, composing, arranging and copying out parts. There had been many uncertainties: in the previous July, Quilter had written to Grainger that the opera was to be performed in the autumn.[41] In August, he had his 'ear to the telephone and a nose to the M.S. papers'.[42] Grainger, who had intended to leave England for New York just before the opening night, generously delayed his departure in order to hear it.

At the end of the first night, Quilter bravely went up on stage, and made a short speech. His family had shown emphatically no interest whatsoever during the writing of *The Blue Boar*, not even his sister Norah, but they came en masse to the first night, and afterwards his nephew Raymond, son of his eldest brother Eley, gave a huge dinner party for the family at one of the major London hotels,[43] at which Quilter also spoke. Though he still had difficulty with his p's and b's, his customary stammer was less noticeable in the marginally less tense surroundings.[44]

Many friends came to the first night too, and not just Ella and Percy Grainger: Cyril Scott called it a 'winner',[45] and reaction from friends and musicians was generally warm and friendly, kind, and sometimes very enthusiastic. Quilter

[39] 'British Music Drama Opera Company', *The Musical Times*, December 1936, p. 1132.
[40] Quilter to Percy Grainger, telegram, 20 October 1936, GM.
[41] Quilter to Percy Grainger, 9 July 1936, GM.
[42] Quilter to Percy Grainger, 24 August 1936, GM.
[43] Possibly the Dorchester.
[44] I am indebted to Mrs Diana Tennant, daughter of Quilter's younger brother Percy, for these recollections, recorded in an interview on 7 January 1997.
[45] Cyril Scott to Quilter, 4 [December 1936], GM.

found this very heartening, after the troubled period he had struggled through to get his 'frivolous, essentially theatrical venture'[46] off the ground.

Reviews were not unkind, but neither were they wild with enthusiasm. They generally commented, quite rightly, on the waltz-tune: 'a most captivating waltz',[47] 'an infectious waltz-tune',[48] and they were moderately restrained about the lead soprano; one reviewer made his opinion of her clear: 'Miss Margaret Bannerman is an attractive countess so long as her part is spoken, which is most of the time.'[49] It was considered to be a pretty comedy, with a happy manner, 'sprightly', 'charming', well-bred and lilting.[50] At least two of the reviewers for *Julia* wrote very favourably of the sets (by Hamish Wilson), especially the scene in which the hero's opera is being performed, as an opera within an opera: 'a clever presentation of the stage seen by the real audience as from behind a transparent backcloth'.[51]

Perhaps the reviewer in *The Illustrated London News*, W. J. Turner, pinpointed the difficulty: 'In a smaller theatre as a popular musical play, "Julia" might have a good success.' Many years later, Stanford Robinson recalled Wilson's 'delightful setting', and expressed his regret that it had not been produced in a more suitable theatre, where it 'would have had success'.[52] Covent Garden was too large, grand and formal for what was essentially a chamber opera to succeed; and its poor showing made it an unattractive proposition elsewhere. Its subsequent modifications are the more understandable. Cyril Scott's comment, written the following day, is perspicacious: he wanted 'to see it having a long run in the West End, away from the stodgy atmosphere of Covent Garden'. He was positively mesmerised by the waltz-tune, and unable to get it out of his head.[53]

Percy Grainger was ecstatic. He had attended some of the rehearsals and had been deeply impressed at Quilter's unwonted temper: he had evidently been rather 'peevish' with the orchestra – probably with worry at the way the rehearsals were going – but Grainger interpreted this as showing Quilter's 'kingly' aspects, that he was 'bigger, nobler, more insight-having & more critical than millions of Englishmen'.[54] He told Quilter to write more operas; he wrote to Margaret Bannerman to praise her in the rôle; he wrote that 'the whole mood of the opera, the whole texture of the music, has a soft intimate magic like Nipples'.[55] Even Ella Grainger wrote, to say that she had felt she was 'in the presence of civilisation'. Three days later, Grainger wrote from the ship taking him to New York, describing *Julia* as 'delicately lovely', and believing it to be a

[46] Quilter to Percy Grainger, 15 December 1936, GM.
[47] Review in *The Illustrated London News*, 12 December 1936.
[48] Review in *The Sunday Times*, 6 December 1936.
[49] Review in *The Times*, 4 December 1936.
[50] These comments are from the various reviews.
[51] *The Times*, 4 December 1936.
[52] Stanford Robinson to Quilter, 9 January 1952, BBC WAC.
[53] Cyril Scott to Quilter, 4 December 1936, GM.
[54] Percy Grainger to Quilter, 8 October 1947, GM.
[55] Percy Grainger to Quilter, 5 December 1936, GM.

possible goldmine. It appealed to his ideals; he found it ravishing and he found it true to Quilter's personal soul and artistic being.[56] He was fascinated that Quilter – unlike him – was able to produce 'a whole evening's entertainment that is aristocratic, sex magical, dream-drenched, love-warm as all yr art always has been'.[57] It was everything he 'never [sic] dreamed it could be'. He urged him to get *Julia* performed wherever and whenever possible, in whatever forms made it more saleable; the paramount need, he stressed, was to get the music heard, in any shape or form. Others, with a different sense of worldliness from Grainger, were not necessarily of the same view; *The Blue Boar* and *Julia* remained unpublished, and the full scores are lost.

There was nevertheless talk of a revival the following autumn.[58] But this was the year that Edward VIII abdicated, there would be a coronation the following year, and the theatrical world was nervous of uncertain ventures. Quilter was pessimistic about the prospects, yet keen to set *Julia* 'on her legs and walking';[59] he had put much of his own money into it, got into debt, and needed to get a concert version out in order to try to recoup his losses. A complete concert version never materialised, but he began to rework the piece, first as *Rosmé*, and then as *Love at the Inn*. He did some work on it as *Love and the Countess*, which perhaps fitted in between. *Love at the Inn* contained largely the same material as *Julia* and was published by Ascherberg, Hopwood and Crew. From the mêlée of this continuously evolving opera, various single songs were extracted and published.

Quilter had dealt with and survived unpleasantnesses and incompetence in the course of getting *Julia* off the ground, and now he was tired. He conducted the opening night of the *Rainbow* season on 16 December at the Holborn Empire and then rested.

Quilter had lived at 7 Montagu Street for twenty-five years and had probably had it on a twenty-five-year lease which was now about to expire. He decided to move to 1 Marlborough Hill, St John's Wood, a district of London, north of Montagu Street, and although he dreaded the upheaval, he looked forward to being 'away from the "madding crowd"'.[60] He moved there in August 1937 but it transpired that the house was very close to the Underground train lines and nearby was a vent from which the smoke erupted visibly. He found the infernal belching and subterranean noises deeply disturbing and though he and his friends nicknamed the house 'The Rumbles' to put humour into the situation, he had to find somewhere else.[61]

The somewhere else was 23 Acacia Road, an elegant house also in St John's Wood and very near to Mark Raphael's home in Woronzow Road; but it was not ready, and at the end of February 1938 Quilter moved temporarily to a flat

[56] Percy Grainger to Quilter, 8 December 1936, GM.
[57] Percy Grainger to Quilter, 8 December 1936, GM.
[58] Quilter to Percy Grainger, 28 March 1937, GM.
[59] Quilter to Percy Grainger, 31 December 1936, GM.
[60] Quilter to Percy Grainger, 24 May [1937], GM.
[61] Interview between Henry Heaton and Dr William Mitchell, late 1980s.

at 1 Melina Court, St John's Wood, while work and repairs were carried out. He went into a nursing home in Beaumont Street, London, to have another operation on his nose, staying there from the end of May until early June, and he recuperated at Harrogate in late July.

He finally moved to Acacia Road in early August 1938. It was an expensive time for him. Although he made more money in 1938 than in the previous year, he was, albeit temporarily, running two homes and he was also helping various Jewish friends. His close association with Mark and Eva Raphael gave him particular insights into the Nazi events and Jewish sufferings and he was increasingly aware of the difficulties facing European Jews. A few whom he knew well, in Vienna and elsewhere, and Eva's concern for her family, who were largely still in Poland, kept the matter high in his consciousness.

Amongst his Jewish friends in England, Germany and Austria was Heinrich Simon, the editor of the *Frankfurter Zeitung* for about thirty years, and whom he had known since at least the early 1920s; in December 1934 Jane and Wilfrid de Glehn had dined with the 'brilliant ugly' Simon at 7 Montagu Street and Jane described him as:

> a man of rare intelligence, a Doctor of Philosophy[,] a splendid musician. . . . A few weeks ago the Nazis came & turned him out & seized his paper. Think what it must be for an elderly man who has had a great position & career to be just adrift. He *loves* Germany too & his family have been there for generations. . . . Think of the withering scorn an enlightened man like that must feel for these brutal clowns who are ruling Germany.[62]

Within a month of moving into Acacia Road, Quilter was sheltering Dr Rudolf Stern, a Jewish scientist from Vienna, and his wife, while Dr Stern sought work. Quilter treated them with a light touch and showed them extraordinary generosity as well as sensitivity. They continued to live in London until well after the war, and Quilter supported them for many years.

When Mark Raphael had given concert tours in Germany, even in the late 1920s, he and Quilter were well aware of anti-Semitic feeling, and he chose the venues for his recitals carefully. Some Jews were able to leave Germany and Austria, and other countries where they were not welcome, but it was rarely a straightforward process. The usual methods of gaining entry to the UK were to have a ready means of employment, or to have guarantors of financial security, so that the immigrants would not be a drain on the state, and it was in this way – by providing the financial guarantees – that Quilter was able to help his Jewish friends.

Grainger could never understand Quilter's desire to help; he felt it was simply interfering with nature. He had nothing against individuals, and indeed nothing against any particular race, and he never quite claimed views of racial supremacy, though his ideas now would certainly be viewed with considerable suspicion. But he saw the Nordic races as having a thoughtfulness and kindness

---

[62] Jane de Glehn to her sister Posie, 10 December 1934, AAA.

lacking in others, and he resented the intrusion and interference of those other races.[63] For Quilter's more direct outlook, however, world events sickened him to his very soul. In a deeply felt and unusually explicit outburst, prompted by Grainger's direct criticism of his actions in sheltering refugees, he wrote to him:

> when I see a fly caught in a spider's web, struggling in despair to get free, & knowing that the spider is coming to eat him alive my heart is wrung with pity & horror and I feel terribly for the fly & rescue him if I can . . . I loathe every form of bullying – most of all that which is done as if it were a *holy duty*, and something that was purging & purifying the one who bullies – that is why I *loath* [sic] the German form of bullying and despise it with every fibre of my being. The Jew is a perfect scapegoat – the world *must* approve of this splendidly organised marvellously carried out persecution. Every great nation has to have its great purges: I've had all this dinned into my ears till I am sick to death. But my spirit revolts & always will revolt.[64]

And this was his philosophy throughout his life, from Eton days to the end: a love for humanity and for the individual, and a compassion for others, founded on a bedrock of justice and equality. As a boy, when he saw a strength of mind, desperation and nobility in the behaviour of the miners on strike, while his fellow-students saw only ingratitude, so now he saw a depth of character in the people he knew and he would be ashamed of himself if he did not use the resources he possessed – spiritual as well as worldly – to help them. This was his religion: not an organised religion, which he hated, but a deeply held belief in the need for humanness, one to another.

1938 was a 'ghastly, horrible year'.[65] War was clearly impending, and Quilter was in a poor frame of mind and thoroughly devitalised.

> I never knew I could suffer so much. I have been through a good deal, at odd times, physically and mentally, but somehow this time my *soul* has come in for it, and has suffered real hurt. It is not a nice experience. . . . I cling to my little bit of human kindness, and try not to get 'downed' by what goes on. . . . I have felt so horribly shocked & miserable.[66]

His dearest nephew, Arnold Vivian, whom he treated as a son, had joined the Army, the Grenadier Guards; Arnold had inherited a love of gardens from his grandmother, had trained as a nurseryman in Edinburgh and at Waterer's Nurseries in Knapp Hill, Surrey, and until Roger Fielding Notcutt's sudden death in 1938, was in the midst of plans to help him in his nursery business at Woodbridge. Now Arnold managed to find solace in the plants he saw, while blacking his boots and doing parade drill. He too had been at Eton, but had fared better than his uncle: he was a more positive character, with a sunny personality, though still sensitive and capable of plumbing the depths. He was

[63] Percy Grainger to Quilter, 25 February 1939, GM.
[64] Quilter to Percy Grainger, 14 January 1939, GM.
[65] Quilter to Lydia Emmet, 5 December 1938, AAA.
[66] Quilter to Lydia Emmet, 5 December 1938, AAA.

young, excited about life and the future, a light tenor who loved to sing his uncle's songs; they shared a common sensibility and love of music, poetry and art, and he was infinitely closer to Quilter than any other member of the family. He was Quilter's godson, and also his heir.

6

The Last Years (1939–1953)

Quilter was always intensely pleased to hear Arnold's news, though his own was much less exciting: his periodic rheumatic troubles flared up in August 1939. He went to Harrogate on 28 August to play in a concert, but it was hard to get through it, partly because of the rheumatism, and partly because he felt the tension of the imminent war so strongly. By 1 September, he was helping to police air-raid shelters, but shortly after war was declared two days later, he went down to his sister Norah at Foxboro', to help with fifteen children, evacuees from London.[1] Norah's elder son, Eustace Miller, had joined up, leaving his wife, mother, sister Ruby and his two children, just 'one lot of women out of millions in the same state'[2] while Quilter distracted himself cutting the evacuees' hair and giving them lessons in geography and arithmetic.[3] He made himself work on his music in the mornings[4] and the good weather helped him though he was 'sick at heart'.[5]

In the panic of the opening weeks of the war, all entertainments were closed down. Quilter clung to his simple faith in children, music and nature, resolving not to be shaken by 'the cruelty in the world, and all the misery brought by it',[6] though his patience was tried by a rash promise he made to his sister-in-law, Percy's wife Gladys, to 'help at a "variety entertainment" (in aid of Red Cross)' in November.[7] He returned to Acacia Road and spent Christmas at the home of his other sister, Maude.

Grainger begged Quilter to go to the Welsh hills, or the Highlands of Scotland, anywhere but London, at least for a few months,[8] but Quilter was determined to remain in London, despite the difficulties of living there. He told Jane de Glehn, 'I *won't* be downed by those bl__dy Germans'.[9] With the tax increases, and the support he was giving to Dr Stern and his family, he was struggling financially – by 1943, he was more than four thousand pounds

---

[1] Quilter to Mark Raphael, 8 September 1939, BL Add. MS 70607, f. 76.
[2] Quilter to Eva Raphael, [10 September 1939], BL Add. MS 70607, f. 78.
[3] Quilter to Mark Raphael, 8 September 1939, BL Add. MS 70607, f. 76.
[4] Quilter to Eva Raphael, 29 September, BL Add. MS 70607, f. 82.
[5] Quilter to Percy Grainger, 24 September 1939, GM.
[6] Quilter to Eva Raphael, 1 November 1939, BL Add. MS 70607, f. 84.
[7] Quilter to Eva Raphael, 4 November 1939, BL Add. MS 70607, f. 87.
[8] Grainger to Quilter, 26 September and 19 October 1939, GM.
[9] Jane de Glehn to her sister Lydia Emmet, March [1940], AAA.

overdrawn – but he refused to worry about it. He needed his domestic servants, he knew no other way of living, and there was nothing to be done.

He suffered agonies over the news, and lack of news, of various relations. His nephew Eustace Miller and a great-nephew David Sutherland (Norah Vivian's grandson) were successfully evacuated from Dunkirk in June 1940, but the intense emotion of the situation left Quilter feeling 'quite dead . . . If only one did not suffer on other people's account'.[10] The strain of the Great War, allegedly the war to end wars, had been enough for him to cope with; another was almost too much to bear.

In January 1941, following an initiative by the Ministry of Information, Dr Adrian Boult, Director of Music at the BBC, commissioned patriotic songs from George Dyson, John Ireland, Quilter and Ralph Vaughan Williams, with Walford Davies in reserve. The brief was for a 'song or lay hymn, with orchestral accompaniment, the *theme* patriotic but not necessarily war-like . . . "England" to be avoided as a synonym for Britain'.[11] The lyrics were to be between six and eighteen lines long, or two to three stanzas, and some poets were suggested, though it was not obligatory to choose one of them: the list included Masefield, Herbert Read, Edmund Blunden, Laurence Binyon, A. P. Herbert and Lord Dunsany, with Robert Nichols, Siegfried Sassoon, Hilaire Belloc, T. S. Eliot or J. C. Squire as reserves.

Vaughan Williams was approached and commissioned first, but he set Henley's 'England, My England' which promptly caused a furore and nearly put a stop to the entire process. Quilter had no wish to compose anything '*too* warlike and flagwagging'[12] and asked if he might interpret the commission in terms of 'liberty'.[13] He initially considered his cousin-in-law A. P. Herbert as librettist, but in the end he set words by Rodney Bennett. It was not an easy commission for him to fulfil. The patriotic music of St George, from *Rainbow*, had come readily, but this was patriotism on demand, hard for one who went 'by nature to flowery meadows, purling streams'.[14]

By 10 April, Quilter had produced a piano sketch, which he sent for initial approval before he continued with the orchestration, and he conducted the first performance on 10 July 1941. On 19 September 1944, all four settings – Vaughan Williams's 'England, My England', Dyson's 'Motherland' (renamed from the original 'England and Her Dominions', of William Watson), Ireland's 'O Happy Land' (a setting of words by W. J. Linton); and Quilter's 'A Song of Freedom' – were broadcast. None was felt to be especially successful: 'the unison song, particularly when coupled with patriotism, seems to be a first-class stifler of inspiration.'[15] Boult thought Quilter's setting a 'mixture of roast beef and

[10] Quilter to Jane de Glehn, [June 1940], AAA.
[11] BBC WAC, R27/58.
[12] Quilter to Jane de Glehn, [early 1941], AAA.
[13] Quilter to Adrian Boult, 16 January 1941, Contributor file (1940–62), BBC WAC.
[14] Quilter to Adrian Boult, 16 January 1941, Contributor file (1940–62), BBC WAC.
[15] MP Organiser (Ronald Biggs) to DM (Adrian Boult), 29 September 1944, BBC WAC.

saccharine'[16] and he regretted the absence of Quilter's more distinctive style. Ireland's and Vaughan Williams's settings were generally thought the best of a disappointing collection, with Quilter's 'A Song of Freedom' inferior to his 'Non Nobis, Domine' of 1934.

When a bombing raid in April 1941 destroyed Jane and Wilfrid de Glehn's house in Cheyne Walk, both they and Quilter felt that an era had ended. Many first performances had taken place there, and many artists, writers and musicians had gathered there. Quilter's house managed to survive all the bombings, though it was damaged by shrapnel: it seemed to provide sanctuary and the garden especially was an oasis of calm. However, over these months Quilter – a fairly thin man at the best of times – lost weight, his hair became much greyer, and he began to have severe headaches.

Nevertheless, he managed to arrange some of his various Shakespeare settings for piano quartet and piano quintet, as well as for small orchestra. His setting of 'Trollie Lollie Laughter', a setting of a poem by Victor B. Neuberg, had been published in 1939, as had been the partsong for men's voices, 'Madrigal in Satin'. During 1940, he had reworked *Julia* and called it *Rosmé*, little remaining of it now except a chorus, 'Youth and Beauty', published in 1941, and a concert waltz for orchestra that uses the waltz-tune 'Love Calls through the Summer Night'. His arrangement of 'The Rose of Tralee' was also published in 1941.

By March 1942, the de Glehns had moved into their new house at Stratford Tony, Wiltshire. Quilter loved its peacefulness, and he often visited them there. Jane was extremely concerned at his morbid insistence on staying in London, but to stay there, in his own home, was one thing for him that was constant – surrounded by so much disruption and destruction, he needed what little stability he could get.

In the middle of June, Quilter's manservant Frank Twiner – who by now had married the cook – had had enough of the bombings, and walked out without a word, but with the cook, leaving Quilter almost helpless.

He advertised in *The Times* for a couple to look after him and the household, and the couple he found began working for him on 4 July 1942.[17] The Heatons were originally from Settle in Yorkshire, Henry (usually called Harry, and formerly a batman in the army) and Ada, a childless couple in their very early forties; they had been married for seventeen years.[18]

Ada Heaton was the stronger personality, a good cook and a stickler for setting a table well. Harry was scatty: they made an odd couple. They ran 23 Acacia Road competently and did indeed look after Quilter, but there were many of his friends who, at best, disliked them and at worst, hated them with a vitriolic intensity, describing Harry in particular as wheedling, obsequious, slimy and insinuating. Others described Harry as somehow lacking the

---

[16] Director of Music to Deputy Director of Music, 27 September 1944, BBC WAC.

[17] The advertisement reads: 'Gentleman (single) requires superior Married Couple undertake entire work small house, St John's Wood; good wages and outings; own sitting room and bath room; good references essential', *The Times*, 16 June 1942, p. 8e.

[18] They were married in Giggleswick on 17 June 1925.

masculine ways that they expected of a Yorkshireman. Some thought he was homosexual. Many people who knew Quilter well claimed that the Heatons took advantage of him in many ways, mostly financially, and said too that Quilter was, at one and the same time, fond of the Heatons, ensnared by them and terrified of them.

In April 1943, Quilter was reworking *Julia*, simplifying the story and incorporating new music, and he mentioned to Grainger that 'someone good' had faith in it, though he did not elaborate.[19] In January 1945, a simplified version was indeed tried out at Leicester; it had four performances, and was scored for string band, piano, single woodwind and percussion.[20] Nothing else is known about it, though it may have been the version of *Julia* called *Love and the Countess*. As with *Rosmé*, this was not published complete, but one of the songs, 'Island of Dreams', was published separately in 1946, with words as well as music by Quilter. Another song was published in 1946, 'Here's a Chapter Almost Ended', but this was shown as being from *Love at the Inn*.

Quilter called his light-hearted choral work *The Sailor and His Lass* a 'folk-ballad'. It was written in 1943 and was performed in manuscript near Leicester in 1945 or early 1946. It was published in 1948 and Quilter attended its first performance after that, in Woodbridge on 14 April 1950. In 1944 he offered it to the BBC; they rejected it gently and kindly, saying they had no suitable space for it at that time;[21] in fact, the readers' reports are very disparaging: from Gordon Jacob, 'It is surprising to find this composer turning out what can only be described as utter tripe. But such, alas, is the case' and from John Ireland, 'This will not add to the composer's reputation – and is better left in obscurity so far as the B.B.C. is concerned'.[22]

Early in 1942, to Quilter's distress, his nephew Arnold Vivian was sent out to the Middle East. Arnold was deeply unhappy: he found his fellow soldiers uncultured and uncongenial, with no one to share his interests. He hated the 'friction and constant bloodyness'[23] and tried to get another posting outside the battalion. By March 1943, he had had four jobs in as many months, but moved to be with the Anti-Tank guns unit which he found more to his liking.

On 17 March, however, he was wounded and captured in the Battle of the Horseshoe, Medenine, Tunisia, and was taken to a prisoner-of-war camp in northern Italy. As the situation in Italy worsened, matters became extremely muddled, and when Italy capitulated in early September, the guards told the prisoners in the camp that they would no longer guard them, and the prisoners were thus free to leave. The officers were strongly advised to remain, however, because the Germans were still fighting the Italian partisans and there was considerable confusion. Arnold and his friend, Norton, Lord Brabourne,

19 Quilter to Percy Grainger, 14 April 1943, GM.
20 Quilter to Percy Grainger, 12 January 1945, GM.
21 Deputy Director of Music (Kenneth Wright) to Quilter, 24 June 1944.
22 Music General – Music Reports 1928–54, R27/614, both reports dated 13 January 1944, BBC WAC.
23 Arnold Vivian to Quilter, 17 January 1943, BL Add. MS 70595, f. 142.

decided to take their chances and walked out, but the situation was as chaotic as they had been told and after a night or two, they returned to the camp, only to find that in the meantime, it had been recaptured by the Germans and they were prisoners again. Everyone was herded onto a train heading for Germany, and on 15 September, while it was stopped just outside Bronzolo, a little station near Bolzano just before the German border, the prisoners were allowed to take some exercise in pairs. Arnold and Norton Brabourne took the opportunity to escape, but from this point on, there was no news of them – only silence.

Arnold's mother Norah was beside herself with worry; Quilter tried to keep her spirits up but it was all but impossible when he was himself so upset. He spent many periods at Foxboro' Hall with her, but by now it was winter, and cold and damp at the Hall, and he felt ill. Then in April 1944, his sister Norah had a letter out of the blue from an officer, expressing condolences on Arnold's death. This was a most dreadful shock, but Arnold's regiment was unable to confirm it and she and Quilter continued to hope, though the strain on them intensified. One of Quilter's finest songs, 'Drooping Wings', a devastatingly bleak setting of a poem by Edith Sterling-Levis, dates from this period. Quilter convinced himself that one day Arnold would return and, in hope, he continued to work on a collection of songs that he had begun some months earlier to cheer Arnold up while he was abroad, for him to sing on his return. The songs – arrangements of English, Scottish, Irish and French melodies – included five that had been published over twenty years earlier: 'Three Poor Mariners', 'Drink to Me Only', 'Over the Mountains', 'The Jolly Miller' and 'Barbara Allen', and there were eleven more, including 'Ye Banks and Braes', one of Arnold's favourites, and 'L'Amour de Moy' that Quilter had arranged for the Harrison sisters but had never published.

He spent as much time as he could with Jane de Glehn, whose presence he found comforting. He was pleasantly distracted by – and pleased to accept – Thomas Dunhill's invitation to join the Council of the Composers' Guild, in the summer of 1944, but he was annoyed with his publishers, Boosey and Hawkes, who were refusing to reprint his songs in piano and voice form, though demand for orchestrated versions was such that they had to publish some of them. Rather disgruntled, he told Percy Grainger 'they bring out quite a number of more modern things, especially those of Benjamin Britten' whom he admitted 'is certainly a very gifted & accomplished young fellow'.[24] Grainger called him a nuisance.[25]

A few more songs emerged at around this time, with the unison version of 'The Cradle in Bethlehem', and the partsong 'The Pretty Birds Do Sing', published in 1945.

At the end of December 1944, Quilter's friend Benton Fletcher died at his home at 3 Cheyne Walk.[26] The two had known each other since at least 1908,

---

[24] Quilter to Percy Grainger, 19 May 1944, GM.
[25] Percy Grainger to Quilter, 25 July 1948, GM.
[26] Fletcher had encouraged the National Trust to buy the property, in which he then lived. A trust fund was set up to support it, and later his collection of musical instruments was installed

when they were in Egypt at the same time, Fletcher involved in the archaeological digs, and Quilter accompanying his parents. In the early part of the
century Fletcher had been a popular guest on the London dinner-party circuit,
and was a regular visitor at Foxboro' Hall even in his later years, but he became
more and more difficult with age. He died in squalor; his house was, by choice,
quite unheated despite the bitter cold, and at his funeral on 5 January 1945,
there were only four mourners, one of whom was Quilter.[27] The others were a
nephew and two colleagues from the National Trust: Fletcher was an extremely
knowledgeable advisor on buildings and their acquisition, and his views were
highly respected.[28] Quilter kept Fletcher's obituary notice; he was deeply upset
by his friend's death and the undignified circumstances in which it had
happened.

The war ended and with it all hope of his nephew Arnold's survival. Richard
Elwes, one of Gervase Elwes's younger sons and now a barrister, was working at
the War Office tracing missing soldiers, and early in May 1945, he told Jane de
Glehn privately that they would not find Arnold alive. At the beginning of June,
Quilter wrote a letter to Percy Grainger. He could not bear to tell him the news
outright, but prattled on about the usual things. In the middle he suddenly –
almost en passant – told him that his nephew was dead.

After Arnold and Norton Brabourne had escaped from the train, just outside
Bronzolo, they found their way to a farmhouse, in an area that was formerly
part of Austria, where most of the locals, including the Mayor, were German-
speaking and pro-Nazi; the occupants of the farmhouse informed the Mayor,
who passed word of the two escaped prisoners to the German officer in charge
of the train, and the two friends were recaptured. The German escort officer –
who may have been an SS officer rather than from the Wehrmacht – had them
taken back to the station, made them kneel on the railway tracks and shot them
in the back of the neck. Their bodies were dragged to the side of the tracks and
left there as a warning to other prisoners.[29] That night, however, in defiance of
the orders:

> The 'partisans' came & took the bodies away & got the village priest – who *risked
> his life* in giving the boys a decent burial. They put a wooden cross, with the names
> on it:– and, think of it, the villagers had kept putting fresh flowers on the grave in
> that little village cemetery.[30]

---

there. These had previously been kept in Old Devonshire House which he had given to the
Trust in 1938; during the war they were stored out of London for safety, a prudent measure
since Old Devonshire House was bombed in 1941. Later 3 Cheyne Walk was sold and the
instruments rehoused in Fenton House, Hampstead. (James Lees-Milne, *Diaries 1942–1945*
(London, 1975); and correspondence between Langfield and the National Trust, 6 July 1998.)

[27] James Lees-Milne, *Diaries 1942–1945*.

[28] Fletcher wrote and illustrated a rather attractive book called *Royal Homes near London* (London,
1930).

[29] Lord Brabourne (Norton Brabourne's brother) to Langfield, 20 November 2000; and archives of
the Grenadier Guards.

[30] Quilter to Percy Grainger, 10 June 1945, GM.

The murders were investigated and treated as a war crime and the officer was executed; Quilter thought that in seeking to find out what had happened to Arnold, he had set in motion a train of events which had consequently led to the German officer's death. This was not so: the investigation had been initiated by the Grenadier Guards more than by Arnold's mother Norah, but Quilter was deeply distressed by the further death.

A memorial service to Arnold was held at St Andrew's Church, Bredfield, near Woodbridge, on 23 June 1945. Arnold was twenty-eight, and Lord Brabourne twenty-one years old when they died; later they were reinterred and now lie side by side in the war cemetery at Padua.[31]

Quilter never got over Arnold's death. He was numbed by it, completely devastated and heartbroken. The repercussions lasted for the rest of his life and his book of songs for Arnold to sing on his return became an epitaph to him instead, *The Arnold Book of Old Songs*.

The rest of the year was spent quietly, trying to pick up the pieces of his life, and to some extent continued normally: on 14 August 1945 he recorded six songs with the baritone Frederick Harvey for the BBC Transcription Service; the records would be sent to broadcasting organisations around the world, but were never released as commercial recordings. In December 1945, however, Quilter had some sort of prostate operation, possibly for cancer,[32] and was in hospital for several weeks. For a chronic depressive, this was the final straw; he was 'very ill & miserable & did not read or write for 3 months'.[33] His mental state broke down during the first half of 1946: Jane de Glehn told her sister Lydia that it 'was the result of the long strain of the bombing, the agonising surprise & grief over Arnold & then the big operation on top of [it] all. He was so extraordinarily controlled and heroic all through these things that there has been a reaction'.[34] In July, Mark Raphael, under some pretext, drove him to the noted mental hospital, St Andrew's Hospital, Northampton, and had him admitted. Quilter wrote Raphael a letter, angry, bitter and accusatory, but action was essential; Quilter had lost his hold on reality. He had changed radically since the operation: he was much ruddier in the face and coarser in complexion, his behaviour changed and he was now overtly homosexual,[35]

---

[31] Sources: Grenadier Guards Archives, Lord Brabourne, and interviews and reported interviews with contemporaries. The information dating from the 1940s is extremely confused. An initial investigation took place immediately after the cessation of hostilities, but the investigation of the war crime did not take place for a further two years, by which time memories had faded, and even in 1945, witnesses readily, and understandably, confused one shooting with another.

[32] So Quilter's godson Roger Frith was led to believe, but it has not been possible to confirm it.

[33] Quilter to Percy Grainger, 1 April 1946, GM. In the same letter, he told Grainger he had two light operas coming on, with one of them due to be performed at the end of May, though there is no evidence to confirm this.

[34] Jane de Glehn to Lydia Emmet, [9 January 1947], AAA.

[35] The reasons for this are not at all clear; there may have been some mild brain damage as a result of the operation itself, or he may have been given testosterone treatment, which can cause an increased ruddiness of complexion and behavioural changes. If he was given this treatment, it is not known over what period he was given it.

offering flowers to young men in the street and laying himself open to the possibility of blackmail. He seemed unable to comprehend the danger. He pursued Raphael's teenage son Roger relentlessly, and on one occasion when Mark and Eva were away from home for an extended period, Quilter's attentions became so intrusive that Roger Raphael and his sister had to flee their London home and stay with a godmother. When staying at his sister's at Foxboro' on one occasion, Quilter accosted the gardener, who, indignant, informed Norah Vivian; it would have been comic if it were not so pitiful.

Quilter stayed in what was probably an annexe of St Andrew's called Eagle House and was there for six months. The records have been lost or destroyed, but he almost certainly underwent the favoured treatment of the time, electro-convulsive therapy, with dosages considerably higher then than they are now, and with partial, but permanent, loss of memory a common side-effect of high dosage.

Quilter wrote music throughout his stay at St Andrew's, but discovered afterwards that it was complete nonsense and he destroyed most of it; those manuscripts that survive are clearly disorganised.[36]

Once he was allowed home, in January 1947, he discovered – much to his amazement, since he had no recollection of it at all – that he had written music before the breakdown, and that it was now being published: 'Hark, Hark, the Lark!' had appeared in 1946, and also the partsong for men's voices 'Farewell to Shan-Avon, Song of the Forlorn Warriors'. Although 'One Word is Too Often Profaned' is dated 1946 (and published a year later), it was probably originally composed earlier.

The hospital fees had been very substantial and although Harry and Ada Heaton ran 23 Acacia Road as best they could, they had eventually run out of money and had had to approach the family for help to pay the bills; by the end of May his accountant Arthur Dickinson had been appointed Receiver by the Court of Protection in order to manage Quilter's affairs and his long-standing bank overdraft of four to five thousand pounds was eventually paid off by selling some of his shareholdings. From January 1946, after his operation, the financial management was erratic – formerly, the Heatons had been paid a regular £10 a week plus a Christmas bonus of £25 or £30, but now the amounts they received were variable.

On 10 June 1947, his younger brother Percy died and was buried at Bawdsey Church, in the family tomb, and six months later, on 10 December, his sister Norah died. She had been forty-six when Arnold was born and she had regarded him as her 'Benjamin' son.[37] She had had heart problems, and had she lived much longer, would have been '*miserable* as a useless invalid'.[38] At last, her 'restless, feverish, spirit [was] . . . at rest'.[39]

---

[36] For example, full scores might have different numbers of bars in different parts (there is one example in the archives held by Leslie East).
[37] Robin Miller to Langfield, 24 November 2000.
[38] Quilter to Percy Grainger, 20 January 1947, GM.
[39] Quilter to Percy Grainger, 11 December 1947, GM.

This was two years after his surgery and one year after his long stay in St Andrew's, and Quilter felt he was still recovering and unable to work properly: he had bouts of neuralgia and various minor ailments, though occasionally he claimed to feel really well. He was conscious of time running out for him and wrote very little new music, if any, reluctant to start something he might not be able to finish. Instead, he revised previous work and prepared it for publication: 'Tulips' in its partsong form is dated 1946; he arranged it as a solo song the following year, and 'Music' dates from 1947 too. Quilter considered reworking the partsong 'Omar Khayām', but this came to nothing and it remained in manuscript.

By October 1947, Boosey had finally published separately all the songs of *The Arnold Book of Old Songs* though they were not published in one volume until 1950 (with Quilter sharing the costs on the initial edition of 250, and receiving a double royalty).[40] Quilter battled with Boosey and with Forsyth for not keeping his music in print, but they, for their part, were battling with paper shortages.

His other sister Maude died on 19 October 1949, and Balfour Gardiner died at the end of June 1950, 'terrible sad & sudden news';[41] Gardiner's memorial concert took place the following April, and Quilter's note in the programme highlighted his old friend's passionate nature.[42] He described the concert to Grainger, recalling Gardiner's 'unspeakable charm and glinting but kind and humorous glance'.[43]

He went abroad on holiday in 1948, probably to France; to Italy and Switzerland in May 1949; and to the Austrian Tyrol and Switzerland in July and August 1950;[44] he took the Heatons with him. He continued his rounds of visiting friends, sometimes timing them around the Heatons' holidays, though when they returned to Settle, Yorkshire, in 1950 to celebrate their silver wedding anniversary, he went with them; it was not by any means the first time they had taken him there.[45] When Quilter used to come up, he would stay at Hazel Dene, the house of one of the local families, or in one of the local inns, while the Heatons stayed with relations. In these post-war Yorkshire years, Quilter met a number of local musicians and corresponded with them, gave them copies of his songs, and sometimes gave them manuscripts.[46]

In May 1950, Hubert Foss, Music Editor at Oxford University Press, was re-editing Philip Heseltine's book about Delius and decided to supplement it with contributions from some of those who had known Delius, Quilter and Grainger

[40] Correspondence between Quilter and Boosey, January 1950, author's collection.
[41] Quilter to Percy Grainger, 21 May 1950, GM.
[42] Reproduced in Stephen Lloyd, *H. Balfour Gardiner* (Cambridge, 1984), p. 218.
[43] Quilter to Percy Grainger, 24 April 1951, GM.
[44] Quilter's passport.
[45] It was a musical area: in earlier years, Elgar had stayed at the house of his friend Dr Buck in the adjacent village of Giggleswick.
[46] These were people such as Frederick Lord, a composer and pianist who had studied in Switzerland and was organist at the English speaking church of Vevey, near Montreux; he had met Quilter while back in Yorkshire visiting his sister.

amongst them. Quilter wrote sensitively, describing what Delius and his music meant to him (about a performance of *Brigg Fair* at Frankfurt): 'I was . . . overcome by the beauty both of the composition and of the performance . . . I became completely charmed and fascinated by him.'[47]

In August 1950, aged seventy-two and frail, Quilter fell in his bedroom and broke two ribs,[48] and at Christmas was laid up with a chill. Inevitably at that time of life, many of his friends and contemporaries were dying: the following April, it was clear that Wilfrid de Glehn, his friend for fifty years or more, had not long to live; he died a month later. Quilter told Grainger that he was writing memoirs. Some autobiographical notes survive, though they are incomplete and may date from various periods in Quilter's life.

Throughout these post-war years, Quilter gave cause for concern to those who cared for him: sometimes he threw tantrums and was moody[49] and on the other hand, at Christmas time, he would tip anybody and everybody who came to the door; he would go out with a pocketful of money and come back with nothing.

Care had to be taken with visitors. One young man, who worked for a music publishing firm, used to write to various composers and ask to meet them. When he came to tea with Quilter, Ada Heaton, fearful of scandal, kept finding reasons for coming into the room, evidently in the interests of the young man, whom Quilter would have accosted otherwise. Quilter sometimes visited the composer Eric Coates, and Phyllis Coates regularly had to rescue her husband from similar attentions; but they had known Quilter for many years and were very understanding and tolerant of his behaviour.

On many occasions, the Heatons refused to allow some of Quilter's friends to visit at all: Marie Bernard, Anthony Bernard's wife, was extremely upset at being denied entrance so often. Her elder daughter, Nicolette, was a god-daughter, and her younger, Christine, was treated as if she were one. In earlier years they had all visited Quilter regularly, and loved being taken out by him, in his chauffeur-driven car, for picnics, or to the ballet, or an outing on the river.[50]

There are many allegations that Quilter was blackmailed in his later years. These can never be proved, but it was clear that Quilter's behaviour had become an extremely worrying liability. Whether third parties were bought off to avoid scandal, or whether people closer to him saw a convenient opportunity, must remain speculation; there are rumours that he was arrested, though no evidence for this has been forthcoming; on the other hand, the Raphaels (Eva especially), the Bernards and the Sterns all mistrusted the Heatons completely, and were totally and utterly convinced that they were blatantly making the very most of the financial opportunities afforded them. Dr Stern's

---

[47] Peter Warlock, *Frederick Delius*, 2nd edn. (London, 1952), p. 156.
[48] Quilter to Percy Grainger, 31 August 1950, GM.
[49] Interview with Harry Heaton's niece, 11 April 1997.
[50] Correspondence and interview with Christine Bernard, March 1998 – December 1999.

daughter Harriet had met Quilter considerably later than had her father, and coming to the scene with a fresh eye, also came to the conclusion that the Heatons were blackmailing him.

At some point, he may have attempted suicide and in November 1951, following a 'nervous brainstorm' as he described it to Grainger, Quilter was readmitted to St Andrew's Hospital.[51] The stay was only five weeks this time and he came home early in January 1952, but it was still expensive. When he gave five pounds to Benjamin Britten that April – the reason is unclear, but possibly his niece Norah Nichols, who was a supporter of the Aldeburgh Festival, asked him to help – he apologised for not giving more and explained that he was heavily in debt, though he promised to come to the Festival that summer.[52]

He busied himself with concerts in Suffolk during March, and in May with sending some clothes for Grainger's museum. As part of Grainger's wish to show, down to the last detail, what makes a creative personality (he also wanted to demonstrate the 'musical links between Britain & Australia'[53]), he wanted his composer friends to send him their old clothes which he would then display. Quilter fought shy of this request for a long time (it was first made in 1941),[54] pleading a more immediate and personal need for the clothes, and pointing out that clothes for a man of his size were expensive. But Grainger was insistent and asked him especially for a suit resembling the one he had worn when the photograph was taken at the Harrogate Festival in July 1929, with Scott and Grainger, and Quilter in the middle. He also asked for, and got, Quilter's measurements, in case he had to have a suit made. The clothes were dressed onto papier-mâché dummies, and were displayed in a cabinet at the museum, Quilter between Cyril Scott and Balfour Gardiner. Quilter usually carried a walking-stick and wore a hat; there is no stick at the museum, however: Quilter asked Grainger if that, and the hat, could wait a little, but never sent anything.

On 18 September 1952, Quilter's remaining sibling, his eldest brother Eley, died aged seventy-nine, and so despite his continual illnesses, Quilter outlived all his brothers and sisters.

During that September, Frank Holliday, a friend of the idiosyncratic and reclusive composer Kaikhosru Shapurji Sorabji, wrote to Quilter to invite him to be a signatory to a letter to Sorabji. The purpose of the letter (eventually sent on 15 May 1953) was to persuade Sorabji to allow his music to be recorded; Holliday also collected donations for a fund that would pay for a recording to be made, so as to make the music more widely available to the public. Quilter wanted 'very much to be associated with the letter', gave five pounds, all he could afford,[55] and finally signed the letter in April 1953, but despite Holliday's heroic

---

[51] Quilter to Percy Grainger, 30 September 1951, GM.
[52] The letter is held at the Britten-Pears Library, Aldeburgh, Suffolk.
[53] Percy Grainger to Norah Nichols, 23 October 1953, GM.
[54] Percy Grainger to Quilter, 18 June 1941, GM.
[55] Quilter to Frank Holliday, 22 September 1952, Mills Memorial Library, McMaster University, Canada.

efforts (it took him two years to bring the project to fruition, corresponding with musicians, writers and editors worldwide) Sorabji refused permission.[56]

Leslie Woodgate persuaded the BBC to mark Quilter's seventy-fifth birthday with a special broadcast tribute on 1 November 1952. The programme was a representative one: *Three English Dances, A Children's Overture,* the *Rainbow* suite, excerpts from *Love at the Inn,* 'Non Nobis, Domine', songs and partsongs, and in the radio programme *Music Magazine,* which was broadcast on 26 October, Woodgate talked to Julian Herbage about Quilter's songs.[57] A party was held at 23 Acacia Road to which about ninety people came, and many were surprised that some of the family were amongst the guests since they were not normally noted for their interest in their composer relation.[58]

In February 1953, Quilter was complaining of a 'tiresome nerve complaint which causes horrible irritation' and remarking that he was fat.[59] By mid-June, he was very weak and from then on never left his bedroom. He lost the use of his legs and the Heatons had to lift him in and out of bed, not an easy task. Harry Heaton wrote later to Percy Grainger:

> [On Sunday evening, 20 September] at 8 o'clock we saw there was a change, & brought a Nurse & Dr. He spoke no more after 7 o'clock & lasted until 6.20 A.M. Monday 21st, & oh so peacefully with Ada & I by his side, he went. We still are so lost, we loved him so. He went out of his music room, where I had him laid, covered in Roses, & to the side of his Mother in the family Vault. We did not mind leaving him it was such a glorious day, but some thing has gone & now 5 weeks after, life is still empty.[60]

This was very touching, but Harry Heaton forgot to mention that Mark Raphael was also present at Quilter's death. Raphael and Leslie Woodgate, deeply mistrustful of the Heatons and concerned over what would happen to the manuscripts, immediately grabbed – literally – armfuls of music and papers, virtually anything they could get hold of, and removed them from the house, though not all was rescued and Quilter manuscripts have occasionally turned up in secondhand bookshops. Those that Raphael and Woodgate took are still accessible.

The funeral was held on 25 September at St Mary's Church, Bawdsey. Leslie Woodgate was there to represent the BBC officially, though he would unquestionably have attended in a personal capacity. Various members of the family were there too, as well as the Heatons, Quilter's accountant Arthur Dickinson, and his solicitor Robert Clarke.

In his will, Quilter made a number of bequests. The beneficiaries included close family members, Percy Grainger, Quilter's secretary William Lambourne,

---

[56] Alastair Hinton, 'Kaikhosru Shapurji Sorabji: An Introduction', *Sorabji: A Critical Celebration,* ed. Paul Rapoport (London, 1992)

[57] *Music Magazine,* broadcast on the BBC Home Service, Sunday 26 October 1952, 11.30pm.

[58] Interview with Harry Heaton.

[59] Quilter to Percy Grainger, 3 February 1953, GM.

[60] Henry Heaton to Percy Grainger, [30] October 1953, GM.

the Musicians' Benevolent Fund, Mark Raphael, and his godchildren. Amongst these were Margaret Bennett (her father had provided lyrics for *Julia* and *Love at the Inn*); Nicolette Bernard, daughter of the conductor Anthony; Jean-Paul Roger de Gebhard, grandson of Dr Rudolf Stern; Roger Frith, whose father Arthur, a baritone, had known Quilter since before the First World War; Geoffrey Golden, son of Herbert, whom Quilter had known from Frankfurt days; Roger Raphael, Mark's son; Rupert Withers, whose father was Herbert, the cellist who had performed with Quilter in the concerts in the First World War; children of more friends, and more members of the family. In total, twelve hundred pounds was distributed among fourteen godchildren. He left his royalties to his niece Norah Nichols and to Leslie Woodgate; Woodgate had the responsibility of looking after Quilter's musical interests.

To the Heatons, he left five thousand pounds, and the contents of the basement flat, which was where they had lived, and when it came to administer the will, it was found that a very great number of items, large and small, had made their way downstairs. In about 1993 – after Harry had died – his nephew Dennis was asked if his uncle had inherited all of the Quilter possessions, which included furniture, valuable china and Bristol blue glass, and he replied, 'Er, yes, we *call* it inherited'.[61] Quilter's accountant, Arthur Dickinson, found the notion that things were finding their way downstairs amusing, and sometimes helped to move them there.

The Heatons had wanted to buy a property in Settle, Yorkshire, for some time, and a friend of theirs had bid for one at auction, unsuccessfully, late in 1952;[62] it is not clear on whose behalf he had been bidding, for the Heatons with their own money, the Heatons with Quilter's money, or the Heatons for Quilter. But the aim seems – perhaps – to have been to have somewhere for them all to stay together. A substantial house called Bond End had come up for auction in the July before Quilter died, but it had been withdrawn from sale.[63] Eight days after Quilter's death, the Heatons bought it, taking out a mortgage which they redeemed the following March when the inheritance came through.[64] Eventually they retired there, living quietly, and on Ada's death in 1966, Harry Heaton sold Bond End and moved to a small cottage at the other end of Settle. He had kept almost everything he had acquired from 23 Acacia Road, and the cottage was consequently rather crowded. He died in 1991.

The Heatons remain shadowy and mysterious. They were almost universally loathed and detested, and they unquestionably took full advantage of the financial situation in which they found themselves, culminating in a very substantial bequest indeed; but on the other hand they equally certainly

---

[61] Tape-recorded interview between Dr William Mitchell and Dennis Heaton, undated, about 1993.

[62] Interview with the successful bidder, Onyx Ralph, October 1997.

[63] Elgar's friend Dr Buck was born at Bond End. See W. R. Mitchell, *Mr Elgar and Dr Buck, A Musical Friendship* (Giggleswick, 1991).

[64] Wakefield Deeds Registry, conveyance dated 29 September 1953; mortgage deed dated the same, 1953/156/828/382; mortgage receipt dated 17 March 1954, 48/145/72. The house cost £2,050.

looked after him to the end. In their terms, they may have been genuinely fond of him, but they were also greedy and highly manipulative. Yet, though they sold some of the items they had acquired, they did not sell much.

On 14 October 1953, a memorial service for Quilter was held at the musicians' church, St Sepulchre's in Holborn Viaduct. Leslie Woodgate tried hard to get the BBC Concert Orchestra together, but it proved impossible to gather sufficient resources, and so only the BBC Singers and Chorus performed; they sang Quilter's settings of 'Lead Us, Heavenly Father, Lead Us' and 'Non Nobis, Domine'. The church was packed: Quilter's family came, and so did some of the Elwes family, and Mark and Eva Raphael. Representatives of the London music colleges, of the Italia Conti school, and of the Musicians' Benevolent Fund were there. Mavis Yorke, who had played Will-o'-the-Wisp in the first performance of *Where the Rainbow Ends*, came, and so did many performers, composers, writers and publishers.

Most touchingly of all, about two hundred strangers came, people who simply wanted to pay their respects to a man of lyrical gifts, whose music they loved.

7

Songs and Choral Works: Part 1

The best of Quilter's songs have an unmistakable sound: an iridescent quality of the harmonies, complexity of part-writing, the textural details, the interplay between voice and piano, and words and music – all these are common elements in his songs, some of which are among the finest anywhere and stand comparison with any; his other songs set these into relief.

Trevor Hold has commented that Quilter emerged 'virtually fully fledged' in about 1905[1] though there were certainly glimpses of the song-writer to come, in 'Und was die Sonne glüht' of 1903, and the original 1897 version of 'Now Sleeps the Crimson Petal'. The best songs appear between 1904 and 1929; quality undoubtedly tails off after that, with the occasional gem. It is not always clear exactly when songs were written – any date shown at the end of the score is only the completion date – but positive datings can be made sometimes from mention in correspondence of specific songs, enough to indicate that generally Quilter's song-writing became simpler as he got older and as the effort became, relatively, greater.

Quilter was but one in a long line of song-writers. Most of these are forgotten: as far as musical content was concerned, their songs were simply vehicles for amateur singers and pianists, a musical equivalent of pulp fiction. By 1910, it is estimated that perhaps one in ten homes had a piano,[2] but that does not mean that every player was competent. The importance of an easy accompaniment was emphasised in a comment made to Maude Valérie White by Alberto Randegger, singing professor at the Royal Academy of Music. He predicted the failure of her first published song, 'Absent Yet Present', of 1879, saying, 'That accompaniment is enough to ruin its chances. You oughtn't to make your accompaniments so difficult'.[3] As it happens, in this instance he was wrong and the song became immensely popular, but the essence of his comment is still valid: accompaniments of the time were usually straightforward. They had to be manageable by keen but not necessarily able pianists. It was important that the pianist did not have to move about the keyboard more than absolutely necessary, so that the notes, once captured, did not escape; for similar reasons, many a young (and not so young) pianist has been grateful for repeated chords. Flourishes at the end for both singer and pianist – out of proportion with the

---

[1] Trevor Hold, *The Walled-in Garden*, 2nd edn (London, 1996), pp. 23 and 24.
[2] Cyril Ehrlich, *The Piano* (Oxford, 1990), p. 91.
[3] Maude Valérie White, *Friends and Memories* (London, 1914), p. 185.

rest of the song – provided a sense of achievement, the musical evening leaving everyone sated without too much effort having being expended. The repeated chords – frequently triplets – were the stock-in-trade of the drawing-room ballad (typified in Stephen Adams's famous song 'The Holy City'), along with chords on the flattened sixth, and dominant ninths, especially in minor keys; word painting, often involving trills in the piano part; sighing motifs, and the piano part regularly doubling the vocal line. The distinction between verses was usually very clear-cut, with a strong sense of reinforcing the opening mood – even if on a different instrument – so that for the third verse there could be a contrast and a climax.

The situation was not unique to England: the French salon was just as demanding of quantity above quality, although the piano was not as popular there as in England. The requirement in both countries was for novelty and the songs were a vehicle to show off the grace and ability of the singer. In France, this gave rise to a somewhat formulaic manner of composition, limiting the originality but bringing to the fore the singer's ability to hold a beautiful line, giving greater glory to the singer and, indirectly, to the hostess of the salon.[4]

In England, the royalty ballad practice sustained the demand which thousands of songs fed; the nineteenth-century English ballad was a sentimental piece, essentially simple, and in its way also demanding of the singer; Balfe's ballad 'The Power of Love' and his more famous 'I Dreamt that I Dwelt in Marble Halls', and Blockley's 'Evangeline' suffer from their texts but otherwise have a simplicity of manner comparable, if not quite on a par, with such bel canto *Composizioni da Camera* as Bellini's 'Bella Nice, che d'amore', his 'Vaga luna, che inargenti' and Donizetti's 'La conocchia' (a Neapolitan song); the Balfe and Blockley songs would probably have gained a better reputation (though scarcely a greater popularity) had they been sung in Italian translation. Both English and Italian songs follow a similar pattern of introduction: a few bars either of the opening melody, or of its cadence; by Quilter's time this had moved on, with a greater sense of the vocal line 'emerging' from and being integral with the piano part.

The popularity of the ballad was to some extent linked with that of the piano, whose popularity was in turn linked with the social changes of the time and the rise of the middle classes: when many homes had a piano and when ballad concerts were readily accessible, the songs were soon publicised. The almost insatiable need for music for home consumption grew: a demand for music, but not demanding music.

Themes of patriotism, nature, the seasons, love, homely sentiments, were typical of the ballad of the early part of the nineteenth century. They remained central for many decades and were more significant than the actual words, which were often banal; they were produced by the hundred. The sheet-music covers – where there was any room left after the names of everyone involved in

---

[4] David Tunley, *Salons, Singers and Songs, A Background to Nineteenth Century French Song* (Aldershot, 2002).

them had been listed – were often decorated with beautifully engraved pictures, to tempt the buyer.

Quilter drew on such themes throughout his song œuvre. When he was a pupil at Pinewood school, he almost certainly heard the popular songs of the day played by his music teacher Mrs Brackenbury, wife of the Reverend Fabian Brackenbury who ran the school,[5] so that when Quilter began composing in 1897, aged nineteen, he was drawing on the language he knew and the repertoire he had grown up with. As a result, his two earliest published songs, 'Come Spring! Sweet Spring!' and 'The Reign of the Stars' (published in 1897 under the pseudonym 'Ronald Quinton'), are strophic and harmonically straightforward. However, the independence of the vocal line from the piano part recognises the earlier contributions of others such as Maude Valérie White (1855–1937), whose music was 'almost [Quilter's] first real love',[6] Amy Woodforde-Finden (1860–1919) and Liza Lehmann (1862–1918); their work is notable (though not exclusively so) for the difficulty of their piano parts which are not safe accompaniments and clearly stretch a moderate pianist's technical capabilities, especially Lehmann's *Bird Songs* and Woodforde-Finden's *Four Indian Love Lyrics* and *Six Songs from 'On Jhelum River'*. Either pianists were stretched beyond their ability – with presumably unfortunate results – or such a level of ability could by now be reasonably expected.

The words – his own – of these two early Quilter songs are not promising poetry, but do provide an acceptable vehicle:

> Come spring, sweet spring,
> Quickly all your treasure bring;
> Subtle perfumes on the breeze,
> Em'rald buds to deck the trees

and so on. On his own copy of the published music, he wrote in 1916 'on no account to be reprinted in any form – under my name'.[7] Quilter later realised the limitations of some of these very early songs: in October 1915, he had the plates for two of them destroyed, 'Come Back!' and 'A Secret'. His 1898 setting of Christina Rossetti's 'Should One of Us Remember' remained unpublished; presumably its limitations were more obvious.[8]

The next songs to appear were the *Four Songs of the Sea*, first performed in March 1901, dedicated to Quilter's mother, and settings again of his own words; the titles of the individual songs indicate the subject matter adequately. Quilter was still finding his feet and these are not especially distinguished, though the piano parts are not unrewarding. The hearty sentiment of the opening song, 'I Have a Friend', is a somewhat watered down (and less satisfying) precursor to Ireland's 1915 setting of Masefield's 'Sea Fever'; it has three verses, set

---

[5] Strongly surmised by Edith Brackenbury's grandson, John Brackenbury, in conversation with the author, January 2001.

[6] Quilter to Percy Grainger, 6 November 1937, GM.

[7] Archives held by Leslie East.

[8] This MS, dated August 1897, was sold at Sotheby's in May 1968 to an untraceable buyer.

strophically, the middle verse having a different accompaniment: the same harmony but with textural contrast. When the set was republished in 1911, this song was omitted and the texts for the second and fourth songs were revised (later still, the original four-song set was reissued): in the second song, 'The Sea-Bird', 'the day was dying in floods of crimson gore' in 1901 but in 1911 'the light was dying o'er Sunset's golden floor' and the 'gleaming' sky of 1901 is 'fading' by 1911. By 1911 too, the waves are 'sad', though they were 'young' in 1901. In the fourth song, 'By the Sea', the waves of 1901 'did trickle and curve' and 'tumbled over my sinful soul' though in 1911, they 'sigh'd and sang to my list'ning soul' and could only 'frolic and curl'.

If the texts of the revised versions are softer and less vibrant, the music is bolder. In 'The Sea-Bird', the 1901 accompaniment for the central section is little more than broken chords where the 1911 version is richer with a countermelody to the vocal line and a wider pitch range, though the harmonies remain the same. The greater bass sonority is maintained but is kept smaller scale in the more youthful version.

Ex. 7.1a, Quilter, 'The Sea-Bird', 1901 version, bars 14–17
© Copyright 1901 Forsyth Bros. Ltd.

Ex. 7.1b, Quilter, 'The Sea-Bird', 1911 version, bars 14–17
© Copyright 1911 Forsyth Bros. Ltd.

The 1911 version is generally richer, with a fuller texture, and Quilter is not afraid to have the piano part much higher than the voice. Minor changes in rhythm result from the word-change: 'floods of' is set to a dotted rhythm where 'Sunset's' is set to even quavers.

'Moonlight' is almost unchanged – extra bass notes filling in the chords give strong support to the 'fairy vessel'.

Ex. 7.2a, Quilter, 'Moonlight', 1901 version, bars 17–20
© Copyright 1901 Forsyth Bros. Ltd.

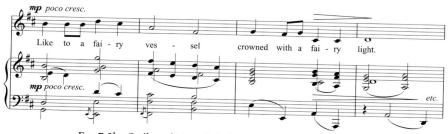

Ex. 7.2b, Quilter, 'Moonlight', 1911 version, bars 17–20
© Copyright 1911 Forsyth Bros. Ltd.

The last song, 'By the Sea', is again richer than its 1901 counterpart and Quilter makes more assumptions about the singer's ability, without being less considerate; there is a greater sense of a duet between singer and pianist.

Ex. 7.3a, Quilter, 'By the Sea', 1901 version, bars 14–15
© Copyright 1901 Forsyth Bros. Ltd.

Ex. 7.3b, Quilter, 'By the Sea', 1911 version, bars 14–15
© Copyright 1911 Forsyth Bros. Ltd.

The Quilter of 1911 is a much more confident one.

'Come Back!' and 'A Secret' were published in 1903, though the manuscript of 'A Secret' is dated 6 May 1898, while Quilter was still at Frankfurt, and 'Come Back!' probably dates from the same time; they were published as a pair and are again settings of Quilter's own words. 'Come Back!', in which the singer recalls dreaming of the loved one, is the more promising, with the common rhythmic motif ♪ ♩ ♪ pervading the first half of the song. When these are turned into triplet chords in the second half, with lush and clichéd chords, the song deteriorates. It is a pity, because the opening, reminiscent of Tchaikovsky's 'None but the Lonely Heart' which also starts with repeated syncopated chords, is intimate, delicate and effective; but Quilter has not learned how to maintain the mood.

Ex. 7.4a, Tchaikovsky, 'None but the Lonely Heart', voice entry

Ex. 7.4b, Quilter, 'Come Back!', opening
© Copyright 1903 Elkin & Co. Ltd.

'A Secret' is a sprightly song, with some similarities to Parry's 'My Heart is Like a Singing Bird', although Quilter's singer describes his or her heart as being locked away with a golden key until the lover comes. The first verse is repeated to put the short song into ternary form and there is a small change in the figuration of the piano left hand, between manuscript and published version, at the end of the central section.

Ex. 7.5a, Quilter, 'A Secret', manuscript

Ex. 7.5b, published version

Quilter's Op. 2 was a set of four songs to German texts, *Four Songs of Mirza Schaffy*, words by Friedrich Bodenstedt (1819–92); under the name Mirza Schaffy, Bodenstedt (a pupil of Schaffy's) published numerous poems which he later admitted were his own. The translation was by Walter Creighton, and the songs were marked 'In remembrance of Frankfurt days'. They were first published in 1903, without an opus number, and were revised with a new translation by R. H. Elkin in 1911 as Op. 2 and rededicated, to friends, J. Walter and Marie English.

In the first song, 'Neig' schöne Knospe dich zu mir' ('Lean, Opening Blossom'/'Come Tender Bud' – Creighton/Elkin translations), the singer tells a flower bud that he wants to clasp it and warm it up, so that it will unfold. Semitonal chromaticism in the middle verse hints at the erotic aspect of the words, even if Quilter was unaware of it, and the motif in the piano introduction appears throughout the song. In the second, 'Und was die Sonne glüht' ('Where'er the Sun Doth Glow'/'The Glow of Summer Sun'), the singer describes his songs as made from the glow of the sun, the wind and well-springs, and the bloom of roses; Quilter treats the song with a light textural hand, beginning on a chord of E♭ major but then rocking ambivalently between

G minor and B♭ major, and returning to E♭ major at the mid-point of the first verse. Imitation between piano and voice provides continuity in the delicate through-composed setting. The third song, 'Ich fühle deinen Odem'; ('I Feel Thy Soul's Dear Presence'/'The Magic of Thy Presence'), recalls the gentle rhythm ♩ ♩ ♩ of earlier songs (by Quilter and others), and though a pleasing enough love song, its predictable four-bar phrases are unremarkable; the other songs in the group show greater invention and freedom of phrase length. The fourth song, 'Die helle Sonne leuchtet' ('The Dazzling Sun is Glistening'/'The Golden Sunlight's Glory') compares the sunlight on the dancing waves with the radiance of the loved one's face; it is in compound time, though Quilter tends to favour simple signatures, and gives a sparkling finish to the set.

The songs sit well in the German text, though there are some awkward vowels in 'Und was die Sonne glüht', with 'Himmel' and 'klingt' on high notes; these are made easier when Elkin sets 'joy', 'heaven' and 'woven' to their notes, and Creighton is similarly kind, setting 'heavens', 'from' and 'that's'. The lack of sophistication masks good writing, and the songs show strong hints of the Quilter to come: a generally fluid tonality, interplay between voice and piano, subdued emotions; in this, Quilter follows Fauré, though in some textural details he draws upon Tchaikovsky and Schumann.

The differences between the two versions are greater than those between the 1901 and 1911 versions of the *Songs of the Sea*, but the harmonies remain unchanged and the nature of the differences remains superficial: the later version is usually richer, but sometimes more spare, sometimes less colourful; the earlier version sometimes shows a greater pitch range.

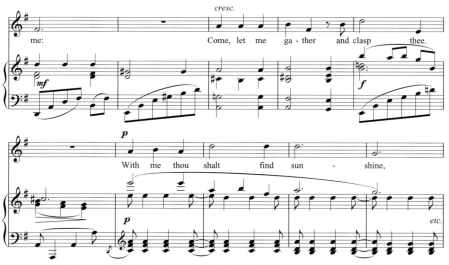

Ex. 7.6a, Quilter, 'Lean, Opening Blossom' (1903/Creighton)
© Copyright 1903 Elkin & Co. Ltd.

Ex. 7.6b, Quilter, 'Come Tender Bud' (1911/Elkin)

The second song is almost unchanged, though the accompaniment under the words 'Und was vom Himmel nieder' is more stark in the younger version.

Ex. 7.7a, Quilter, 'Where'er the Sun Doth Glow' (1903/Creighton), bars 23–25

Ex. 7.7b, Quilter, 'The Glow of Summer Sun' (1911/Elkin)

The third song is similarly almost unchanged; on the whole, the earlier version has thicker chords.

The piano figuration in the fourth song shows the greatest change: the rhythm of the 1903 version proceeds in half-bar steps:  but by 1911 has a more forward momentum: .

Ex. 7.8a, Quilter, 'The Dazzling Sun is Glistening' (1903/Creighton), introduction
© Copyright 1903 Elkin & Co. Ltd.

Ex. 7.8b, Quilter, 'The Golden Sunlight's Glory' (1911/Elkin), introduction
© Copyright 1911 Elkin & Co. Ltd.

Ex. 7.9a, Quilter, 'The Dazzling Sun is Glistening' (1903/Creighton), end
© Copyright 1903 Elkin & Co. Ltd.

Ex. 7.9b, Quilter, 'The Golden Sunlight's Glory' (1911/Elkin), end
© Copyright 1911 Elkin & Co. Ltd.

The later version has a slightly extended and better balanced ending.

In most of these early songs, Quilter shows that he uses the words as little more than a vehicle for the music, in the way that so many other composers did; yet he shows too a remarkable awareness for depths within the words, layers of meaning that his music is already bringing out with beauty and subtlety.

Quilter translated and set another Bodenstedt poem later, 'My Heart Adorned with Thee', in two versions, solo and duet (mezzo and baritone); both were published in 1953, and an autograph manuscript score of the solo version is inscribed 'Autumn 1951', the date of its gift to the recipient (one of the musical amateurs he met in Yorkshire). It has much the same economy and simplicity of the earlier settings: pedal notes on the dominant settle on to the tonic, relaxed and calm, and textural contrast is provided by placing the accompaniment at the opening of the second verse higher than in the first. The solo manuscript version has numerous changes that alter the proportions, such as a change of phrase shape in the introduction, an extra bar's accompaniment between the verses, and an extra bar at the end; these are worthwhile differences. The translation is sometimes a little pretentious ('Thou giv'st it light') but is otherwise effective.

Ex. 7.10a, Quilter, 'My Heart Adorned with Thee', introduction, manuscript solo
© Copyright 1953 Trustee of the Roger Quilter Estate

Ex. 7.10b, Quilter, 'My Heart Adorned with Thee', introduction, published solo
© Copyright 1953 Elkin & Co. Ltd.

The manuscript is in pencil, over-written in ballpen, and is a rare example showing how Quilter revised work before publication, usually simplifying it and making the piano part more stable, and in this instance, losing some of the harmonic richness in the process. The change of phrase sequence in the introduction had an inevitability in the manuscript version that is lost in the published one.

Ex. 7.11a, Quilter, 'My Heart Adorned with Thee', central section, manuscript solo

Ex. 7.11b, Quilter, 'My Heart Adorned with Thee', central section, published duet

There was one other setting of a German text; it was unpublished and undated, but to judge from the compositional style and the writing was an early work. 'Mond, du bist glücklicher als ich', dedicated 'To Cyril Meir Scott from the composer', is a setting of an anonymous text, quite short – twenty-four bars – with a simplistic accompaniment of repeated chords, slightly redolent of Wagner's *Wesendonck Lieder* but without the lushness.

Quilter's two Binyon settings, 'At Close of Day' and 'The Answer', published in 1904, and his setting of Nora Hopper's 'June', published in 1905, were musical makeweights, little more than pot-boilers. But 'At Close of Day' is one of the earliest of his songs to show his ability to go beyond mere vocal line plus accompaniment: the texture of the piano part changes as the verses change – the first and last (of four) contain flowing quavers; in the second, gently rippling semiquavers colour the emergence of magic light, and in the third, with the whispering of the fairies come chattering, repeated quaver chords. The eight-bar melodic phrases in verses one, two and four are diatonic and remain broadly unchanged, but the third verse, like the words, 'grows strange' and extends over twelve bars. The 'solid ground a dream' is mirrored in the harmonies which shift smoothly via pivot notes from C major to A major and back, and over a bass line that sinks gradually and sometimes chromatically from Db through a minor ninth to the tonic C at the start of the fourth verse.

Ex. 7.12, Quilter, 'At Close of Day', third verse
© Copyright 1904 by Boosey & Co. Ltd.

The second Binyon setting is mundane, and full of clichés and a rhythmic motif whose too frequent repetition irritates, and in late 1927 or early 1928, Boosey destroyed the plates, at his request.

Ex. 7.13, Quilter, 'The Answer'
© Copyright 1904 by Boosey & Co. Ltd.

'June' was published a year later, greatly inferior to 'At Close of Day' but equivalent to 'The Answer'; strophic, all three verses set to pairs of four-bar phrases, the last verse extended to enable the words to be similarly extended: 'That's the way of June, the way, the way of June.' Textural changes across the verses fail to disguise the repetition of the predictable harmonies; the song harks back to the worst of the formulaic royalty ballads and regrettably remains popular.

'A London Spring Song' was performed on 21 November 1904; the words were by Julian Sturgis, from *A Book of Song*, but it remained unpublished until 1928, when Quilter offered it to Boosey as long as it appeared under a pseudonym, C. Romney; the title was amended to 'A London Spring'. Quilter wished it, and Boosey, well, but it remained in oblivion. Some Sullivanesque melismas and precision of text-setting make it an attractive song, less pretentious than 'June', and had it been published in 1904, it might have fared rather better.

These songs mark the end of Quilter's apprenticeship – from now on, his style was mature and did not develop substantially further. The poets Quilter set were drawn from two broad periods of lyric poetry – Shakespeare and the seventeenth-century poets; and the nineteenth-century poets and Quilter's contemporaries. He set very little from the eighteenth century; what he set was, notably, Blake. The remainder of this chapter describes the song-settings of the older poets, and the next chapter, those of the more recent ones. *The Arnold Book of Old Songs* is placed within the next chapter.

Quilter's Shakespeare settings span his output and provide an overview of the way he approached song-setting throughout his life. The earlier songs are undoubtedly more interesting than the later, and show greater invention, but if the later settings say little that is new, some at least do have something to say that is worth hearing.

With the first set of *Shakespeare Songs*, Op. 6, published in 1905, comes greater consistency than before. Shakespeare provided the texts for twenty of Quilter's songs; some, such as Ariel's *Tempest* songs, were intended as songs quite specifically, but in any case, all had been set before and so were familiar to singers. Quilter responded strongly to Shakespeare's freedom of rhythm and metre, and because the texts were already widely known, he had further freedom to make assumptions about how the texts were perceived.

The words of the first two songs of the first set are from *Twelfth Night*, 'Come Away, Death' and 'O Mistress Mine'; the last, 'Blow, Blow, Thou Winter Wind', is from *As You Like It* and the set was dedicated to Walter Creighton. This is a fine set of songs, found frequently and justly in recital programmes, showing the astute attention to the words that is so notable in Quilter's best work. In addition, the songs are – unusually – linked by key, and are well-matched in mood; a strongly unified set.

'Come Away, Death', harmonically rich but tonally stable, modulates briefly to the dominant major at bars 9–10 ('slain by a fair cruel maid') and 28–9 ('where my bones shall be laid'), and with only fleeting glimpses of the relative major, at bars 12 ('My shroud of white'), to give some relief, remains securely in its home key of C minor with descending bass lines constantly reinforcing the key. The accompaniment to the first part of the first verse is in the mid to low range, and contrasts with the blank simplicity of the piano part accompanying 'My shroud of white'. In the second verse, however, it begins two octaves higher than in the first, figured in delicate triplet arpeggios, and the bass line moves inexorably downwards from middle C, eventually reaching C two octaves lower; the accompaniment at 'A thousand, thousand sighs' is an octave lower, and fuller than in the first verse. A Russian influence, that was gradually infiltrating western music via France, can be heard perhaps in the melismatic *cri de cœur* on the final 'weep';[9] the decorated descending scale, melodic minor form, from 3̂ through 1̂ to the lower 5̂, picks up elements of the melody and imitative piano part from the words 'fair cruel maid': unusually dramatic for Quilter and highly effective.

Ex. 7.14, Quilter, 'Come Away, Death', end
© Copyright 1905 by Boosey & Co. Ltd.

The vocal line, through the constant harping on the dominant note, almost becomes a monotone, albeit an ornamented one: nearly every phrase ends on g^1, being reached by a four-note pattern from 8̂ to 5̂. The tension so created is maintained to the very end: even the piano part picks up the four-note pattern and remains unresolved until the penultimate bar.

'O Mistress Mine', is in the relative major, E♭, and opens with a series of descending second inversion chords. The falling scale, that Quilter so often associates with melancholy, initially seems happy here: the major key gives a warmth. But the poet is pleading with the loved one not to delay, not to wait for an uncertain future but to make the most of the present, and therein lies the sadness. The word-setting is very precise, and built around the exact word stresses, so that it can be sung almost to speech rhythm, with a very elastic and fluid pacing. Performance practice was once such as to pause on 'love', the third word in the second verse, and to pause on 'mine' in the last phrase (which repeats the opening phrase, altered to end on the tonic, not the dominant), and this is a practice that is consistent with the manner of Quilter's word-setting. He sets the dactylic text in a triple metre to allow flexibility, often ♩ ♩ ♫ but sometimes ♫ ♩ ♩ or ♩. ♪ ♫ .

Ex. 7.15, Quilter, 'O Mistress Mine', beginning of second verse
© Copyright 1905 by Boosey & Co. Ltd.

---

[9] See Richard Taruskin, ' "Entoiling the Falconet": Russian Musical Orientalism in Context', *The Exotic in Western Music*, ed. Jonathan Bellman (Boston, 1998).

Ex. 7.16, Quilter, 'O Mistress Mine', end of second verse
© Copyright 1905 by Boosey & Co. Ltd.

The last song, 'Blow, Blow, Thou Winter Wind', returns to the key of the first. The song is marked *Non troppo allegro, ma vigoroso e con moto* – not too quick and lively, but vigorously and with movement. This marking is crucial, since if sung too quickly, the song loses all sense of bitterness; unfortunately it is usually sung as a jolly drinking song, descending into the banality of which Goddard accused Quilter in his substantial article about him: 'the weather "Blow, blow thou winter wind," and the mention of ingratitude and forgetting of friendship, both done in the same hearty manner . . . it is quite false in sentiment but how charming!'[10] However, Mark Raphael rightly commented on the song's 'acid lilt'.[11] The chorus, though in the tonic major and marked *Poco più allegro*, is not especially quick – the metronome mark is only ♩ = 88 – and is not marked *forte* until the piano interlude that brings back the tonic minor. Falling fifths on 'Most friendship is feigning, most loving mere folly' reflect the falling fifths from 'Come Away, Death' on 'My shroud of white, stuck all with yew' and the V–I, with suspensions, in the passing modulation into F major at 'This life, this life' is reminiscent of the falling sequence at the opening of 'O Mistress Mine', though this is also a harmonic motif that Quilter often employs.

All the songs in the first set were arranged for various instrumental combinations, though it is often difficult to be certain which were Quilter's own arrangements and which were those by Boosey's in-house arrangers, since Quilter's hand-writing varied. 'O Mistress Mine' in a version for voice and string orchestra was published in 1944, and one of 'Blow, Blow' for the same combination was published in 1945; these are certainly Quilter's own arrangements.

Three songs, with piano accompaniment, were published in 1919 as *Songs from 'As You Like It'*: 'Under the Greenwood Tree', 'Blow, Blow, Thou Winter Wind' and 'It was a Lover and His Lass'; the last was a duet. It was normal for songs in the theatre to be performed with an orchestral accompaniment, and there is no reason to think that these songs were treated any differently, although the orchestrations that exist (and which are in Quilter's autograph) have different instrumentations for each of the three songs and were probably written – as with the Op. 6 set – according to demand.

---

[10] Scott Goddard, 'The Art of Roger Quilter', *The Chesterian*, vol. VI, no. 47 (June, 1925), pp. 213–17.

[11] Mark Raphael, Obituary, 'Roger Quilter: 1877–1953, the man and his songs', *Tempo*, vol. 30 (1953–4), p. 20.

The first and third songs (the second, 'Blow, Blow', having already been published in the first set, Op. 6) were incorporated into the second set, *Five Shakespeare Songs*, Op. 23, which were published in 1921, and contained 'Fear No More the Heat o' the Sun', 'Under the Greenwood Tree', 'It was a Lover and His Lass', 'Take, O Take Those Lips Away' and 'Hey, Ho, the Wind and the Rain'.

'Fear No More the Heat o' the Sun' from *Cymbeline*, Act 4 Scene 2, is dated 1921 and was dedicated to the memory of Robin Hollway, Quilter's Oxford friend who committed suicide in March 1921. F minor, a melancholy key, sets the mood, and the modulation down to the flat submediant Db major seems only to depress the spirits further; as the text travels through lightning, thunder, slander and all the perils of life, so move the keys, the Db changing enharmonically to C♯ and thence treated as the dominant to F♯ minor; through Eb major, and though aiming for F major, passing through its Neapolitan Gb major and its flat submediant Db major (skating either side of the dominant note C) before settling into the tonic major, with flattened sevenths to the end. The use throughout of major and minor to reflect the words precisely is poignant, the rise to the relative major offering brief but forlorn hope; rhythm – quaver movement much of the time, but resigned towards the end to static crotchets – is used to still the motion to nothing. Quilter chooses to set the subdued aspects of the text, not the furious ones, and has been greatly criticised;[12] but his perfumed setting suggests the strength of feeling that Quilter evidently had for his friend.

'Under the Greenwood Tree' is from Act 2 Scene 5 of *As You Like It* and is set in the forest of Arden; it and the following song, 'It was a Lover and His Lass' were dedicated to Quilter's friend Walter Creighton. It makes much use of parallel fourths, and the first four lines are set rhythmically in a straightforward manner, but Quilter then draws out the three 'come hithers', producing a three-bar phrase followed by a fluid five-bar phrase. This is light music, and together with the next song, is on a par with Quilter's songs from his light opera *Julia*; it should be judged as such. Goddard, in his highly critical article on Quilter's songs, writes of texts that are so well known 'that they have become covered with a patina of insignificance' and dismisses Quilter's Shakespeare settings (especially 'Under the Greenwood Tree' and 'Blow, Blow') as 'unimaginatively done'. But a theatre environment calls for a light-handed treatment; nor is there discredit in setting familiar words, and that is what Quilter does here and with 'It was a Lover and His Lass'; the immediate appeal of these songs especially is entirely appropriate: not every song must try to plumb unmeasurable depths of greatness.

'It was a Lover' is from Act 5 Scene 3, and in its original form is a duet for two of the banished Duke's pages, which they sing to Touchstone; it is scored for soprano and alto, in G major. The solo version of the song (in E major) simply omits the lower part and only in one place makes any attempt to fit it into the

---

[12] Scott Goddard (1925), and Trevor Hold (1996).

piano part; all the parallel thirds and sixths that characterise the part-writing and which illustrate the pages' comment that they are 'both in a tune like two gipsies on a horse' – and at the beginning, the piano has four bars of two-part counterpoint by way of further illustration – are thus lost. That notwithstanding, the writing is fresh, light and detailed, with delicate semiquavers at the end of the first chorus and a chiming bell and tonic pedal in the piano part at the first occurrence of the words 'When birds do sing' that draws rhythmically upon Point's song from Gilbert and Sullivan's *Yeomen of the Guard*, 'I Have a Song to Sing-O'.

Ex. 7.17, Quilter, 'It was a Lover and His Lass', end of first verse
© Copyright 1921 by Boosey & Co. Ltd.

Ex. 7.18, Sullivan, *The Yeomen of the Guard*, 'I Have a Song to Sing-O' (Point),
part of chorus

'Take, O Take Those Lips Away' is from *Measure for Measure*, Act 4 Scene 1; it was dedicated to Quilter's friend Bertie Landsberg, another of the Oxford circle, and had started life as a piano sonata theme from his Frankfurt days.[13] This is a remarkably introverted song, the vocal range only a minor seventh, the intervals mostly seconds and thirds, with a few fourths, and only two fifths, in both cases from $\hat{6}$ to $\hat{2}$. The lines continually diverge and converge, expanding and contracting until the insistent rising thirds, on 'but sealed', of the vocal line's last phrase. It is perhaps too introverted for its own good and never quite manages to arrive anywhere, but by the same token, it does not outstay its welcome. Quilter recorded it in an arrangement for piano quartet (Frederick Grinke, violin, M. Gilbert, viola, Herbert Withers, cello), with Mark Raphael, in 1934.

The last song, 'Hey, Ho, the Wind and the Rain', comes from *Twelfth Night*, Act 5 Scene 1, and like the other theatre songs in the set, Quilter dedicated it to Walter Creighton. He set four of the five verses, omitting the fourth verse concerning toss pots. Again, he treats his text lightly, playing between four- and five-bar phrases, and using the motif ♩♫♩ to set a dance rhythm. There is no word-painting of wind or rain, but since the words are almost a nonsense refrain, it is not necessary.

The set is an assemblage of songs, not linked as are the songs of the first set. Two are serious, three are in a light music style. There is no key interconnection – F minor, D major, E (duet) or G (solo) major, D♭ major, C major – and there is no particular need to perform them as a group; the *As You Like It* songs make a more homogeneous group, with 'Hey Ho' added for good measure.

The partsong 'What Shall He Have that Killed the Deer?' (which is from Act 4 Scene 2 and which was used in Lilian Baylis's 1921 production of *As You Like It*) is set strophically, with the words 'then sing him home' treated as a brief chorus and inserted accordingly; the four resultant verses are sung by the baritone and the line 'the rest shall bear this burden' is omitted in accordance with some theories that it is a stage direction. The rhythm, with its frequent changes of time signature, is free and the dominant note A echoes throughout, rather like an Immovable So, rather than Grainger's Immovable Do: the first, second and fourth verses sound the rhyming words on this note: deer, wear, scorn, horn, born; the third verse moves up one note. The brief choruses resonate around the tonic chord, except in the third chorus, whose cadence is interrupted; the final cadence is approached by way of the flat mediant. A strangely haunting song, this, its simple structure offering scope for variety of harmonisation in the chorus, and flexibility of line.

---

[13] From notes taken of an interview between Professor Stephen Banfield and Mark Raphael, 28 February 1974; I am indebted to Professor Banfield for allowing me access to the notes.

Ex. 7.19, Quilter, 'What Shall He Have That Killed The Deer?', ending

The third Shakespeare set, Op. 30, contains four songs, most written and published in 1933, but the first is dated 1926 and was published in 1927. 'Who is Silvia?' (from *The Two Gentlemen of Verona*) is dedicated to Nora Forman, a warm-hearted and very knowledgeable patron of music. The song is strophic, like the well-known Schubert setting, but more varied. The piano introduction itself starts tentatively, questioningly, by commencing on the second quaver of the 3/4 bar and rising. the vocal line has a range of only a minor sixth, but because of the use of sequence, does not feel limited: the first phrase is centred around f♯ and a, the second – sequentially – about g and b and the third about a and d^1; the shape is supported by the piano part. In Quilter's usual manner, the second verse has a higher-placed accompaniment, sometimes taking over the melody, falling to the original tessitura, and there are small changes to the vocal line; the interlude between verses two and three is compressed from four bars (as between verses one and two) to two, and disguised by the prolonging of the voice. Thus the third verse starts almost impetuously, without ado, to match the words 'Then to Silvia let us sing'.

'When Daffodils Begin to Peer', by its title (it is from *The Winter's Tale*, Act 4 Scene 3), seems innocuous enough and Quilter treats it in rather a hey-nonny-no manner. The song is in ternary form; he shifts to the mediant major at the end of the central section and slips back again. If Quilter did not realise the meaning of tumbling in the hay with his aunts, Grainger would surely have told him eventually. It was dedicated to Mark Raphael, and the next song, to Mark's wife Eva.

'How Should I Your True Love Know?', from *Hamlet*, Act 4 Scene 5, is delicate and sad, one of Ophelia's songs sung in her madness. The simple and well-shaped phrases of the outer verses (though some of the chromaticism is too predictable) frame the middle one, in the major, that is almost a monotone, on the tonic. The Aeolian mode is doleful and Quilter, unusually, ends on the tonic, with a strong sense of finality; a small song, but compelling, and as Trevor

Hold points out, genuinely a woman's song, a rare thing in Quilter's song output.[14]

It is followed by a hey-nonny-no song, 'Sigh No More, Ladies', from *Much Ado about Nothing*. Quilter's nephew Arnold Vivian was eighteen when it was dedicated to him, in 1933, and doubtless sang it with the lightness and joy it needs. Quilter makes no attempt to discern the callousness of the song as it appears in its play context: it is utterly straightforward, with standard four-bar introductions to each of the two verses and an altered ending to the second to finish on a high note. There are no overdone chromaticisms, just a quick light touch, a blink of an eye and a page-turn or two, and it is over.

The set, like the second set, is a strangely mixed one, no unifying factor, simply some songs with texts by Shakespeare and grouped together for convenience, as are the two songs of the final set, Op. 32, published in 1939.

'Orpheus with His Lute' (written in 1938) starts inauspiciously, with hackneyed secondary sevenths just before the voice entry. The 6/8 time signature, with arpeggiated chords and grace notes, is clearly intended to suggest a lute. Clinton-Baddeley, writing on the union of words and music, describes how composers can so change the emphasis of the words as to make nonsense of them, and he explains how Sullivan does so in his setting of this text, which is a hundred and twenty-two bars long, compared with Quilter's economical thirty-eight.[15] The length of Sullivan's setting is largely accounted for by the repetition of the text: for example, the first three lines are repeated, the third line again. The real distortion of meaning occurs in the last verse, when the text runs:

> In sweet music is such art,
> Killing care and grief of heart,
> In sweet music is such art,
> Killing care and grief of heart.
> Fall asleep, or hearing die,
> Fall asleep, or hearing, or hearing die.

This runs counter to the intended meaning of the words by dividing the sentence wrongly. It is the care and grief that fall asleep: 'killing' is an adjective. Quilter does not repeat the text in the same way; instead, his text runs:

> In sweet music is such art,
> Killing care and grief of heart
> Fall asleep, fall asleep, or hearing, die.

This is as it should be and achieves the proper effect, and his setting of that particular section is languid and beautiful, though it has to be said the rest of the song does not match it. A misprint in the original key edition of C major is corrected in the high key, E♭ major version: the final piano semiquaver in the ninth bar from the end should be a G♮ not a G♭.

---

[14] Trevor Hold (1996), p. 41.
[15] V. C. Clinton-Baddeley, *Words for Music* (Cambridge, 1941), p. 12.

Ex. 7.20, Quilter, 'Orpheus with his Lute', ending
© Copyright 1939 by Boosey & Co. Ltd.

'When Icicles Hang by the Wall' (written in 1938) is a curious little song. It switches from minor to major for the 'tu-whit' chorus and repeated semiquaver chords are presumably intended to suggest brittle icicles. It is a light song, but really without the sparkle of Quilter's intentionally light music.

The remaining Shakespeare settings could quite easily have been grouped into another set, since there was little enough reason to group the others, except for the Op. 6 set. But these songs are post-war, and it was probably easier, in publishing terms, to issue the songs as they came, and not incur further cost by republishing them in a set. 'Hark, Hark, the Lark!', published in 1946, is a pretty song, the piano part, with a similar texture to 'Love's Philosophy', clearly imitating the song of a skylark, but stylistically it says nothing new and the vocal line is routine. The fingering shown in the piano part under the word 'lies' relates to the D major edition, original key.

Quilter's songs were falling out of fashion by this time, and where in earlier decades they would have been seized upon and sung until audiences were familiar with them, neither songs nor audiences had such opportunities any longer, and the later songs are little known. Sometimes this is justifiable, but not always. 'Come unto These Yellow Sands', one of Ariel's songs from *The Tempest*, was published in 1951 in just one key, indicative of the generally fading interest. It is an attractive lyrical setting, rather than a feat one, with some surprises: Quilter responded to the 'bow wow' with strident dissonances and there is an abrupt harmonisation on 'the burden bear' when what seems as if it will be a perfect cadence in C major veers suddenly into the tonic E♭ major, and into C major again for 'Hark, hark! The watch dogs bark'. The song deserves to be better known.

'Tell Me Where is Fancy Bred' was also published in 1951; it has a passing resemblance to 'Take, O Take Those Lips Away', but lacks the intricacies and flexibility of rhythm; the marking *ben legato* describes the entire song.

The fifth edition of Grove's *Dictionary of Music and Musicians* lists two more Shakespeare settings, though these are lost: 'Full Fathom Five' and 'Where the Bee Sucks', both Ariel songs.[16]

The rest of this chapter follows the poets in broadly chronological order, adjusted where it enables a set of songs to be considered in its entirety.

'An Old Carol' is a setting of an anonymous fifteenth-century text ('I sing of a maiden/ That is matchless'), written in 1923, published in 1924, and dedicated to Constance Wathen. Katherine Wathen was an old friend of Quilter's mother, the same generation, and Constance may have been a daughter. The song is not in the same league as the Shakespeare settings but is disarmingly simple and has much to commend it. Although set in 2/4, there are places where the barring is flexible, replaceable with the occasional 3/4 bar; the four-bar phrases are not rigid. Colour comes with the raised $\hat{4}$ and passing modulations to the mediant major (G♯ major), and flat mediant (G major), with Quilter's gentle play between major and relative minor in between for a mildly modal touch. It was included as the third song in the Op. 25 set, and was also published without change (and without opus number) as a unison song, in Winthrop Rogers's 'Festival Series of Choral Music'. Mark Raphael gave it its first performance, on 8 December 1923 at the Wigmore Hall, and it was also published in the December edition of the YWCA Magazine 'Our Own Gazette'.

Another anonymous setting was of 'Amaryllis at the Fountain', a sixteenth-century text that Quilter performed in 1904, though the song was not published until 1914, and is dated that year; it is the second in the set of *Three Songs*, Op. 15, and was dedicated to Percy Grainger's mother Rose. The text can be found in A. H. Bullen's *Lyrics from the Song-books of the Elizabethan Age*, first published in 1887. It has much of the simplicity of the first two of the *Child Songs*, Op. 5, 'The Good Child' and 'The Lamplighter', which date from about 1904, and they share a similar melodic phrase of three notes rising by step, $\hat{1}$–$\hat{2}$–$\hat{3}$ followed by $\hat{5}$; though in 'A Good Child', the notes are harmonised over a chord of the relative minor, but over a tonic chord in 'Amaryllis' and 'The Lamplighter'. It shares harmonic similarities too with *To Julia* with the striking change to a flat second inversion (exx. 7.21a, b).

Amaryllis swears immortal faith, and writes the words in the sand, but the wind blows the sand – and her faith – away. The harmonies become richer as she swears her love, the texture becomes more elaborate as she makes her oath, and the pitch of the piano part rises, as the wind blows. The texture becomes spare once faith has been blown away, with a return to the opening child-motif.

---

[16] H. C. Colles, 'Roger Quilter', Grove's *Dictionary of Music and Musicians*, 5th edn, ed. Eric Blom (London, 1954).

In just twenty-four bars, Quilter and the anonymous poet have painted a clear picture of a fickle Amaryllis.

Ex. 7.21a, Quilter, 'Amaryllis at the Fountain', bars 8–9
© Copyright 1914 by Boosey & Co. Ltd.

Ex. 7.21b, Quilter, 'Prelude' from *To Julia*, bars 5–6
© Copyright 1906 by Boosey & Co. Ltd.

'The Fuchsia Tree' is a setting of a Manx ballad, the words attributed to Charles Dalmon, but the melody all Quilter's; the manuscript is dated 18 February 1923, and it was dedicated to Leslie Woodgate. Its modal sound arises from the flattened sevenths, its 6/8 rhythm lilts gently and Quilter has taken care not to overdo the harmonies and accompaniment. The melody is haunting, with a more arpeggiated accompaniment in the second verse, and following a drop in the vocal line of an octave and a half over four bars (a wide pitch range by Quilter's standards) it ends with a short melisma, very unusually for Quilter, and a Picardie third. It is a very beautiful song indeed, and the recording by Carmen Hill, of 19 December 1923, is particularly so.

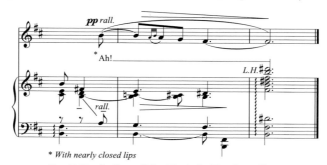

* *With nearly closed lips*

Ex. 7.22, Quilter, 'The Fuchsia Tree', ending
© Copyright 1923 by Winthrop Rogers Ltd.

'Love is a Bable', a setting of a text that appeared in Robert Jones's *Second Book of Songs and Airs*, of 1601, remains lost and unpublished.

Ex. 7.23, Quilter, 'Good Morrow', second verse

'Good Morrow, 'tis St Valentine's Day' is also unpublished, but for no obvious reason. It is an arrangement of a melody based on one from D'Urfey's 'Wit and Mirth' of 1707, and it exists in two forms (both in Quilter's hand), one a piano conductor score, for voice, string quartet and harp, and the other a version for voice and piano; the score (containing both versions) is marked 'written Oct 1917 altered Oct 1919 RQ'. The second version has an altered title, 'Saint Valentine's Day, old English Song'. The versions – they are light-hearted lyrical settings – are essentially the same, beginning with a four-bar introduction in 3/4, continuing into a further six-bar introduction in 6/8, in which time it remains to the end. It has one verse, and that is repeated, though with a slightly varied accompaniment. What it was intended for is not known, though it has an air of the theatre about it.

Quilter's SATB setting of a poem about the spring, 'The Pretty Birds Do Sing', by Thomas Nashe (1567–1601) was written in 1945 and published the following year by Ascherberg, Hopwood and Crew, in their 'Mortimer Series of Modern Part Songs'. A simple verse and refrain setting, the third verse has different harmonies, but a broadly similar melodic shape, and its refrain is the same as the first two. Quilter's partsongs are invariably chordal settings, rather than contrapuntal, and this is no exception; it is colourful and extremely attractive.

Ex. 7.24, Quilter, 'The Pretty Birds Do Sing', last verse and refrain

The *Seven Elizabethan Lyrics* are amongst Quilter's finest work and are justly performed and recorded frequently. On 3 August 1907, he wrote to Percy Grainger that two of them were already done:[17] these were 'Weep You No More' and 'Damask Roses'. On 14 August, he told Rose Grainger that a friend of his, a singer called William Higley, liked the first of the set, 'Weep you no more, sad fountains', the 'best of all [his] stuff'.[18] On 3 January 1908, he wrote to Grainger that he had had to reject two of the songs, on the grounds of poor quality, and had replaced them with two others, probably 'Brown is My Love' and 'My Life's

---

[17] Quilter to Percy Grainger, 3 August 1907, GM.
[18] Quilter to Rose Grainger, 14 August 1907, GM.

Delight'.[19] He had intended them to be ready for a concert Gervase Elwes was giving in February 1908, but in a letter to Rose dated 27 March 1908, he wrote that he had played them through to him, which suggests that they had not yet been premièred.[20] Elwes appears not to have been overly enthusiastic about them, and though Quilter himself thought four 'were passable',[21] Elwes' reaction made him defensive and unsure of them. Nevertheless, Elwes performed them on 19 November 1908 at the Bechstein Hall with Quilter accompanying and this may have been their first performance.[22] Elwes also recorded an impassioned performance of the last song, 'Fair House of Joy', despite any reservations he may once have had. The set was dedicated to the memory of Elwes's mother, Alice Cary-Elwes, who had died in March 1907.

All the songs set love lyrics of one kind or another. Quilter's sources for the texts are unknown; no single volume containing all the texts has yet been traced, and though all the texts were set in one or other of the various books of Ayres such as Dowland's ('Weep You No More' occurs in the *Third Book of Ayres*) and Campion's ('My Life's Delight' occurs in his *Third Book of Ayres*), there is no evidence that Quilter knew these works. Four of them appear in Palgrave's *Golden Treasury of Songs and Lyrics*, first published in 1861: 'Weep You No More', 'Damask Roses', 'The Faithless Shepherdess' and 'Fair House of Joy', and the first five appear in Bullen's *Lyrics*. In 'Fair House of Joy', Quilter sets 'rich fruit' in the second verse instead of the original 'ripe fruit': 'rich fruit' was published in Bullen's anthology, by Quiller-Couch in *The Oxford Book of English Verse*, and also in the *Golden Treasury of Songs and Lyrics*, but this is not enough to identify Quilter's source positively.

In the songbooks of the sixteenth century, it was normal for texts to be anonymous, and it was by no means the case that the composers wrote both words and music. Four of Quilter's settings are to anonymous texts, a fifth setting is of a text by Thomas Campion ('My Life's Delight') and a sixth, of a text by Ben Jonson ('By a Fountainside'). The remaining song, 'Fair House of Joy', is a setting of the text 'Fain would I change that note'. This was first set by Tobias Hume, the song being published in his *First Part of Ayres*, also called *Musicall Humors*, in 1605;[23] although the text is anonymous, it '[has] a deeply-felt quality and an individuality of expression which [finds] echoes in [Hume's] other writings' so that there is the possibility that it may indeed be by Hume.[24]

Quilter was fond of the first song, 'Weep You No More, Sad Fountains' and so were others: it was sung often and was one of the three from the set most

[19] Quilter to Percy Grainger, 3 January 1908, GM.
[20] Quilter to Rose Grainger, 27 March 1908, GM.
[21] Quilter to Rose Grainger, 27 March 1908, GM.
[22] The programme is held in the archives of the Wigmore Hall (formerly the Bechstein Hall).
[23] See E. H. Fellowes, ed., *English Madrigal Verse*, 3rd edn, ed. Frederick W. Sternfeld and David Greer (Oxford, 1967), p. 540. There is useful information too in Peter Warlock, *The English Ayre* (London, 1926), p. 82.
[24] David Greer, ed., *The English Lute-Songs*, series 2, vol. 21 (London, 1969), p. vi (the edition of Hume's songs). I am indebted to Professor Greer for his help and insights.

frequently performed singly; the others were 'The Faithless Shepherdess' and 'Fair House of Joy' though oddly 'The Faithless Shepherdess' has not been recorded separately.

The manuscript of 'Weep You No More' is dated July 1907.[25] Its long, liquid lines glide effortlessly between major and minor, in an exquisitely prolonged expression of hope. There are three stresses to each of the first four lines, the stresses placed in different parts of the bar. Lines five, six and seven contain seven stresses between them, spread out over five bars, the first four stresses in two bars and one in each of the next three bars.

But *my* Sun's *heav'nly eyes* View *not* your *weep*ing, That *now* lies *sleep*ing

So the pace slows down; in addition, Quilter repeats the last word and draws it out over two bars, slowing it down still further.

Quilter plays on the repeated 'softly'; the rhythm is gently rocking, ('softly now'), as of a lullaby, and the chords use pivot notes to shift harmonies smoothly, calmly. The two verses are the same, except for one significant change, where in the second verse, the piano and voice parts are reversed, so that the vocal line falls and throws attention onto the piano part: this begins with a descant to the sung line, highlighting the recurrent figure $\hat{3}$–$\hat{2}$–$\hat{1}$. It recollects the first stanza and so becomes assimilated into the sung line: simple and direct.

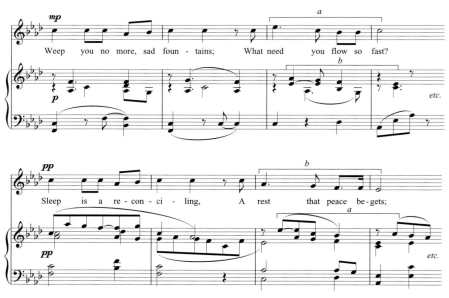

Ex. 7.25, Quilter, 'Weep You No More', first 4 bars of each verse
Both extracts © Copyright 1908 by Boosey & Co. Ltd.

[25] The MSS, showing dates of composition, for all these songs are held by Leslie East.

The underlying harmonic structure follows the sense of the words – the bass line first rises in thirds, F – A♭ – c, matching the upward vision of mountains, and then falls, again via thirds, A♭ – F – D♭, as the reader's view is brought earthward, down. The images and the bass line have the same outline in the second stanza, arching upward with the sun, with a fall for the end of the day, and a return to the weeping sentiment of the opening at the very end.

The song harps poignantly upon the note c^2, providing both a pivot and a constant question, whether the note is to be treated as $\hat{5}$ in the key of F minor, or $\hat{3}$ in its relative major, A♭; Quilter maintains the ambivalence by avoiding the raised seventh, E♮. Mark Raphael rightly said of it that it was an instance 'where melody and eloquence are perfectly blended'.[26] Its limpid simplicity belies the complex construction and support for the text.

In 1939, an arrangement by Quilter for women's voices in two parts was published; it is pleasant but not distinguished.

Campion's poem, 'My Life's Delight', has some similarities with his contemporary Shakespeare's 'O Mistress Mine' (from *Twelfth Night*), in that both appeal to the loved one to come quickly to the lover, but where Shakespeare's lover pleads for no delay, the recipient of the affections evidently being a little reluctant, Campion's has no such subtlety. This lover is young and impassioned and Quilter's setting (of December 1907) reflects the urgent mood by starting *in medias res* on a second inversion dominant. The bass line rises quickly and almost chromatically to $\hat{6}$, and the voice enters on the resolution of a perfect cadence (chains of descending fifths throughout the song give immense forward momentum): no question marks here, no hesitation – the singer comes tumbling in with a confident and infectious enthusiasm.

As so often with Quilter – and he was particularly good at it – the vocal line follows the word stresses closely, with several points at which the stress is drawn out and emphasised. The crotchet rest that follows 'to me' enables both a restorative breath after the previous long, breathless phrases, and an opportunity for the singer to be – in a dramatic sense – lost for words while trying to think of something with which to compare the lover's flight. Campion makes comparison with heavenly light, and Quilter supports it, by way of inverse emphasis, with the lowest note of the song, D_1. The phrase in the second verse takes nine bars, where the equivalent place in the first is given only six, yet the phrase does not seem unnaturally stretched or forcibly lengthened.

In this song, the mood of excitement is immediately and vividly captured by the accompaniment; the quaver movement is almost continuous with only the occasional hiatus, and nearly every bar begins with rising motion. At the end of the first verse, the brief cessation of quaver movement mirrors the words 'depriv'd of thee' at the same point, and towards the end, under the words 'swift to me', the bass line rises an octave and a half within the bar, and two bars later, when the quaver movement ceases altogether, the bass line rises by a leap of two

---

[26] Mark Raphael (1953–4), p. 20. He applied this comment to 'Cherry Valley' and 'Autumn Evening' as well.

octaves. In the third bar from the end, the initial fall is immediately offset by a rapid rise to the highest note of the song, d^3, in the penultimate bar, followed by a drop of four and a half octaves, surely indicating a collapse from complete exhaustion.

Ex. 7.26, Quilter, 'My Life's Delight', last bars
© Copyright 1908 by Boosey & Co. Ltd.

'Damask Roses', dating from July 1907, is a difficult poem to set: the basic argument – the confusion between lips and roses – is a delight, but the poem's multiple conceits and long lines – four of pentameter and two of hexameter – are intrinsically complex and cluttered. The pentameter lines each contain eleven syllables, not ten, so that there are pairs of unstressed syllables across line-ends, and the final hexameter lines distribute thirteen and fourteen syllables respectively over a heady mixture of dactyls, spondees, trochees and iambs.

The unstressed syllables betray the text's Italian origins – Wilbye's sixteenth-century setting was of a translation of Angelo Grillo's 'Quand'io miro le rose' – and the multiple unstressed syllables would surely be more liquid in that language: the variety of syllabic weight and length is a potent element of English, but is here decidedly heavy.[27] Quilter does not let air into this setting; there is very little break and the variety in the way he places word stresses within the bars seems laboured rather than fluid.

The shift to the flat mediant – F major – for the fifth line, while supporting

---

[27] Rohrer has written lucidly on the significance of Purcell's word-setting and the 'tension between stress patterns and poetic metrical schemes', and has examined the connections between those and the compositional interpretation, paying particular attention to variety of syllabic lengths. (Katherine T. Rohrer, 'Interactions of Phonology and Music in Purcell's Two Settings of "Thy genius, lo"', *Studies in the History of Music*, vol. 1, Music and Language (New York, 1983).)

the change in metre, seems routine and pedestrian; it moves via F♮ as pivot note to D minor, back through F major to B♭ major, to D minor and thence via a kind of false tierce de picardie, to the tonic D major. The busy nature of the text is neither clarified nor enhanced by the music.

'The Faithless Shepherdess' is deceptive – its outward directness and simplicity conceal great invention. It is an elusive poem with a variety of metres: the first four lines of each verse are tetrameter and the next two ('Three days endured your love to me/ And it was lost in other three') double as both coda to the verse and an introduction to the refrain of lines 7–9, 'Adieu, Love, adieu, Love, untrue Love,/ Untrue Love, untrue Love, adieu, love!/ Your mind is light, soon lost for new love'. Lines seven and eight have only three stresses to the line, and a radical change of pace as a result; the last line (a pentameter line) can be stressed in alternative ways:

Your mind is light, soon lost for new love.

or

Your mind is light, soon lost for new love.

or

Your mind is light, soon lost for new love.

Much indeed of the poem can be scanned in alternative ways, giving an indication of the flexibility of its rhythm – and indicating too the waywardness of the shepherdess herself. Quilter ends each verse in slightly different ways; he was clearly aware of the various possibilities and this is what he does:

(first refrain)
(second refrain)

The original poem contained four stanzas; Quilter omitted the middle two, although since his source is not known, he may never have known all four. The missing verses are:

Another shepherd you did see,
To whom your heart was soon enchained.
Full soon your love was leapt from me,
Full soon my place he had obtained.
Soon came a third your love to win,
And we were out and he was in.

Sure you have made me passing glad
That you your mind so soon removed,
Before that I the leisure had
To choose you for my best beloved.
For all my love was past and done
Two days before it was begun.

These fill out the story, rather than add anything significant to it, and Quilter was wise to set just two verses – the point is made strongly enough without the extra lines.

The descriptive simplicity of the poem is reflected in the outward simplicity of the musical setting – a simple time signature of 3/4, simple divisions into quaver/two semiquavers, or two semiquavers/quaver groupings. Yet from the start, there is a deliberate confusion. The first four beats sound exactly as if they make a 4/4 bar, and this is confirmed by the two pairs of crotchets that follow – actually the second and third beats of bar 2, and the first two beats of bar 3 – which are treated sequentially. The next crotchet's worth – in fact the third beat of the third bar – sounds as if it is an extension to the sequential repeat, and the introduction rounds off with a tripping downward scale, sounding disconcertingly like someone laughing at our gullibility.

Ex. 7.27a, Quilter, 'The Faithless Shepherdess', alternative barring
© Copyright 1908 by Boosey & Co. Ltd.

Ex. 7.27b, Quilter, 'The Faithless Shepherdess', original barring
© Copyright 1908 by Boosey & Co. Ltd.

Brief, descending scales appear in the verse, but more cunningly, in the refrain: the voice has a six-note scale from f^2 down (with the piano broadly in tenths below), until it reaches a♮ when, with the turn in the words from 'Adieu, Love' to 'untrue Love', it turns upon itself and goes back to c¹. This is immediately repeated, but the hesitancy is now gone: while the voice stays the same, the piano line continues its parallel tenths down to f, and beyond, down to d♮, as if a decision has been made – not simply 'untrue Love' but definitely 'adieu, Love'.

In 'Brown is My Love', written in December 1907, the poet compares the brownness of his beloved with whiteness, but he is curiously ambivalent: the first line starts with a criticism 'Brown is my Love' and follows with a compliment 'but graceful'; but the comparable line in the second half of the poem reverses the order: the compliment comes first, 'Fair is my Love', and is followed by a criticism 'but scornful'. The piano part matches the ambivalence: it starts on a chord of B♭ major, but immediately moves down by step to the relative minor, G minor, when the voice enters with an octave leap downwards. The lower note, g¹, heralds a four-note motif that appears eleven times, in nearly as many bars (ex. 7.28).

Ex. 7.28, Quilter, 'Brown is my Love', 4-note motif
© Copyright 1908 by Boosey & Co. Ltd.

Six of these start on the note G (one uses only the first three notes, but following closely on the heels of another occurrence, is a clear echo of it); this insistence on the sixth degree of the scale constantly calls into question the tonality of the song: B♭ major or G minor. There is a secondary ambivalence throughout the song, too, between the notes G (the relative minor) and F (the unresolved dominant of B♭ major).

Quilter sets word stresses as follows:

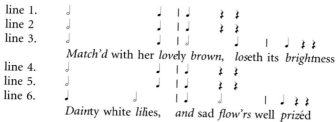

The differences between lines 3 and 6 (pentameter lines) accommodate the words: in line 4, fitting the first three syllables 'Match'd with her' into one crotchet, as happens with 'Dainty white' in line 6, would be unkind and unclear. Similarly, 'brown, loseth its' and 'and sad flow'rs well' are treated differently, so as to allow a break after 'lilies', punctuation which is important in separating the sentiments of despised white lilies, and prized sad flowers.

Most of the first half of the poem extols the lady's virtues, yet the constant play between F and G implies doubt, and the tonic chord is not heard again (except as a passing chord on the third beat, under the word 'renownéd') until five bars from the end. By the time the poet reaches 'but scornful' at the end of line 4, he is sounding a little anxious, and indeed in saying that some people despise lilies, which would normally be regarded as lovely, and that they similarly prize 'sad flow'rs' he is clearly making excuses for the behaviour of his lady. His anxiety is reflected in the chromatic music of the second half. At the point at which the poet seems to have made his argument – with the arrival of the tonic chord on the final syllable of 'prizéd' – there is still a doubt, expressed in raised fifth, db^2, rather than the c^2.

The poem ends here, but Quilter takes the story a little further. In returning to the music of the beginning, and repeating the opening line (with an added chromaticism in the piano part) he is attempting to support and console the poor poet, by reminding the listener that the loved one is graceful, after all. But the singer has two adjacent octave falls to contend with now, one on 'prizéd' and one on 'Brown is'. They are falls, first from f^2 to f^1 and then from g^2 to g^1, the very notes that gave rise to ambivalence in the beginning. And Quilter repeats 'but graceful' as if the poet continues to feel a need to justify his lady's behaviour. However, at the last moment, Quilter makes the poet's mind up for him: the db^2 makes a determined effort to rise up to $d\natural^2$, whence it can resolve through c^2 and on to bb^1. At last the stable tonic, so long denied and delayed, can be affirmed and the poet need no longer find fault with his loved one.

Ex. 7.29, Quilter, 'Brown is my Love', last 6 bars
© Copyright 1908 by Boosey & Co. Ltd.

The pentameter metre that predominates in 'By a Fountainside' (written in November 1907, to a text by Ben Jonson, 1572/3–1637) is unusual in Quilter's work; he generally prefers tetrameter, whose regular hold he often loosens by distributing it across a triple metre. Here he distributes the five stresses over four bars, for each of the first four lines:

This division has a pattern within a pattern; the internal rhythm of same–same–different–same within the line is found across the lines themselves:

same–same–different–same, a subtle symmetry. The final alexandrine 'Since nature's pride is now a wither'd daffodil' is extended by word repetition and occupies over a quarter of the song. (Quilter's other Jonson setting was of 'Drink to Me Only' which is discussed in the next chapter, in its context as one of the *Arnold* songs.)

The atmospheric, almost claustrophobic nature of the song derives partly from the extended pedal C♯/D♭, which permeates the whole song; it dominates, for example, seven out of the first eight bars. The heaviness of the words is supported by the highly repetitive motif, two notes falling by step, which in the upper voices provides a sighing effect, and elsewhere is the stuff of suspensions; particularly poignant are those in bars 9 and 10, under the words 'slower, yet', made so because of the semitonal dissonance in bar 10, D♯ against E, and by the slower movement of the word-setting, imitating the word itself.

Ex. 7.30, Quilter, 'By a Fountainside', bars 9–10
© Copyright 1908 by Boosey & Co. Ltd.

So a significant proportion of the song is based firmly upon C♯/D♭; and while this gives the song a comforting security, it also imprisons it; all attempts to escape are suppressed. The voice's opening motif is a concentration of the two-note motif as it appears elsewhere; it forms a loop, returning to whence it began.

Ex. 7.31, Quilter, 'By a Fountainside', opening of vocal line
© Copyright 1908 by Boosey & Co. Ltd.

The similarity of bars 36–40 with the last of Schumann's song-cycle *Frauenliebe und -leben* is unmistakable: the gentle part-writing, the suspensions in sequence, the resolutions of ninths on to the octaves, and the use of sixths, immediately relate the one to the other. Quilter surely knew the cycle, given that he had trained at Frankfurt where Clara Schumann had held sway for so long. The bitterness of the lover is perfectly clear in Quilter's interpretation, with his strong focus on the last line, and the image of the withered daffodil. Bars 27 to 29, with the crescendo to support the rising line, are some of the most haunting and heart-rending bars that Quilter ever wrote, and their intensity is maintained until the final tierce de picardie has died away.

Ex. 7.32, Schumann, postlude from *Frauenliebe und -leben*

The link between this song and the last, 'Fair House of Joy', is a tonal one. Both were written in November 1907; the one is in the minor, the other in the tonic major, wholeheartedly joyful, the other side of the coin.

The song is very straightforward and apparently routine, with conventional cadential modulations to the dominant and the relative minor. The singer has an almost continuous line, with only eight rests, and quaver rests at that; no other break, except for a scant bar and a crotchet's rest between the verses. It is predictable, and it ought to be dull, but has instead a sense of glorious abandon, achieved through simplicity and fluidity of line, and teasing changes of stress.

Each verse has ten lines, and most of the lines have three stresses; the seventh and tenth in each verse have two; in whatever way one cares to scan the text, it would be easy to set it in stultifying four-bar phrases. Quilter sideslips the danger, by using a time signature of 3/4, and by dividing the first four lines into two pairs, and setting each pair to a three-bar phrase: the double layer of triple metre impels the movement onward. Lines 5, 6 and 7 coalesce and are given an expansive five-bar phrase, and the last three lines settle back into a more comfortable four-bar phrase.

The words are unusually flexible and Quilter treats many as multiple upbeats – 'to which fond' and 'When thy rich fruit is', for example, the emphasis thus being thrown on to the next word and the first beat of the next bar. This is a device Quilter used very notably in 'Now Sleeps the Crimson Petal' and it makes the listener hold the breath, waiting for the main beat.

But this is not all: every line has a different rhythm, and the placing of the stresses within the bars also varies:

Line 1.	♩ ♩ | ♩	*Fain* would I *change* that *note*
Line 2.	♩ | ♩ ♩	To *which* fond *Love* hath *charm'd* me
Line 3.	♪ ♩ ♩ | ♩	Long, *long* to *sing* by *rote*,
Line 4.	♩ | ♩ ♩	*Fancying that* that *harm'd* me:
Line 5.	♪ ♩ ♩ | ♩	Yet *when* this *thought* doth *come*
Line 6.	♩ | ♪ ♪ ♩ | ♩	'*Love* is the *perfect sum*
Line 7.	♩ | ♩	Of *all* de*light!*'
Line 8.	♩ | ♩ ♩	I *have* no *other choice*
Line 9.	♪ ♩ ♩ | ♩	Ei*ther* for *pen* or *voice*
Line 10.	♩ | ♩	To *sing* or *write*.

There is an ebb and flow in the setting of the metre that is a constant surprise and delight. One further surprise is the amount of alteration that Quilter made for the transposed, low voice, setting. The drop in key of a minor third set the piano tessitura into a muddy region; on the whole, and especially in solo piano sections, where the bass line would drop from D♭ to B♭₁, it rises instead to B♭, but otherwise, when the voice is singing, the piano part continues to drop a third. Sometimes the texture is reduced in the transposed version. Overall, the transposed version has a greater pitch range, compared with the original.

Ex. 7.33a, Quilter, 'Fair House of Joy', first 5 bars, original key
© Copyright 1908 by Boosey & Co. Ltd.

Ex. 7.33b, Quilter, 'Fair House of Joy', first 5 bars, transposed key
© Copyright 1908 by Boosey & Co. Ltd.

The songs comprising *Five English Love Lyrics*, Op. 24, were published separately before being brought together as a set. 'Morning Song', to a text by Thomas Heywood (*c.*1574–1641), was written and performed in 1922 and published in the same year by Chappell's, and became the second in the set; it was dedicated to the singer John Coates. It is a pretty and cheery song though its four-square phrases irritate slightly; some of the final words are repeated to make a climax. It is set strophically, but not rigidly so: there are a few small melodic and rhythmic changes between the two verses. The poet instructs the birds to sing to the loved one: the lark, nightingale, blackbird, thrush, starling, linnet, sparrow, robin – all are mentioned and the result is a veritable dawn chorus.

The fourth in the group was a setting of Thomas Dekker's 'O, the Month of May', written in 1926, published in 1927 and dedicated to the composer Maude Valérie White, whom Quilter admired greatly. Dekker (1570?–1641?) was known primarily as a dramatist, and the text is from his play of 1600, *The Shoemaker's Holiday*. Birds appear in this song too: the nightingale entreats the maid Peggy to listen to her poet's tale; but, against the tonic minor, the poet shows his dislike of the proximity of the cuckoo, denoted by falling thirds. Much of the vocal line revolves around the dominant note A, and despite its sprightly mood, the song seems to have an underlying question, resolved when the poet finishes decisively on the tonic.

'Go, Lovely Rose', to a text by Edmund Waller (1606–87), is one of Quilter's finest songs. Waller achieved fame as a poet in his own day, largely on account of this poem. The poet asks a rose to tell his love to come forth and be seen and admired, in case she should die through lack of praise. Maude Valérie White also set it, in 1885; Quilter's setting dates from 1922, it was published and performed (by its dedicatee, the tenor Hubert Eisdell) the following year and although Quilter probably knew White's setting, there is no apparent point of contact between them. Her setting is in 6/8, the four verses paired to make a two-verse strophic setting; Quilter's seems at first to be strophic too, but slides away into a through-composed setting, varying between 4/4 and 3/2. Hers, marked 'Andantino arioso', is very lyrical and smooth, to match the smoothness of the poem. It is a pleasing enough, shallow, setting, making minimal demands on singer, pianist and audience; Quilter's is a world away. Yet it is from her work, and from that of others such as her, that Quilter's work emerged: all the lyricism of the nineteenth-century song could be taken for granted, as a foundation for his own work and his own world.

His setting has a fluidity based upon the text, not upon the melody, and there is a remarkable degree of unifying motivic writing.[28] In the first two bars, a rising bass line (unusually positive for Quilter) is placed against the notes of the tonic chord; the voice enters with a four-note descending scale counterpointing the rising bass line of the start; here it accompanies reference to the rose, but when later inverted, seems more associated with the loved one.

---

[28] This is also highlighted by Trevor Hold (1996), p. 37.

Each verse has five lines, the first and third with two stresses, the others with four, so that the sense is to repeat, and in the repetition, to prolong, something which Quilter reflects in the opening of the vocal line: its first bar contains two significant notes, D♭ and A♭: they repeat and insist on being heard, by being prolonged across the next two bars.

Ex. 7.34, Quilter, 'Go, Lovely Rose', graphical chart, first 5 bars

The bass line arches up to b♭ and then falls to the starting G♭ for the second verse, the piano left hand now an octave higher than at first, and the bass line falls again, separating from the voice line, as if in sympathy with the lonely desert 'where no men abide'.

Ex. 7.35, Quilter, 'Go, Lovely Rose', bars 14–15

It falls further, to the lowest note so far, the submediant E♭ major (a key Quilter regarded as warm and resonant), as the poet speaks of his loved one, on a rising four-note motif. Three sustained bars over the E♭ give way to a sonorous tonic G♭ chord, full of feeling, under the word 'die', which is what the rose must now do, to show 'how small a part of time they share'; 'how small' are the only words of the poem that are repeated. The coda makes reference to the rose's motif, with echoes of the opening of the piano part. The G♭ on 'die' is not to be sung loudly, however, despite its importance: it is preceded by a *diminuendo* and there is a *crescendo* on it, but across the whole song, the loudest dynamic marking is *mp* and that is at the beginning. This is a song requiring not vulgar passion, but emotional intensity.

All four verses have seven bars each (up to the start of the very last note). In the first verse, Quilter sets line 4 into a 3/2 bar; in the second, he sets the very end of line 5 into a 3/2 bar, and the third verse is entirely in 4/4; the variation follows the word stress and length. Part of line 2, and line 3, are together set into a bar of 3/2 and lines 4 and 5 are set to a 4/4 bar and two 3/2 bars but greatly extended by the 3/2 bars. Throughout, the pacing of the vocal line is dictated by the text, free from bound rhythm, though it is by no means recitative; the listener is eavesdropping on the poet's intensely personal thoughts.

The poets of these three settings were exact contemporaries with Robert Herrick (1591–1674). The prolific Herrick inspired fifteen settings by Quilter, compared with twenty inspired by Shakespeare, and the earliest of these were two unaccompanied SATB partsongs , 'To Daffodils' and 'To the Virgins', both published in 1904, and without opus number. The sound of Quilter's partsongs is quite different from his solo songs; they explore choral texture rather than delve deep into the textual meaning. Quilter freely repeats words, though not whole lines, so that in 'To Daffodils' (likening the brevity of the life of a daffodil, which is associated with the spirits of the dead, to the brevity of human life), the opening words 'Fair daffodils' are repeated, and so are the words 'As yet' in line 3. The speed of word-setting varies: 'Stay, stay' is set to two semibreves, where the movement is normally crotchets and quavers; parts are paired, sopranos with basses, then altos with tenors. Quilter does not stray far from the tonic D major, except via pivot note to B♭ major. Parts exchange, so that the melody first on sopranos is then heard on tenors, and both verses end with spiced chords that Quilter had probably found at the piano.

Ex. 7.36, Quilter, 'To Daffodils', last 5 bars
© Copyright 1904 by Boosey & Co. Ltd.

'To the Virgins' is the well-known text 'Gather ye rosebuds while ye may' and as with 'To Daffodils' is driven by choral texture and the shape of the vocal line; unexpected turns of harmony surprise, but are a delight to sing, deriving from the use of pivot notes; individual parts are each interesting to sing in their own right. Only marginally less inventive than 'To Daffodils', 'To The Virgins' has a lovely touch at the very end, when sopranos, tenors and altos chase the rhythm 'gather ye' round each other, by way of coda. Neither setting is exactly simple or straightforward, yet the appeal is direct. These songs, like the set of *Five Lyrics of Robert Herrick*, have fallen into unjustified disuse.

Herrick was noted for his themes of nostalgia, of the fleetness of time, to which Quilter responded strongly and he selected themes of love, death, flowers, and seizing the day: all themes rich in opportunity and not treated complete within themselves as the metaphysical poets tended to do. Herrick was also noted for his finely-detailed writing, which again found resonance in Quilter's own way of working.

Ex. 7.37, Quilter, 'To the Virgins', last 4 bars
© Copyright 1904 by Boosey & Co. Ltd.

The date of composition of the unaccompanied partsongs, *Five Lyrics of Robert Herrick*, Op. 7, is unclear. They were probably begun in 1905, hot on the heels of the previous settings, and were certainly finished by June 1907;[29] Quilter seems to have first offered them to Boosey (who had published the first two Herrick settings), though they were eventually published by Forsyth, in October 1907.[30] Quilter dedicated them to his 'dear friend, Percy Grainger'.

'Cupid' is a light-hearted fast-moving melody with chordal accompaniment, strophic, with numerous consecutive fifths that presumably taxed Quilter to the point where he yielded to the inevitable and left them in; the result however is a sequence of very evenly spread and well-balanced chords.

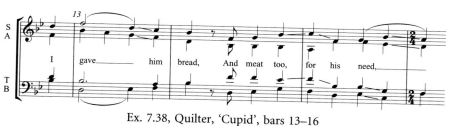

Ex. 7.38, Quilter, 'Cupid', bars 13–16
© Copyright 1907 Forsyth Bros. Ltd.

'A Dirge' is in the relative minor to 'Cupid' and contrasts with it. Imitative writing is assigned to different voices in the two verses (the original text is eight lines long; Quilter has divided it into two) and it is extended in a coda. Parallel chords are arranged with interleaved parts, and the chromatic writing is treated very lightly. There is a small misprint on page 8, penultimate bar, soprano line, where the quaver on 'est' should be a crotchet.

---

[29] Quilter to Percy Grainger, 14 June 1907, GM: '[Boosey have] done two, & there are five more.'
[30] Quilter to Rose Grainger, 17 October 1907, GM: 'My Herrick choruses will be out soon. I've just corrected the proofs.' A copy in the Grainger Museum is inscribed from Quilter to Grainger and dated 1 November 1907.

Ex. 7.39, Quilter, 'A Dirge', bars 14–17
© Copyright 1907 Forsyth Bros. Ltd.

Ex. 7.40, Quilter, 'A Dirge', bars 21–22
© Copyright 1907 Forsyth Bros. Ltd.

'Morning Song' (not to be confused with the Heywood setting, Op. 24, no. 2) is a playful song in 6/8, which takes its cue from the words which are in the original already repeated ('old, old age' and 'evil, evil days'), so that brief phrases are repeated more than usual. Marked *Molto allegro marcato*, it has the lightness and energy of 'The Night Piece'; it is in ternary form (as a Da Capo), with the outer sections in C minor; the central section is in C major, 2/4, without the racing rhythms of the 6/8, but with a not entirely predictable passing modulation to the submediant major.

'To Electra' is the only poem that Quilter set twice; there were several that he set for solo voice and then arranged for chorus, or vice versa, but this poem had two completely different settings, with the solo song eventually given the title of its first line, 'I Dare Not Ask a Kiss' though one manuscript gives its title 'To Electra'; it was written in 1925 and published by Boosey in 1926, the third of *Five Jacobean Lyrics*. The choral setting is strophic, in 4/4 with simple rhythms, and a coda that sets an extra line derived from the first two: 'I dare not ask a kiss, a smile'; the solo song is through-composed, in 2/2 with triplet crotchets, resultant cross-rhythms, and quavers only at the very end. The thoughtful mood is similar, however, with the solo song marked *Andantino quasi allegretto* and the partsong, *Poco allegro semplice*. Both have a directness, the solo song because the words are not repeated (it is twenty-three bars long, including five bars of piano introduction and postlude), the partsong – twenty-eight bars long – because of its simple harmonies; sequential repetition (down by step) harmonises and mirrors the word repetition gracefully. Yet despite the simplicity of the partsong, it has a range of pacing, with the lines set thus:

‖: | 𝅗𝅥 𝅘𝅥 𝅘𝅥 | 𝅘𝅥 𝅘𝅥 𝅘𝅥 :‖
| 𝅗𝅥 𝅘𝅥 𝅘𝅥 | 𝅘𝅥. 𝅘𝅥 | 𝅘𝅥. 𝅘𝅥 | 𝅘𝅥.

The second line is a reflection of the first, and the last takes elements of the others. The second phrase of the solo version repeats the first, a third higher sequentially, with a bass line rising by step. The text does not sit so happily on the partsong as it does in the solo song, but Quilter's aims were different; the partsong aimed to satisfy a choir (with low F for the basses, and variety of phrase shape for all), while the solo version aimed to satisfy a single vocalist. There is a fleeting glimpse of things to come at bars 11–12: at the same point – the beginning of the second half – in 'Take, O Take' of 1921 is heard the same melodic shape and a similar harmonic outline; both are in D♭ major, and both express similar sentiments of forsworn love:

Ex. 7.41a, Quilter, 'I Dare Not Ask a Kiss', bars 11–12
© Copyright 1926 by Boosey & Co. Ltd.

Ex. 7.41b, Quilter, 'Take, O Take', bars 11–12
© Copyright 1921 by Boosey & Co. Ltd.

The final song, 'To Violets', is again strophic, praising violets, symbols of modesty, but pointing out that being modest, they are likely to be neglected. So it is a modest setting, and has indeed been neglected. Its beauties of fluid phrase length – five bars (one for each petal?), then another five bars, extended by word repetition to eight – go unnoticed, despite their delicate proportions.

Grainger thought very highly of these partsongs, and over many years had Quilter send multiple copies to numerous choirs around the world.

Quilter's next Herrick setting was his Op. 8, *To Julia*, which he dedicated to Gervase Elwes; it was composed over the summer of 1905, performed in October that year, and published the next year. This – his only song cycle –

was for voice and piano but he arranged it for piano quintet some years later; in 1954, Leslie Boosey gave Leslie Woodgate permission for Sargent to orchestrate it for a Prom.[31] Quilter chose six songs from *Hesperides*, Herrick's vast collection of poems published in 1648. All six refer to Julia, and all extol her various aspects. She has a melodic motif, one which also appears in an approximate inversion (exx. 7.42, 43).

Ex. 7.42, Quilter, Julia's theme
© Copyright 1906 by Boosey & Co. Ltd.

Ex. 7.43, inversion of Julia's theme
© Copyright 1906 by Boosey & Co. Ltd.

The cycle begins with a prelude for piano solo which presents these two themes; it starts in D major but passes through increasingly flat keys, never settling, until eventually G minor emerges as a subdominant, cadencing on to D minor – the tonic minor – with a statement of the inverted form of the theme. This is imitated at the start of the first song, 'The Bracelet' (which describes how Julia has captured her lover), and Hold interprets this version of the theme as perhaps representing Herrick,[32] as if introducing the listener to Julia via the poet, though Julia's theme, with its distinctive pairs of falling thirds, dominates the rest of the cycle.

The turbulent writing of the extremely pianistic accompaniment is supported by the irregular but fluid phrase lengths. In a way that he has not done before, Quilter breaks away completely from the rigidity of four stresses to a line. The introduction is six bars long, extended from a conventional four by judicious use of sequence and a rise and fall in tessitura; from the repetitions of the rhythmic motif ♩. ♫ ♪ the voice emerges, its line punctuated with comments from the piano. The vocal line of the first half of the poem (which is treated as if it were divided into two verses) takes fifteen bars in all, nine plus six. The word stresses in the first half are spread across bars as follows:

line 1.			❘	♩ ♩	♩	❘	♩		
line 2.			❘	♩	♩	❘	♩ ♩		
line 3.	♩		❘	♩ ♩		❘	♩		
line 4.	♩	❘	♩	♩	❘	♩			
line 5.	♩	❘	♩ ♩		❘	♩			
line 6.	♩	❘	♩	♩	❘	♩			

[31] Leslie Boosey to Leslie Woodgate, 27 July 1954, WAC 2nd contributor file 1940–62, BBC WAC.
[32] Trevor Hold (1996), p. 29.

This rich variety is retained for the most part without change in the second verse (which is divided from the first by three bars that use material from the introduction, but with a higher tessitura, compressing some motifs, prolonging others). Only the second line differs, to suit the sense of the words: the line rises to f^2, on 'free'.

line 2. | ♩ ♩ | ♩ ♩

The melody otherwise repeats that of the first half, though the words 'fast bound' are now given equal quavers, where the first occurrence set a dotted rhythm for 'how in'; the final phrase stretches up first to Ab^1 and then to the dominant, $A\natural^1$, and the postlude subsides into D major before rising again to end in D minor.

The agitation and harmonic interplay between dorian mode and D minor yields to the serenity of 'The Maiden Blush', which opens with a clear statement of Julia's theme in the relative major of F major, and remains harmonically static for six bars. Thence to A minor, the mediant, and via falling fifths to the dominant, C major; parallel first inversion chords recall 'Now Sleeps the Crimson Petal'. Quilter returns to the F major tonic; the bass line climbs to a Bb, falling by step to D, in D major, and then by falling fifths again, but this time going beyond the dominant by falling one more fifth on to the tonic (with a fleeting flattened seventh at the final cadence).

Instead of spreading four-stress lines across a triple metre as in 'The Bracelet', Quilter now spreads four-stress lines across a quadruple time signature (the last line is greatly extended, and so falls outside the scope of this brief rhythmic examination):

line 1.   ♩ ♩ | ♩ ♩
line 2.   ♩.   ♩ | ♩ ♩
line 3.   ♩ ♩ | ♩ ♩
line 4.   ♩ ♩   ♩ | ♩
line 5.   ♩ ♩ ♩ | ♩
line 6.   ♩   ♩ | ♩
line 7.   ♩ | ♩ ♩ ♩
line 8.   ♩ ♩ | ♩ ♩ ♩
line 9.   ♩   ♩ ♩ | ♩

With no two lines the same, this is an extraordinarily inventive and fluid word-setting even by Quilter's standards; it is offset against the simple harmonic outline, and leaves the listener with the sense of the song being sung in one remarkable breath. This matches the sense of the words, a single statement describing Julia's appearance when she blushes.

The introversion of 'The Maiden Blush' leads on to the sunnier mood – though no less gentle – of 'To Daisies', which asks the simple flower, since there is still daylight, to stay open until Julia has fallen asleep. The line only loosely derives from Julia's theme, taking notes four to seven, the repeating adjacent notes, and giving them to the accompaniment. It retains the serenity of the second song by remaining on its tonic chord, D♭ major, for five bars, and makes a brief foray into the world of E♭ major before sliding back to home territory. The shift of a major third, from the F major of 'The Maiden Blush' to the D♭ of 'To Daisies', was one of Quilter's favourite key relationships; nor was such a relationship especially unusual: it is commonly found in Schubert's music and allows a different kind of key relationship since it is based not on harmonic connections, but on pivot notes – the note F is common to both keys.

Quilter sets the song strophically: the first two lines of each verse are the same (with minor variations to fit the words) and the vocal lines for third and fourth lines for verses one and two are similar, higher in verse two, over the same harmony. In verse three, the line moves higher still and is prolonged; the bass line is substantially the same. This is a very simple treatment; its lack of sophistication is appealing, and is a foil for the richness of the previous song, and for the excitement of the next.

The fourth song, 'The Night Piece', combines both forms of the theme, the inverted in the piano part, and the main in the vocal line; Quilter enjoys the consequent contrary motion, though for the most part, it is the accompaniment that initially gives the shape as it rises and falls in the first two verses, mirroring the dancing sparks of fire of the fifth line; chromaticism and staccato articulation add to the picture. The first two verses start similarly but go off at different tangents, each ending with short melismas, that for 'sparks' a sequence of dotted rhythms, and that for 'ghost' more wailing. The third verse starts a minor third higher and moves up sequentially by the same interval, through E minor and G minor to B♭ minor; thence through a bass line rising chromatically from D♭ to a sudden F major, which, with its block-chord change of texture and equally sudden cessation of movement, cuts through as clearly as the words 'tapers clear' that it carries. In such turbulent writing, the lover wants to protect Julia – there is almost a sense of casting spells and certainly a sense of magic – and now, with a change of voice, asks Julia to come to him. The change is indicated by a change to the tonic major – C♯ minor to D♭ major – and by an expansive version of Julia's theme on piano, accompanied by chords and rising arpeggios, which melt back into the texture of the opening, remaining in the major; evidently Julia has acceded to the request.

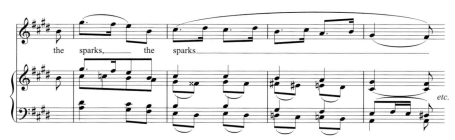

Ex. 7.44, Quilter, 'The Night Piece', end of first verse

It is a tight, well-controlled, sparkling song, nothing overplayed – Hold calls it a 'deft scherzo'[33] – and it is easy to see why it was encored at its first performance.

Ex. 7.45, Quilter, 'The Night Piece', end of second verse
© Copyright 1906 by Boosey & Co. Ltd.

The twenty bars of the fifth song, 'Julia's Hair', make it easily the shortest song in the cycle. The inverted theme on a single line, musing on the beauty of Julia's hair, starts on an F, apparently the third of the tonic chord from 'The Night Piece'. This is then treated as the tonic of F minor (a major third away from the previous tonic) but it finally settles into A♭ major.

Ex. 7.46, Quilter, 'Julia's Hair', bars 10–16
© Copyright 1906 by Boosey & Co. Ltd.

Four simple statements follow, the first, second and fourth based on Julia's theme, interspersed by further versions of her theme in the accompaniment,

---

[33] Trevor Hold (1996), p. 29.

and supported by parallel chords; the third statement is underpinned by a
sinewy line that falls almost completely chromatically from c^1 to c; Julia's hair
must surely be loose and unbraided. It provides eloquent contrast to 'The Night
Piece' and is an exquisite gem.

After such a contemplative song, the brief piano interlude that follows (again
based on Julia's theme) provides a breathing space; modulating through sundry
keys, it seems to settle on A major but finally resolves onto a cheerful F major
for the exuberant 'Cherry Ripe'. This is something of a disappointment,
however: insensitive, succumbing to the call for a rousing finale, and determined to be happy. Its main shortcoming is its length, forced by the extension
and repetition of the eight lines to create a ternary form song, and additionally,
lines 5 and 6 are duplicated to create the contrasting central section:
1234567812–56–1234567812. These are Quilter's repetitions, not Herrick's,
but he was by no means the only composer to do so: Charles Horn's well-
known setting also repeats lines freely. The other songs do not suffer such
treatment, often through-composed, or if strophic, treated very lightly. There is
much to commend it nevertheless: the accompaniment is splendid – it has the
same kind of exuberance as 'Love's Philosophy' – and the rising bass lines
contribute to the rising excitement; but the marketplace 'Cherry Ripe!'
exclamations chafe against the broader and more intimate mood of the rest
of the cycle.

The piano solos within the cycle have been likened in principle to the piano
interludes in Lehmann's cycle *In a Persian Garden*[34] but the similarity between
the cycles ends there; her setting, which incidentally was hugely successful, is a
strange mixture of recitative and four-bar phrases using perceived exotic
idioms. Here though, Quilter's freedom and fluidity of line, his balance and
interplay between voice and piano, his use of keys, key relationships and
chromaticism, is developed to the full, and fine though some of his previous
songs are, we see just what he is capable of.

The piano quintet arrangement was recorded on the Columbia label and
issued in November 1923, sung by Hubert Eisdell, with an unidentified string
quartet and directed by Quilter; it is safe to assume that Quilter directed from
the piano. The string parts often double what is in the piano, but not always,
and there is rarely a break for the piano, the opening of the Prelude, 'The
Maiden Blush' and 'Julia's Hair' being exceptions. There are a few minor
differences of figuration between the score and the recorded version. It is a pity
that Quilter does not more often contrast string-only texture with piano alone,
or use the resources of a piano quintet as an instrument in its own right, as
Vaughan Williams had done so many years earlier in his 1909 cycle *On Wenlock
Edge*; overall, the arrangement was just that, a version that had parts for string
quartet, and Quilter saw no need to rework the cycle in any way, or to develop
the concept of a work for voice and piano quintet. The arrangement still pleases,
but the missed opportunity annoys as well.

---

[34] Stephen Banfield, *Sensibility and English Song* (Cambridge, 1985), p. 116.

Malcolm Sargent arranged the cycle for voice and orchestra, and it was performed by Alexander Young, one of the finest singers of Quilter songs of his generation, in a Promenade concert on 15 August 1959.

Quilter's last Herrick setting was 'Tulips'; it was originally written as an unaccompanied partsong and published in 1946, and as a solo song, published a little before Christmas 1947. The solo song takes the soprano line of the partsong, and Quilter added a piano accompaniment, consisting essentially of the entire four parts, with repeated crotchet chords turned into minims, and the occasional arpeggio to open out the texture.

Ex. 7.47a, Quilter, 'Tulips', partsong bars 7–9

Ex. 7.47b, Quilter, 'Tulips', solo song, bars 9–11

The solo song inevitably lacks the fluidity of text setting normally found in Quilter's solo songs, and its phrase extension is not quite enough to redeem it; it works better as the partsong, though some of the chromaticism is disappointingly syrupy and lacking in imagination.

The remaining songs of the *Five Jacobean Lyrics*, Op. 28 (the third one being a Herrick setting), were love-lyric settings of poets slightly later than Herrick. Quilter set them all in 1925 (including the Herrick setting), and Boosey published them a year later, except for the first, 'The Jealous Lover' which was written for Mark Raphael in 1923 and published the same year. The second and fifth songs are settings of Sir John Suckling (1609–42), whose writing was recognised for its wit and verve and seen to advantage in these songs, 'Why So Pale and Wan?', advising a lover who is unable to woo his lady successfully to give up ('The *devil* take her!'), and 'The Constant Lover', where the poet expresses astonishment that he has loved the same lady for three days, where normally he would have loved a dozen in the same time. Quilter was anxious that Mark Raphael should like them,[35] but he had no cause for concern: 'The Jealous Lover' and 'I Dare Not Ask a Kiss' were both included in the group of seventeen songs that Quilter and Raphael recorded in 1934.

The keys of all five songs are clustered together, starting and ending in D major, the second in C minor, the fourth in Eb major, and the central one in Db major; variety is achieved with the range of moods: adoration, lack of perseverance, shyness, the liberty of love, and its inconstancy. 'Why So Pale and Wan?' is a spirited song, in the form AAB; the first section ends on the dominant and the second – with small changes to the vocal line – resolves on to the tonic, and the third begins by seeming to be a continuation of the same, but breaks off in a decisive dénouement: the character of the poet is vividly portrayed in the staccato chords, impatient and dismissive of the unmoved lady; Quilter rarely selects texts that conjure up such a specific scene, from the pedal tonic at the beginning of the first two verses, under the speaker's question, to the impetuous speech rhythms of the last verse.

Quilter's setting of 'The Constant Lover' misses the cynicism of the poem (as Michael Pilkington points out in his *Guide*[36]) by repeating the first two verses, those that marvel at the poet's full three days of being in love with the same lady; the repetition enables an exuberant high-note ending for the song, and for the group, but it is a forced restatement and though it is musically balanced, textually it is not.

'To Althea from Prison' is the fourth *Jacobean* setting, the text by Richard Lovelace (1618–58). Lovelace's poetry is considered somewhat inaccessible and his poetic arguments rather convoluted, and Quilter's ternary-form setting meanders too, only beginning to find its way at the return of the A section (the beginning of the third verse), at the well-known text 'Stone walls do not a prison make,/ Nor iron bars a cage'. The phrases are four-bar and four-square, with phrase extension only at the end of the second and third verses; however, in such tortuous, busy composition, Quilter has captured the nature of Lovelace's style admirably; it is certainly a different kind of writing from the others in the group and manages to be hearty and sentimental at the same time.

'The Jealous Lover' is the first of the *Jacobean* songs, and also the first to be written; it was published in 1923. The poet, the second Earl of Rochester (1641/7–80) was known for his licentiousness, and the subject matter of his poem – about the lack of constancy of his mistress, so that he is loath to leave her for even a day – could equally be applied to him. Quilter seems to have taken the words at their face value, however, and this is a pleasing song. Like 'To Althea', it is too much set in four-bar phrases, but it is at least unpretentious.

The other of Quilter's settings of Rochester was 'To Wine and Beauty', the first of a group of *Three Songs for Baritone or Tenor*, Op. 18, all written in 1913, published separately in 1914, and as a set in 1920. Three further songs were added in 1914 and 1916, and the complete title amended to *Six Songs*. It is a

---

[35] Quilter to Raphael, 1 December 1925, BL Add. MS 70607, f. 38.
[36] Michael Pilkington, *English Solo Song Guides to the Repertoire: Gurney, Ireland, Quilter and Warlock* (London, 1989).

motley set, though the first three songs make an excellent group. 'To Wine and Beauty' was dedicated to Theodore Byard, an actor friend with whom Quilter had stayed in Venice in May 1914. It is an unfailingly hearty song, its words made very much more polite and its line order altered from the extremely bawdy original; Quilter's source for the text remains unknown. The four-bar phrases are predictable and so are the harmonies; there is little finesse.

The third of the Op. 18 set was Quilter's first Blake setting, 'The Jocund Dance'. This and 'Dream Valley' were both originally called 'Song' and published in 1783, although written when Blake was still a youth. The text of 'The Wild Flower's Song' was first published in 1905, and that of 'Daybreak' (originally entitled 'Morning') was published in 1874; these two poems came from Blake's sketchbooks and commonplace books. Quilter presumably had the collected edition.

Blake (1757–1827) uses words very directly; there is not the Cavalier elegance as found in Quilter's earlier poets and his austere style can be difficult to work with. He has a simple eloquence nonetheless and Quilter's 'The Jocund Dance' has a comparable simplicity, of a kind that recurs in his 'Under the Greenwood Tree' of 1919. The rustic mood of this gentle love song is set with the tonic-dominant pedal under the first five bars of the voice entry; Blake uses simple, short words, and Quilter uses simple rhythms in short, 2/4, bars. It was dedicated to Quilter's friend Frederic Austin, singer and composer.

'Dream Valley' was the first in the set of *Three Songs of William Blake*, Op. 20, first performed on 14 December 1917, by Muriel Foster, at the Wigmore Hall; the manuscript is dated 18 September 1916, and the poem muses upon the melancholy of memory. Its opening piano introduction falls by steps and thirds, with the occasional twist upwards; Vaughan Williams, in his settings of *Ten Blake Songs for Voice and Oboe*, written in 1957, responded in a similar way to Blake's style, and employed a similar melodic shape in the opening song, 'Infant Joy'.

Ex. 7.48a, Quilter, 'Dream Valley', opening
© Copyright 1917 by Winthrop Rogers Ltd.

Ex. 7.48b, Vaughan Williams, 'Infant Joy', bars 5–6
© Copyright 1958 Oxford University Press

The setting is strophic, but there are changes to the vocal line in the second verse; the various musical lines are sometimes repeated, prolonged slightly, the prolongation sometimes aided by a 3/2 bar, and the phrases characterised by a gentle rise and fall. The song is very delicate, atmospheric and understated, and Mark Raphael said of it that it 'flows gently on, as if in a trance'.[37]

Quilter arranged it for violin and piano: the score is marked 'for May Harrison', and she performed it with Quilter on 5 June 1917 at the Wigmore Hall. The vocal line is assigned to the violin which takes over part of the piano postlude; there are some tessitura alterations. He also added a cello obbligato part to the song (this score marked 'Monica Harrison' and was evidently intended for her to sing, with her sister Beatrice playing the cello part); the cello doubles the vocal line throughout, in unison, and doubles a fragment of the piano part in the postlude.

'The Wild Flower's Song' has a spareness similar to that of 'The Jocund Dance', with a hazy quality created by pedal notes, and parallel sixths which descend regardless of the harmonic clashes they cause. The pedal notes frequently are clusters of fifths sounding together: $\hat{1}$, $\hat{5}$, $\hat{2}$, $\hat{6}$. The central line 'But I met with scorn', as the wild flower tells how it seeks the delight of the morning and describes the adverse reaction it receives, is treated unusually, with a static accompaniment, and it has an unadorned – though very brief – directness and a harshness of harmony, before returning to the simplicity of the beginning.

Ex. 7.49, Quilter, 'The Wild Flower's Song', bars 18–20
© Copyright 1917 by Winthrop Rogers Ltd.

The first verse is repeated (Quilter's repetition, not Blake's) to make a *da capo*, like an echo, and with a child-like air. The song was finished on 3 March 1917, and the last song in the set was finished the following day.

'Daybreak' starts unpromisingly, as if it is determined to be robust at all costs, but the words inspire Quilter to an extraordinarily colourful and chromatic setting, akin to his Shelley settings. All the effort is in the piano part, supporting a slow-moving vocal line; Blake's images of a journey, a new beginning and

---

[37] Mark Raphael (1953–4).

mental strife are complex, and Quilter colours the sound at once with a major $\hat{6}$ in the minor key (E♭ minor); the slip to the tonic major (E♭ major) as the sun comes up towards the end of the song is that much easier as a result. The broadly falling piano line contrasts with the vocal line that soars upwards at its entry, its three-note motivic unit $\hat{5}$–$\hat{6}$♮–$\hat{8}$ seized upon by the piano part, to emerge ever more frequently until the sun finally begins to climb. Birdsong permeates the sound, while the singer-poet stands stock still, revelling in the joyous activity that surrounds him, that increases throughout the song.

These four Blake settings are very different from each other, and capture different facets of Blake's wonder and joy in life.

Articles in the journals of the day emphasised Quilter's attention to detail, the refinement, his grateful writing for the voice, and his debt to Elwes, which Quilter himself acknowledged. They commented on, and sometimes criticised, his lack of development of style, but were broadly agreed on the 'unforced natural charm which is the peculiar glory of the English countryside'.[38] In 1929, Hermon Ould wrote thankfully of Quilter's 'sound musicianship' and 'artistic conscience' in 'a desert of Stephen Adamses'.[39] In the broadcast of the radio programme *Music Weekly* on 23 October 1977, the singer Astra Desmond reported Quilter's comment about his love of poetry: 'You know, the trouble is, I almost love poetry more than music', and this was a claim he made throughout his life. Quilter's style demonstrates an extremely acute awareness of the layers of meaning in the texts, and his understanding is reflected in detail in the music: Mark Raphael pointed out that 'his accompaniments, harmonically fragrant, sweetly lyrical and rhythmically interesting, are a joy to all sensitive pianists'[40] and there is a tight integration between voice and piano, and craftsmanship at every point. This is especially noticeable in his settings of the earlier poets, whose complexity and intricacy of thought are so in tune with his own.

[38] Roger Holdin, 'Roger Quilter', *The Musical Mirror and Fanfare*, vol. XI (May 1931), pp. 158–9.
[39] Herman Ould, 'Two English Song-Writers: Roger Quilter and Cyril Scott', *English Review*, vol. XLVIII (April 1929), pp. 478–82.
[40] Mark Raphael (1953–4).

8

Songs and Choral Works: Part 2

In 1933, Ralph Hill summed up Quilter's style thus:

> The style of poetry that he is attracted by is the exact counterpart of his own musical style: polished workmanship, delicate sentiment, and graceful rhythm and imagery. Thus, if it is not Shakespeare and his contemporaries or the Jacobean poets, it is the fragrant lyrics of Blake, Shelley, or Tennyson. Quilter writes with intimate vocal understanding, and his melodies are flexible and expressive; but of equal importance are the accompaniments, with their colourful harmony and delightful turns of phrase: simple and unaffected, they are yet full of subtlety and point.[1]

On the other hand, Eric Blom commented – perhaps a little unfairly – 'His songs add music to poems as Arthur Rackham used to put pictures to books. They are always in the same manner, whatever the subject may be, but the manner is personal and tasteful'.[2] Scott Goddard, writing in 1925, was wholly scathing; he was clearly of the school that disliked English song, had no understanding of or sympathy for the validity of the Victorian drawing-room ballad, would much rather Quilter had been foreign, and damns him with faint praise: 'Influenced by the ballad composers of his youth, not untouched by the pertness of Sullivan, he yet towers above those of his kind. If in the company of Ravel and Pizzetti he is not to be noticed, in that of Teresa del Riego, Wilfred Sanderson and Graham Peel, he shines with a greater brilliance than any of them.'[3] He criticises Quilter because he finds his style 'confidential' and he seems quite unaware of Quilter's detailed interpretation of the texts. He was not the only one to find fault with Quilter's style: the columnist in *The Liverpool Echo* wrote, after a recital on 1 March 1923, 'One suspects that Mr. Roger Quilter finds it just a little too easy to write a song. Melody, one feels, is inherent in him, and he has only to turn on the tap, so to speak, for it to flow out. But the flow is not of even strength, and sometimes he writes very good melodies and sometimes not so good'.[4] The apparent ease of the finished product successfully hid the effort that went into a song.

---

[1] Ralph Hill, 'Exquisite Miniaturist', *Radio Times*, 25 August 1933.

[2] Eric Blom, *Music in England*, revised edn (West Drayton, 1947), pp. 267–8.

[3] Scott Goddard, 'The Art of Roger Quilter', *The Chesterian*, vol. VI, no. 47 (June 1925), pp. 213–17.

[4] *The Liverpool Echo*, 2 March 1923; the recital was by Dorothy Ledsome, with Quilter accompanying.

Quilter's opus numbers give an indication of when he began a composition, regardless of when he finished it. He worked slowly on all his compositions: he worked on them to a certain point and then left them to 'simmer' – this was clearly the process with 'Now Sleeps the Crimson Petal', 'Passing Dreams', 'Amaryllis at the Fountain' and for piano, 'Summer Evening' and the first Study, Op. 4, no. 1; it was also the process with the last four of the set of Jacobean lyrics. His view on melody was that 'melody must have an unbroken line', even if it sometimes made it difficult to decide where to breathe.[5]

Quilter's song-setting is rarely rigid or fixed, unless for special effect; he was acutely aware of English declamation and his vocal lines always allow the wide variation in stress that is part of the language.[6] What shows repeatedly is his extraordinary attention to detail and his total commitment to the words: his response to the text was at an immediate level, resulting in many instances where more layers of meaning are to be found in the songs than it would seem at first sight or hearing. He was aware of every nuance of a poetic phrase;[7] not for nothing did he claim that poetry meant almost more to him than music.[8]

His choice of subject is always acceptable – themes of love and nature are the most common, with many references to flowers and birds. Generic, indefinite images prevail, nothing taxing; so there is no Yeats, nor Hardy; nothing so robust. So far, so innocuous; but his song endings – that is, the notes on which the songs end – rarely feel definite, since he seldom gives the singer a tonic note on which to end: the *joie de vivre* that often accompanies an exuberant ending may give an initial feeling of certainty, but ultimately there is almost always a question mark, a suggestion of an alternative viewpoint and a reluctance to commit himself – or the singer – to something conclusive.

The seventeenth-century poets plainly found favour with Quilter: their detailed ideas, intricacies and conceits were in keeping with his own style. Blake was different, and his timeless themes brought out an altered quality; and the later poets are different again, much less involved in the complexities of the thoughts behind the words, than with the conjuring of images and feelings.

The setting of 'There be None of Beauty's Daughters', Op. 24, no. 1, is one such example. This, the first in the set of *Five English Love Lyrics*, was Quilter's only setting of a poem by Lord Byron (1788–1824); it dates from 1922, was published that year and dedicated to Roland Hayes. It compares Beauty's daughters unfavourably with the loved one, whose voice lulls the waves and the winds, and the continued description is mirrored in the through-composed

---

[5] Mark Raphael: notes for BBC Radio talk of October 1977. Not all the notes found their way into the final broadcast.

[6] Donald Tovey, *Words and Music*, from *Essays and Lectures in Music* (Oxford, 1949), pp. 202–19, especially p. 213.

[7] In Sir Quintin Hill's obituary ('Roger Quilter: 1877–1953', *Music and Letters*, vol. XXXV (1954), pp. 15–16), Hill explains, 'Once when repeating Ophelia's song [Quilter] remarked; "You and I would have been pleased with 'At his feet a stone'; but Shakespeare says 'At his heels a stone'"'.

[8] Astra Desmond reminiscing about Quilter in a programme broadcast on BBC Radio 3 on 23 October 1977; see p. 163.

setting (though the two verses have a similar introduction), and the calmness of the waves is described using adjacent chords of B♭ major and A major (against a tonic of E♭ major). Harmonically, the song is unadventurous but this matches the still sentiment of the poem.

After Shakespeare and Herrick, Quilter set more Shelley (1792–1822) than any other poet and his first Shelley setting became one of his most famous songs. 'Love's Philosophy' was published in 1905 and was grouped with two others – one, 'Now Sleeps the Crimson Petal', already published – to make the set of *Three Songs*, Op. 3; Quilter wrote in Elwes's Visitors' Book a brief quotation from it during a visit probably in late 1904, suggesting a composition date of around that time; the quote is marked 'Quick and passionate', a more vivid instruction than the published 'Molto allegro con moto'.

The accompaniment, though difficult, is extremely pianistic, but the phrases are four-square and symmetrical – rather dull compared with the balanced asymmetry so often found in his better songs – the two verses are broadly the same, the second altered to make a high-note climax, and the harmonies are straightforward. However, the evocation of distant images typical of Shelley seems to have inspired a particular kind of sound in Quilter, a mercurial quality common to all his Shelley settings. Despite the words not matching the music – the plaintive lover wants a kiss from the beloved, a mood at odds with the cheerfully bubbling texture – the sheer exuberance of the music makes the song a showpiece and the lover presumably wins a kiss during the piano's postlude; Delius takes the end of his earlier setting in a more subdued direction, the mood matching the text rather better.

It was some time before Quilter set Shelley again, the years between being largely taken up with the seventeenth-century poets. It was a worthwhile wait, although Quilter's Shelley style did not emerge fully until his setting of the Indian Serenade, 'I Arise from Dreams of Thee'. In the meantime appeared the mellifluous 'Music, When Soft Voices Die', the fifth of *Six Songs*, Op. 25, each song published separately and then brought together as a set. This – it concerns love and memory – was written in 1926 and published in 1927 and was dedicated to Quilter's niece, Norah Nichols. The use of sequential phrases, each higher than the previous, links each of the statements to each other; within the warm tonic of A♭ major, all the phrases are made harmonious by parallel thirds or sixths between voice and piano, and the highest note for the singer is at the start of the fourth statement, on the word 'Love'; it is the climax, but very subdued – the loudest dynamic marking is *mp*.

Exotic images – the Arabic, the Indian – were readily found in texts and songs throughout much of the nineteenth century;[9] Shelley's poem 'From the Arabic, An Imitation' was one example. Quilter's setting (he renamed it 'Arab Love Song') is highly dramatic, its duple quavers in the voice against piano triplets imitating hoofbeats, the cross-rhythms turbulent and urgent. The words are

---

[9] See Jonathan Bellman, *The Exotic in Western Music* (Boston, 1998) for a collection of excellent essays on the broad topic.

written from the woman's view, she feeling faint and aware that her lover is so far away, comparing her thirst for him with that of a hind thirsty for water at noon. Against a tonic of C minor, the harmonies shift constantly, with frequent, implied, changes of key, never actually resolving, continually avoiding a decision. Against F minor, the dominant C major chord with added seventh and ninth is juxtaposed with a subdominant chord: the raised D♮ and E♮ lift the colour, and the second inversion chords create a sense of anticipation and onward movement – their strange sound coming from the strong diminished fifths – backed by downward scales in the bass, often chromatic.

Ex. 8.1, Quilter, 'Arab Love Song', bars 10–11
© Copyright 1927 by Hawkes & Son (London) Ltd.

'Arab Love Song' was the fourth in the Op. 25 set; it was published in 1927 and was dedicated to Mary Kinsley Rogers, Winthrop Rogers's widow.

'I Arise from Dreams of Thee' was a text that was frequently set, and more usually known as the 'Indian Serenade'. Quilter's offering, Op. 29, was known primarily as a song for tenor and orchestra, though there are earlier manuscripts for voice and piano (and it was the voice and piano version that was published). One, in C♯ minor, is not in Quilter's hand, though it has annotations that are, and it is dated 1928; the hand has marked similarities with scores known to have been written by Leslie Woodgate, who was working for Quilter until 1929. Another manuscript, in the same key, is in Quilter's hand; it has numerous small differences from the other manuscript and is undated. The published version of the song (in E♭ minor and C minor) is close to Quilter's autograph manuscript, but also has further differences; it is dated 1929 and was published in 1931. The unpublished orchestral score, in E♭ minor, is in Quilter's hand and is marked 'for Tenor Voice and Orchestra' – Quilter wrote to Grainger that 'I arranged it also for rather high *baritone* but *tenor* is the original key'[10] – and it was first performed at the Harrogate Festival in July 1929, with Mark Raphael. Later, Grainger wrote to Quilter, discussing the scoring, that 'the voice did not come thru, but then, it was a baritone & not a tenor'.[11] The opus number suggests that it was begun in the mid-1920s.

[10] Quilter to Grainger, 9 July 1932, GM.
[11] Grainger to Quilter, 17 April 1935, GM.

Ex. 8.2a, Quilter, 'I Arise from Dreams of Thee', 1928 MS (Woodgate)

Ex. 8.2b, Quilter, 'I Arise from Dreams of Thee', published voice and piano version (dated 1929), and MS (Quilter)

Ex. 8.2c, Quilter, 'I Arise from Dreams of Thee', 1929 orchestral score
(transposed to C♯ minor)
© Copyright 1931 by Boosey & Co. Ltd.

The precise circumstances of the creation of 'I Arise' thus remain enigmatic. It seems probable that the original version of the song was – as usual with Quilter – for voice and piano, that it was in E♭ minor (with Mark Raphael singing it a tone lower), and he then orchestrated it, in response to the need for an item for the Harrogate Festival. Examples 8.2a–c, following the key of the oldest manuscript, illustrate the differences between the versions. The 1928 version is slightly thicker than the later voice and piano versions; the orchestral allows more inner melodies. One of the most notable differences between the versions is that the Woodgate manuscript sustains the very last chord over one bar and a crotchet, and all other versions sustain it over two bars and a crotchet. The published score (for voice and piano, in E♭ minor) is the one considered here, because of its accessibility. Quilter opens with an atmospheric use of major thirds, descending chromatically, over a dominant pedal; when the voice enters, it is on a short rising scale, $\hat{5}$–$\hat{6}$–$\hat{7}$ of the melodic minor scale; when the line drops to $\hat{3}$, the resulting augmented triad reinforces the sense of being in another world.

Ex. 8.3, Quilter, 'I Arise from Dreams of Thee', tenor entry
© Copyright 1931 by Boosey & Co. Ltd.

As with 'Arab Love Song', the harmonic changes are swift and ephemeral, with hints of keys to come, avoided at the last moment: E♭ minor, A♭ major, G♭ major, D♭ major, G♭ major again. None of these is definite, but suddenly from the mêlée of chromatic chords emerges a shift to D major and a modicum of stability (in the C♯ minor version, this brief section – just a bar and a half, from bar 19 to partway through bar 20 – is on white notes only; in the E♭ minor version, the result is a shift from flat to sharp keys), as the poet – dreaming of his loved one – finds himself led to her window. (In the orchestral score, this section, bars 19–24, is notated in D major; in all the voice and piano scores, the opening key signature is retained, with accidentals as required.) A suggestion of a cadence in A♭ major metamorphoses into one in G major, and the cluttered, claustrophobic texture of the opening dissolves into more sparse triplets of 'the wand'ring airs'. A pentatonic melody appears three times, starting on different notes of the G major chord; at the last appearance, the voice enters; and birdsong imitation accompanies mention of the nightingale, which remains audible to the end. The harmonic changes arise through use of pivot notes, passing through G major, B major, back to G major, D major, A major; a diminished seventh chord on A that includes C♯ slips to C major; falling major thirds – linking to the opening – with brief forays to F major and finally an enharmonic shift F♯/G♭ back to the recapitulating E♭ minor, as the poet proclaims his imminent demise. At the end, an inversion of the opening falling thirds, against the tonic major, proclaims clearly and with relief that dawn has come.

The vocal line on the whole remains subdued – most of the dynamic markings are *piano* or *mezzo piano*, with only one *forte* to relieve the tension of such relatively wild harmonies. The piano part is complex, though it was not the first time Quilter had painted such colours: his piano piece 'Summer Evening' has similar touches of impressionism, and images of dusk, night and dawn triggered a particular reaction from him. The orchestral version, sparkling with a particularly French colour, opens with horns, haunting and distant (and marked *misterioso*), and tremolo strings which soon emphasise the words 'night' and 'winds'; Quilter uses the clarinet in his customary melancholy way and a solo violin accompanies the poet to his lover's chamber window, not returning until the very end. The lower brass is used sparingly and is silent once the solo violin returns, at which point the harp adds gentle splashes of colour.

Generally, the scoring provides a very sympathetic support for the text although Quilter and Grainger discussed alternative orchestrations, including the use of a muted trombone with pizzicato strings, to accommodate singers with smaller voices. The original orchestration consisted of two flutes, one oboe, two clarinets, one bassoon, two horns, two trumpets, three trombones, timpani, harp and strings, and when it was broadcast in a Promenade Concert on Sunday 7 May 1933, its instrumentation was the same, but with double woodwind; Heddle Nash was the tenor soloist. Grainger told Quilter, 'You wrote of not being satisfied with the orchestration – but it seems to me the orchestration at

Harrogate was lovely & effective'.[12] Grainger arranged the first performances of 'I Arise' in Australia; it was performed in Adelaide, broadcast on Australian radio, performed in Sydney in September 1935, and in Dunedin, New Zealand, in November the same year. It is, however, many years since it was last heard in its orchestral version.

'I Arise' has a disturbed quality, as if the poet is struggling to find his way out of a nightmare. Quilter cannot treat these words as he treats Herrick. Those settings are responses to the refined precision of the texts, but in Shelley's words he found an emotional madness to which he responded in a different way. The strange magic of the song and its shimmering textures are achieved with augmented harmonies, multiple cross-rhythms, and layers upon layers of sound. The song – in both piano and orchestral versions – is perfumed, passionate, highly emotional, intoxicating, indulgent and gloriously sensuous. It was dedicated to Robert Allerton, Quilter's lover from before the First World War; there is no explanation for the extended gap between their relationship and the dedication, other than the long gestation period that some of Quilter's songs needed.

'Music and Moonlight' is a very muted song in comparison. It is dated January 1935; one manuscript has minor differences from the published version, one of which is the opening direction, which shows *Allegretto grazioso con moto* where all other manuscripts, and the published version, show *Un poco allegro con grazia*. The song was published by Chappell in 1935. It has a similar chromaticism to 'I Arise', an inner line e♮^{1}, f^1, f♯^{1}, g^1, that adds a gleam to the sound, especially the e♮^{1} (ex. 8.4).

Ex. 8.4, Quilter, 'Music and Moonlight', introduction to second verse, MS version

Its lilt comes from the 6/8 time, and the strummed arpeggios were clearly influenced by mention of the guitar. Its harmonies are driven by pivot notes again, with chords of F major, A♭ major, and the dominant seventh (the tonic is E♭ major), and the raised $\hat{2}$ and $\hat{4}$ in the penultimate chord add a final piquant splash of colour. It is set at night (again) and compares the 'soft splendour' of the moon, against the starlight, with Jane's voice, which gives soul to the guitar strings. It has a filigree delicacy, but surprisingly it has no opus number, nor a dedication, but it does come in a version for duet.

The next setting, 'One Word is Too Often Profaned', is especially sad. It is

---

[12] Grainger to Quilter, 9 August 1932, GM.

dated 1946 (and published in 1947); in the latter half of that year, Quilter was in St Andrew's Hospital, and in the first half, his mental state was deteriorating and this song was presumably written during those early months. The poet asks the loved one to accept not love, but worship, in a flowing but very diatonic and unexciting setting.

In 'Music', Quilter redeems himself a little, though it harks back disappointingly – because so unoriginally – to the toccata nature of the accompaniment to 'Love's Philosophy'. Quilter set only the first two verses (Shelley did not complete the others), repeating the first to make a ternary-form song. Shelley's direct images 'My heart in its thirst is a dying flower' receive a direct treatment, but the song says too little that is new, and there are too many clichés. It is dated 1947, and was published in 1948.

Ex. 8.5, Quilter, 'Music', opening 6 bars

'Far, Far Away' is included here because although it is incomplete – unreconstructably so – it is typical of the best of Quilter's Shelley settings. Melodically, it has some resemblance to 'Music, When Soft Voices Die' though it clearly is meant to move more quickly: it is marked *Andante moderato ma con moto* and the piano part is marked *Poco appassionato*. It bears more resemblance, however, to 'Drooping Wings' of 1944 and the sentiments are similarly bleak. What little there is in the extant manuscript is more than enough to be tantalising (see ex. 8.6). It is clearly work in progress; why Quilter never finished it is unknown, though it may be that 'Drooping Wings' is in fact a major reworking of it. Its date is unknown. There is a fragment of another Shelley setting ('To Night', which begins 'Swiftly walk over the western wave', another atmospheric lyric), but it shows extremely confused and nonsensical writing, and may date from Quilter's time in St Andrew's Hospital.

Ex. 8.6, Quilter, 'Far, far away', first verse

There were several exceptions (not least the Shelley settings), but the poems of the late eighteenth and nineteenth centuries that Quilter chose to set were all too often uninspiring and rarely provided more than barely adequate vehicles for him; one can only wonder why he chose them. They were generally products of his later years, too, and the combination of simple texts, often homely in idiom, and the reduction in Quilter's compositional effort as he grew older was an unprofitable one.

'Where be You Going?', a simple love lyric and a quasi folk song by John Keats (1795–1821), the second of *Six Songs*, Op. 18, is an unprepossessing text and Quilter perhaps realised it. It was a moderately popular text, set by Bridge (in 1903), O'Neill (in about 1910) and Holbrooke (in 1909), so that Quilter's setting was very much of its period. Unusually, the voice ends on the tonic and Quilter enjoyed the opportunity, presented by the outdoor scene, for birdsong. The 4/8 time signature is unique in Quilter's output. It was published in 1914 and dedicated to Harry Plunket Greene, son-in-law to Sir Hubert Parry. Greene was a fine singer, and an exponent of the art of singing; he well understood the nature of phrasing, and probably made more of a success of this song than it deserved.

'To a Harebell by a Graveside' was one of two Darley partsong settings; George Darley (1795–1846) was an acerbic Irish critic, more known for his prose than his poetry, with a great interest in the style of the Elizabethans. In this song, he values a humble flower over man's hypocrisy. Set for sopranos and altos, with piano accompaniment, it is dated 1938 and was published that year. Pivot note modulations are predictable and provide some small variety, and it is simple and pretty, but overall the song does very little more than add to the SA choral repertoire.

'Farewell to Shan-Avon' is a curious choice of text: not Quilter's usual kind though he clearly saw some choral possibilities in it. It was set for unaccompanied men's chorus (two tenor lines, baritone and bass) and was published in 1946. The score explains that the poem is from 'The Fight of the Forlorn' and that it is a 'romantic ballad founded on the History of Ireland'. It opens with a vigorous battle cry which punctuates the song at intervals, and though the texture varies, it is mostly close harmony, albeit with good part-writing. Dissonances on the word 'Long' emphasise the word within its line: 'Long, Oh! long in vain'. The song is subtitled 'Song of the Forlorn Warriors', the warriors mourning their departure from the river Shannon ('Shan-Avon') and the Mountains of Mourne.

An unpublished song 'What Will You Do, Love?' was an arrangement of a song by Samuel Lover (1797–1868), another Irishman, one of many talents, being novelist, playwright, song-writer, poet and artist. The manuscript is marked 'for Arnold' and dated June 1942, about the time Arnold Vivian was sent out to the Middle East. The words describe Quilter's feelings: 'What will you do, love, when waves divide us . . . I'll still be true, And I'll pray for you on the stormy ocean, In deep devotion.' The words are repeated in their entirety, the second time with the accompaniment an octave higher to rend the heartstrings, but as so often with Quilter's arrangements, there is a beguiling simplicity that appeals. Why Quilter left it unpublished is unknown; possibly it was too clearly personal.

'The Time of Roses', with words by Thomas Hood (1799–1845), was written in 1928 and published that year, and is the fifth and last of the *Five English Love Lyrics*, Op. 24; the poems in that set thus span a period of over two hundred years. The wistful text tells of love that began in the time of roses, but ends in the twilight of winter time. Melodies within the introduction (which starts in the minor) hint at the vocal line to come; the vocal line starts in the major, and the tonality mingles and alternates until the end, when, in a mood of regret, it briefly considers the possibility of a cadence on to the relative major but sideslips instead onto the tonic major, rather as Quilter did a little later in 'If Love Should Pass Me By', from *Julia* and *Love at the Inn*. This pleasing little song was dedicated to Quilter's sister Maude.

Quilter's setting of 'If Thou Would'st Ease Thine Heart' by Thomas Beddoes (1803–49) was unpublished and its whereabouts are now unknown.

The three songs comprising Op. 3 were grouped together arbitrarily. Quilter thought the central one 'no good at the time . . . but it [became] one of his most popular works'.[13] 'Now Sleeps the Crimson Petal' is one of Quilter's best-known songs; it is recorded frequently, and regularly broadcast. Elwes sang it extensively from early on in his career and his gracious artistry was an effective advertisement. Though it draws criticism now for its alleged 'cloying sentimentality',[14] it did not do so then. Its very unity, simplicity and consistency seemed to speak directly to performers and audience.

The manuscript is dated March 1897; it was revised substantially before publication in 1904. It was revised further in 1946, but the changes were generally minor, though the most significant one was made at Mark Raphael's suggestion: the group of four semiquavers at the end of the second verse ('slip into my') are changed to a triplet ('into my'), thus retaining the original words ('slip' is otherwise repeated) and making it easier to sing since the double consonant 'sl' is not easy to sing softly on a high note. However, many performers retain the original semiquavers while adopting the other changes, and some post-1946 singers retain the 1904 version in its entirety.

The poem was by Alfred, Lord Tennyson (1809–92), from *The Princess; A Medley*. This was Tennyson's first large-scale work, written in 1847 when he was 38, but 'Now Sleeps' was not in the original version; he added it and the other lyrical poems (most were placed between the cantos, though 'Now Sleeps' is placed within canto 7) for the second edition of 1850. The poem consists of 14 lines, grouped 4–2–2–2–4, each group of lines beginning with the word 'Now' and ending with the word 'me':

> Now sleeps the crimson petal, now the white;
> Nor waves the cypress in the palace walk;
> Nor winks the gold fin in the porphyry font:
> The firefly wakens: waken thou with me.
>
> Now droops the milk-white peacock like a ghost,
> And like a ghost she glimmers on to me.
>
> Now lies the Earth all Danaë to the stars,
> And all thy heart lies open unto me.
>
> Now slides the silent meteor on, and leaves
> A shining furrow, as thy thoughts in me.
>
> Now folds the lily all her sweetness up,
> And slips into the bosom of the lake:
> So fold thyself, my dearest, thou, and slip
> Into my bosom and be lost in me.

The poem is set at dusk and the imagery of the outer verses is inward, downward and firmly earthbound, in strong contrast with the outward-facing

---

[13] Donald Brook, *Composers' Gallery* (London, 1946).
[14] Stephen Banfield (1985); however, in his sleeve notes for David Wilson-Johnson's recording of Quilter songs (1986), he relaxes his strictures somewhat.

central couplets, with the outdoor peacock, the distance of the ghostly image and the images of stars and meteors. Quilter focused wholly on the introverted level, and omitted the central six lines, leaving two balanced stanzas under-pinned by a series of descending scales of E♭ major, which focus attention on the ever-descending mood. Britten also set the poem (in 1943, for tenor and orchestra), but set it in its entirety; he too seems to have been aware of the sense of direction, since the musical lines for the central stanzas continually rise.

In his original manuscript, Quilter's piano introduction comes to a full stop before the first voice entry, but by the time of the first published version, he has found a way to develop the line more fluidly, while retaining the pattern of alternating 5/4 and 3/4 bars. The vocal lines are long and extended – generally, each vocal phrase begins with a quaver rest and the last note in each poem's line falls on a main beat; the last lines in each verse are treated slightly differently.

Though Tennyson's text was often set, it was Quilter's setting that dominated the field and its influence on later settings is often very clear – Eric Thiman's setting of 1938, for example, also omits words (only the central couplet) but has a prolonged upbeat, and alternates time signatures, though less so than Quilter, and only uses 3/4 and 4/4. Britten's setting is more rigid rhythmically, but is set in compound time; its lullaby rocking motion is reinforced by the hypnotic ostinato accompaniment; Quilter's setting was, incidentally, a favourite of Britten's mother.

In the original poem – 'so fold thyself, my dearest, thou, and slip / Into my bosom' – so many commas slow the movement, while 'slip' is short, leading readily and fluently on to the next word. But Quilter's repetition of the word 'slip' marks and highlights the start of one of the structural E♭ major scales – the last one, after which all will be still; this was the only word repeated in the 1897 version. The 1897 and 1904 versions, in repeating 'slip', set it into semiquavers. The triplet version of 1946 changes the stress radically, highlights what can only be seen as a minor word 'into', and eliminates what was otherwise a strong point well made. It would have been better had Quilter retained the original figuration, and the sense of balance that he so surely had even as a nineteen-year-old. On the other hand, the change in the bass line in bars 5 and 16 is beneficial and the counterpoint is smoother by virtue of the contrary motion that is introduced. This is the only song that Quilter revised that was published in both versions; the differences are shown in ex. 8.7. Quilter arranged the song for voice, strings and piano or harp, but it was not published, nor dated, though it is later than 1946.

The partsong 'The Starlings', text by Charles Kingsley (1819–75), first made an appearance in 1904 but was not published until 1938, and nothing was heard of it in between. It is possible that the 1938 two-part SA setting with piano accompaniment has no connection with the earlier version, which had been performed as a solo song; but on the other hand, the alto part is to be found almost completely within the piano part, raising the possibility that it was derived from the accompaniment. The soprano line is independent. It is a fresh-sounding, pretty song, delicate, with a touch of wistfulness: the starlings are sad

Ex. 8.7, Quilter, 'Now Sleeps the Crimson Petal', differences between the 1904 and
1946 version

in March that they are weary with nest-building, and in autumn they are sad
that the year is 'all but done'.

There are two settings of Christina Rossetti (1830–94), 'Should One of Us
Remember' and 'When I am Dead, My Dearest'. The manuscripts exist but are

untraceable, although the second one may be the same as 'A Song at Parting'. This strophic setting, with four-bar phrases, was appropriate to an older demand for ballads, but not in 1952, when it was published. Quilter missed opportunities, prevented any kind of sympathetic treatment by setting it in a stultifying common time, and could not break out of the prison he had made for himself. Although the manuscript is undated, the song may have been written in 1898, as was the other Rossetti setting. Ireland's lovely setting of 1928 is very fluid, despite being in 2/4.

Quilter said of the translation to his partsong setting of verses from 'Omar Khayām' that it was made by E. A Johnson, the father of a female friend; assuming that the young lady was a contemporary, the father might thus have been born in the 1840s or so, but the song is placed at this point, because 'Omar Khayām' (whatever the spelling) is inescapably identified with Edward Fitzgerald (1809–83). The unaccompanied five-part setting is for alto, tenor, second tenor (or baritone), first and second basses, the score is dated 31 May 1902, and the text reads:

> Bring wine, for wine alone may quench the fire
> Of fleeting hope and unfulfilled desire,
> Wake! for in waking sleep shall find its crown,
> Youth's ardour faileth fast, the strong shall tire
> Bring wine, for wine alone may quench the fire
> Of fleeting hope and unfulfilled desire.
>
> Perchance the cup to which my lips are pressed
> Has lived and loved ere yet it sank to rest,
> The very handle that my fingers clasp
> Has lain in rapture on a woman's breast.
>
> Drink! in forgetfulness thy wounded soul
> May find a moment's peace though round thee roll
> The wildest floods of grief, thou need'st not fear.
> Thine ark of safety is the brimming bowl.

This is Quilter's first extant partsong, and in it he established his style of choral writing – broadly chordal, with some imitative writing, some repetition of words, the melody moving around the voices, with twists of harmony as the parts move slightly. Grainger was as enthusiastic as ever when he wrote to Quilter about it:

> And this is what I worship in you more than all yr other lovely gifts – the way you modulate away into a new key-lane, the way a moving part lands you in a new harmony. That is why I like the Omar Khayām chorus especially (its text leads to a bolder spread of FORM that [sic] Elisabethan verse) – that it throws itself around & UP_HEAVES more unexpectedly.[15]

The outer sections are in C major, the central one, treated far more chromatically, in A♭ major; at first hearing, the words seem independent of

---

[15] Grainger to Quilter, 21 July 1947, GM.

the setting, but there is some musical cohesion within its through-composition, though more variety of texture would have relieved the dense writing. The use of second inversions at the start of phrases is reminiscent of the style of a reverential church anthem, though Quilter had worked this out of his system by the time of his first published partsongs, the two Herrick settings of 1904. But the wistful nature of the text, in spite of its drinking-song context, was bound to appeal to Quilter, and his response, though restrained, is a genuine one.

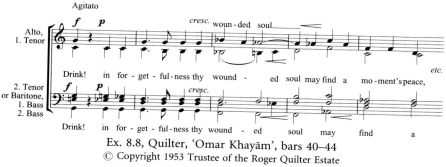

Ex. 8.8, Quilter, 'Omar Khayām', bars 40–44

In the third and last of the Op. 3 set, 'Fill a Glass with Golden Wine', published in 1905, Henley's words start each verse positively, a mood that Quilter responds to, with a drinking-song exuberance, but the cynicism of the words is not matched by the music; the regularity of the phrase length rides roughshod over the varying line lengths of the test, the music for 'Ev'ry kiss' sounding as if it is a new phrase, rather than part of the previous one. The first verse is repeated, with a word repetition 'Leaves us less of life, less of life to live' to enable a high note on the second 'life'.

Ex. 8.9, Quilter, 'Fill a Glass with Golden Wine', bars 7–12

Quilter would have had much sympathy with William Henley (1849–1903), who had severe ill-health to contend with throughout his life. Besides 'Fill a Glass', Quilter set two other Henley lyrics, both included in the Op. 14 set of *Four Songs*, published in 1910 and dedicated to Robin (music critic of the *Daily Telegraph*) and Aimée Legge. The first of these was placed third in the set, 'A Last Year's Rose', a bubbling song and one which did not tempt Quilter to imitate birdsong, despite the significance of the nightingale.

Henley's turn of phrase is deft, treated thankfully and fairly flexibly, the ten lines (two of them with only two stresses, compared with normal four) set to twelve bars in both verses but in different ways. 'Fading' is repeated in the first verse, and 'silence' in the second, reinforcing the sentiment. The nightingale sings exultingly to the rose, and the boldly rising lines of the piano introduction are exultant too, but each verse ends poignantly.

Ex. 8.10, Quilter, 'A Last Year's Rose', end of first verse
© Copyright 1910 by Boosey & Co. Ltd.

The last Henley setting was fourth in the set of *Four Songs*, 'Song of the Blackbird', not to be confused with Cyril Scott's extremely popular 'Blackbird's Song', which was to words by Rosemary Marriott Watson. The words provide plenty of opportunity here for imitative birdsong, and Quilter based the opening on a blackbird's song that he had once heard, but that is all the words can do: 'The Nightingale has a lyre of gold,/ The Lark's is a clarion call,/ And the Blackbird plays but a boxwood flute,/ But I love him best of all' does not augur well. Yet Quilter's setting is an especially happy one, marked *brillante e scherzoso*, musically undemanding, not amongst his best songs by any means, but with a warm chromaticism that lifts it. Elwes's recording of it (and Frederick Kiddle's fine playing) shows what it is capable of.

The powerful poetry of Sir William Watson (1858–1935) was often a response to political events; it is imaginative and strong. Generally, those poems would not be amenable to setting to music, certainly not by Quilter, and indeed it was not one of that style of Watson's that he set. 'April', the second of the *Four Songs*, is a pretty little song despite embarrassing words: 'April, April,/ Laugh thy girlish laughter;/ Then, the moment after,/ Weep thy girlish tears'; its balletic waltz lilt comes from the emphasis on the second beat of the bar. Voice and piano are linked motivically by leaps of fourths, fifths and octaves.

The first of that set was 'Autumn Evening', to words by Arthur Maquarie from *The Wheel of Life*, a collection of poems published in 1909: it is set at a graveside and the original title of the poem was 'Allerseelen'. The text verges on the maudlin, but is rescued by the setting, whose stillness, established by a pedal tonic and by slowly moving thirds and sixths and the mournful Aeolian mode, is most moving. Mark Raphael commented that 'on the words "the breath of Autumn evening chills," the change of mood momentarily creates an icy tenseness'.[16] He misremembered the words: it is 'early evening', not 'Autumn evening', but the fleeting move, up a semitone to the flat supertonic, on a second inversion for added tension, is indeed as telling, as the move to the relative major for the middle verse is magical. The piano part is closely integrated with the voice line, and imitative, and the phrases in the outer verses are adjusted to suit the punctuation and sense of the text. Quilter is often at his best when he writes conversationally, fluidly following the natural word rhythm, and this song, one of his finest, is one such example. At the end, the voice's descent by step to 5̂ is heart-breaking.

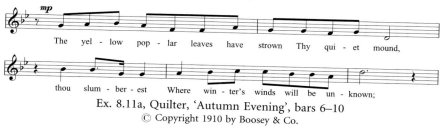

Ex. 8.11a, Quilter, 'Autumn Evening', bars 6–10
© Copyright 1910 by Boosey & Co.

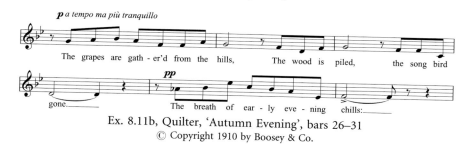

Ex. 8.11b, Quilter, 'Autumn Evening', bars 26–31
© Copyright 1910 by Boosey & Co.

By the opus number, Op. 5, the *Four Child Songs*, settings of Robert Louis Stevenson (1850–94), date from 1905; the manuscript date is 1914, but this only indicates the date of revision, ready for publication the same year. The original manuscript is lost or destroyed and the fourth song is no longer performed because although its jingoism was normal for the time, a century later it is deemed excessive, even though it is jingoism in the mouth of a child.

Quilter dedicated the set to his sister Norah: she had two young children, Eustace and Ruby. The poems are taken from Robert Louis Stevenson's *A Child's Garden of Verses*, though – as Stephen Banfield comments – whether the

---

[16] Mark Raphael, Obituary, 'Roger Quilter: 1877–1953, the man and his songs', *Tempo*, vol. 30 (1953–4), p. 20.

poems are intended for a child, or display wishful thinking on the part of an adult, is debatable.[17]

The regular stresses of the first song, 'A Good Child', hold any setting in a deadly embrace. Quilter tries to avoid the rhythmic straitjacket by setting it in 3/4 and extending the phrases, either by repeating a line or by adding in an extra bar of accompaniment: artificial ploys. Simple tonic–dominant harmonies fit simple words. The second song, 'The Lamplighter', also restrictive in its rhythmic possibilities, is set in 4/4, with simple rows of quavers and the occasional dotted rhythm.

These first two songs describe mundane scenes: a day in the life of a good child, and at bedtime, watching the lamplighter going his rounds. The words of the third song, 'Where Go the Boats?', are more open, with more far-reaching images. Quilter sets a secure tonic pedal which lasts through the first ten bars before moving to a conventional dominant. Above it, part-writing allows quavers to weave between the voices, constantly overlapping, and the voice itself picks out certain notes to create its line. The dactylic word rhythms remain a restriction, but the song is calm and supports, by its stillness, the sense of the strong ever-flowing river. It is one of Quilter's simple, haunting songs, and it lingers in the mind.

The last song was considered 'very bright and winsome';[18] Quilter circumvents the restrictive rhythms of its text inventively (ex. 8.12).

Ex. 8.12, Quilter, rhythm of 'Foreign Children'
© Copyright 1914 Chappell Music Ltd., London W6 8BS. All Rights Reserved

Parallel fourths and fifths are a common code to indicate that we are in exotic climes; one familiar example is Luigini's *Ballet Egyptien* of 1875 wherein abide all manner of fourths, fifths and pentatonic scales, and such devices were used typically in films of the 1920s and 30s (and later) to indicate a change of scene to the Orient, or the presence of Chinese or Japanese elements; Hoagy Carmichael's song 'Hong Kong Blues', from the 1944 film *To Have and Have Not*, is a memorable example.[19] Overall, the *Child Songs* are disappointing; Quilter let himself be distracted by pretty words and – except for 'Where Go the Boats?' – could not rise above them. In 1945, Chappell published a partsong arrangement by him of it, for soprano and alto. It is a tone lower, in G major, and there are

[17] Stephen Banfield, *Sensibility and English Song* (Cambridge, 1985), p. 114.
[18] George Lowe, 'The Music of Roger Quilter', *Musical Opinion and Music Trade Review*, vol. 496 (Jan 1919), pp. 210–11.
[19] See Bellman (1998) for a wider discussion of the whole area.

some changes to the accompaniment, affecting the sonorities of the bass line slightly, but it is otherwise unaltered and makes an unpretentious and attractive piece.

Quilter's next settings of Stevenson, *Two Songs*, Op. 26, are very different. Stevenson's verses are considerably richer than those used for the *Child Songs*, and inspire Quilter to far greater things, though equally remarkably, it is 'Over the Land is April' that has been recorded, a privilege apparently denied 'In the Highlands', despite it being the more satisfying song.

When Quilter set later poets, he tended to choose simple texts, calling for a simple approach, on straightforward themes of nature, the seasons, and love: the bread and butter of the Victorian ballad. Occasionally a text takes one of those themes and captures something beyond the obvious, and so it is here. 'In the Highlands' opens conversationally and musingly, in nostalgic mood for the Highlands of Scotland, the vocal line matching the word rhythm, pentatonic for three bars. The key shifts play around a diminished chord, from the tonic Eb major, to Gb major, back through the tonic and to C major. After setting the scene with images of the people of the land, the first change of key, to Gb major, accompanies 'essential silence'; then back to the tonic for the music of the spirit of the hills, with again an almost completely pentatonic line. As the singer becomes more agitated with longing and memories, the harmonic rhythm accelerates, moving down to C major, then up to E major and G major, to G minor as the night falls, finally coming to rest as the singer dreams of being there and at peace; although the song is in ternary form, the recapitulation is harmonised with a second inversion tonic chord, not the root position as at the beginning; the anticipation is exquisite. The atmosphere of the song in the central section derives from the wash of sound, in the piano triplets, cross-rhythms, hints of birdsong; the open texture matches the quiet imaginative voice of the outer verses, and the final phrase, as with the end of the first verse, falls gradually across an octave and a fourth. Stevenson's pacing is clear from the text, and Quilter has seen it, accepted it, and clothed it.

'Over the Land is April' was the second of the pair; they were both dedicated to Quilter's friends Louis de Glehn and his Scottish wife Dinah (who doubtless appreciated the choice of Stevenson), and both songs were written in June 1922 and published that year. 'Over the Land' is attractive, but superficial, and far inferior to 'In the Highlands', though Quilter and Raphael chose to record it in 1934, and Raphael wrote that 'audiences . . . enjoy the throbbing urge of "Over the Land is April"'.[20] In simple ternary form, the third verse is a repeat of the first; the text was unfinished, and Quilter adapted the words to suit his purpose; that does not matter, except that the words are repetitive: by the end, the listener is secure in the knowledge that the mountain is both high and brown. Diatonic writing is interspersed with modulations to the mediant major (E major), laboured and just a little cloying, but the modulations to the flat

---

[20] Mark Raphael (1953–4), p. 20.

mediant (E♭ major), which 'In the Highlands' tends to favour, are sweet and colourful.

Stevenson's vigorous style comes off well in the accompanied soprano–alto partsong 'Windy Nights'. The song is in common time, treated largely as 12/8, given the presence of a man riding; the piano part is an integral part of the song, since it is this, so to speak, that provides the horse. Quilter brings urgency to the setting with the canonic treatment of 'Late in the night/ When the fires are out'. Short, strophic, and sweet, it is over almost before it is begun, but since the horseman is galloping by, that is as it should be; it is an excellent partsong.

Ex. 8.13, Quilter, 'Windy Nights', bars 13–16

The settings of two poems by Mary Coleridge (1861–1907) reflect the tinge of mysticism for which she was admired: 'Through the Sunny Garden' has a sense of the stillness of a hot summer's afternoon, arising from its use of a tonic and dominant pedal for much of the first verse (the D♯ major chord under the word 'bees' has a descriptive piquancy), and the whole-tone sequential shifts in bars 11 and 12, with consequent augmented sound, are delicately magical. The repeat of the first two lines, with different harmonies for the humming bees (a flat submediant), adds to the atmosphere. Both songs were dedicated to the contralto Muriel Foster, and were published as a pair in 1916, called *Two September Songs*, Op. 18.

Ex. 8.14, Quilter, 'Through the Sunny Garden', bars 11–12
© Copyright 1916 Elkin & Co. Ltd.

The second song, 'The Valley and the Hill', plays between D minor and D major; its original metronome marking was ♩ = 120, altered to 138, the original marking of *Allegro poco con moto* changed to *Allegro con moto e poco appassionato*, and the *con passione* in the recapitulation, under 'I shall love them', was originally *molto espressione*. It describes how much a picturesque landscape means to the poet; it is lively and youthful (and hard to envisage its première by a contralto). A sequence of colourful chords, falling chromatically, has no counterpart in the second verse, and Quilter omits the third verse, which tells much more directly of fir trees, dogs and five-bar gates, stopping at 'I shall weary of Heaven to be there'.

Quilter was not a church composer, but occasionally produced anthem-like compositions: 'Lead Us, Heavenly Father, Lead Us', 'Non Nobis, Domine', 'Freedom', and 'Hymn for Victory'. 'Hymn for Victory' is mostly straightforward, but with an attractive sequence that gives rise to poignant major sevenths. 'Lead Us, Heavenly Father' (words by James Edmeston, 1791–1867) is better known in the chorale version, as altered by Filitz, but Quilter's setting – very definitely an anthem – is a solid, business-like one, SATB in the first verse, tenor solo in the second, and tenor solo providing a descant in the third. The published score is dated 1908, the manuscript is dated 22 July 1909, but it was not published until 1924, dedicated to Ida Legge.

Quilter set words by Kipling (1865–1936) only once, but it was a memorable setting, 'Non Nobis, Domine'. Quilter's piece was commissioned by his friend Walter Creighton (Kipling's words were already in existence) and it was soon published by Boosey and Hawkes in a number of forms – SATB, three part women's chorus, two-part men's chorus, unison, with strings, piano, organ or full orchestral accompaniment.

Although Quilter's 'patriotic' melodies were indubitably English, the best were those that he wrote primarily in response to some need where the patriotism was secondary: St George's theme from *Where the Rainbow Ends* portrayed a character within a wider context, and here, it was in response to a semi-theatrical pageant, and one instigated by his friend. When, during the Second World War, he was commissioned to write something overtly and directly patriotic (and not within a theatrical environment), it was not so successful.

When the melody first appeared, in the Pageant of Parliament, it was heard several times throughout the performance; it would seem that it was used to punctuate and unify the tableaux. The words at these points were not Kipling's, and may have been Creighton's:

Who prays the king for right
To none will he say nay
He justice will not sell
Nor suffer its delay
Unswerving Rule and Law
Shall make a people free:
Since out of justice man is made
To live in liberty.

The statesmen who for love
Her high behests obeyed:
Her people strong, whose rights
On loyal love are stayed;
These served the Queen with joy,
Accounting this for gain;
The brightest glory of her crown
Was by their love to reign.

The crown we freely give
To Kings who keep the lay
The rights our fathers won
Are as the breath we draw
Let Parliament and King
Henceforth no more be twain
While freedom he upholds,
We will the King maintain.

The first and third verses were in D major, the second and 'Non Nobis' itself in E♭ major; it was the last musical item in the Pageant. Its bold rising fourth at the start, from $\hat{5}$ to $\hat{8}$, and back again, is immensely positive, expressing 'an incoming emotion of joy, an acceptance or welcoming of comfort, consolation, or fulfilment'.[21] The modulations are exactly as they should be (to dominant, and in passing, to relative minor and subdominant) and even at first hearing – coloured by memories of 'Now Thank We All Our God', 'Let All the World in Every Corner Sing' and other stalwarts – it sounds faintly familiar, so firmly rooted is it in the sound of English hymnody. Mildly chromatic harmonies in the third phrase and plentiful suspensions reinforce the sense of nostalgia; it is a fine, sturdy piece.

The printed, unpublished, music of the pageant is entirely anonymous, but another item in it, 'You've Money to Spend', was identified as Quilter's in a separate manuscript version, orchestrated by Cyril James Clarke;[22] this raises the possibility that much of the other incidental music was also by Quilter, though

[21] Deryck Cooke, *The Language of Music* (Oxford, 1959), pp. 159 and 167.
[22] Held by the BBC Music Library.

most seems to be no longer extant. 'You've Money' is a verse and refrain song for the chorus. It accompanies a street scene set in a market, with different parts of the chorus advertising their wares: small coals, vinegar, dressmakers, lace-threaders, tinkers, hatmakers and so on. Quilter's waltz lilt pervades the song, with its emphasis on the second beat, and Viennese hemiolas, and the setting is admirably fit for its purpose.

Ex. 8.15, Quilter, 'You've Money to Spend', ending

Quilter's *Songs of Sorrow*, Op. 10, were mostly new work, dating from spring 1907, finished that June, and published by Boosey in 1908; the manuscript copy calls them *Voices of Sorrow*. They were settings of poems of Ernest Dowson (1867–1900), published in 1896 and 1899, and were dedicated 'To my friends Wilfrid, and Jane von Glehn'. He chose flat keys, except for the bright E major of the fourth song, 'In Spring'. 'Passing Dreams', which Mark Raphael thought the most poignant of the set,[23] was a revision of an earlier song of 1904.

The songs are all slow and make a sombre group, though an extremely effective one, and are surprisingly neglected. The first, 'A Coronal', is a strophic poem about the death of love, indulgent in its mourning; the lines 'Violets and leaves of vine' and 'We gather and entwine' appear six times in both poem and song, like a refrain, each verse beginning in the same way musically as well as

---

[23] Mark Raphael (1953–4), p. 20.

textually, but diverging thereafter, in more extreme manner as the song progresses; the nine lines of each verse translate into ten bars of music. The bass line ranges widely, tending to prefer a low Bb_1, and the use of fourths becomes oppressive: the opening phrase is focused upon the tonic Bb major, falling to the F below, and rising to the Eb above; in the second verse, the Ab is added, then the Db, Gb and Cb, bringing the key to the flat submediant, at the most chromatic at the strongest images of death.

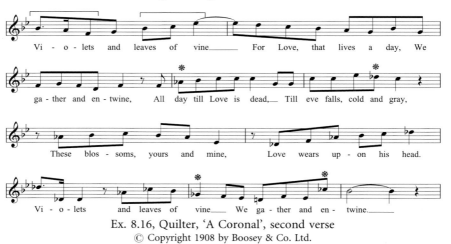

Ex. 8.16, Quilter, 'A Coronal', second verse
© Copyright 1908 by Boosey & Co. Ltd.

The second, 'Passing Dreams', is the only song of the group in the minor key. At its opening, it is accompanied by soft-treading chords, and the vocal line starts with a three note motif that opens 'Autumn Evening', to similar autumnal effect; the song compares the transience of the days of love and hate with the transience of the days of wine and roses. Dowson's poem, and indeed the fragile style of his work generally, had made a considerable impact on literary society, and this poem had been published only eight years before Quilter set it.

Ex. 8.17a, Quilter, 'Passing Dreams', opening
© Copyright 1908 by Boosey & Co. Ltd.

The second verse, initially warmer and harmonically richer, and on the words 'days of wine and roses' more lyrical, soon chills again and becomes small, stifled in the attempt to escape fate; twenty-three intensely focused bars. Although Quilter had obviously already responded to the poem, by 1907 there were further layers of meaning for him – the text surely came very close to reflecting Quilter's experiences, of the previous autumn and winter, when he was so seriously ill.

Ex. 8.17b, Quilter, 'Autumn Evening', bars 6–7
© Copyright 1910 by Boosey & Co. Ltd.

The third song, 'A Land of Silence', is again strophic, the six five-line verses grouped into two pairs, and two single verses; the textual repetition between the outermost verses is reflected in the music, with the last verse almost the same as the first. As usual, the strophic treatment is not precise, with changes in texture and pitch, and the second double verse modulates to the mediant major, F major; he holds that for a few sunny bars before returning to the tonic D♭ major, though the bass line rises briefly, in contrast with its appearance in the first verse, before falling back home.

The fourth song, 'In Spring', plays around the tonic E major, but for the refrain-like repetition of the words 'the spring of the soul' and in the second verse, 'the flowers of the soul', moves imperceptibly to the relative minor, highlighting the movement from the spring (the bud), to the summer (the flower), and by implication, to the fruit, the autumn. Grainger's mother was fond of this song, with a '*personal* poignant pathos' at the words 'the spring of the soul cometh no more for you or for me'.[24] In writing to Quilter, Grainger continued:

> You once wrote to me 'You are the wind that blew thru my garden.' Truly I can say to you that the wind of your songs has blown thru my garden. Indeed I should not count my composing in vain if it has brought anyone the comfort & delight yr songs always brought to me, & always will. On the most personal & most impersonal grounds, both, they were & are deeply dear to me. I relish keenly the last vocal phrase of 'In spring' – an inspired close.[25]

The song approaches its end with a suggestion that it will remain in the relative minor, though at the last moment it slips back into the major, bringing an unexpected warmth.

---

[24] Grainger to Quilter, 31 August 1923, GM.
[25] Grainger to Quilter, 31 August 1923, GM.

Quilter set three poems by Nora Hopper (1871–1906). The first was 'June', discussed in the previous chapter; the next was 'Blossom-Time', written and published in 1914, one of the Op. 15 set, *Three Songs* (the others being 'Cuckoo Song' and 'Amaryllis at the Fountain'); and the third, also written and published in 1914, was 'Spring is at the Door', the fourth of the Op. 18 set, *Six Songs* (the first three of which were republished as *Three Songs for Baritone and Tenor*; the last two were the *Two September Songs*). Texts of Nora Hopper's type abound in the song literature of the period and earlier; they are at the other end of the spectrum from the crafted virtuosity of the Elizabethan and Cavalier poets. 'Blossom-Time' was dedicated to Frederick Kiddle, and was later arranged as a duet and published in that form in 1934; the second voice sometimes adds harmony, and sometimes provides imitative counterpoint; the accompaniment in both versions is almost identical, with small changes in the postlude. 'Spring is at the Door' was dedicated to Madame Louise Kirkby Lunn and opens with birdsong. The first two verses are trite, and are repeated to make a ternary form song, but the relative richness of the central section is astounding given the material with which Quilter was working; there is no disguising their superficiality.

Quilter's two settings of Alfred Williams (1877–1930) were nine years apart; both came from Williams's book of poems *Songs in Wiltshire*, published in 1909. The first became one of *Three Songs*, 'Cuckoo Song', Op. 15, no. 1, and the second, 'Song of the Stream', became one of *Six Songs*, Op. 25, no. 1. The manuscript of 'Cuckoo Song' is dated 26 July 1913, published November 1913, and dedicated to Dame Nellie Melba, and that of 'Song of the Stream' is dated 6 November 1921, published in 1922, and dedicated to Pauline Hill.

Williams's poem 'Cuckoo Song' contains nine verses, most of them four lines long, plus a refrain 'Cuckoo! Cuckoo!'; Quilter sets five of them and repeats the first. He starts in a bright D major, with rippling semiquavers in the piano – presumably imitating the winds of May – and the phrase lengths, regular at first but offset by the two-bar call of the cuckoo, become more irregular as the song proceeds, especially in the central section; this is in B♭ major, with a broader quaver-triplet figuration, where the opening employed semiquaver-triplet figures. At the 'iron frost', the piano plays *staccato*, and both piano and voice become more agitated before a brief return to the opening phrase, accompanied by wider-ranging arpeggios than at first. The sense of development and of rising excitement is clear, as the cuckoo anticipates the music of spring. Quilter does not attempt to match Williams's short, punchy and joyful lines, but takes their brisk elements and adds musical description to them.

'Song of the Stream' was renamed from Williams's original 'The Brook', a forty-line poem. Though the lines are short, it is a long poem for Quilter to set, and he divides it into five eight-line verses, treated broadly in ternary form: the first two strophic, the next two through-composed, as a central section, and the last as a recapitulation, entirely appropriately, since the words for the last eight lines are an altered version of the first eight. Phrase lengths vary across the first two verses, following word sense as usual, though the shortening of the phrases in the second verse make the pace move on a little in anticipation of the stream's journey; in changing the title, Quilter saw the poem in terms of the *song* that the stream was singing. Williams's short lines get the better of Quilter, and the central section is dominated by two-bar phrases; a pity, since the harmonic movement is rich and shows a strong Fauré influence: the song opens in E major, but by the beginning of the central section, which describes the sand, pebbles and the weather that the stream sees, it is in C♯ minor, and over the next ten bars, it translates to the tonic major, D♭, briefly to G♭ major, enharmonically to F♯ major, thence to B major and F♯ major again, by sequence to E♭ major (with A♯/B♭ as pivot note). It slips chromatically down to F♯ minor and the pace – thankfully – eases up for the calmer travels through woods, an open texture, and a return to the opening; the piano part is thicker here for a few bars but reverts to the original figuration and a gentle ending.

It is a difficult song to sing because of the modulations, and it is a long song to sustain, but it is highly descriptive with a strong sense of a journey, and shows well Quilter's response to modern poetry.

The next group of songs show Quilter's response to his own texts, which were never published on their own, but were always written for the purpose. Many texts, on their own, are hardly outstanding poetry, though they can give rise to outstanding songs, but unfortunately this is not the case here. Some of his early songs were to his own texts; these remaining songs are from later years. None has an opus number.

'Fairy Lullaby', written and published in 1921, was dedicated to the singer Hilda Blake. It is a graceful little song, and the words serve their purpose well, being a means to an end; it is not as twee as one might have expected. Quilter arranged it for women's voices in three parts, too, and this version was published in 1939.

In 'Spring Voices', Quilter used a pseudonym, Romney Marsh, as the poet's name; it was something of a joke between him and his nephew, Arnold Vivian. The song (published in 1936) uses his toccata style of accompaniment, but lacks a sense of direction; he deals with musical cuckoos more effectively in 'Cuckoo Song'. The song shows no dedication, though a Miss Grace Moore wrote to Quilter to thank him for his dedication of a new song;[26] it may have been this one, or 'Wind from the South', though that shows no dedication either.

Quilter used the same pseudonym for the poet of 'Summer Sunset', an accompanied partsong for soprano and alto, and very routine; the modulation to the mediant major is predictable, and it lacks the interest that Quilter usually shows in his choral writing. It was dated 1938, but published in 1949.

'April Love' has a similar piano figuration to 'Spring Voices' and a similar lack of interest; they sound like diluted versions of Rachmaninov's 'Spring Waters'. In the early years of Quilter's career, songs were often published in three keys, sometimes (as with 'Now Sleeps the Crimson Petal') in four. This

---

[26] Grace Moore to Quilter, 7 June 1936, BL Add. MS 70605, f. 41.

one is in one key only, indicative of its quality and likely sales. It was published in 1952, date of composition unknown, and it was dedicated to Newton Goodson, of whom nothing is known.

'Dancing on the Green' was published in 1954; the score claims Leslie Woodgate as its editor, and he presumably worked it into a performable piece, perhaps from sketches. He made a good job of it and it is a merry little unaccompanied partsong for SATB, though its opening has strong hints of army songs.

Ex. 8.18, Quilter, 'Dancing on the Green', opening
© Copyright 1954 Ascherberg, Hopwood & Crew Ltd., London W6 8BS. All Rights Reserved

How much of it is his, and how much is Quilter's is arguable; probably more the former than the latter.

The remaining poets discussed were younger than Quilter, and many were women. His sources of texts are not so often the slim volumes published by his contemporaries, relatively easy to track down, and to deduce how he came across them; some of these later poets are certainly of that kind, but increasingly many of Quilter's selections are clearly individual pieces, of the kind that would have been published in a journal in a regular 'poet's corner', and which happened to catch Quilter's eye. For many reasons, the older poets whom Quilter set were men; for the same reasons, there was more possibility for the later poets whom Quilter set to be women.

Quilter only set one poem by James Stephens (1880–1950), the last of the Op. 25 set, 'In the Bud of the Morning-O'. Stephens was Irish, and famous for his liveliness and complete involvement in his writing, and although he was barely four feet six inches tall, he was once described as 'quite big inside, large and roomy'.[27] The poem – it was published in a slim volume – is fresh, with a dainty

---

[27] The fourth Earl Grey, in presenting a copy of a volume of Stephens's poems to a friend, described him thus (Oliver St John Gogarty, 'James Stephens', *Dictionary of National Biography* (Oxford, 1959)).

setting, but his words are strongly rhythmic, and are not altogether satisfactory when set to music. The manuscript is dated 1926, it was published in 1927 and it was dedicated to Evelyn Marthèze Conti, Italia Conti's sister.

Stephens was the only Georgian poet whom Quilter set; he was quite depressed enough, without Housman's, Owen's, Sassoon's and Thomas's sepulchral images of lost youth. Many of the contemporary poets whom he set died young, and their sense of melancholy, frailty and decadence (especially Dowson's) was very much in sympathy with Quilter's sensibility.

Seosamh Mac Cathmhaoil's more pronounceable name was Joseph Campbell and he continued a sporadic correspondence with Quilter over some years, from at least March 1907, the fruits of which were Quilter's settings of three of Campbell's poems, 'I Will Go with My Father A-Ploughing' (better known in Gurney's setting), 'Cherry Valley' and 'I Wish and I Wish', in a group which Quilter nearly called *Cherry Valley: Three Songs* but eventually called *Three Pastoral Songs*. Quilter negotiated for 'The Seeding-Song' and 'Harvest Home', with a view to setting them for chorus and orchestra as two of *Three Country Songs for Chorus*, but that was as far as it went. The manuscripts are dated 1920, and they were published as a set, Op. 22, in 1921; they were dedicated to the singer Monica Harrison, one of the four Harrison sisters. They are written for voice and piano trio, and a version for voice and piano was published at the same time. The violin and cello parts are obbligato parts, and are doubled, either in unison or at the octave, by the piano; but in the recording of 'Cherry Valley' that Mark Raphael made with Quilter, Quilter suppressed some of the piano part, allowing the violin and cello to show through the better.

Campbell's poetry is of a kind with that of Alfred Williams – observant of the world around him and nostalgic – but Campbell is more rose-tinted than Williams, and he calls forth rose-tinted settings. 'I Will Go with My Father' follows the natural word stress in a way that Gurney's song (written and published in 1921) does not attempt. Gurney's word-setting is often unexpected, and strong; his song strides forth, where Quilter's is milder, and tells a gentler story. Quilter follows the text in two-bar phrases, adjusting the last line of each verse, letting the song speak for itself; its rhythm has more in common with the stroke of the scythe than does Gurney's.

Ex. 8.19a, Gurney, 'I Will Go with My Father', opening
© Copyright 1921 by Boosey & Co. Ltd.

Ex. 8.19b, Quilter, 'I Will Go with My Father', opening
© Copyright 1921 Elkin & Co. Ltd.

The lyrical and atmospheric 'Cherry Valley' is the best of the set. It holds all the elements of Quilter's style: fast harmonic rhythm in the middle section, with plenty of secondary sevenths and chromaticism, birdsong, cross-rhythms, textural variety, flattened sevenths, strong inner part-writing, and a valid response to the text itself. The writing is delicate and crystalline, and the fairies, visible in the moonlight, can just be discerned in the light repeated chords that illustrate their footsteps. Mark Raphael thought highly of this song.

One need only consider the enormous interest shown in the Cottingley fairies[28] to realise how much interest there was in the supernatural, in the early years of the century and especially in the immediate post-war years. However, the opening words of 'I Wish and I Wish' are inescapably trite:

> I wish and I wish
> And I wish I were
> A golden bee
> in the blue of the air,

and though the rest of the song has a happy, child-like quality, similar to that of Quilter's Stevenson settings of the *Child Songs* (especially 'Where Go the Boats?'), with the play between 6/8 and 9/8 lightly and neatly handled, it is unquestionably and irretrievably damaged by the text.

There remain Quilter's settings of Rodney Bennett's poems, his collection *The Arnold Book of Old Songs* and those that can only be described as of the miscellaneous variety. On the whole (though not always) these songs were rather run-of-the-mill, with unfortunately little to commend them; there was one absolutely outstanding exception.

Bennett was born in 1890, and his work was important to Quilter. Bennett may not have written especially good poetry, but he did know how to write words for music.

---

[28] The 1919 hoax, in which Frances Griffiths and her cousin Elsie Wright 'photographed' fairies at the bottom of their garden; the photographs were published around the world. The apparent proof of the existence of fairies was accepted unequivocally and with little or no question by many, including (after initial scepticism) Sir Arthur Conan Doyle, the creator of the ultra-rational Sherlock Holmes. Controversy still reigns, despite the confession by the perpetrators in the early 1980s that they had taken trick photographs, using cut-outs and hatpins.

'Madrigal in Satin' was written and published in 1939, for unaccompanied men's chorus, TTBB; a melody line can be sung by the second tenors or as a baritone solo. Much of the solo line is accompanied by humming, that lends itself to smooth part-writing. The second basses provide sonorous B♭ tonic pedals and the first basses are assigned neat chromatic lines, raising $\hat{5}$ through F♯ to G. The nine- or eleven-bar 'fa-la' refrain provides the madrigal element.

> Lady the light is gone
> When you're away
> Though bright the day;
> The birds forsake their lay:
> Until your light renew the Spring,
> They fold their wing,
> Forgetting how to sing.

The varied stresses free Quilter to be his best fluid self. He picks up the mock-Elizabethan style, mixing it with the mood he created within *Julia* (during the scene set back in an earlier period), adds his own measure of colour, and produces a wistful, plaintive song.

The Sailor and His Lass is a short, light-hearted work for soprano and baritone soloists, with chorus and orchestra; it tells a story of a lass whose sailor-love goes away, deserting her. Another sailor comes to woo her, but she remains true to her lover's memory, despite the offer of gold, silver and a wedding ring. The sailor then says that he is in fact her love and he was merely testing her constancy. It was written in 1943 though the score is marked 1945, and was published in 1948, the year of Bennett's death. The music is continuous, with choruses, no solos, one duet, and the rest, solo comment accompanied by the chorus. It was given a very poor report when Quilter offered it to the BBC: the readers were Gordon Jacob and John Ireland who, like the critics of Quilter's operetta *Julia*, probably expected a different Quilter, the Quilter of the refined artsong, and when they were given the other one, objected. Having said that, however, *The Sailor and His Lass* certainly lacks variety of texture, and in austere post-war years found no willing home. Because there is no spoken dialogue, the action is carried solely by the music, but it is tired, and its paucity of harmonic and melodic invention is disappointing.

Quilter was commissioned to write 'A Song of Freedom' in early 1941, and he conducted its first performance on 10 July 1941; it was published the same year, under the simpler title of 'Freedom', for unison singing, with optional SATB chorus and orchestral or piano accompaniment; for SSC; as a song with piano and string accompaniment; and for solo voice and piano; in this edition, the cover of the score shows a V for victory overprinted by the cover words.

The most remarkable aspect of the melody is its close similarity with Eric Coates's 'Dam Busters' theme: Coates was asked to provide music for the film *The Dambusters* in 1954, and eventually, and reluctantly, provided a concert march; it is said that he picked up something he happened to have lying on top of the piano.[29] Coates and Quilter had known each other since at least 1923, and Rodney Bennett, under the pen-name Roydon Barrie, wrote lyrics for Coates. It seems highly unlikely that the plagiarism was intentional, since Coates was eminently capable of writing melodies without help from others: rather more that it was an indication of a common language, or perhaps an affectionate tribute.

Ex. 8.20, Quilter, 'Freedom' and Coates, 'Dam Busters March'
against the upper stave (Quilter): © Copyright 1941 by Boosey & Co. Ltd.
against the lower stave (Coates): © Copyright 1954 Chappell Music Ltd., London W6 8BS.
All Rights Reserved

The passing modulations to relative minor and dominant are simple, but well-placed and strong, and the German sixth, carrying the G to which 'fettered' is sung, through G♭ to F on 'wind', is very powerful; it is brought out more clearly in the orchestration, played by clarinets and violins.

Ex. 8.21, Quilter, 'Freedom', bars 5–8
© Copyright 1941 by Boosey & Co. Ltd.

The setting is strophic, with an open-textured accompaniment for the first verse, sung by trebles. Martial triplets and more percussion accompany the second verse, and SATB choir added to the trebles, with descant on flute and violins, accompany the third. The words match the loyal sentiments of St

---

[29] Interview with the composer Ernest Tomlinson in May 1998. Ernest Tomlinson knew Coates, and was also a Director of the Performing Right Society, with particular knowledge and experience of investigating instances of plagiarism.

George, from *Where the Rainbow Ends*, with 'Sing a song of Freedom', 'Fight the fight of Freedom' and 'Oh! Raise the flag of Freedom' the focal points of the three verses. The BBC were perhaps a little hard in their criticism: the military fanfares that punctuate the last verse especially were surely what were needed, though Quilter works them rather too much. It was, however, functional and workmanlike music, written for a particular purpose, but it did not have the opportunity to become well-known in the way that 'Non Nobis' did: 'Non Nobis' was repeated several times within each performance of the Pageant of Parliament and the whole was performed nightly for a month. Nor did 'Freedom' have the opportunities afforded by use in a film, though it is clear that Coates's verse and refrain structure is effective, and the march, with the melodic and harmonic change in its final appearance, very emotive.

The score of 'The Cradle in Bethlehem' is dated 1945 and it was first published by Michael Joseph in 1945 in *Voices on the Green*; it was then, with minor changes, published in 1949 as an accompanied unison song, by Curwen, and in a two-part version for high voices in 1950, again by Curwen. There is also an accompaniment for strings. Its generalised nativity words are gentle; the 6/8 rhythm slips smoothly into an occasional 3/4, and irregular length lines, and 9/8 bars and duplets allow a fluid, lullaby character. A typically Quilterian flattened seventh in the postlude is soothing.

Bennett's remaining lyrics are those within the collection, *The Arnold Book of Old Songs*, all dedicated to Quilter's nephew, Arnold Vivian, though those that had first been published in 1921 had then borne different dedications. Grainger wrote of the set that

> they are a lovely string of gems, most touching in their humanity & typical of the heart-revealing skill you have built up of weaving such tune-enhancing arabesques & comments round the melody in the accompaniment – comments that inject new meaning into the line & text of the melody. . . . How *right* of you to have prepared this nose-gay for your beloved Kinsman, & to have dedicated them to his memory, since he could not return to enjoy them. I hardly know what we should consider worth thinking & feeling about these days (& all days) if it is not about the sweet & noble young men lost in war.[30]

Grainger's reaction and comment on Arnold seems rather automatic and matter-of-fact, almost to the point of callousness.

Bennett provided translations for two French texts to old French melodies, 'Le Pauvre Laboureur' ('The man behind the plough') and 'L'Amour de Moy' ('My Lady's Garden'). The former tells of the ploughman, always working, come rain or shine, always singing; he would not change places with a duke or a lord. The 6/8 setting is simple and robust, depending almost entirely on the tonic chord.

Vaughan Williams's setting of 'L'Amour de Moy' was first performed in 1904; it is feasible that Quilter heard it, though Vaughan Williams's treatment

[30] Grainger to Quilter, 2 January 1948, GM.

is different from Quilter's quadruple with an all-pervading accompaniment of triplet crotchets, and with different harmonies. Quilter's arrangement of it ('moy' is sometimes spelt 'moi'; the melody is fifteenth century) appears many years later in various guises. It exists as an autograph manuscript, arranged for cello and piano, undated but earlier than another arrangement for cello and piano; this manuscript, also autograph, was Beatrice Harrison's copy and is a piano reduction of an orchestral version (presumably the arrangement of March 1933 that she had asked him to make for HMV). Both cello versions are in Eb major and marked *Andante moderato*. It exists as a song, with untranslated French words, again in undated autograph manuscript, but now in Db major; there are fairly substantial differences between it and the first cello version, more than can be accounted for by the change of solo line or key, but it is similar to the second cello version, though still not quite the same. The only published form is in *The Arnold Book*, where it is again in Db major, but with further differences in the piano part from the other versions. Both sung versions are marked *Moderato un poco andante*. The song, and Quilter's arrangement – in whatever form it is heard – is exquisite and delicate.

The original melody contains a brief melodic figure as a haunting refrain (ex. 8.22).

Ex. 8.22, Quilter, 'L'Amour de Moy', recurrent melodic figure

The song versions have two verses, and a brief return to the beginning; the cello versions omit the return, retaining the two verses. (Vaughan Williams's setting follows this latter structure.) Where Quilter's repetitions sometimes pall, here the return to the opening brings the song full circle; the limpid setting is diatonic, until the chromatic chords at the very end, and is enriched with suspensions and added sixths and sevenths. The translation is not especially felicitous, unfortunately – the French language carries a very different kind of sound from the English, and Bennett's translation uses short words, against the generally longer, more evenly balanced and liquid ones of the original.

Ex. 8.23a, Quilter, 'L'Amour de Moy', ending, undated autograph MS copy,
for cello and piano

Ex. 8.23b, Quilter, 'L'Amour de Moy', ending, Beatrice Harrison's autograph MS
copy; orchestral version 1933

Ex. 8.23c, Quilter, 'L'Amour de Moy', ending, undated autograph MS copy,
for voice and piano

Ex. 8.23d, Quilter, 'L'Amour de Moy', ending, 1947 published copy,
for voice and piano

In 'The Ash Grove', the last of the sixteen songs of the set, Bennett's text is
altogether different. It provides an alternative to the traditional text, retaining
the idea of being parted by death, but emphasising the impossibility of
knowing what the future will bring. The traditional text was not sufficiently
personal to Quilter's needs; Bennett's text is a direct response to Arnold
Vivian's death:

> The voices of friends that the long years have taken,
> Oh faintly I hear them, the song and the word.
> How much in the heart can so little awaken:
> The wind in the leaves and the song of a bird!

and:

> How little we knew, as we laughed there so lightly,
> And time seemed to us to stretch endless away,
> The hopes that then shone like a vision so brightly
> Could fade as a dream at the coming of day!

Although Quilter never claimed to be a competent arranger of folksongs, his arrangements are extremely clear, and, uncluttered, allow the original voice to come through.

The five songs published in 1921, *Old English Popular Songs*, were 'Drink to Me Only', 'Three Poor Mariners', 'The Jolly Miller', 'Barbara Allen' and 'Over the Mountains'.

'Drink to Me Only' was first published in 1917 in an arrangement for violin and piano, and also for violin, cello and piano, as one of *Two Old English Tunes* (the other one being 'Three Poor Mariners'), and in 1921 it was published as a song, dedicated to the baritone Arthur Frith. It is a chromaticised setting (though not as convoluted as Cyril Scott's arrangement) of the well-known melody by Colonel Mellish, with words by Ben Jonson (1572/3–1637). In 1927 it was published, again in Quilter's arrangement, for piano solo. All three are essentially the same, all fairly thick-textured, though with variations in figuration and fullness of chord, and Grainger was entranced by it. In the second verse, for example, the instrumental versions are placed an octave higher; in the song version, the voice – not surprisingly – stays at the same octave, but it is the accompaniment, enriched, that is placed an octave higher.

Ex. 8.24a, Quilter, 'Drink to Me Only', opening of second verse: violin and piano (1917)
© Copyright 1917 by Winthrop Rogers Ltd.

Ex. 8.24b, Quilter, 'Drink to Me Only', opening of second verse: piano solo (1927)
© Copyright 1927 by Winthrop Rogers Ltd.

Ex. 8.24c, Quilter, 'Drink to Me Only', opening of second verse: voice and piano (1921)
© Copyright 1951 by Boosey & Co. Ltd.

The ending of the instrumental versions is a bar longer than that of the vocal setting, a more rounded finish.

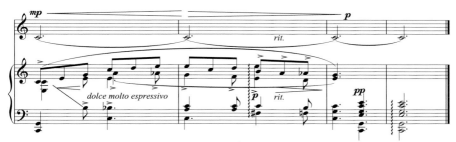

Ex. 8.25a, Quilter, 'Drink to Me Only', ending: violin and piano (1917)
© Copyright 1917 by Winthrop Rogers Ltd.

Ex. 8.25b, Quilter, 'Drink to Me Only', ending: piano solo (1927)
© Copyright 1927 by Winthrop Rogers Ltd.

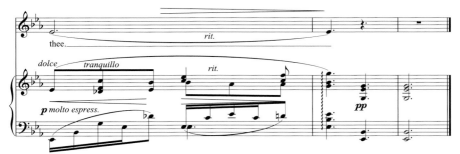

Ex. 8.25c, Quilter, 'Drink to Me Only', ending: voice and piano (1921)
© Copyright 1951 by Boosey & Hawkes Ltd.

The other song, arranged for *Two Old English Tunes*, was 'Three Poor Mariners'. In the song version (dedicated to Guy Vivian, Arnold's father, the score dated 1920), it has a straightforward setting, two verses, the accompaniment much the same in both, but with extra octaves, hearty and strong. The instrumental version is a different matter; it is a free arrangement, greatly developed over the simple song version, with extended interludes between the verses; the melody transfers to the piano left hand in octaves in the second verse, with the right hand taking over at the halfway point of the melody, and for the third verse, it is an octave higher than at the opening. It is a very merry arrangement, a real duet between violin and piano, though in the interludes it sometimes rather loses its way: there is just an inkling that this might have been a student piece once, with Quilter required to work certain effects into it, but it is robust and happy, with a glorious and all too rare sense of fun; this was Quilter's humour expressing itself in his music.

'The Jolly Miller' was dedicated to Joseph Farrington; the melody is called 'The Budgeon it is a delicate trade' (a 'budge' being a thief) and the text was partly taken from Arne's *Love in a Village*, of 1762, which was revived by Nigel Playfair at the Lyric Theatre, Hammersmith, in April 1928, so that the revival clearly postdates Quilter's arrangement of the song. Only the first verse seems to have been used in the original *Love in a Village*; in Playfair's production the song, sung by Frederick Ranalow in the rôle of Hawthorn, had two extra verses, possibly derived from *The Convivial Songster* of 1782, and it is this text that Quilter used. Quilter was well acquainted with both Alfred Reynolds, who arranged the music for Playfair's production, and Ranalow.

The song is more familiar in Britten's arrangement of it, though there are similarities, particularly in the semiquaver movement that in both cases illustrates the movement of the miller's wheel. Britten's miller is more efficient, however, since his wheel-music is continuous. On the other hand, Quilter's miller is drinking with cronies, and the wheel turns only when the miller remembers. Grainger especially liked the chords under 'rejoice and sing' in the last verse.

It was to Frederick Ranalow that 'Barbara Allen' was dedicated; the words are claimed as traditional, though they appear in Percy's *Reliques*, with fifteen verses; Quilter selects six (differing slightly from the selection in Hatton's edition of *The Songs of England*). Each verse is treated differently, with countermelodies as undercurrents; the opening words are set against a subdominant chord, clashing with the vocal line immediately; the 'merry month of May' is set against a simple tonic. As Barbara Allen approaches Jemmy Grove, the bass line climbs inexorably, to end with a chord of E major as she tells him he is dying; the line falls as he dies and is buried. A bell – an octave B, with bare fifth – tolls on the third beat of alternate bars in the fourth verse, with strident chords and harmonies on its last line, 'Woe to Barb'ra Allen!' and in the piano interlude before the fifth verse, a touch to which Grainger reacted positively. The last two verses are calmer after the outburst of the fourth, with another E major chord to accompany Barbara Allen's declaration that she too will die. This is a powerful text, rendered justice by Quilter's setting.

'Over the Mountains' was dedicated to Theodore Byard, the actor; he was also a singer. The text is found in Percy's *Reliques*; Quilter sets four of the five verses, omitting the middle one that claims that no matter how weak or cowardly a suitor, love will find a way. The four verses are harmonised in similar fashion, with different textures, but overall, it is a simple and unsophisticated setting; it was a particular favourite of Grainger's.

Quilter's Irish arrangements were to words by the Irishman Thomas Moore (1779–1852), from his volumes of *Irish Melodies with Symphonies and Accompaniments*, the music by Sir John Stevenson. 'Believe Me, if All Those Endearing Young Charms' is flowing and unpretentious, claiming that fondness will grow with age; as with many of these settings, Quilter lets the song speak – or sing – for itself. The other song, 'Oh! 'tis Sweet to Think', is a defence of inconstancy, treated suitably lightly. The melody is a jig and needs to be quick, but Quilter has marked it Allegretto, with ♩. = 80, which renders it a rather sedate jig; Moore's original is marked 'playfully'.

Robert Burns provided the texts to two more settings, 'Ye Banks and Braes', a lyrical melody that Quilter sets in G♭ major; the wide pitch-range of the accompaniment gives a depth of feeling to the song of regret. It was one of Arnold's favourite songs, though it is not clear if Quilter had arranged it before Arnold was called up, or if it was simply a favourite melody.

The mournfully Aeolian 'Ca' the Yowes to the Knowes' uses every note within the range of a tenth, c^1 to e^2, except for the sixth degree of the scale, f^1; the note has been stolen as the poet's heart has been stolen. Like 'Ye Banks and Braes', it is a beautiful melody, with a deceptively artless accompaniment.

'Charlie is My Darling', Quilter's third Scottish arrangement, is marked as a 'Scottish Jacobite marching tune 1775' and it is the march elements to which Quilter responds; fife and drum are clearly present, together with drones; this is a delicious setting.

Ex. 8.26, Quilter, 'Charlie is My Darling', interlude between verses 1 and 2
© Copyright 1951 by Boosey & Co. Ltd.

Grainger found 'these French tunes . . . very engaging – particularly "Pretty Month of May" bewitches me'.[31] This was an anonymous translation of 'Joli Moi de Mai' wherein a young man promises to love a young shepherdess if she will love him, it being May. The light-hearted song is treated lightly, an attractive descant on piano introduced in the second verse.

---

[31] Grainger to Quilter, 2 January 1948, GM.

'Since First I Saw Your Face', another of the English songs, was a melody by Thomas Ford, from his *Mvsicke of Svndrie Kindes* of 1607; Quilter's source was probably Bullen's *Lyrics from the Song-Books of the Elizabethan Age.* The three-versed sorrowful love song has long lines, and Quilter does not prolong them further; there is a two-bar interlude between the first two verses, but the third continues straight on from the second. The dejected and disdained lover has a simple line, decorated somewhat in the second verse; it is a pretty setting.

'My Lady Greensleeves' was given new words by John Irvine, a poet with whom Quilter corresponded during the 1940s and probably earlier; Irvine had had poems published in *The Irish Times* and at some point sent a poem of eulogy to Quilter, in beautiful calligraphy. The song was first published in 1942, as a two-part song for women's voices, SA, in G minor; in the solo version, it is in F minor; a manuscript copy is in E minor, marked 'for Arnold' and dated June 1942. The accompaniment has a justifiably predictable hint of a harp, and the text is suitably laudatory to the Lady Greensleeves. The piano part is identical in both versions, and the second chorus part simply provides a harmony line, usually in thirds below the melody.

Since the melodies were fixed, attention is focused on the accompaniments in a different way from usual; the songs cover a wide range in Quilter's output, from the simple, unaffected and unsophisticated arrangements, such as 'Pretty Month of May' and 'Since First I Saw Your Face' to the scintillating 'Charlie is My Darling', and the powerful 'Barbara Allen'. They are worthy companions to the mainstream of Quilter's work, and as Trevor Hold has pointed out, make excellent alternatives to the usual folk-song fare served on the concert platform.[32]

Quilter set another poem by Irvine, 'Wind from the South', dated and published in 1936. It starts unpromisingly, with yet another bird, and sure enough, in the second verse is 'a bird calling/ In the blue haze/ From the dim woodland'. But the poem is atmospheric, and Quilter produces an atmospheric song. The first verse establishes the tonic, E♭ major; from there the central section moves through various harmonic diversions, in Quilter's normal manner, before returning to the tonic for the recapitulation; Quilter's passing modulations have every appearance of having been found at the piano, but the resultant lack of direction creates a sense of stillness.

'The Passing Bell' is a setting of words by Winnifred Tasker. She wrote a book of poems called *Songs of Wales and Devon*, but this poem is not in it, and was probably a single poem published in a newspaper or journal, that caught Quilter's fancy. He offered it to Boosey, but though the firm made persistent efforts, it was unable to trace Tasker, and because copyright permission could not therefore be obtained, the song was never published. The score is dated 1934, though Quilter was likely to have been working on it from late 1933. It is graceful, of course, but not, unfortunately, a very exciting setting.

---

[32] Trevor Hold, sleeve note to Jeffrey Benton's Symposium recording of *The Arnold Book* (1993).

Bawdsey Manor (by courtesy of Steven Plunkett)

Mary Ann Quilter with her sons: clockwise from top left, Roger, Arnold, Eley,
Percy and Eustace (by courtesy of Robin Miller)

Quilter's father
(by courtesy of David Tudway Quilter)

Quilter's mother
(by courtesy of Mrs Jane Szilvassy)

Pinewood, Farnborough, Quilter's prep school (by courtesy of Percy Vickery)

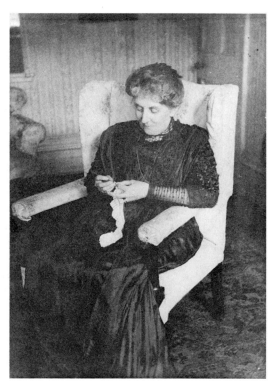

Edith Brackenbury,
Quilter's music teacher
(by courtesy of John Brackenbury)

Quilter's brother,
Colonel Arnold Quilter
(by courtesy)

Quilter's nephew Arnold
Vivian (by courtesy of
Mrs Jane Szilvassy)

Quilter aged 22 (by courtesy of Robin Miller)

The brothers: Arnold, Eustace, Percy, Eley and Roger Quilter, Bawdsey, December 1903
(by courtesy of David Tudway Quilter)

Quilter, portrait by Herbert Lambert (by courtesy of Jenny Letton,
administered by Composer Prints Ltd)

Quilter's music room at 7 Montagu Street (by courtesy of Mrs Irene Raphael)

Walter Creighton (by courtesy
of Mrs Hugh Creighton)

Robert Allerton ('Man in
Black' by Glyn Warren
Philpot) (by courtesy of
the Tate Gallery, Tate,
London, 2001)

Quilter and Arthur Frith
(by courtesy of Roger Frith)

Quilter and Lawrence Brown
(by courtesy of Leslie East)

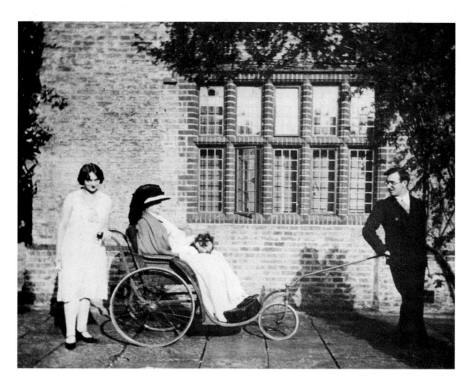

Quilter's mother, with Mark and Eva Raphael (by courtesy of Mrs Jane Szilvassy)

Quilter in Paris with Lawrence Brown, Eva Raphael, Roland Hayes,
and Mark Raphael (by courtesy of Mrs Jane Szilvassy)

Quilter and Grainger at Harrogate
(by courtesy of Mrs Jane Szilvassy)

Quilter with Joan and Rodney Bennett
(by courtesy of Mrs Jane Szilvassy)

Quilter in garden (by courtesy of Mrs Jane Szilvassy)

Leslie and Lena Woodgate (by courtesy of Mrs Jane Szilvassy)

Bertie Landsberg, Quilter, Baroness d'Erlanger, unidentified man (by courtesy of Mrs Jane Szilvassy)

Norah and Robert Nichols (by courtesy of Mrs Jane Szilvassy)

Quilter, portrait by Howard
Coster (by courtesy of the
National Portrait Gallery,
London)

Harrogate, July 1929:
unidentified man, Basil
Cameron, Beatrice Harrison,
Grainger, unidentified
man (by courtesy of
Mrs Jane Szilvassy)

Quilter, by Wilfrid de Glehn RA
(by courtesy of the National Portrait Gallery, London)

Quilter and the Heatons, his housekeeping couple (author's collection)

Quilter in his last home, 23 Acacia Road (author's collection)

Ex. 8.27, Quilter, 'The Passing Bell', opening

'Come Lady-Day' is a solo song, in G major, and also a partsong for soprano and alto, in F major, to words by May Pemberton; another of Quilter's light, attractive, unpretentious songs: routine but agreeable. The piano parts are the same, with a few notes omitted in the partsong at the beginning of the third verse; the four verses are grouped into two pairs. Both versions were written and published in 1938.

Olive Mary Denson wrote 'Wild Cherry', a poem in praise of the loved one; the song was written and published in 1938, and an archive copy is dated 21 July 1938. Like 'Come Lady-Day', it is pleasing and well-written, and like 'Come Lady-Day' says very little. Its triplet accompaniment flows smoothly.

'Trollie Lollie Laughter', written and published in 1939, to words by Victor B. Neuburg (1883–1940), is an enchanting song with pale purple harmonies (though its 2/4 time signature gives a trotting gait) but its words are irrecoverably disastrous: 'Trollie, lollie laughter!/ Swallows skim the sky;/ Nightingales come after,/ When the moon's up high'.

In 'The Rose of Tralee', Quilter redeems himself a little; the setting for solo voice was published in 1941, and that for accompanied SATB in 1951; it is an arrangement of Charles Glover's well-known melody, with words by E. Mordaunt Spencer. The piano parts are the same, with some small differences of figuration; in the choral versions, the sopranos have the melody, and the lower parts have straightforward harmonisation, either with words, or humming. Occasionally there is a small change – the partsong may show a minim where the solo version has a dotted crotchet and quaver rest. One word differs slightly: in the solo version, the first line has only one mountain, but the choral version has 'mountains'. It is a simple setting, with some slight (and pleasant) surprises in the harmonies.

'Daisies after Rain' was another song (to words by Judith Bickle) available both as a solo song (published in 1951) and as a partsong (for two soprano lines and published in 1952); it is indicative of the nature of the song that it should be susceptible to choral or solo setting; it is no surprise to find that it is about the short life of some flowers, and the happiness of daisies. However, although the two songs are clearly the same, there are considerable differences of figuration in the piano parts, with the choral accompaniment much fuller; the solo song accompaniment is very spare. It was written first and Quilter seems to have found its rich harmonies a little too strange; in the partsong he steps back, altering them to something smoother (exx. 8.23a, b).

Ex. 8.28a, Quilter, 'Daisies after Rain', solo version, bars 11–16

Here for two bars, the solo version is the equivalent of a tone higher than in the partsong: the solo version moves up from C to D♭ major, where in the partsong, the shift is down, from E to E♭ major; The different harmonies and different figurations (the solo piano part extremely spare, the partsong introducing triplets) respond in their different ways to the imminent demise of the roses and poppies. The partsong setting is considerably more inventive.

'The Walled-in Garden', words by Arthur Heald, was published in 1952, an unadventurous song, but gentle and pensive, its words a love song; Trevor Hold sees its title as encapsulating Quilter's career.[33]

For Marian Anderson's début recital at the Wigmore Hall on 15 June 1928, Quilter arranged a Negro spiritual, from Harry Burleigh's arrangement, one of a group of spirituals. Originally called 'Heav'n, Heav'n', he renamed it 'I Got a Robe'. The arrangement takes no risks, but supports the melody and is delightfully fresh.

As Quilter grew older, he set less and less of the kind of poetry that had inspired his most detailed settings, the kind where the music underpins a subtext and reveals its glories gradually. Later poetry, and that of his contemporaries, drew a very different approach from him, in a sense harking back to his earliest settings, which had drawn upon the drawing-room song for their

---

[33] It gives the name, of course, to his monograph on Quilter's songs.

Ex. 8.28b, Quilter, 'Daisies after Rain', partsong version, bars 11–16

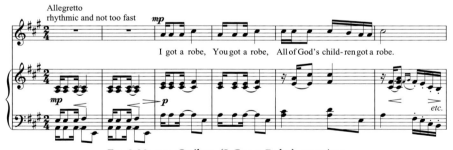

Ex. 8.29, arr. Quilter, 'I Got a Robe', opening

inspiration in terms of both musical language, and their texts and sentiments. The later songs are still cultured, and the better ones are extremely atmospheric, matching the mood that the words seek to set, but they are frequently formulaic in their manner – almost always three pages long, strophic or ternary; in the latter case, the central section with more complex harmonies, sometimes for their own sake rather than justified by the lyrics. Rarely in later songs does Quilter invoke time changes; note-lengths are frequently overly simple; many are beautifully written, excellent fillers for concert programmes, but the dessert, not the main course.

One song, however, is in an altogether different league. 'Drooping Wings', the words by Edith Sterling-Levis – Quilter's source for the text is unknown – has a depth of emotion and anguish not to be found in any other song, moving though many of them are. The score is dated 1944, published in 1945, there is no dedication, and the whereabouts of the manuscript are unknown; it is presumably destroyed. It is in G minor, a key Quilter reserves for a particular kind of melancholy: 'How Should I Your True Love Know?', Op. 30, no. 3 and 'Autumn Evening', Op. 14, no. 1, are also in G minor.

In the accompaniment, the opening appoggiatura, from d^1 resolving onto c^1 (*a*), with a resultant dissonance, reinforced by repetition of the right hand chord, sets the tone; the fall to the b♭ below completes a three-note motif (*b*) that pervades the song (ex. 8.30a, opening). It is immediately imitated by the voice's opening notes, doubled by the piano, in the tenor range; the voice continues the downward scale to d^1 (ex. 8.30b, bars 3–4 (*b1*)); the motif is echoed in the next line, a third higher, with a temporary move to the relative major; pairs of notes in the bass line sigh as they fall from e♭ to d, doubled by the voice at the end of the phrase and recalling the e♭^{1} to d^1 on 'drooping wings' (ex. 8.30c, bars 7–8); the first verse comes to an end, seemingly complete, but the piano now harks back to the voice, recalling its opening notes, and emphasising the fall to d^1 by adding a chromatic e♮^{1} (ex. 8.30d, bars 11–12 (*c*)).

Ex. 8.30a, 'Drooping Wings', opening

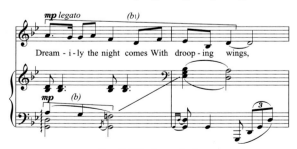

Ex. 8.30b, bars 3–4

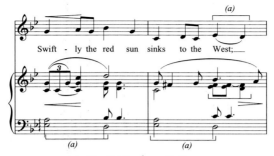

Ex. 8.30c, bars 7–8

Ex. 8.30d, bars 11–12

Ex. 8.30e, bars 17–18

Ex. 8.30f, 'Drooping Wings', last 5 bars

An abrupt shift to G major draws the curtain aside, allowing a moonbeam brief entrance, a ray of hope. An exquisite A major chord, second inversion, prolongs the possibility, the 'whispering wind stirs' and the vocal line rises in sequence, but it is held back by the pedal e♮ in the bass (ex. 8.30e, bars 17–18); at the very point of escape, escape is withdrawn, the dream dies and we are drawn back to the opening. The voice has been silenced, and its music (*b2*) can only be heard on the piano, over a bass G, sustained until it falls a further octave to the end (ex. 8.30f, last 5 bars).

Interestingly, Poulenc's wartime song 'C.', which was written in 1943 and published in 1944, contains a similar chord to Quilter's A major chord, in a similar context, though the chronology is such that neither could have known the other's song; 'C.' is likewise to do with lost hope.

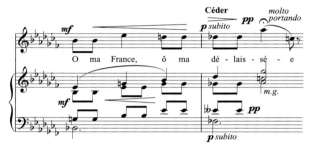

Ex. 8.31, Poulenc, 'C.', bars 37–38
© 1944 Éditions Salabert

'Drooping Wings' has all the depth and detail of a setting of an older text; the desolation of the poem clearly addressed Quilter's soul, when, worried about his nephew, he was more than usually vulnerable.

John Irvine's poem,[34] written for and about Quilter, and using familiar flower images, captures the man and his music:

> *To a Great Artist (Roger Quilter)*
>
> There is a magic flower, the natives say,
> That grows in the high mountains of Peru,
> And having known its perfumed breath but once
> Man must return again from near or far,
> So subtle, and so lasting is the spell
> That all his senses crave that breath again.
> Thus hath your music charmed me through the years,
> The deep poetic impulse, and the grace
> That clothes in beauty your most lovely songs.
> Delighting in your notes I turn again
> From other voices, haunted by your own;
> A rich expression of a perfect art.

---

[34] Irvine acknowledged Quilter's letter of thanks in February 1943.

9

Where the Rainbow Ends – The Story of a Journey

Clifford Mills's story emerged in the aftermath of the jingoism of the second Boer War; that war lasted from 1899 to 1902, a time when, with the British Empire under threat, the Englishman regarded himself as being worth several foreigners,[1] and a time when Queen Victoria's Diamond Jubilee celebrations a few years earlier in 1897 were still fresh in the memory. The Boer War also brought forth a quantity of war poetry; though overshadowed by that of the Great War, it was nevertheless notable because it was the first war in which the common soldier had been literate and articulate to such a degree. Even after (or perhaps because of) the Great War, there were still many who believed – or wanted to believe – in such creatures as the Cottingley fairies. In the theatre, the strong flavours of escapist melodrama remained highly popular and mad scenes jostled happily with evil aristocrats and innocent children, or to take it more basically, the unreal alongside the good and the bad.

The story

The play tells the story of a brother and sister, Crispian and Rosamund Carey. Their parents have been missing for some months following a shipwreck, and the children are being looked after by wicked Uncle Joseph, a solicitor, and wicked Aunt Matilda, who are helped by a nasty wheedling little bell-boy called William. Crispian is a naval cadet at Osborne, and immensely proud of his smart uniform, which he wears even when not at school; he and Rosamund have a pet lioncub, called Cubby, a very protective creature, who is occasionally given a pleasant dose of Colonial Mixture to help him continue to grow brave and strong. The children discover a book in Joseph's library, which had belonged to their good Cousin Matthew, until his death – unfortunately he had died intestate thanks to his hatred of solicitors in general and of Uncle Joseph in particular. The book is called *Where the Rainbow Ends* and it tells of the land where all lost loved ones are found. Joseph, who has purloined all Cousin Matthew's property, tells Crispian that he is to leave his beloved school and become an office boy, and a German dealer, Schlapps, is called in to buy the

---

[1] South Staffordshire Regiment, *Handsworth News*, 10 March 1888, as quoted in M. D. Blanch, 'British Society and the War', *The South African War, The Anglo-Boer War 1899–1902*, ed. Peter Warwick (Harlow, 1980).

books. The dealer is interested in one particular book, only to find that it is missing from the shelves – Rosamund has it, and is hiding with it under the table in the library, listening to the conversation. The book of course is *Where the Rainbow Ends.*[2]

Shortly after, the children find that Cousin Matthew had left a magic carpet in the library, complete with a matching genie, who can be summoned by reciting special words. The genie gives them two wishes each: Rosamund asks for their uncle and aunt to begin their dinner all over again, thus giving them more time to escape and Crispian asks for his school friend, Jim Blunders, and his young sister Betty to come with them. Rosamund also asks for St George. This wish seems to go wrong, for a decrepit monk-like figure in a long cloak appears, who does not look at all how a patron saint ought to look, but when he realises that there is a maiden in danger and asking his aid, he is transformed instantly into a glorious knight in shining armour. (In the original libretto, he is described as a 'tall, beautiful youth in ragged garments but of a most splendid and courtly mien'.[3])

They leave, with Cubby the lioncub, for the Land Where the Rainbow Ends, but just as they do so, Joseph and Matilda discover their disappearance thanks to William the sneak. With the aid of a piece of the magic carpet which William had torn off, Joseph and Matilda are able to summon the evil Dragon King, green and scaly, and he takes them to the magic country too.

At the beginning of Act 2, all parties are on the island of the magic country, and the curtain rises on the outskirts of the Dragon Wood. The Wood, stage left, is dark green, and a light green mound, from which St George's flag flies, is stage right. The Genie tells the children that while they stay on the light green mound, they are protected by St George, but should they leave its safety, they are prey to all the evil creatures that abound in the Wood. Rosamund, reading the Book, learns that the path to the Land Where the Rainbow Ends leads through the Wood which comes to power after sunset, so that it is crucial that they do not enter it between then and sunrise. Will-o'-the-Wisp, an Ariel-like sprite, appears briefly.

The audience is introduced to Dunks, the Dragon King's Chief Minister, and to the Sea Witch, in thrall to the Dragon King, who sends her to find an England-bound ship and conjure up a storm that will drive the ship to the island. The Dragon King intends the ship to rescue Mr and Mrs Carey – Crispian and Rosamund's parents – before they have a chance to be reunited with their children. In that way, he will be avenged upon Joseph, since Joseph will thus lose the estate that he has falsely obtained.

Joseph and Matilda arrive; Herr Schlapps/M. Bertrand comes too, but finds

---

[2] In 1915, Schlapps was converted into a Frenchman, Monsieur Bertrand, and remained so in later versions of the novel and in all the published versions of the libretto, although in the 1932 production he was translated further, into a 'foreigner'. (Letter dated 18 November 1937, inserted into the Lord Chamberlain's copy of the libretto, from Italia Conti, detailing the changes that had crept in over the years, BL LCP 1911/19Q.)

[3] Lord Chamberlain's copy of the libretto, BL LCP 1911/19Q.

Joseph's derision of St George's flag deeply offensive and leaves him. (In the revised 1979 version of the play, however, he stays behind in the library at the end of Act 1 and plays no further part in the story.)

Joseph and Matilda meet Dunks and then attempt to catch the children. But the children are on the mound and thus protected: because of the attempted abduction, St George appears and forces Joseph and Matilda to retreat. The children decide to spend the night on the mound; the boys go to find firewood, and Rosamund goes to find some strawberries, leaving Cubs to guard Betty. But evil Fairies and Elves enter and, despite Cubs's best endeavours to prevent them, entice Betty off the mound and into the Wood, and he goes in after her. Rosamund returns to find only Betty's shoe, and also goes after her, and the boys, returning a little later, follow too. It is sunset.

In Act 3 Scene 1, the sun has set at the Witch's Cove and the audience meets the children's parents, Vera and John Carey. The Sea Witch tells the Careys about the ship she has brought to the island, and Vera sends John to see if the witch is telling the truth. Will-o'-the-Wisp appears and tells Vera about some bad people – Joseph and Matilda – whom he has led into a bog. When he also tells her about the children he has found, she realises he is talking about her own children. In the distance, they hear John hailing the ship – the Witch was indeed telling the truth, and Will promises to lead Vera to it, so that the ship can take her to where the rainbow ends, and to where her children are.

Scene 2, set back in the Dragon's Wood, sees Betty being pinched and teased and tormented by the Elves. Cubs finds her and rescues her, and while they exit the stage trying to find a way out of the forest, Crispian and Jim Blunders enter, dishevelled after a fight with a leopard. The audience meets briefly two highly memorable characters: first the Slitherslime, half man, half worm, who leaves a trail of sticky slime, and whose eyes, though blind, illuminate the path; and the enticingly aesthetic Slacker, who has given in to the Dragon King's power, and consequently gives off a desirable, eerie green glow and exits laughing maniacally; it was a sought-after rôle.

Cubs appears and draws the boys to him, leading them off to Betty, and leaving the field open for Joseph and Matilda, fresh from the bog that Will had led them into. The trees have branches like arms, and one of the trees steals Matilda's scarf. (In the first version of the novel, we are told that the tree was once a high-born dragon.) Matilda and Joseph spot Rosamund, capture and gag her, and tie her to that tree, leaving her to be eaten by the Hyenas whose howls they can hear in the distance. But the tree removes the gag, she is able to summon help and consequently all the children and Cubs are reunited. The tree flings down the scarf, the Hyenas then follow Matilda's scent, and they devour her. A Black Bear stalks Joseph who is doubled up in mirth at Matilda's fate, and eventually a similar fate overtakes him. (In both versions of the novel, Joseph, hungry and thirsty, finds the bottle of Colonial Mixture which had been dropped in error, and drinks it for its strength-giving properties, not realising that it is lethal to those without true hearts: thus is he poisoned as well as being eaten by the Hyenas. In both published versions of the play, he drinks the

Colonial Mixture much earlier in the action, at the beginning of Act 2, but it only tastes bitter, and does not poison him.)

The final scene of Act 3 takes place at the lake that lies beyond the Wood. This is the domain of the Spirit of the Lake, the Lake-King's daughter, and she and Will dance together in the moonlight. The children emerge from the Wood, and start to cross the water over stepping-stones, but flying dragons swoop down, capture them, and take them to the Dragon King's Castle.

In the first scene of Act 4, the children and Cubs are on trial before the Dragon King for placing themselves under the protection of St George. Where the Dragon King's flag is flying, St George cannot come to their aid, and they are all sentenced to death: they will be thrown from the ramparts of the castle – Cubs included – as the dawn breaks. Cubs has other ideas; fully sentient, and lacking merely speech, not intelligence, he manages to convey the suggestion that the children should take the Dragon King's castle for their own, by striking the flag and replacing it with that of St George. Resourceful children that they are, they contrive to make a flag out of handkerchieves and ribbons, held together with pins that they have fortunately brought with them. When the sentries turn away, the boys climb the pole and strike the Dragon King's flag, but they are noticed and dragons rush in, taking up the two girls to throw them from the battlements. The boys work feverishly to hoist the flimsy replacement, and just as the sun's rays mark the dawn, they fly St George's flag and summon him to their aid.[4] St George appears in a flash of blinding light, and fights the Dragon King to the death. Victorious, he points with his sword to where a rainbow appears in the sky and the Rainbow children can be heard singing in the background.

Their trials are not quite over; in Scene 2, they have still to go right to the end of the Land to find their parents. Mr and Mrs Carey are about to embark on the boat to take them out to the ship that the Sea Witch had brought ashore in the storm, but Mrs Carey lingers, and hears the voices of Crispian and Rosamund. They are reunited amidst proper scenes of rejoicing. Finally, the figure of Hope, in her boat, is transformed into St George, come to accompany them to England, against a vision of a rainbow across the back of the set.

The story is a thoroughly satisfying one; it is well paced, vivid, and written in a direct style. Despite the stereotyped characters – the archetypal goodie of St George and baddie of the Dragon King; the beautiful mother Mrs Carey and masculine father Captain Carey, the silly girl Betty, and the stout-hearted Crispian and Blunders – it remains an exciting story with plenty of action, helped by the variety of characters (gender issues and patriotism notwithstanding) and considerable detail in the telling. And the goodies win in the end.

---

[4] A larger flag was hidden in the tower and substituted for the small one at the suitable moment.

The production and the contractual arrangements

The production rights of 1911 were granted to one Peter Laye, by the owners of the rights, Clifford Mills (her real name Emlie Clifford) and John Ramsay (his real name Reginald Owen), and the contractual arrangement was that the decision to revive the production had to be made before 31 August 1912, or the rights would revert to them. The revival had to take place before the 31 December 1912, and in these circumstances, the agreement was then extended until 31 August 1913.[5]

So an annual pattern was established. However, the whereabouts of the 1917 production are unknown, though it seems to have happened since advertisements for later productions that showed the number of seasons so far suggest that there had been no break. The story in the years 1920–5 is unclear: Peter Laye certainly went bankrupt, probably in 1920;[6] it seems that the rights may then have been assigned to a Mr R. Oswald, for a specified period, probably a year, and were then leased by the Kirby family (famous for their theatrical flying effects) in 1921;[7] they arranged to make a film.[8] A year later, in 1922, Italia Conti bought the rights and billed *Rainbow* as an Italia Conti production for its first season at the Holborn Empire, and her ownership dates from this time. In about 1930, she founded the Rainbow League, a non-sectarian, non-political League of Hope charity, with Noël Coward as its President at one stage (certainly in 1936), to help establish 'Rainbow Beds in British Hospitals, or to help any movement for the good of Children, for the Vocational training, and for their better education in their duties as future Citizens of our Empire'.[9] Its aims were 'to foster friendship and understanding, first among all young people of the British Empire, secondly among the Youth of the World . . . to carry on the fight against evil, to break down class prejudice, and by a right understanding of National Pride and the love of Country and Race, to extend to all other Nations a like understanding of their love of Country and Race'.[10] Its objects were 'to produce or arrange for the production of dramatic, musical and other kinds of plays, vaudeville, ballets, revues, pantomime,

---

[5] Some of the details are from the British Library and elsewhere, but an enormous amount of information – contractual, production, story, personalities – came from Italia Conti's niece Ruth Conti; she ran the school from just after the Second World War until she sold it in the late 1960s. I am inordinately grateful to her for her infinitely patient answers, shrewd, vivid and always a joy to read, to my never-ending questions.

[6] Samuel French archives record that this was in 1923, and that the rights were then assigned to Italia Conti; but she appears to have bought them in 1922.

[7] Ruth Conti to Langfield, 2 January 1999.

[8] This is stated in an article by Brian Doyle, 'Remembering the Rainbow', *Story Paper Collectors' Digest*, December 1993, pp. 30–3, and January 1994, pp. 16–20. However, no sources are cited, and it is unclear whence this information was gleaned. Not all of it is accurate, though much can be confirmed.

[9] Advertisement reproduced in *Story Paper Collectors' Digest*, April 1995, p. 4.

[10] From a programme for *Where the Rainbow Ends*, 1936 season.

concerts, cinematograph exhibitions, musical comedies, operas, operettas and the like'.[11]

The requirement to stage a revival within the year was flexible: it was merely the intention to revive that needed to be notified and the owners needed merely to be reasonably satisfied that the lessee would be in a position to fulfil the obligation.[12] Certainly it was usually revived at Christmas, but there were two seasons when it was not, and it frequently went on to tour after finishing the four-week season at the Holborn Empire.[13] During its nearly fifty-year history, it was staged at various London theatres (see Appendix B), and during the war toured the provinces, this being within the scope of the rights agreement; it reached Morecambe and Bournemouth. The ban on theatre productions, imposed as a panic measure on 4 September 1939, the day after war was declared, had been lifted by the middle of October 1939, just in time for *Rainbow* to be produced that Christmas season. In the Blitz of 1940, Italia Conti's school in central London was bombed and so was the Holborn Empire, that had been home to the production for eighteen years. The production transferred to the New Theatre for that season; the original full score survived (and a copy was made at about that time), and later wartime productions were generally on tour. Those hard days of touring took their toll on Italia Conti's health, and she died in 1946. Her sister, Mrs Bianca Murray, took over the school, the *Rainbow* production, and the rights. In this she was helped enormously by her niece, Ruth Conti, daughter of her brother Ferdinand who had emigrated to Australia years before. Ruth Conti had come to England in 1932, and was heavily involved both in the running of the school, and in the production: she sang the 'Slumber Song' (which occurs at the beginning of the play), and played various rôles.[14]

During the difficult wartime touring conditions, the scenery had become very dilapidated – some was the original[15] – and it became hard to find a theatre and adequate stagehands; after the war, which he had spent in the States, the charming and charismatic Anton Dolin became involved, bringing much-needed capital with him. Born in 1904 as Patrick Healey-Kay and known as Paddy, he had danced with Diaghilev's ballet company, was associated with Alicia Markova, and was a favourite of Bianca Murray, Italia Conti's sister. For the season at the Royal Festival Hall on London's South Bank in 1954 and for some of the productions later still, he brought Markova in to play the cameo rôle of the Spirit of the Lake, which from 1911 until the mid-thirties had been

---

[11] It was a registered company (BL Add. MS 70606B).

[12] This is according to Peter Laye's original producer's agreement.

[13] Ruth Conti to Langfield, 1 February 2001.

[14] When she sold the school and returned to Australia, she presented various items to the British Library, including the full score of *Where the Rainbow Ends*.

[15] A photograph of the Dragon King's Castle shown in *Play Pictorial* is strikingly similar to a watercolour painting of the Castle in Evelyn Shillington's autograph book. (The autograph book is in the possession of Mrs Jacy Wall.) Evelyn was in her late teens when *Rainbow* was first produced, and the painting is likely to date from then or soon after, which would suggest that the set probably changed little in the intervening years. This is confirmed by Ruth Conti.

played, in a manner suited to her first name, by Grace Seppings. As an inducement to Markova, music by Tchaikovsky was added and the dance with Will-o'-the-Wisp was therefore curtailed.

As time went on, it became apparent that the text of the play was outdated and its jingoism too strong. Mills had died long since, and Owen had decamped to the States, having given Mills's daughter Evelyn a free hand to decide on any appropriate changes on behalf of both of them. For a very long time, she resisted any change whatsoever, but in 1979, a revised version of the libretto was published, with the patriotism toned down. The Colonial Mixture – originally consisting of 'equal parts of Canadian, Australian and New Zealand Iron mixed with Indian and South African Steel' – now was simply Lion-cub Mixture, ingredients unspecified. Crispian and Jim were at school, with not a Naval Cadet in sight.

However, despite the financial success of the show, and the capacity houses, it became ever more difficult to find a theatre in which to stage the production. The last professional production was at the Granada Theatre, Sutton, in Surrey, in the 1959–60 season, with Anton Dolin still taking the part of St George. It was billed as the forty-seventh season; in calendar terms, it should have been the forty-ninth. The two missing years spoil the run, of course, but it was unquestionably successful and for years part of the regular Christmas scene, along with *Peter Pan* (which had been premièred seven years earlier in 1904). Since its last professional season, it has been performed regularly by amateur groups all over the country.

For one of the most exciting effects of the production, Charles Hawtrey used a stage trick devised by Maskelyne and Devant, the famous illusionists of the turn of the century. Hawtrey describes it in *A Message from Mars*, a production he first put on at the Avenue Theatre in 1899 with occasional revivals, and which he took on tour to the United States during the winter season 1902–3:

> This coat was always somewhat of an anxiety to me, as so much in the play depended on it. It was put together so that it might, at the proper moment, fall from my shoulders and down through a trap door in the floor of the stage. The coat was made in several pieces which were laced together, and it was necessary that this should be very carefully done to prevent anything going wrong. I stood in front of the trap door. . . . There was a ring attached to the laces at the back of the coat, in the lining at the bottom. When this ring was jerked the laces were released, and in a flash the coat fell away and down the trapdoor.[16]

In *Rainbow*, it involved the cloak worn by the hermit-like figure who appears in answer to Rosamund's summons for St George. It was very heavy, and was threaded with gut so as to enable it to be held in place; it took half an hour to thread, and had to be reworked for every performance. The actor playing St George had to stand on his mark just in front of the trapdoor,[17] and during the

---

[16] Charles Hawtrey, *The Truth at Last* (London, 1924).
[17] Ruth Conti recalls (Ruth Conti to Langfield, 6 April 1998) that on another night, a stand-in lost his balance and fell down backwards into the trap; he was badly shaken but not badly injured.

course of the scene, the thread was pulled out by stagehands standing below the trap. At the cue, they tugged the cloak extremely hard, it disappeared into the trap, there was a mighty flash of light from a magnesium flare, and St George was revealed, resplendent in armour. It was always a most exciting trick, though nerve-wracking – Jack Watling, who played St George in 1939, recalls that one night he missed the mark. The stage-hand popped his head up through the trapdoor and called out 'Over 'ere, mate!'[18] Eventually the trick was replaced: in later productions when Anton Dolin took over the rôle of St George, the cloak was whisked off into the wings with strings – not as spectacular, but more reliable.

For perhaps thirty years, St George wore metal armour which was substantial and effective, but which could give rise to problems. Jack Watling also recalls how one night during the fight to the death, the knee joint jammed while he was on the floor, effectively pinning him there: he was obliged to hold his sword up and whisper to the Dragon King to impale himself upon it.[19]

Florence Woodgate played in *Rainbow* in the 1920s, first probably as an elf, and later as Will-o'-the-Wisp and then Rosamund; her uncle was Leslie Woodgate who during this period was Quilter's secretary. Another uncle, Walter Woodgate, was in the first performance of *Rainbow* in 1911 and her father Albert (he had been in *The Two Hunchbacks*, under Italia Conti's instruction) kept a record book showing each day that his daughter worked. According to this record book, a film was made in 1928, but no further details can be found. A 5,000-foot film – about two hours' worth – was certainly made in 1921, directed by H. Lisle Lucoque, and produced by the British Photoplay Film Company, but there appears to be no extant copy.

Reception

The Times was happy to report that there was no singing, apparently ignoring the Lullaby (later known as the 'Slumber Song') and thus presumably referring only to children's singing.[20] These early reviews were full of praise – 'masterly', 'marvellously trained crowds of little folk-dancers', 'the score has tune and dramatic meaning, and answers its purpose very well',[21] with some deliberately ignoring any allegorical aspects, and others pointing them out. The *Daily Telegraph* said of the opening night that 'the reception could not have been more enthusiastic',[22] though as decades passed and *Rainbow* became more of an institution, there was less to be said. Reviews dating from the 1930s tended to comment on the longevity of the production; those from later still were, however, less kind: G. F. in *The Spectator* in January 1953 wondered if the

---

[18] Jack Watling to Langfield, 7 June 1998.
[19] Jack Watling to Langfield, 7 June 1998.
[20] *The Times*, 22 December 1911, p. 9.
[21] *The Illustrated Sporting and Dramatic News*, 27 January 1912, p. 952.
[22] *Daily Telegraph*, 22 December 1911.

play could keep up with modern tastes, while acknowledging the value of the illusory quality of the theatre. Four years earlier, in December 1948, *The Spectator*'s reviewer (the same?) had attended with a world-weary child who had responded adversely to St George's rhetoric, clasping her head in her hands after thirty seconds of it, as the reviewer had responded adversely to the stereotyped characterisations. Finding the concepts too unsophisticated, the reviewer damned its innocence with faint praise: 'As spectacle it is undoubtedly gorgeous; and if the gorgeousness is of the sort generally found on the lids of jigsaw-puzzle boxes, no child is going to complain of that.'[23]

In 1935 Royal endorsement came when King George V's granddaughters, the Princesses Elizabeth and Margaret, were in the audience with their mother for the Silver Jubilee performance, celebrating the twenty-five years since the accession.

Before that, however, an issue in 1932 of *Play Pictorial* was devoted to *Where the Rainbow Ends*, celebrating its twenty-first year of production; the photos include outdoor shots, taken from the film of 1921, as well as contemporary shots from the staged version. These photographs show an exaggerated, somewhat stylised manner of staging, with the Dragon King, in armour, looking like a pantomime villain; Joseph would not look out of place in a music hall. The most effective set is that for Act 1, the library, because of its realistic heavy wooden panelling. The dark timelessness of this, in the opening scene, must have contributed enormously to the sense of timelessness of the fundamental elements of the story. The heavy, claustrophobic pressure, reinforcing Rosamund's smallness and insignificance against the inevitability of the events to come, contrasts strongly with the openness and lightness of the second act – indeed with the rest of the play, since only Act 1 is set indoors – in which she is able to transcend the limits of being a child, showing that only a child's faith could reach beyond the library's limits.

The music

The reasons for the popularity of *Rainbow* are not hard to discern. The whole package was well constructed – play, production and music. The story was strong, essentially simple, fast-moving, with a happy ending. No concessions were made to the child-actors: professional standards were required and achieved. The music supported the character and mood of the story, and illustrated the individual characters. The story itself also suited Quilter, lost in a world of if-only: if only his health were better, if only all things were beautiful, if only marriages were made in heaven, if only his family were not so appalling, if only his realisation that he was homosexual were not so *difficult*, if only all women could be boyish, if only everything could be right with the world. So too is the story an if-only tale of longing for things to be as they should, for all the

---

[23] *The Spectator*, 31 December 1948, p. 869.

things that are wrong to be put right, for order to be restored from chaos. The Edwardian middle-class milieu was a comfortable one: the early action takes place in the library, which defines a minimum size for the house, and its nature; there is a bell-boy, an unseen cook, and an implication of other servants. Crispian is set for a career in the navy, as is his friend Jim. Jim's sister, Betty, is a silly feminine character, who in later years will presumably marry well, and stay empty-headed. Quilter's delicate music supports this unspoken framework.

There are two versions of the full score. The original, and very well-used, autograph copy is scored for flute, oboe, clarinet, trumpet, timpani, side drum, full string complement, and piano;[24] few of the numbers are given identities. The other copy is also well used and is for a slightly larger orchestra: flute, oboe, clarinet, bassoon, two horns, cornet, trombone, percussion (triangle, tambourine, side drum, cymbal), timpani, strings and a harp part added later, and is in a copyist's hand; the cue numbers are identical.[25] Despite the greater resources, much of the orchestration is on a smaller scale, and it is perhaps this that gives rise to the comment on the first page 'reduced score'. The recording of a selection from *Rainbow* that Quilter himself conducted uses this orchestration. A third copy is a clean score – probably a security copy – identical with the 'reduced score', though some markings have been omitted in error.[26]

The 'small orchestra' parts available for hire generally follow the scoring given in the older score, although the orchestration is inconclusive, since some of the parts are missing and there is no full score for this arrangement. It is scored for at least flute, oboe, clarinet, trumpet, percussion (triangle, tambourine, side drum, cymbals, glockenspiel), timpani and strings. There is also a piano reduction in a copyist's manuscript; the various numbers in both the piano reduction and in the parts follow those in the second full score.

The orchestration is extremely competent, though Quilter was not as a rule happy about orchestrating his work, and occasionally was advised by his fellow student from Frankfurt, Norman O'Neill, who achieved a huge success in the realm of theatre music. There is no evidence, however, that Quilter availed himself of his friend's advice on this occasion.

In the older score, the Prelude incorporates the themes representing St George, the Land Where the Rainbow Ends, and St George again; in the 'reduced score', it includes the Dragon King's music, the Land Where the Rainbow Ends, Slumber Song, then the dance of the Moon Fairies and the Fairy Frolic, St George and Rosamund; and the piano reduction follows the autograph score.

This is light music. The requirement for brevity suited Quilter, and the musical construction is straightforward – generally simple time signatures rather than compound (in common with the rest of Quilter's output), simple rhythms and simple textures.

[24] BL Add. MS 54208.
[25] BL Add. MS 72086–7.
[26] BL Add. MS 72088.

Of many outstanding items, perhaps the loveliest is that for Rosamund; certainly Grainger thought so, referring to it regularly throughout his long correspondence with Quilter, and calling it 'kingly . . . and weal-bestowing'[27] and 'soul-feeding'.[28] He had heard it early on in its career and towards the end of its second season asked if he might go to hear it again.[29] As late as 1947, he was still urging Quilter to enlarge it, and to develop it into something of symphonic proportions, to 'weave a truly symphonic adumbration' of the *Rainbow* material, Rosamund in particular.[30] However, this was alien to Quilter's nature and abilities, and, given the increased intensity of Quilter's chronic depression (and at the time Grainger wrote this, it was scarcely six months since Quilter had been discharged from a mental hospital), impossibly demanding.

What was it that Grainger heard in the music that made him want to hear a developed version? How did the music help the story? A clue lies in Ruth Conti's comment that her aunt Italia drew more and more music from Quilter, so that the play became bound up with the music, and the music with the play.

Rosamund is the lynchpin. Her importance is stated at the outset: the audience sees her first, seated alone and quietly in the darkened library, and holding the stage. She is a dreamer: if only she and Crispian could find their parents again, all would be well; but she is practical with it: she finds a way to make the dream a reality. She is quick-witted: in choosing her two wishes, she asks for her aunt and uncle's dinner to start again, thus buying her more time. She thinks laterally: she asks for help from an archetypal St George, where Crispian, with less vision, merely asks for his friend and, as companion for Rosamund, his friend's sister. Rosamund spurs on the others, encouraging them, exhorting them to persevere, to exceed that which they thought their limit. She leads from the front, but observes the conventional gender rôles when she expects Crispian and Jim to climb the flagpole: this is men's work, and her strengths are intellectual ones, not physical. She is intelligent, unlike Betty who against all instructions (stock character as she is) allows herself to be tempted away from the safety of the light green mound. Rosamund confronts her own fear, acknowledges her right to be afraid, but never wallows in defeat. She is open-minded: as she accepts the resources of the Book, of the Genie, of St George, she accepts also the resources of Cubby. She is renewed by his ideas, stimulates the others to find the materials to make a flag, and thus enables them all to summon help again. Rosamund is a rounded character of great strength and serenity, set into relief by the other generally more superficial characters.

The music to accompany and illustrate Rosamund is therefore vital. It consists of a simple balanced melody supported by some detailed part-writing, and the opening statement, scarcely altered in its later appearances except to be extended, is ten bars long: two pairs of two-bar phrases, the fifth, a coda-like phrase.

[27] Grainger to Quilter, 8 October 1947, GM.
[28] Grainger to Quilter, 26 March 1917, GM.
[29] Grainger to Quilter, 17 January 1913, GM.
[30] Grainger to Quilter, 21 July 1947, GM.

Ex. 9.1, Quilter, *Rainbow*, Rosamund's theme, Act 1
© Copyright 1912 Elkin & Co., London WC2H 0QY

It is firmly in E major, a warm, golden key. Though a chord of E major in a
tonic context appears in nearly every bar, the tonic note is seldom heard in the
melody, the theme simply twining itself about the note E, and never settling:
even at the very end of this first statement, the final melody note is the
dominant. The ever-present delay and evasion induce a feeling of wistfulness
and a longing to settle down. In some later statements of Rosamund's theme,
this need is met when the tonic is finally reached; but not at this early stage. The
opening four notes rise and immediately lift the music and its expression
positively: in Deryck Cooke's terms, affirming joy calmly and emphatically,[31]
and the following fall is soothing and comforting.[32] This melody, like
Rosamund, is central to the play and pervades its furthest corners.

Quilter's music variously accompanies stage action, accompanies ballets,
underscores dialogue, announces a character, creates or sustains atmosphere.
The item that follows Rosamund's theme, the Lullaby 'Rock-a-Bye Slumber',
performs the last function: it serves to reinforce the wistful mood. When this song
was published separately (as the 'Slumber Song'), it was given another verse, but
in the play contains only one. (The song was also arranged as a piano solo and for
piano with violin or cello.) The rock-a-bye motion is established with a 6/8
rhythm and it is set in another warm key, A♭ major. The tonic chord permeates the
song, usually with added sixths for further warmth, although a few coloured
chords hint at passing modulations. The tonic note occurs mostly only on weak
quavers and semiquavers, but lands firmly in the closing two bars, a final bolt of
security.

---

[31] Deryck Cooke, *The Language of Music* (Oxford, 1959), p. 105.
[32] Deryck Cooke (1959), p. 106.

Ex. 9.2, Quilter, *Rainbow*, 'Slumber Song', Act 1
© Copyright 1912 Elkin & Co., London WC2H 0QY

The wistful mood having been clearly set, dramatic action continues, introducing Joseph, Matilda, Cubs, and Herr Schlapps (Crispian and William having appeared before the Lullaby); the next music accompanies stage business just before the reading of the instructions to summon the Carpet Genie, whose exotic status is indicated by open fifths – of necessity undefined tonality – and flattened sevenths over a pedal E.

Ex. 9.3, Quilter, *Rainbow*, Genie Music
© Copyright 1912 Elkin & Co., London WC2H 0QY

A trumpet fanfare announces the translation of St George from monk to shining knight, followed shortly after by a full statement of his stirring melody. St George's theme is the first appearance of any of Quilter's patriotic tunes; the style is seen in the later partsongs, 'Non Nobis, Domine' and 'Freedom', which are all linked by the immensely confident leap from dominant to upper tonic: St George's patriotic message is clearly stated in the music, played underneath an equally stirring verbal description of the Battle of Agincourt by St George (with a passing nod to *Henry V*) (exx. 9.4a–c).

Ex. 9.4a, Quilter, *Rainbow*, St George's theme
© Copyright 1912 Elkin & Co., London WC2H 0QY

Ex. 9.4b, Quilter, 'Non Nobis, Domine'
© Copyright 1934 by Boosey & Co. Ltd.

Ex. 9.4c, Quilter, 'Freedom'
© Copyright 1941 by Boosey & Co. Ltd.

The personification of evil, in the form of the Dragon King, is marked by augmented chords (ex. 9.5).

Ex. 9.5, Quilter, *Rainbow*, Dragon King's motif, Act 1
© Copyright 1912 Elkin & Co., London WC2H 0QY

Ballets punctuate the stage action, pacing it, allowing both a breathing space after fast-moving events, and a sense of calm before action to come, setting it into greater relief. They are not used in a real-world setting, nor when there are adults present, with one exception: when Joseph and Matilda dance grotesquely to the music of the 'Fairy Frolic'. This dichotomy between two worlds, children/ adults, fairy/real, and how they are perceived is seen also in *Peter Pan*, where only the children are able to fly (it is explored further in Steven Spielberg's film *Hook* of 1991, where a grown-up Peter Pan is unable to fly until he returns to a sense of the child), and in the film *The Wizard of Oz* where the 'real' world is shown in black and white, and only the magical world is in colour. Joseph and Matilda have crossed the boundary into the fairy world by believing in and summoning the Dragon King: hence their participation in the dance. But because they are evil, they cannot reap its benefit: hence also therefore their violent demise. The Fairy Frolic is not heard again until Joseph and Matilda have been eaten by the Hyenas.

Thus there are no dances in Acts 1 or 4, and the first ballet, the 'Fairy Ballet', occurs as the sun begins to set, towards the end of Act 2. The sequential repetition of melodic shape in the second phrase, over a tonic pedal, together with the accompaniment figure of crotchet plus minim (or two crotchets plus rest) which throws the stress on the second beat, shows distinct hints of Gounod's *Faust* ballets and betrays its origins in French ballet music.

Ex. 9.6a, Gounod, *Faust*, ballet music – waltz

Ex. 9.6b, Quilter, *Rainbow*, 'Fairy Ballet', Act 2
© Copyright 1912 Elkin & Co., London WC2H 0QY

The expansive melody of the central section (what if it is a little close to Tchaikovsky's 'Waltz of the Flowers'?) is punctuated by a shift of metre, a hemiola device that Quilter used elsewhere in triple-metred pieces, one much used in a waltz context by Tchaikovsky. 'Fairy Ballet' indeed owes much to the French dance tradition and to Tchaikovsky, but it has a lightness that is Quilter's own; a delicate gem.

Ex. 9.7a, Quilter, *Rainbow*, 'Fairy Ballet'
© Copyright 1912 Elkin & Co., London WC2H 0QY

The tension created during this long scene, culminating in Betty's disappearance into the Wood, is maintained by continued stage activity and is then released at the beginning of the next act, with the calming influence of Rosamund's music, illustrating not Rosamund herself this time, but the appearance of her parents; it is also used to remind the audience of her words of faith in the future, that she spoke in Act 1. The long dance for – effectively – the corps de ballet is now balanced by a substantial solo dance, in which Will-o'-the-Wisp dances to his shadow.

Ex. 9.7b, Tchaikovsky, *Serenade for Strings*, Op. 48, Waltz

Will-o'-the-Wisp's light, triple-time dance is one of the finest examples of Quilter's delicate touch. Lilting triplets and mordent-like grace notes establish a hesitancy and a darting quality that describes Will's ephemeral character eloquently. The dance is a constant play of mild harmonic tension between dominant chords with added sevenths and ninths over a tonic and dominant pedal, and the resolution on to the tonic with added sixths, under an arch-shaped melody.

Ex. 9.8, Quilter, *Rainbow*, Will-o'-the-Wisp's theme, Act 3
© Copyright 1912 Elkin & Co., London WC2H 0QY

A secondary motif is more lyrical; at the end of the rising bass line it tumbles back into the decorations of the opening motif, and thence to a restatement of the main theme. The central section changes metre (from triple to duple) and texture (from light and staccato to sustained), as if Will is taking a rest or as if something has caught his attention. It is based on a tonic pedal in C major with occasional forays into the relative minor, and plays between C major and E major, using the mediant, Fauré-like, as a pivot-note. A warm chromaticism with liberally scattered secondary sevenths enhances the lyricism and a trill imitates a bird call, or perhaps Will's piping. Towards the end of the section, the music sinks down onto a gloriously rich Delian chord, C major with added minor seventh, ninth and thirteenth, before Will seems to wake up again and reiterate his main sprightly theme. His music, as wayward as he is, flits melodically and texturally.

Will blows a kiss to the Lake-King's daughter before they dance together in 'Moonlight on the Lake'; the scene is romantic, even sensual, yet sexless. He cares about no one, indifferent to the children's fate, malicious in the way he leads Joseph and Matilda into the bog, but he is not malevolent and he responds to Mrs Carey and wants to please her. He is responding to the depth of character in her – in so far as we are allowed to see it in the short characterisation that she is given – but it is nevertheless a depth that is found also in Rosamund, a serenity that counterpoints his own capriciousness.

The start of Will's conversation with Mrs Carey is underscored by the first section of his music, repeated so that it fills the space needed; it is thus integral and not merely a vehicle for a single dance, and indeed whenever his music appears, so does he. This does not happen in reverse, however: on the one occasion when he appears and his music does not, it is when – and because – he is mimicking Matilda. His conversation with Mrs Carey revolves around past events: how Will has found other people on the island. At the point where she realises that Will has seen her children, however, the underscoring uses the central, lyrical section, with its yearning theme (initiated by a powerful rising sixth, dominant to mediant), to accompany the conversation about future intentions: how Mrs Carey wants Will to show her the way to where the rainbow ends. The 'Delian' chord is intended to be reached at the point where Captain Carey, offstage, sees the ship that Will had mentioned and hails it.

Will-o'-the-Wisp dominates the scene, and his music underpins a subtle change in its viewpoint, from looking back to looking forward.

The next dance follows immediately, the first part of the second scene. Like the 'Fairy Ballet' in Act 2, it allows plenty of activity: it opens with a sequential fourths figure after a stock introduction, all in 2/4, and the rustic sound derives from the flattened sevenths. It leads into the 'Dance of the Mischievous Elves', a medley of the fourths figure, a light polka and the Elves' jeering laughter as they tease Betty. A three-note whole-tone rising motif marks the entrance of the Black Leopard/Bear and frogs enter to imitative low orchestral croaks. There is almost no spoken dialogue; the Elves sing a few words in chorus, and Betty, bewailing her lot, has but little to say. The action is carried wholly by the bustling music, the short and choppy movement well suited to the brevity of the individual items, and giving an urgency – almost irritating, certainly frenetic – to the action.

It is a relief then, after this activity, after the excitement of meeting the Slitherslime and the Slacker, and after the gruesome deaths of Joseph and Matilda, to be soothed by the serenity of the interlude between the second and third scenes. 'Moonlight on the Lake' was a favourite of Percy Grainger who played it regularly in his concerts. It is not a ballet as such but acts as a preliminary for the 'Dance of the Spirit of the Lake' – actually a duet for the Spirit and Will, which like much of the other ballet music is in ternary form. The introduction to

Ex. 9.9, Quilter, *Rainbow*, 'Dance of the Mischievous Elves', Act 3
© Copyright 1912 Elkin & Co., London WC2H 0QY

the dance again shows clear influences from Tchaikovsky; the graceful quaver melismas feel as if they are introductory passages, though they turn out to be part of the thematic material. Although this dance is, like Will's solo dance and the Fairy Ballet, in triple time, it is not until the central section that a waltz appears, tantalisingly short and owing much to the waltz songs of German and Sullivan in its chromatic rising bass lines. It eases back adroitly to the quaver melismas of the main dance and towards the end there is a hint of the Dragon King's music – denoted by augmented chords on double-dotted crotchets – which alerts the audience to the entrance of two green dragons: the Spirit lives on the Lake by the Dragon King's castle, and is ever in his shadow.

Ex. 9.10a, Tchaikovsky, Piano Concerto no. 1, slow movement

Ex. 9.10b, Quilter, *Rainbow*, 'Dance of the Spirit of the Lake'
© Copyright 1912 Elkin & Co., London WC2H 0QY

The pace of the action, presently calm and serene despite the dragon undercurrents, is slowed further with a short 'Dance of the Moon Fairies', introduced with the same motif as introduced the Spirit of the Lake and followed by a short, light dance in 3/2, a most unusual time signature for Quilter. After the two-bar introduction, the succession of three-bar phrases give a length of line that has a folk music lilt – something Quilter tried again in the piano piece 'Pipe and Tabor' (from *Country Pieces*, 1923) and in the theatre piece 'Shepherd's Holiday', from the suite for *As You Like It* (1920). The effect is enhanced by a tonic pedal under the first two phrases; the third and fourth phrases have a chromaticism that acknowledges Sullivan (and particularly 'Three Little Maids' from *The Mikado*).

Ex. 9.11, Quilter, *Rainbow*, 'Dance of the Moon Fairies'
© Copyright 1912 Elkin & Co., London WC2H 0QY

Quilter reminds us of the presence of the Spirit of the Lake with a melodic hint of her introductory music before launching into the 'Fairy Frolic', now in its proper context and no longer sounding grotesque. It is in the familiar musical language of Sidney Jones or Edward German, but even in Quilter's lighter moments, he never forgets his natural grace and elegance, and there are delightful glimpses of a lyrical chromaticism.

Ex. 9.12, Quilter, *Rainbow*, 'Fairy Frolic'
© Copyright 1912 Elkin & Co., London WC2H 0QY

Quilter's views on Wagner are infrequently documented, but in 1948, Quilter wrote to Grainger: 'I . . . went to "Tristan" and "Walküre", and thoroughly enjoyed myself – I had rather sickened of Wagner, after wallowing in him too much when I was young – but this time, I was able to judge better, and so appreciated the good things very keenly.'[33] The following year he wrote to

---

[33] Quilter to Grainger, 8 April 1948, GM.

confirm his impressions: 'I . . . had a Wagner "come-back": not quite the drunken emotion of my first wallowings, but a warm appreciation of his lovely impulses and his masterliness.'[34] He almost certainly saw his first Wagner operas while studying in Frankfurt, and musical references are to be found on rare occasions: after the Dragon's King motif is heard in Act 4, the Dragons enter to a steady march in C minor which ends with the giants' motif from *Das Rheingold*. A connection can be made between the Giants as puppets of fate, and the Dragons as puppets of the Dragon King; in both cases, an apparent inevitability in the course of events is altered at the last moment.

Ex. 9.13a, Quilter, *Rainbow*, Entry of the Dragons
© Copyright 1912 Elkin & Co., London WC2H 0QY

Ex. 9.13b, Wagner, *Das Rheingold*, Giants' motif

The chase connotations of fugue (as used in, for example, Tchaikovsky's fugal treatment illustrating the fight in his Fantasy Overture *Romeo and Juliet*) are brought into play in the extremely effective, if brief, fugue that accompanies St George's fight with the Dragon King. Fugue is rare in Quilter's output; one other fugal treatment occurs in 'A Children's Overture', with the tune for 'A Frog He Would A-Wooing Go', a different kind of chase. The fight fugue is conventional and in three parts; the voices do not necessarily stay with their first instrument, and the trumpet generally picks out the main melody notes, rather than the entire fugue subject.

---

[34] Quilter to Grainger, 9 March [1949], GM.

Ex. 9.14, Quilter, *Rainbow*, Fight between St George and the Dragon King, Act 4

Music accompanies the drama from this point until the epilogue – under-scoring, building dramatic tension, reflecting the action, and after some glancing modulations (while the curtain is down for a rapid scene change) that hint first at C♯ major and then slide through high F♯ major chords that sound like shafts of sunlight, the key slips at last, via the submediant and an enharmonic change, into A♭ major for the main statement of the theme for the 'Land where the Rainbow Ends'. The sense of anticipation, achieved over a dominant pedal, resolves just before the curtain rises and the Rainbow children enter. Then follows a résumé of the main themes – the Slumber Song juxtaposed with the music for the Land where the Rainbow Ends, followed by a 'Song for the Rainbow Children'. Will's appearance links the children – both 'real world' and Rainbow – with Captain and Mrs Carey whose entrance after Will's is accompanied by the Slumber Song; its positioning at the end of the story, a mirror-image of its appearance at the beginning, frames the drama, binding all its elements and thus symbolising the family and unity, and security and faith in the future.

The function of the music

Where the Rainbow Ends was as much part of the theatrical Christmas fare as was *Peter Pan* (which was premièred in 1904) and there are clear similarities between them – children, magic and a happy ending. In both cases, parental absence is a significant factor, as it is also in Enid Blyton's *Famous Five* books, where it is parental absence that enables the children (two girls, two boys and Timmy the dog) to have their adventures. The *Swallows and Amazons* adventures of Arthur Ransome are also safe, set against a secure and unchanging background.

Most of these stories start from a stable scenario (as indeed any disaster story does, whatever the level of disaster). In *Rainbow*, however, the opening situation is already unstable. The children are not safe: they are at risk, because of their uncle Joseph and Aunt Matilda. Along their journey, they learn many things; patriotism is only one of them: tenaciousness is another, and personal integrity.

Other characters are either helpers, 'goodies', or hinderers, 'baddies': the Genie helps and so does Cousin Matthew, though he was also largely responsible for their predicament. St George is the figure for archetypal good, and the Dragon King that for archetypal evil. Joseph and Matilda hinder, as do the Forest animals. Various characters exert control over others, and it is essentially the change of state, from the children having no control over their circumstances, to having control, that makes the story.

The change of state from being controlled to controlling entails a journey, a theme that runs through many stories and myths: Dorothy's quest in the *Wizard of Oz* is to find the way home; the final quest in *Lord of the Rings* is to take the ring to Mordor to destroy it; it is to be found in the Arthurian Quest of the Holy Grail and Sir Galahad's ultimate achievement of it; and in the Ring cycle where there are quests too numerous to mention. There are journey elements too in J. M. Barrie's *Mary Rose* of 1920, where Mary Rose seeks her lost son (to notable music by Norman O'Neill), and in Walter de la Mare's play *Crossings* of 1919 with music by Armstrong Gibbs, where the children have to discover if they can be happier when left quite alone to fend for themselves in a strange place, than when looked after by an extremely strict spinster aunt. *The Starlight Express*, based on the story *A Prisoner in Fairyland* by Algernon Blackwood, with music by Elgar, was seen by its producer in 1915 as having a 'mystic quality' which would 'help people to bear the sorrows of the war';[35] the journey there is for Minks, the chief protagonist, and indeed all the other adults to regain their childhood innocence and peace. In *Rainbow*, the children must reach the Land Where the Rainbow Ends, where all lost loved ones are found, so that they can be reunited with their parents. Their own real world has left them helpless; it is only to unreal sources of help that they can respond, and only unreal sources – the magic carpet and the book – can help them.

The children's journey to regain control begins once they have the book (which gives them hope and knowledge) and the carpet (which gives them power so they can summon the Genie of the Carpet), and in beginning to take control of their situation, they are given wishes, one of which they use, most importantly and significantly, to summon St George, as archetypal good. Once the initial quota of two children has increased to include Jim and Betty, the resulting unit then bears a marked resemblance to that of the later *Famous Five*: Cubby the lion-cub is essentially a dog, raised for Colonial and jingoistic reasons to the status of a lion. The Famous Five's Anne is equivalent to Betty; Julian, Anne's brother, links to Crispian as the dominant male figure, with Dick, Julian's younger brother, as the secondary male player, equivalent to Betty's brother Jim. George (really Georgina) cannot be written off as merely a tomboy. She too defies convention assertively and relates to Rosamund.

The move of the various adults – Joseph and Matilda, Vera and Jim Carey – into the unreal world, is paralleled by loss of control over their real-world lives; conversely the children's arrival in the unreal world signals the start of their journey to regain control, the start of their change of state. The magical creatures, being a permanent part of the unreal world, do not change.

The music provides a vivid and descriptive backcloth, with a fresh, immediate appeal, but it also provides a subtle support for the story, since those with control have their own music, a musical motif of some kind, and those with no control have none. Thus there is no music to represent Cousin Matthew, Schlapps the book dealer, the parents, the children – except for Rosamund, or Cubby the lioncub (he is in any case part of the unit of children). Joseph and Matilda only have music while they are in control; once they lose that, they lose the music too, and the music that they do have is any case a caricature, restricted to the music used later as a Fairy Frolic.

Seeds for the children's ultimate success are sown early, with the strong statements made about Rosamund. The children, as a unit, have no control; it is Rosamund who takes control for all of them. It is her vision and faith, her strength, her refusal to yield to circumstances that enable her to take up the

---

[35] Lena Ashwell (the producer) to Elgar, late 1915, quoted in Robert Anderson, *Elgar* (London, 1993), pp. 122–3.

offer presented to her in the form of the book, the carpet and the Genie. So she has her own music, and it permeates the entire play.

The music that accompanies the first appearance of Rosamund's parents has an entirely different effect from that when Joseph and Matilda have music. This is music for the 'other set' of real-world adults. Joseph and Matilda's music had not been heard before and so gives the initial impression of being their own music, but Captain and Mrs Carey's music has been heard already and it has already acquired meaning: it is Rosamund's theme; it is not their own. It signifies her calmness and serenity, and her faith in the future and her ability to transcend all difficulties and hence hope for her parents too, that all will come right. So Captain and Mrs Carey look backwards to music heard earlier, to provide them with a future, where Joseph and Matilda, unwittingly, are looking ahead, with music that will be heard later.

The Genie facilitates the transfer of the children between real and unreal worlds, and permits them to use the powers they have been given. They control him, since they summon him, but he – albeit at their command – summons St George; and so there is music for the Genie.

The various Forest creatures exist only because of the Dragon King but nevertheless exert considerable control over others: over Joseph and Matilda of course, whom they devour – and for a time, over the children, since they entice the youngest, Betty, off the safety of a magic mound, and the other children and Cubby are obliged to risk the power of the evil Forest, in order to find her. So there is music for the forest creatures, for the fairies, the Mischievous Elves, and a Black Leopard or Bear.

The Spirit of the Lake neither controls nor is controlled and she has no independent music, but she dances with Will-o'-the-Wisp, who alone of all the characters is controlled by no one.

By the end of the story, the children and Cubby have journeyed right through the Wood, and in the process the forest creatures have been unable to retain control over them. Joseph and Matilda's journey has ended with their deaths. Although the children are captured by a swarm of dragons and are on alien ground, they devise a means by which they can call St George to their aid – they can control him.

St George's music and that of the Land Where the Rainbow Ends frames the entire play; St George's underlying support runs throughout. The serenity of the music for the Land Where the Rainbow Ends indicates a successful outcome to the children's journey; its appearance at the start of the play, in the Prelude, shows that in the present is perhaps also the future – and that there will at any rate be a happy ending.

Postscript

By the 1920s, Quilter was usually conducting just the opening performance, leaving Leslie Woodgate to conduct the subsequent performances; he rarely conducted in the later seasons. The percussionist James Blades, who called himself the 'drummer' in the show, described Quilter as 'a musician's conductor – *so* gentle and appreciative'.[36] In the early years, at the end of each season, Quilter held a party for the whole cast at a hotel, usually the Savoy, but later it was limited to the five child principals, the elves, and the mothers of the younger children and held at Quilter's home. They would play games – musical chairs (with Quilter, or in the 1920s, Leslie Woodgate, playing the piano), hunt the slipper, hunt the sixpence, matchboxes passed from one nose to another, blind man's buff, charades, pin the tail on the donkey, and so on. There were prizes, displayed on the Bechstein so as to show the choice better, but in any event, no one left the party without a present.[37] Children were warned, however, to behave and be quiet, as Miss Italia Conti informed them that Mr Quilter disliked overexcitement, and the room was crammed with nick-nacks with a consequent risk of breakages. At the last performance of the season, Quilter had boxes of chocolates presented to the principals on stage, but before that, all the understudies had had their chance to play their rôles, in a special understudies' performance.

Perhaps the last words are justly given by Ruth Conti, who was closely involved with the production for many years, and ran the stage school, and Christine Bernard, sister of one of Quilter's godchildren. Christine Bernard described going to see *Where the Rainbow Ends*, and of going backstage afterwards: 'I remember his anxieties . . . the way he was treated there, all the things that tell you, however young you are, that your Uncle Roger is a part of this particular show.'[38] Ruth Conti wrote of singing the mother's 'Slumber Song' under the stage,[39] then 'turning . . . and watching the men preparing to reveal St George in his armour from the monkish figure. The tension and quietness of it all. The music – the darkness – the words – the stillness set the play firmly on its magic journey.'

[36] James Blades to Langfield, 14 March 1997.
[37] Florence Woodgate Konczewska to Langfield, 28 January 1998; and George Hammond to Langfield, 23 February 1998.
[38] Christine Bernard to Langfield, 5 September 1998.
[39] Ruth Conti to Langfield, 27 July 1998.

10

Light Music, Genre Pieces and the Miniaturist

Quilter's loves were words, the voice, the theatre and simple entertainment; from these elements springs all his compositional output.

Many of his instrumental works are arrangements of other pieces, and his instrumental arrangements of songs – where those arrangements were separately published or recorded – are discussed with the songs, for the sake of relevance to the original idea. He wrote original piano music, made piano arrangements of other pieces, and wrote short orchestral pieces, some light chamber music and incidental music; *Rainbow* has its own chapter. The effort that went into writing even a short song was enormous, and to write an extended work was out of the question: Vaughan Williams's comment to him at a dinner, suggesting that he write a symphony – 'they're ever so easy' – can only have been tongue in cheek.[1]

The Piano Music

The body of piano music is small, but it is all exquisite and highly pianistic: *Three Studies, Three Pieces for Piano, Two Impressions,* and *Country Pieces.* Of the other music that he arranged for piano, in most cases it lies under the hand so felicitously that it can be regarded as original piano music, even where the original concept was instrumental. However, Quilter felt his piano technique was non-existent (in a letter to Mark Raphael, he claimed he had 'no technique as a pianist'[2]); yet he had studied with a reputable teacher, Ernst Engesser, at Frankfurt.

All are short, characteristic pieces – the longest takes just under five minutes – defining a mood ('Summer Evening') or a type of piece (the *Studies*). Quilter uses simple ternary and binary forms throughout, though they are sometimes fairly loosely applied.

One small piece, called 'Theme', dates from 1899 and was unpublished, a sixteen-bar chorale-like piece, marked 'for pianoforte or organ' and written largely in four parts; words have been added, though they do not scan well. It is very correct, though juvenile and rather saccharine, but at the same time suggests a potential use as a Theme and Variations.

[1] Stephen Banfield, interview with Mark Raphael, unpublished note.
[2] Quilter to Mark Raphael, 15 September [1924], BL Add. MS 70607, f. 24.

The *Three Studies*, Op. 4, were published in 1910, the first one separately, and the three together, and dedicated to Madame Pura Heierhoff-de Castelaro. The scores are dated 1909, although another manuscript of the first Study is dated March 1901; it has some differences from the final version.[3]

All three studies are quite short, and are fast, textural and motivic pieces, concerned with touch and overall sound, as well as dexterity. They form a cohesive group and are remarkably free: in his piano accompaniments, Quilter is normally extremely considerate, forever eliminating possible sources of embarrassment for a pianist with limited abilities; not so here.

The first study opens in A minor with a simple melody divided between the hands, and an arpeggiated accompaniment figure that also alternates between bass and treble; the merging of one phrase with the next creates the sense of the whole of the first page being in one breath. The published score is marked *Molto allegro con moto*, a direction omitted in the 1909 manuscript. Evelyn Suart performed it at the Bechstein Hall on 8 June 1903; it was not indicated as being a first performance but it must have been one of the earliest.

The central section (the study is in ternary form) is in the tonic major, with a chordal texture, but the repeat half way through makes for an awkward fall from $f\sharp^1$ to e^1 and back to the $c\sharp^1$ at the beginning of the repeat. A sequence of diminished chords building to a brief climax delays the return to the opening section; a short coda rounds the piece off.

Ex. 10.1a, Quilter, *Study*, Op. 4, no. 1, 1901 MS, end of central section

[3] MS held by the National Library of Scotland, MS 21864.

Ex. 10.1b, Quilter, *Study*, Op. 4, no. 1, 1909 MS, end of central section

The second study, in F♯ major, is in binary form and encourages the use of the thumb on black notes. It is a flowing piece, with almost constant quaver movement, marked *Molto allegro amabile*, changed from the manuscript *Vivace ma amabile*. The melody is picked out by the top notes of the right hand, but they occur off the beat, on the second quaver of each crotchet, and this gives the piece a never-ceasing hesitancy; it feels very slightly apologetic. The flowing wistfulness is very reminiscent of Brahms's *Intermezzo*, Op. 117, no. 2, in B♭ minor.

Ex. 10.2a, Quilter, *Study*, Op. 4, no. 2, bars 2–4

Ex. 10.2b, Brahms, *Intermezzo*, Op. 117, no. 2, bars 2–5

The third study, marked *Vivace misterioso e legato* (changed from the manuscript *Molto allegro ma misterioso e legato*), reverses the tonality of the first: it opens in A major, and its middle section is in A minor. This is a lush, rich, very Brahmsian piece, with a wide dynamic and pitch range; it is moderately demanding and turbulent, with large chords and exposed and rapid octaves in the right hand. The opening section is in an arch shape, starting in the lower part of the piano's register, climbing steadily to octaves at the top, and gradually sinking again to the end of the section; there is a sense of yearning.

The middle section makes substantial use of augmented chords, contrasting with the diminished chords of the first study. The tension rises until the resolution onto a second inversion chord on the subdominant leading back to the recapitulation and the piece flies to its end. A typical Quilter chord appears at the final cadence, in the third bar from the end: a diminished chord on the subdominant, but with the supertonic raised chromatically to B♮, acting as a passing note, the whole acting as a dominant substitute. The study uses the full resources of the piano.

The *Three Pieces for Pianoforte*, Op. 16, were published in 1916, separately and in a set, though they were written at various times.[4] The first, the light and airy 'Dance in the Twilight', became very popular, but like the rest of the piano music, is now forgotten. It was sketched at much the same time as the Studies were finished, in 1909, though not finished until 1915; at the end of each graceful phrase in the opening and closing sections, Quilter uses the dominant-substitute chord that is heard so effectively in the third Study. The playful, and slightly faster, middle section passes through several keys, with a freedom of tonality allied with harmonic tension, but easing gently back to the opening section; this is substantially a straight repeat, but using sequence builds to a climax on a second inversion tonic chord and then settles to an extended perfect cadence.

The original pencil manuscript shows a few small changes: a few extra notes, adding the occasional octave; some details of accentuation and performance direction are added in the published score.

'Summer Evening' is atmospheric and impressionistic, with traces of Debussy (exx. 10.3a, b).

---

[4] The MSS of the *Three Pieces* are held by Leslie East.

Ex. 10.3a, Quilter, 'Summer Evening', bars 44–45, showing manuscript time
signatures in bar 45
© Copyright 1910 by Winthrop Rogers Ltd.

Ex. 10.3b, Debussy, 'La Chevelure', from *Chansons de Bilitis* (1897), opening

It opens calmly, marked *Andantino moderato, Tempo rubato, cantabile espressivo
e molto rubato*, in a steady 3/4, the first sixteen bars of the right hand following a
broad arch shape. The second section, *Poco con moto, sempre tempo rubato*, is
very free rhythmically, with many changes of time signature, and its substantial
(and highly pianistic) use of fourths create an open texture. There are colours
and hints of Vaughan Williams throughout this middle section, as well as of
Delius, whom he had met some years before, and whose music he so much
admired. The piece is also notable for its ornaments, commonly found in
Quilter's piano writing but especially prevalent here: crushed notes, double
grace notes and arpeggiated chords. Occasionally the notes are written out in
full, indicating the requirement for exactitude; sometimes they are used to
indicate birdsong.

The piece is serene and evocative. In 1902, its dedicatee, Charlotte Emelia
Bellot, wrote most movingly to Quilter, that the doctors had told her she had
only a very short time left to live, but that she felt no pain and really did not feel
as if she was going to die.[5] The peace within the music matches the peace in her
writing to Quilter.

As with 'Dance in the Twilight', the manuscript shows fewer performance
directions than in the final published score; one particular ·change of config-
uration of time signature is worth noting (ex. 10.3a). At this point, a 9/8 bar

---

[5] Charlotte Emelia Bellot to Quilter, 31 December 1902, BL Add. MS 70602, f. 10. She died the
following September.

replaces the original 5/8 plus 2/4 bars, giving a very different emphasis to the bar; the accents placed on the second, fourth and seventh quavers in the 9/8 bar are better supported by the original time signatures.

'At a Country Fair' is different again. It is vigorous and robust, with a strong folk-song flavour, and employing three-bar and irregular length phrases; fluidity of phrase-length is one of Quilter's hallmarks.

Ex. 10.4, Quilter, 'At a Country Fair', opening
© Copyright 1916 by Winthrop Rogers Ltd.

The piece was written and published in 1916, and dedicated to Leo Ornstein, the American virtuoso pianist and composer of Russian birth. The first section, with its generosity of notes, feels unfettered and as if it is in one breath, though leaving one slightly breathless (much as the first study does). Quilter again uses parallel fourths; where in other pieces this might give a mock-oriental flavour (as it does in 'Lanterns'), here it gives a rustic colour.

After the brittleness of the F♯ minor opening, the substantial central section is calmer, marked *Meno allegro, tempo poco rubato, cantabile espressivo e legato.* It brings a lull in the frenzy of the fair, and its sweet poignancy is emphasised by being in the submediant D major, with a more subdued mood. It meanders through various keys, then halfway through a perfect cadence (albeit with a raised dominant) changes its mind and, using the raised dominant as a pivot note, shifts neatly into F major, another subdued key.

The last section is introduced by three bars over a dominant pedal, before launching back into a repeat of part of the first section. An extended coda is fast and furious; it develops the melodic intervals throughout a nine-bar phrase, repeated a diminished fifth downwards. A recurring rhythmic motif, two semiquavers followed by a quaver, is unable to contain itself any longer, repeats itself, awards itself a quaver and becomes a 5/8 bar; the 5/8 pulse takes over, augmented to alternating bars of 3/4 and 2/4, and the last page, beside itself with excitement, is variously 3/4, 2/4, and 5/8, with a change in nearly every bar.

Differences between the pencil manuscript and the published version are again intriguing; the performance directions were originally rather milder. The manuscript clarifies a misprint in the published score: in bar 25, left hand, second beat, the c♯^{1} should be c♮^{1}; and in the forty-sixth bar from the end, the manuscript shows an extra semiquaver:

Ex. 10.5a, Quilter, 'At a Country Fair', manuscript
© Copyright 1953 Trustee of the Roger Quilter Estate

Ex. 10.5b, published score
© Copyright 1916 by Winthrop Rogers Ltd.

This is probably Quilter's most exciting piece, a world apart from the serenity of 'Now Sleeps the Crimson Petal'. He paints a vivid picture of a frenetic country fair, culminating in an extraordinary outburst of activity. Its energy in the outer sections is relentless: this is Quilter with the lid off, unrepressed.

The first of the *Two Impressions*, Op. 19, 'In a Gondola', was written in May 1914, the second, 'Lanterns', was finished in 1919, and they were published as the pair, in 1920, dedicated to Percy Grainger. Like the *Three Pieces*, they are descriptive: 'In a Gondola' lives up to its original name 'Barcarole',[6] being a dreamy and languorous piece, largely in 6/8 time. Quilter uses Debussian parallel fifths (p. 3, line 1, bar 2 left hand), and as well as using many clearly defined ornaments, the rhythms are again delicate, and precisely notated, with inner parts marked clearly. The texture, like that in 'Summer Evening' and 'At a Country Fair', is intricate, and the use of whole tones in thirds, again very Debussian, is notable. Unusually, in the pencil manuscript, a very occasional fingering is given, but this is not shown in the published copy.

The central section moves a little faster, the half bar sometimes treated as a light waltz; this is especially noticeable in the all too brief *cantabile* section, which is expansive, and suggestive of Quilter's later waltzes. The whole-tone thirds are supplemented by a parallel line a diminished fifth below the lower

---

[6] The MSS of 'In a Gondola' and 'Lanterns' are held by Leslie East; that of 'In a Gondola' shows the title 'Barcarole' rubbed out and replaced by 'In a Gondola'.

Ex. 10.6, Quilter, 'In a Gondola', twenty-fifth bar from the end
© Copyright 1920 by Winthrop Rogers Ltd.

notes of the thirds. The waltz motif reappears, marked *appassionato* as well as *cantabile*, before a condensed recapitulation of the opening section.

'Lanterns' is a sparkling piece with crisp rhythms and a dance feel. A nine-bar introduction sets the tone of a lively piece in 2/4, whose rhythms constantly surprise. The middle section, in the subdominant, is calmer, but the three-bar phrases deceive the ear into expecting a regularity which never comes. Minor sevenths and perfect fourths are plentiful, and blend the central and last sections happily. The broken fourths figuration of the last section is a common toccata-type, very reminiscent of 'At a Country Fair' and 'Love's Philosophy'. A coda is in the shape of a 'reverse' arch: the pitch generally drops, then rises to a climax, marked *brillante*. This piece is not as innocuous as it at first seems on paper: there is an edge of brilliance, a clarity, that catches the imagination.

In contrast, the four *Country Pieces for Piano*, Op. 27, written in 1923, are disappointingly straightforward. They are relatively easy to play, and it is probably significant that these are the only pieces where any fingerings are given in the final published version. Nevertheless, they are pleasant, and delighted their dedicatee, Quilter's former music teacher Edith Brackenbury.

The first of the set, 'Shepherd Song', is just that – an instrumental song. In ternary form, the entire first section is in conventional four-bar phrases, in the form ABA, and is thus satisfactorily shaped, if predictable. The central section, in the flat submediant, is solid, though still flowing, with simple cross-rhythms mixing the basic 6/8 with a temporary 3/4. The final section is shortened to eight bars, allowing a short eight-bar coda, plus an additional final chord. The whole is enormously charming, and unpretentious; all it lacks – and that is a matter for discussion – are words.

The second, 'Goblins', is once more a characteristic piece, with a pianistic texture and simple syncopation over a staccato left hand. It starts in C minor, moves to a more lyrical relative major, and a lighter central section is in C major, retaining the bright texture with continued use of fourths. It asserts a motivic rhythm ♪ ♫ ♪♫ within a very strong 2/4; the heavy, *marcato* feel is supported by the shape of the notes in the left hand, frequently repeating the second and third quavers, and the fourth and the first. A falling chromatic scale in the top line, from the tonic to the dominant, colours the piece, but the potentially sinister atmosphere is never quite realised, and it ends with a shimmering glissando to the top of the piano, presumably as the goblins disappear.

Ex. 10.7, Quilter, *Country Pieces*, 'Goblins', opening
© Copyright 1923 by Winthrop Rogers Ltd.

'Forest Lullaby' is an excellent foil to 'Goblins', lyrical, as is 'Shepherd Song', and again simply constructed. The first section, in A major, is in ABA format, with a simple 2/4 melody. The warm central section is predictably in the flat submediant, F major, making the whole a warm reflective piece. The rhythmic figure here is in quavers, in pairs, each pair slurred heavily, and it eases conventionally back into the opening section. The essence of the lullaby is its simplicity, and, like the *Shepherd Song*, is unpretentious.

'Pipe and Tabor' is marked *Allegro giocoso* and lives up to its name. The first section is generally in three-bar phrases in 3/4, but the pace is increased at the end of the section with the change to three two-bar phrases. Yet, despite its crisp and sparkling rhythms, it lacks the inventiveness and imagination of 'At a Country Fair'. The comfortable *amabile* central section in E major retains its brightness, but makes a brief excursion into a distant A♭ major – the underlying bass line climbs up the notes of the E major triad, treating the G♯ enharmonically – before recapitulating and finishing with a brief coda. This is neatly done: like the end of the first section, it speeds up the overall motion, this time by shifting to 2/4 in all but name, bringing the piece, and the set, to an effervescent end.

Throughout all these piano pieces, Quilter uses simple, and basic, devices, particularly sequence, which is an effective way to build harmonic (and, on a miniature scale, dramatic) tension, and arch structures, which in his songs are not available to him in the same way, simply because they would put the song out of a normal singer's vocal range; very often, the arch replaces the structure that the text of a song supplies.

Quilter's piano music, though pianistic, is remarkably difficult to memorise. The usual devices that are used by pianists – these may include extracting patterns within the music, to enable conscious memorisation – simply do not work; Debussy's swathes of notes, in contrast, conceal patterns which can be memorised. Because Quilter composed at the piano, the sequence of chords is often driven by the shape of the chord rather than by a theoretical logic, resulting in a vertical feel to the music. Musical progress within any of the pieces is thus at two levels: the overall harmonic structure and direction, with relatively conventional modulations, and the placing of individual chords, the one leading on from the previous, and liable to alteration in any later repetition; at every turn, something is done differently.

Other piano pieces are arrangements: the delightfully fresh solo and duet versions of the *Three English Dances*, which certainly stand on their own merits, the incidental music to *As You Like It*, and the beautiful piano solo version of 'Drink to Me Only with Thine Eyes' that conjures up an image of Quilter playing it late at night on his Bechstein grand. There are other pieces – for example *Where the Rainbow Ends* and *A Children's Overture* (solo version by Quilter, duet version by his friend Anthony Bernard) – which are more properly regarded as piano reductions than as piano arrangements. The orchestral parts to the incidental music to *The Rake* include a piano part which is complete in itself, and was published on its own, without alteration, as an arrangement for piano solo; it betrays its instrumental origins, however, and is also best regarded as a piano reduction.

Orchestral music

The *Serenade*, Op. 9, was scored for small orchestra (double woodwind but with single oboe; four horns and two cornets, timpani, percussion and strings). It was performed only twice, on 27 August 1907 (at a Promenade concert, conducted by Henry Wood) and on 13 November of the same year, and Quilter then withdrew it, pending reworking. It has three movements, and lasts twelve minutes; it was dedicated to Quilter's composition teacher at Frankfurt, Ivan Knorr.

The *Serenade* is at odds with Quilter's other work; it is unlike anything else he wrote in scale, construction and thought. As *The Times* reviewer said after its first performance, it is a very engaging piece:

> [it] is really a diminutive symphony in three movements, of which the last is a Rondo. The whole work shows the lightness of touch and freshness of idea that have characterised [Quilter's] earlier writings; and if the third movement does not add very much to what has already been said in the first two, the andante is so engaging, with its simple, straightforward scoring and unaffected melodies, that one is ready to forgive the echoes in the Finale. The opening allegro, which strikes the buoyant note that marks the whole serenade, contains a good deal of bustling counterpoint, which is none the less clever for being unobtrusive and melodious; and the scoring here and in the other movements shows a nice appreciation of the 'partialities' of the various instruments – an appreciation which is too often neglected by some of the more advanced of the modern instrumentalists.[7]

This is a very fair assessment, even if the last movement is not a rondo, but like the first, cast in sonata form. The first movement opens in C minor, with a second key group in E♭, the relative major. The opening motif is imperious, but agitated, on clarinets, bassoons, violas and cellos, and extends effortlessly over six bars (ex. 10.8).

---

[7] *The Times*, 28 August 1908, p. 6, c. 4.

Ex. 10.8, Quilter, *Serenade*, first movement, opening theme

There is plenty of material here for development, and Quilter focuses especially on the rhythmic motif ♩♪ and the syncopated repeating chords, and one of the melodic shapes, which is at once taken up by the violins in bar 6 and promptly imitated on woodwind; it is derived from the third bar of the main theme, shown by (a). The motif, heard on oboes, is derived from the same source (ex. 10.9).

Ex. 10.9, *Serenade*, first movement, secondary motifs

This metamorphoses into the calm secondary theme, heard on woodwind, and accompanied by open-textured sustained chords on strings, with no brass or percussion (ex. 10.10).

Ex. 10.10, *Serenade*, first movement, secondary theme, bar 26

In the development, Quilter explores the opening theme still further, dividing its rhythmic and melodic elements across the woodwind, and using the brass to punctuate the texture. The timpani are silent throughout until the moment of recapitulation, which is heralded by the cornets accompanied simply by triplets on violins, and the secondary theme appears in the tonic major. All proceeds normally until an interrupted cadence initiates the coda, which brings the movement to a bustling conclusion. The writing is tight and economical in length, though there was some criticism at its first performance of too much repetition; there is plenty of air in the orchestration.

The pastoral second movement is in ternary form; its simple, opening melody, full of sighing, consists of a series of beautifully shaped phrases of varying lengths, falling naturally and conversationally. It is heard on oboe accompanied by muted strings (ex. 10.11).

Ex. 10.11, Quilter, *Serenade*, second movement, opening melody

The first section is short and to the point, gently; the middle section is in the tonic minor, F minor, and picks up a triplet motif introduced briefly towards the end of the first section; it is dainty, with a splash of triangle, and pizzicato accompaniment to the flutes, brass used sparingly; when the lyrical melody returns, it is on horn and cellos, with a countermelody on violins, a fuller orchestration; a brief visit to D♭ major dissolves into a point of subdued climax, and a short coda, with hints of the rhythmic ideas from the central section, and a final statement of the melody on a single clarinet in its chalumeau register.

The last movement is again in sonata form, in C major with a vivacious motivic theme in 3/4; hemiolas proliferate (ex. 10.12).

Ex. 10.12, Quilter, *Serenade*, third movement, main subject

A subsidiary theme on woodwind and pizzicato violins emerges in A♭ major and from this arises the secondary theme in the dominant G major. The exposition ends with a sequence of descending chords that modulate sharply into E major for the start of the development section and this explores the ideas heard so far, treating them largely sequentially. The recapitulation is conventional and sweeps into a coda based on the opening theme, with a final concluding flourish.

Although the work is of small proportions, it put Quilter in a vulnerable situation; there were no words to anchor him and it reached beyond the familiar. It plumbs no particular depths, though it sometimes hints that it might have liked to, and his own comment was that he wanted to lengthen the last movement and rework some of the orchestration – perhaps an excuse more than anything, to avoid the risk of being judged on something where he lacked confidence. But it is perfectly acceptable as it is, and there is much to be said for leaving well alone, and not prolonging a piece beyond its capacity.

The *Three English Dances*, Op. 11, were first performed at a Promenade concert on 30 June 1910, and were dedicated to Percy Grainger, who was overjoyed by them, so much so that the opening of the first is heard briefly but quite clearly in Grainger's 'Gay but Wistful', from the suite *In a Nutshell*; Grainger told Quilter:

> Yr English Dances fetch me much more than the Children's Overture, delightful tho the latter is. But I like the turns of your CREATIVE Form better than the form of folksong. I greatly prise [sic] the middle voice melody of the trio of the 2nd dance, with the lovely waving descant above. And I love the A flat section (letter C) of the 3rd dance. All 3 are the most perfect thinkable examples of CREATIVELY UNFOLDING FORM. And this is what I worship in you more than all yr other lovely gifts – the way you modulate away into a new key-lane, the way a moving part lands you in a new harmony.[8]

The *Dances* come in several forms: Quilter's original orchestration for full orchestra, published in 1910, and various other orchestral versions, one of which, for small orchestra, was by Percy Fletcher, and is the only readily available published arrangement; it came out in 1912. Other arrangements (including one for military band) are listed in various catalogues, though the arrangers are unknown. Quilter also arranged it for piano solo and piano duet, and these editions were published in 1910; the piano duet version especially is enormous fun.

The first Dance, in 4/4, is sprightly, with tonic pedals for rusticity, and long-spun phrases; a passing modulation to the dominant D major is balanced, on the reprise of the main melody, by a passing modulation to subdominant C major. The calmer, more static, central section – the Dances are all in ternary form – is in the tonic minor and is closely linked with the main section, with a rhythmic motif derived from the second phrase.

The second is in a playful but pastoral 6/8, Sullivanesque in its extension of phrases; it opens in C minor, but the central section instead of going to an expected relative major, drops down to the submediant A♭ major; the melody conspicuously omits the fourth and seventh degrees of the scale, though their presence in the accompanying countermelody prevents a pentatonic sound.

Repeated tonic–dominant open fifths launch a lively dance in 2/4; the central section is again in A♭ major, though this is now the key of the flat submediant. The texture is suitably different, and marked *cantabile e sostenuto*. In all movements, there are no codas beyond a few brief chords to bring each dance to a suitable conclusion and while there is certainly a sound of Sullivan, the dances are closer to Edward German, and his *Nell Gwyn* and *Merrie England* dances, though without German's jigs and dotted rhythms. The orchestration is competent, bright and clear, and the sound is indubitably English.

A Children's Overture, Op. 17, is an unfailingly delightful work, with a light-

8 Grainger to Quilter, 21 July 1947, GM.

handed orchestration and skilful weaving and linking of the nursery rhymes, and its clear sound equates approximately to the clarity of the illustrations in Walter Crane's *The Baby's Opera* which had inspired it. Grainger wrote of its 'fine sparkling effects', its 'beautiful use of detached woodwind with pizzicati' and 'the soothing groundswells of legato emotions, vibrating strings, breathing brass'.[9] Quilter arranged it for Chappell's 'Popular Orchestral Edition' and it was published in that form in 1921, having been first performed on 18 September 1919 at a Promenade concert. He dedicated it to his brother Percy.

The numerous recordings on 78 – which include those by Maclean, Sargent, Barbirolli and Weldon – all differ slightly in their content depending on the number of record sides and the exact length required; even those that are nominally complete may be adjusted slightly at the ends of record sides, in order to make a clean finish. Despite Winthrop Rogers's difficulty over the cost of publishing score and parts, many recordings use the original scoring (possibly using the original parts): Maclean's of 1922, Sargent's of 1928, and George Weldon's as late as 1952; Barbirolli's of 1933 uses the Popular Edition. Maclean's score, though clearly the original full version, nevertheless has a few altered details of orchestration that enrich the sound.

The original scoring is for full orchestra and the Popular Edition for small orchestra, the reduction being chiefly in the brass, reduced from four horns, three trumpets, three trombones and tuba, to two horns and two cornets. The only full score appears to be for the original version; the Popular Edition has a piano conductor score, labelled 'piano accompaniment' and a first violin conductor score; the piano solo version stands alone, independent of any orchestral version.

From the opening horn call, taken from the first four notes of 'Baa, Baa, Black Sheep' the mood is set: this is a nostalgic look at the world of nursery rhymes. Quilter sometimes contrasts sections of the orchestra, sometimes plays one instrument off against another, or allows one to complement another conversationally; he emphasises the haunting qualities of the horns and clarinets and it is hard sometimes to recall the original melodies, so felicitous are Quilter's fantasias. Above all, it is the countermelodies that enchant, providing so much detail, invention and variety that there is something new to be heard at every playing. 'Over the Hills and Far Away', like many of the rhymes, never quite finishes in the familiar way, but meanders away along with its title. A curious little fugato section, lasting only a few bars, heralds 'The Frog and the Crow', but 'A Frog He Would A-Wooing Go' is given full fugal treatment, initially in C minor, but opening out into a triumphant C major.

The keys are frequently the same as shown in Crane's book, and Quilter arranges the tunes so that, very broadly, those in sharp keys frame those in flat keys, using pivot notes to link the material and inevitably giving rise to modulations to the mediant and flat submediant (for example, 'I Saw Three Ships' in F♯ major, followed by 'Sing a Song of Sixpence' in B♭ major).

[9] Percy Grainger to Quilter, 30 September 1924, GM.

The Overture was rightly popular, but eventually the BBC, having broadcast it on many occasions, designated it a 'class D' piece: not up to standard for inclusion in a Promenade concert, although suitable for a light-music programme.[10] Light music it certainly is, and totally captivating.

Quilter took part of the Overture – 'A Frog He Would A-Wooing Go' – when asked to provide a fanfare for use at a Musicians' Benevolent Fund dinner in about 1930;[11] he called it 'Fanfare for Children' and the extant score (in a copyist's hand) shows that it was scored for four trumpets, four trombones, cymbal and timpani. It avoids the fugal treatment that the rhyme has in the Overture, and is a free arrangement of the final section, building up to a small climax appropriate for its mere twenty-eight bars.

Robert Atkins was producer at the Old Vic theatre in London from 1920 to 1925. He was noted for the simplicity of his productions coupled with swift action, and his attempts to return to the kind of performances that might have been seen in Shakespeare's day, and he produced *As You Like It* in 1920. The apparent simplicity of Quilter's score may well have appealed to him and supported his vision of the play, though the musical director, Charles Corri, was known to be not much impressed with Quilter's music generally.

Quilter's music to the play is readily assimilated, yet retains the hallmarks of his songs – flattened sevenths, intricate inner melodies, flowing lines, felicitous phrase-balance and piquant chromaticism. It was originally scored for single woodwind (flute, oboe, clarinet, bassoon), horn, two first violins, two seconds, viola, cello, bass, and harp, thirteen instruments in all.[12] The incidental music no longer survives, but Quilter made a Suite from it; it is very short, lasting barely nine minutes, and he rescored it for small orchestra: flute, oboe, two clarinets, bassoon, two horns, two trumpets, trombone, timpani and percussion, harp and strings.

The first of the four items in the Suite, 'Shepherd's Holiday', opens with a bell-chime, as if to call the people away from their work; its 6/8 lilt is reinforced by the slight syncopation. The main statement is twelve bars long, in three four-bar phrases; Quilter also uses triple phrasing in 'Pipe and Tabor', the last of the *Country Pieces*, and the lack of symmetry (though beautifully balanced) evokes an image of inept country dancers. The last of the three phrases bears more than a passing resemblance to the chorus of 'Blow, Blow, Thou Winter Wind', from the same play, at the words 'Most friendship is feigning, most loving mere folly'.

Ex. 10.13a, Quilter, *As You Like It*, 'Shepherds' Holiday', bars 31–34
© Copyright 1920 by Boosey & Co. Ltd.

[10] BBC WAC, R27/177/1.
[11] This is described in Eugène Goossens's autobiography, *Overture and Beginners* (London, 1951).
[12] Quilter to Percy Grainger, 9 February [1919], GM.

Ex. 10.13b, Quilter, 'Blow, Blow, Thou Winter Wind', refrain
© Copyright 1905 by Boosey & Co. Ltd.

Any bitterness implied in the words is whirled away in the energy of the restatement of the theme. The piece is in ternary form, the central section, in the relative F♯ minor, continuing the pastoral sound with flattened sevenths and a drone bass, and a neat continuity with the outer section is provided by use first of a similar rhythm, and then of a similar melodic outline, before the return of the main theme.

'Evening in the Forest' has a similar tranquillity to Rosamund's music from *Where the Rainbow Ends*; it is a simple presentation of an attractive melody. Quilter uses horns in a melodic way, as he does in the *Serenade*, and the oboe is used very plaintively. The chords towards the end, alternating between tonic and submediant, and tonic and flattened seventh, result in semitonal play between F and F♯, and between D and E♭ and add a gentle colour.

Ex. 10.14, Quilter, Suite: *As You Like It*, 'Evening in the Forest', ending
© Copyright 1920 by Boosey & Co. Ltd.

'Merry Pranks' opens with a vigour worthy of Grainger, though its steady, lively 3/4 melody is soon disturbed with extended phrases. Hemiolas and light triplet figures on the second and then the first beat of the bar disturb further, and a silent first beat completes a gentle disintegration of the pulse and the regular phrase length. The brass call order, and a harp glissando dissolves the mild chaos, introducing a central section with the grace of a minuet. Confusion returns, but a perfect cadence emerges, and the piece ends before the prankster can do any more damage.

'Country Dance' too has a strong sense of rhythm in a folksong idiom, with the recurrent figure ♩ ♪♪ reversed as ♪♪ ♩ so that, as well as simple repetition, there are sometimes two adjacent crotchets and sometimes a sequence of four quavers. The cadence points are made very solid when the second figure is augmented to two crotchets and a minim, and the opening of the third eight-bar phrase of the main statement turns the cadence rhythm about, to a minim and two crotchets; the result is lively and varied. Pivot notes and parallel chords surprise to the end (ex. 10.15).

Ex. 10.15, Quilter, *As You Like It*, 'Country Dance', ending

The music that was published as the Ballet Suite *The Rake* was orchestrated by Sydney Baynes for small orchestra, from Quilter's original version, which was almost certainly, as with *As You Like It*, for a theatre band. Baynes's score also included a piano part, and this was published separately without alteration as the music from *The Rake* for piano solo; it was thus complete within itself. It is not, however, a piano conductor score – the first violin contains the instrumental cues, not the piano part. The ballet was first performed on 17 March 1925, in Manchester, as an item within C. B. Cochran's revue *On with the Dance*, for which Noël Coward wrote most of the words and music.

The time signatures are symmetrical across the suite: 6/8, 2/4, 3/4, 2/4 and 6/8; all but the last item are in ternary form and all have different characters. The sound is that of British light music at its best, and although Quilter's original orchestration and thus Baynes's exact contribution is no longer known, the orchestration is certainly attractive and shows off Quilter's work effectively; the composition is tight and compact.

The first and last movements are both in G major and are linked by their openings, identical three-note fanfares, D, down to A, then up to C, all three notes on strong beats; they are identical not only to each other, but also to the opening of 'Shepherd's Holiday' from *As You Like It*. The main statement of the first movement is derived from the fanfare, and the syncopation that follows is bright and sharp, giving Massine an opportunity to show the wit and vigour for which his choreography was noted.

Ex. 10.16, Quilter, *The Rake*, 'Dance at the Feast'

The first and last movement frame the inner three, allowing different moods. The second movement – 'The Light-hearted Lady' – has melodic and rhythmic similarities with 'Pipe and Tabor', from the *Country Pieces* for piano of two years earlier, and its use of parallel fourths mirrors a similar usage in 'Goblins' from the same set of pieces. An intriguing brief sequence of octave jumps on pizzicato strings in its introduction suggests a ticking clock and the passing of time, though the central section has a light pastoral flavour, courtesy of pedal notes in fifths; the whole has a slight, offbeat touch.

The third movement, 'The Frolicsome Friend', is a fairly slow waltz, as if the dancer is gracious but rather clumsy. The main rhythmic motif runs ♩ 𝄾 ♪ ♩ | ♩ and hemiolas disturb the easy flow; inner parts moving chromatically in contrary motion maintain Quilter's usual level of intricacy. The melody sweeps easily across two octaves in broad gestures, and its long line staggers upwards to the return of the main motif, which with the quaver rest, and well-marked third beats slurring heavily on to the first beat, sounds as if the frolicsome friend is a drunken one.

Ex. 10.17, Quilter, *The Rake*, 'The Frolicsome Friend', opening

The fourth movement, 'Allurement', is in C minor and is initiated by a three-note motif (*a*) repeated sequentially in bars 3 and 4 to give an exotically sinuous six-note chromatic scale which insinuates itself throughout the whole piece; the result has a remarkable intensity of feeling and a strong mood of yearning.

Ex. 10.18a, Quilter, *The Rake*, 'Allurement', opening

Ex. 10.18b, 'Allurement', bars 41–42

A lighter section, in descending staccato triplet chords, seems to dismiss the mood of the first section, but a brief inner melody, moving stepwise upwards then back, soon gives opportunity for the sinewy motion to return, agitatedly, building up to a climactic chord based on the opening motif. With further recollections of the opening motif and a sense of resignation, the piece ends on a Picardie third. This is a remarkable piece – fifty-three bars and a mere ten lines of piano score – yet there is packed into it a complexity and unity of construction that is unusual for Quilter's light music.

The intense emotion is swept away in an instant with the opening of the fifth movement, 'Midnight Revels'. In its first part, the eight- and sixteen-bar format is routine, but its sharp, brittle quality lifts it out of its predictability. The second part modulates abruptly from G to E major, changes tempo to 2/4 and inverts and reverses the three-note fanfare; it is accompanied by off-beat quavers, and behaves like an extended coda. The Suite as a whole is well-structured, well-written and underrated.

Chamber works

'Gipsy Life' is subtitled 'Fantasy Quintet' and in accordance with the contemporary conventions, it is for string quintet with piano, six players in all. It has only the occasional signpost to show that it is Quilter, and is a strange piece: light music with a mock Hungarian colour. It is in sections, of varying tempi, and is dominated by the piano part which has no break; the lack of variety is tiring and the piece would undoubtedly have benefited from a change of texture. It was published by Goodwin and Tabb in 1935, in their 'English String Series' and dedicated to Leslie Bridgewater.

Quilter made several instrumental arrangements of songs and orchestral pieces; details are given in the catalogue of works, and generally there is little else to say. The arrangements were made for a purpose; pieces were arranged for piano solo to popularise them and increase sales: the piano suite from *Where the Rainbow Ends*; the *Music from 'Where the Rainbow Ends'*; 'Slumber Song' and the *Two* and *Four Dances from 'Where the Rainbow Ends'* are such instances – practicable versions of the 'best bits'.

Where the Rainbow Ends generated many other arrangements: 'Moonlight on the Lake' and 'Water Nymph' were arranged for small orchestra and also for piano sextet, all published in 1937; a piano quintet version dates from 1922. A manuscript score of 'Water Nymph' in Quilter's hand is the piano conductor score of the 1937 arrangement but has a copyright date of 1952; other parts within the same manuscript, although incomplete, appear to be for a chamber combination; a cello part is marked 'for trio version'. In addition, a manuscript score of 'Moonlight' is the piano conductor score of the 1937 arrangement, though it has been given a copyright date of 1936, and another of 1947.

'Slumber Song' came arranged for piano solo, for violin and piano, and for cello and piano, all published in 1912. 'Fairy Frolic', arranged for piano trio, was published in 1929, and a manuscript version of 'Fairy Ballet' was partially rescored for full orchestra by Quilter, and completed by Leslie Woodgate.

Quilter arranged songs from the cycle *To Julia* for instrumental combinations: the third song, 'To Daisies', and the fifth, 'Julia's Hair', were arranged for cello and piano, both published in 1919. 'Julia's Hair' was also published for violin and piano in the same year; the sixth song, 'Cherry Ripe', was published in 1919, for violin and piano, as 'Love Song to Julia' and was performed in 1917 though the manuscript is dated 1918, its date of finishing.

Two of the *Old English Popular Songs*, 'Drink to Me Only' and 'Three Poor Mariners' were arranged for violin and piano, and also for violin, cello and piano (simply an additional cello part), published in 1917 and called *Two Old English Tunes*; a piano solo version of 'Drink to Me Only' was published in 1927.

On the whole, the arrangements of songs for small chamber groups, while attractive, are not particularly interesting, the string parts, where they are not simply the voice part, being obbligato lines rather than contributing anything of significance; those arrangements that do not include piano are often more satisfactory. They were written for friends (and especially for the Harrison sisters) or because there was a popular market for them. The original works, however, show an understanding of miniaturist forms; he stayed, not within his limits, since that implies an unnecessary criticism that he did not attempt larger-scale forms, but within what he understood. Those works are invariably fresh, almost always highly inventive, and display a full appreciation of the environment for which they were intended.

11

The Opera: *The Blue Boar – Julia – Love at the Inn –* et alia

The Chinese Opera

This was Quilter's first full-scale attempt at an opera, but in all probability never got further than the planning and sketch stages of early 1911; nothing remains of it. The story behind *The Never-Ending Wrong* of Po Chü-I was one of political intrigue, rebellion and tragedy: the Emperor Ming Huang loves T'ai Chên; she lives within the confines of the palace and has a brother, Yang Kuo-chung, who is the Minister of State. The translator Cranmer-Byng set the scenario neatly: 'The Emperor is fleeing with a small, ill-disciplined force before the rebellious general An Lu-shan into the province of Ssuch'uan.'[1] The Emperor's soldiers are tired, ill-fed and on the point of revolt, and believing Yang to be a traitor, cut off his head and demand the death of Yang's sister too, on the grounds that she must surely be implicated in his supposed treachery. To appease his soldiers and prevent a full-scale revolt, he hands over T'ai Chên and she is strangled.

Po Chü-I's poem is 208 lines long in Cranmer-Byng's translation, and deals less with the appalling events than with the epic qualities exhibited by the characters, in particular, with Ming Huang's ultimately successful search for T'ai Chên's spirit, and her forgiveness of him. In Quilter's letters that refer to the proposed opera, images of 'white hibiscus bowers' abound; phrases such as 'Music on the languid breeze/ Draws the dreaming world to love' had an obvious appeal to Quilter's sensibilities. Edith Sitwell made wise suggestions concerning the opening, and how to provide a context; Quilter evidently had an idea to have a 'crane flying homeward across the sunset' and to have a 'song [sung] in semi-darkness, before the curtain is raised' both of which notions pleased her.[2] How much of the original story Quilter planned to set is unknown; it is hard to imagine him responding to the bloodthirsty aspects of the story, though the redemptive qualities of Po Chü-I's interpretation were clearly a different matter.

Although it ultimately came to nothing, it was nevertheless valuable experi-

---

[1] L. Cranmer-Byng, *A Lute of Jade* (London, 1909).
[2] Edith Sitwell to Quilter, 16 May 1911, BL Add. MS 70602, f. 91.

ence for Quilter. Other projects never got even that far, until his collaboration with Rodney Bennett on *The Blue Boar*, in 1929.

The Blue Boar, Julia, Rosmé, Love and the Countess, Love at the Inn, The Beggar Prince

This was basically one light opera, in several different versions, the stories containing common elements, but varying in the detail. *The Blue Boar* came first, broadcast as a one-act version of the written three-act opera on 23 October 1933, and given a second performance the following evening. *Julia* came next, on 3 December 1936. In some of Quilter's own autobiographical notes, probably dating from the 1940s, he refers to 'a light opera called *Julia* (since renamed *Rosmé*) . . . given at Drury Lane a few years ago',[3] and further notes sometimes cross out *Rosmé*, and replace it with *Love at the Inn*. There are three copyright dates for *Love at the Inn*, 1940, 1948 and 1949, and it is likely that this arose because certain numbers were published at different times; the copyright date in the libretto is 1949. The discussions between Jeffrey Lambourne, who wrote the book for it, and Quilter also suggest that the intention was that it should be completed and issued much sooner than happened and Lambourne was extremely annoyed at the publisher's procrastination. *Love and the Countess* probably preceded *Love at the Inn*; one song attributed to it, 'Island of Dreams (Venetian Serenade)', was published in 1946. A further version was evidently in the offing, for in an envelope amongst Quilter papers labelled *The Beggar Prince* are incomplete lyrics for another light opera, which bear some similarities to the others. These papers are undated, and there is no mention of anything identifiable as *The Beggar Prince* in any extant correspondence; a letter however from Rodney Bennett relating to some sort of operatic venture, and held with the lyrics in the same envelope, is dated 13 January 1938.[4] Quilter and Jeffrey Lambourne began a collaboration on a light opera to be called *The Golden Mantle*, but Lambourne started work on the libretto in 1952, and the work never came to fruition.[5]

The Blue Boar was never heard in its entirety and so *Julia* was a major attempt to make it better known; the variants came about because although no version was especially successful, the music was good and for once Quilter knew it, and he was anxious to give it a broader appeal and make it more marketable. This may not have been such an issue between *The Blue Boar* and *Julia* but accounts for the differences between *Julia* and *Love at the Inn*; the remaining versions were probably little more than work in progress.

Complete libretti exist for *Julia* and for *Love at the Inn*. Rodney Bennett wrote the book for *The Blue Boar* and the lyrics for that and for *Julia* and *Love at the*

---

[3] Archives held by Leslie East.
[4] Archives held by Leslie East.
[5] Letters from Lambourne to Quilter, dated June–September 1952, author's collection.

Inn. The book for *Julia* was by Vladimir Rosing and Caswell Garth, and that for *Love at the Inn* was by Jeffrey Lambourne. There are many letters from Quilter to Bennett covering the period during which they wrote *The Blue Boar*, but, beyond Quilter writing perhaps that he was working on or had just finished a particular song, it is clear that they rarely discussed operatic matters by letter, reserving that task for their frequent face-to-face meetings: Bennett would often come to stay at Montagu Street, and they would sometimes go on to the theatre in the evening. When the time came to place the work, they had both moved on to other things, and so discussed those difficulties in correspondence.

Plot details

These exist for *The Blue Boar* (from the *Radio Times*), *Julia* (from the programme and libretto) and *Love at the Inn* (from the libretto) and some character details are known at least in part for the other three variants, though the degree of knowledge of the musical content varies. *Love at the Inn,* having been published, has a clearly defined musical content, but determining what was in the others is dependent upon various sources – reviews, previews and the existence of various manuscripts of the music and the lyrics.

Where they can be determined, the plots are light and unpretentious. Where they cannot, the situation is unlikely to be any different.

The Blue Boar. The story was originally inspired by a 1759 painting by Boucher called 'Madame de Pompadour' and was derived from a French story Quilter had once read. Anne, Countess of Clovelly, is a rich young widow and the ward of the Duke of Chelsea, who, in connivance with Anne's sister-in-law, Lady Sophia, wants her to marry his nephew, Charles, Marquis of Melford. Charles has been pursuing a singer, La Mancinelli, who is a former amour of the Duke. Anne celebrates her birthday, but despite the Duke's best intentions, Charles fails to meet her on this occasion, being summoned away to La Mancinelli by his manservant Robert. His uncle follows him there, but meets only La Mancinelli's disgruntled husband, and sensing an ally, invites him to a grand garden party he is giving the following day.

Meanwhile, Jenny Rollick, of *The Blue Boar* inn, has a wedding party later that day. The Duke visits *The Blue Boar* on occasion, disguised as 'Mr Jenkins', and in that capacity plans to visit the inn for the wedding party. Lucy, Anne's maid, also plans to visit the inn, as does Robert, who is much smitten with her. Robert arranges matters so that Charles meets La Mancinelli there too. So now at the inn are the Duke, disguised as Mr Jenkins, Lucy, Robert, Charles, and also Anne, who has disguised herself for the part. She recognises the Duke, but not he her. He is much attracted to her, as is Charles, who, to present himself on more equal terms, discards his fine clothes for more humble attire, and palms La Mancinelli off on Robert. With all three in disguise, the Duke gives Charles away to Anne. Lady Sophia appears on the scene, following Lucy and looking for Anne.

At the garden party the next day, all falls into place: Anne and Charles are together, the Duke and Lady Sophia are paired off, as are Robert and Lucy, and La Mancinelli and her husband.[6]

In *Julia*, set in 1840, Julia, Countess of Clovelly, is another rich young widow. This time, the intrigue is that her husband had dictated in his will that she should only marry one or other of two suitors chosen by him, or she would lose her fortune. Persuaded by her maid Lucy and by two singers, Kate and Jane, from a travelling players' company (managed by Montague Broscius), she runs away for a night to *The Blue Boar* in disguise. While disguised, she meets there a young composer, David Wycombe. Julia agrees to sing in a new work to be presented by the company, but only on condition that it is a new work by Wycombe; it is thus fortunate that the new work is an opera by Wycombe. Julia's two suitors, Lord Baldoyle and Sir John Pepperley, have managed to follow her to the inn, but are fooled by Kate and Jane and by Julia's disguise. The opera (set in the eighteenth century) is performed, not in the barn as originally intended, but in Julia's own private theatre. Unfortunately, Wycombe discovers Julia's true identity on the opening night, and thinking she has been merely amusing herself at his expense, turns for solace to Broscius's daughter Nancy. Julia, in her turn thinking she cannot escape her destiny, chooses one of the suitors, Lord Baldoyle, but on meeting Wycombe again at the inn, decides to choose love rather than title or position. Nancy is paired off with another member of the acting troupe, Dick; Lucy the maid is paired off with Robert the footman, Broscius, the manager of the troupe, is paired off with Jane, one of the actresses, and Sir John is paired off with the other actress, Kate.[7]

Love at the Inn opens at *The Blue Boar* country inn, in June 1780 or 1785 (both dates are given in the libretto), amidst scenes of ale-quaffing jollity. Morland is a portrait painter who alternates between states of wealth and poverty, the latter exacerbated by too much drinking. While painting a portrait, he fell in love with Jenny, a maid, and she with him. Now Jenny has come to look for him, but on her arrival at the inn, a footman, Robert, falls in love with her too, which is as well because it becomes clear that Morland no longer loves her. He meets Anne, who pretends to be a humble farmer's daughter, since it transpires that Morland dislikes anything to do with the aristocracy, and they fall in love with each other. It is arranged that Morland should paint the portraits of the family of Anne's friend Sophie Longton, daughter of Sir William Longton, and this causes great excitement at Longton Hall. During the evening's entertainments at the Hall, preparatory to the portrait painting, Morland sees Anne in her finery and thinks she has been deliberately misleading him. He taunts her, comparing her with the subject of Hogarth's 'The Harlot's Progress'; this infuriates Sophie's father, but Jenny comes forward to support Morland. He therefore feels obliged to return to London with her, but Anne's brother James,

[6] *Radio Times*, 20 October 1933.
[7] Programme for *Julia*, 8 December 1936.

an engraver, intervenes and brings Morland and Anne together again, while Jenny makes do with second best, in the form of Robert.

The characters in the story were based on real people: there was indeed an artist called George Morland, 1763–1804, who led an artistically foppish and dissolute life, but he did have a period of stability when he was married to a young woman, Anne Ward; her brother was an engraver, but was called William, not James.[8] Deliciously, Morland also turns up in Hugh Lofting's *Dr Dolittle* stories.[9]

The scraps of libretto that comprise *The Beggar Prince* indicate elements found in both operas and folk tales, and is evidently based on the story 'King Thrushbeard', as told by the brothers Grimm. There is a king, whose daughter has suitors; she is required to choose but does not know how. A beggar appears, and agrees to take the princess as wife. He, still presenting himself as a beggar, returns with her to a palace, where he sends her to work in the kitchen, preparing for the marriage celebrations of the prince. When she enters the ballroom, the court also enters, and amidst whisperings and a chorus of laughter, it is revealed that her beggar is the prince himself.

Since Quilter himself wrote that *Julia* was renamed *Rosmé* it is reasonable to suppose that the plots are at the very least similar. One can likewise deduce common ground with *Love and the Countess*, by virtue of the character named in the title.

Common strands run through the variants: where a setting is known, it is consistently an inn called *The Blue Boar*, and apart from the obvious lead soprano and tenor and the secondary leads, there is an innkeeper, with or without a wife, a comedic baritone rôle (played in *The Blue Boar* by Mark Raphael) and various diversionary characters.

All versions use a period setting, varying between late eighteenth and early nineteenth centuries, and throughout there runs an element of disguise involving one or more characters; invariably the disguise is to hide high birth. In *The Blue Boar*, the leading couple are of equal birth, but in the case of *Julia* and *Love at the Inn*, the leading man is lower down the social scale, despises the upper classes because of their lack of judgement and artistic sensibilities, and falls for a woman who represents all he hates. This was a subject dear to Quilter's heart, embodying the attitudes that sickened him, the falseness and lack of understanding of the moneyed upper classes jarring against those with the artistic sense to be indifferent to social position, but without the means to be able to afford to be so.

Love at the Inn has never been performed by a professional company. It was intended for the domain of the amateur operatic society world, and has remained within it, being regularly so performed in the very early 1950s. The publishers, Ascherberg, Hopwood and Crew, had been persuaded to take it in

---

[8] William Cosmo Monkhouse, 'George Morland', *Dictionary of National Biography* (Oxford, 1894).

[9] Hugh Lofting, *Dr Dolittle's Post Office*.

the first place, and in 1962 tried to interest the BBC in it; but acerbic comments in an internal memo point out that in the 'age of Pinter and Osborne, it would be a brave man who would attempt to revive [an] operetta' that belongs 'somewhere between German's *Merrie England* and Novello's *Perchance to Dream*'.[10]

Music

Love at the Inn was published as a complete vocal score, and its orchestral parts are extant, many in Quilter's autograph. A number of the songs had been used in *Julia*, which, from those and from manuscript sources, can therefore be almost completely reconstructed, though orchestrations are not always available; only the instrumental numbers such as the Overture and the Entr'actes and a few songs are elusive.

Table. Comparison, *Julia* and *Love at the Inn*
(Items in bold appear in both versions; music for the items in italics is missing; an asterisk beside an item indicates that it was known to have been used in *The Blue Boar*.)

Julia	Key	*Love at the Inn*	Key
ACT 1 SCENE 1 (JULIA'S HOUSE)		ACT 1 SCENE 1 (THE BLUE BOAR INN)	
Overture		Overture	D
Hail, Happy Birthday (chorus)	A	John, Fill Up Our Glasses (chorus)	E
*What's a Kiss (duet)	A	Mademoiselles and English Maids (trio)	F
If Love Should Pass Me By (solo)	F	*Here's to the Ladies (solo + chor)	D
*Hurry, Scurry (quartet)[11]	E	When Love is Ended (duet)	Em
Entr'acte		Interlude (*Love Calls)	E
ACT 1 SCENE 2 (THE BLUE BOAR INN)		ACT 1 SCENE 2 (THE BLUE BOAR INN)	
Here's to the Ladies (solo + chorus)	D	The Same in the End (duet)	D
Clinkety Clink (quartet)	B♭	**If Love Should Pass Me By** (solo)	F
*On a Morning in June (solo + chor)[12]	F	**Love Calls through the Summer Night**	
Polka with chorus[13]	D	(duet)	E
*Refrain of '**Waltz Love Song**' (duet)		**Clink, Clink!** (quartet)	B♭
*Little Moth (solo)	F	**Country Dance: Oh Come and Dance**	
Finale		**Your Cares Away** (chorus)	G
Entr'acte		Exit of chorus to Country Dance	G
		*Love Calls	E♭
		When, When Shall I See You Again?	
		(finale)	Em

[10] Julian Budden (Music Assistant, Music Programmes Dept. (Sound)) to Douglas Cleverdon (Producer, Features Dept.), 3 September 1962, BBC WAC.

[11] Quilter wrote to Bennett about introducing '4 ladies', which almost certainly refers to this song (Quilter to Bennett, September [1929]).

[12] One title page says 'in June' and another, 'of June'; neither appears to be autograph.

[13] Score marked 'Orch[estrated] Ernest Irving'.

Julia	Key	Love at the Inn	Key
ACT 2 SCENE 1 (BARN – THEATRE)			
		ACT 2 SCENE 2 (LONGTON HALL)	
*A Ribbon Here (duet[14])	D	All is Bustle, all is Haste (chorus)	Em
Flowers Here (chorus)		Hail, Happy Birthday (chorus)	A
*Patch (quartet + male chorus)	Gm	Exit	A
Short part of Finale to Act 2		*Little Moth[15] (solo)	F
Exit of Chorus to 'Flowers Here'		*The Patch (quintet)	Gm
*Love Calls through the Summer Night		*Hurry, Scurry (quartet)	E
(duet)		Dance, Dance, Gypsies (solo + chorus)	Em
Entr'acte		Ballet	Gm
		*Interlude/Gavotte[16]	D
		*Love Calls	E
ACT 2 SCENE 2 (JULIA'S PRIVATE THEATRE)		ACT 2 SCENE 1 (LONGTON HALL)	
On the Mall (chorus)		You Cat![17] (duet)	Gm
*The Serenade: Under Thy Window		What Can Compare [Minuet] (chorus)	F
(duet)	Eb/Ebm	*Gavotte[18]	D
Minuet (on inner stage)	F	Here's a Fuss! (finale)	B
Finale: Song of Denunciation (probably			
similar to the Act 2 Finale, Love at			
the Inn)			
Entr'acte			
ACT 3 (THE BLUE BOAR INN)		ACT 3 (THE BLUE BOAR INN)	
Country Dance (chorus)	G	Bread, Cheese and Beer (chorus)	D
*Blue Boar (solo) (probably 'The Jolly		Emma, Oh Emma (solo)	Eb
Blue Boar' (solo + chorus)	Cm	*The Jolly Blue Boar (solo + chorus)	Cm
When Youth and Beauty Meet (sextet)	G	Sailor Man, Soldier Man (chorus)	Em
Laugh at Love (solo)	Dm	Laugh at Love (solo)	Dm
*What's a Kiss? (duet)	A	Exit of chorus	Em
Finale		*What's a Kiss?[19] (duet)	A
		Farewell (solo)	Bb
		Are Men so Simple? (trio)	Gm
		Finale (*Love Calls)	E

[14] Score shows 'Quartet' crossed out and replaced by 'Duet'; it is in piano score only. There is a 'Dance' at the end.

[15] In an MS copy dated Autumn 1951, mostly not in Quilter's hand, the word 'Countess' in Quilter's hand is crossed out and replaced by 'Anne'. If the Countess is Julia, then this makes sense. This copy is headed 'Lovers Meeting' in Quilter's hand. In both the MS and the published vocal score, it is shown as no. 15.

[16] In the MS, this is shown as number 20, from Love at the Inn, Act 2 Scene 2, then as the Interlude before Scene 2, and as 'ballet – scene 2', number 25; then the title 'Rosmé' is crossed out, and the comment 'better without voice' has been added in pencil; all amendments in Quilter's hand. The MS includes a voice part, marked 'Kate', and was presumably originally used, or intended, for Julia. In the published vocal score for Love at the Inn, the music provides the Interlude, no. 19 and the Gavotte, no. 23. It was published in 1941, as 'In Georgian Days, Gavotte for piano and strings, from the light opera Rosmé'.

[17] The Times review of 4 December 1936 refers to a 'catty' duet, which was probably this one; in other words, this song seems to have been used in Julia, though it is not shown in the libretto, and its exact placing is therefore unknown. It was probably a duet for Jane and Kate.

[18] It is mentioned in a letter from Quilter to Bennett, 9 April [1929], and was used in Act 3 of The Blue Boar.

[19] A 'kissing duet' is mentioned in the Times review of Julia, 4 December 1936; it is mentioned by name in the Quilter–Bennett correspondence, and included in the published vocal score of Love at the Inn.

From this it appears that there is more music in *Love at the Inn* than there is in *Julia*; the dramatic pacing of *Julia* is tighter, it makes its points more quickly and the songs punctuate the text, while *Love at the Inn* provides more for the chorus to do. *Julia* requires more sets: *Love at the Inn* evidently assumes the average amateur operatic society has fewer resources available and the work feels forced into something suitable for amateur performance, where *Julia* has a greater integrity. *Julia*'s sub-plots involving Kate, Jane, Lord Baldoyle and Sir John Pepperley are entirely missing from *Love at the Inn*, though they provide contrast from the main story in *Julia*.

The Blue Boar/Julia/Love at the Inn were in a respectable tradition of light costume opera: Alfred Cellier's *Dorothy* of 1886, to a book by B. C. Stephenson, and the ballad opera *Love in a Village* (originally produced in 1762) with music arranged by Alfred Reynolds in 1928, had been very popular; both were set in the eighteenth century and were but two out of many. Thirty years previously *Julia*'s central issue of love overcoming class barriers would have been a standard and acceptable one, with the protagonists usually turning out to be of the same class (as happens in *The Blue Boar*), or at least a high-born male lead rescuing the lower-born female lead from a lesser existence: some form of the Cinderella story. *Julia*'s appearance was perhaps unfortunate in the wake of Edward VIII's abdication, which had brought issues of marital and class distinction into relief. *Julia* also came at the end of the heyday of such period pieces and was quite simply past its time.

Whether its drawbacks could have been successfully negotiated had it been produced a generation earlier is debatable. There were certainly light operas, with eighteenth-century settings or dealing with class issues, which did manage to have a measure of success – Thomas Dunhill's *Tantivy Towers*, to a libretto by A. P. Herbert, was one such, produced at the Lyric Theatre, Hammersmith, in January 1931 by Nigel Playfair, who a few months earlier had rejected *The Blue Boar*: the story is unusual because the artist, refusing to go hunting and instead shooting the fox to put it out of its misery, in the end fails to get the lady. In February 1929, *Mr Cinders*, with music by Vivian Ellis, told the Cinderella story with reversed gender (hence the title), and managed to incorporate a scene (a coming-of-age party) requiring an eighteenth-century set. As late as 1949, Ivor Novello's *King's Rhapsody* was a success for a number of reasons – Novello himself, the music and an exotic Ruritanian location with opportunity for spectacular costumes. Success can be fickle: an operetta might be successful with only a few memorable numbers, and the rest could be quite routine. Quilter's music is at the least adequate; it also has some good songs, one especially good song, and a splendid waltz.

The waltz, 'Love Calls through the Summer Night', appears frequently, following the lovers around and clearly in both *Julia* and *Love at the Inn* making ingenious excuses for its reappearances. Over a simple harmonic line, the melodic shape of the waltz is graceful and well-rounded. It opens hesitantly, and immediately launches into a sequence of hemiolas, the rhythmic device common in Baroque music but more importantly in Viennese waltzes: hence the particular lilt of Quilter's waltz. Edward German used the same device in his waltz song from *Tom Jones*. As so often in Quilter's melodic lines, he avoids the tonic note in a tonic context, using it instead in a variety of contexts. Finally, he comes to rest on it on the last note; the resultant sense of constant delay, the restraint, is pure Quilter.

Ex. 11.1a, Quilter, 'Love Calls through the Summer Night'

Ex. 11.1b, German, *Tom Jones*, Waltz Song 'For Tonight' (lyrics by C. H. Taylor)

The full flowering of the waltz occurs in Act 2 of *Love at the Inn*, a verse and chorus arrangement. Four highly chromatic bars, with a downward shape, introduce the verse in E minor, and with the entrance of the soprano, the bass line moves chromatically downwards. Melismas linked with the ornamentation in the introduction lead in to the waltz refrain. Though hints of Quilter's waltz-writing ability peep above the parapet from time to time throughout his composing career – less obviously in the songs, but certainly in the piano piece 'In a Gondola' – this is a gloriously potent mixture of Lehár, German and Offenbach. Quilter arranged it for orchestra, called it 'Concert Waltz' from *Rosmé* and Ascherberg, Hopwood and Crew published it in 1941.

The songs from *Julia* are presented first, in story order, followed by the remaining songs from *Love at the Inn*.

'Hail, Happy Birthday' is routine, a straightforward choral setting of straightforward words, the servants rejoicing that today is Julia's birthday. A drone on tonic and dominant, suggesting rusticity, supports an effective lumbering triple time, with an accompaniment motif that is so close to that in Schubert's 'Gretchen am Spinnrade' that one looks for stage business involving spinning wheels.

Ex. 11.2a, Schubert, 'Gretchen am Spinnrade', opening

Ex. 11.2b, Quilter, *Love at the Inn*, 'Hail, Happy Birthday!'

The duet 'What's a Kiss?', a patter song, is an attractive vehicle for amusingly predictable stage business between Lucy and Robert, Julia's maid and major-domo respectively; it appears twice in both *Julia* and *Love at the Inn*.

'If Love Should Pass Me By', a simple, two-verse song for Julia, has a tonal ambivalence – D minor or F major – that matches the ambivalent mood of the words: caught in a trap of wealth while longing for love. It starts with wind instrumentation only, the strings entering with the voice.

Ex. 11.3, Quilter, *Love at the Inn*, 'If Love Should Pass Me By', opening

At bar 15, a three-note motif appears, very reminiscent of Rosamund's theme in *Where the Rainbow Ends*; it appears in a wistful context, and even though F major has apparently been established as the key, the verse ends with a melancholy modal cadence in D minor. The introduction to the second verse is a little fuller (harp and strings again silent), emphasising a motif of repeated falling, sighing, thirds, and the singer's third-last bar places the voice higher than in the first verse, but the final cadence this time ends with a piquant Picardie third.

Ex. 11.4a, Quilter, *Love at the Inn*, 'If Love Should Pass Me By', last 11 bars

Ex. 11.4b, Quilter, *Rainbow*, Rosamund's theme, Act 1

This song is a real gem; it has a haunting, artless innocence that distinguishes it from the other songs in the opera.

The next song, 'Hurry, Scurry', is another delight. This quartet for the four female singers (Julia, Lucy and the two actresses Kate and Jane) shows Quilter at his lightest, never dwelling on or belabouring the point. Strong bass lines, with a clear sense of direction, underpin and shape the song; familiar but uncloying harmonic changes are to be found also in his light orchestral music, while at other points the song is affectionately reminiscent of the waltz song from German's *Tom Jones* and so has links to 'Love Calls'. It comes at the point where Julia has decided to run away to the Blue Boar Inn, with Lucy and the actresses. (In *Love at the Inn* it is sung by Anne, Lucy, Sophie and Jenny and shifted to Act 2, where the ladies are preparing for the later visit and portrait painting by George Morland.)

'Here's to the Ladies', a comfortable drinking song for Wycombe, with choral interventions, is variously in triple and quadruple time, and opens Act 1 Scene 2, introducing the audience to the host of the Blue Boar (he is called Rollick in *The Blue Boar*) and to Broscius, the actor-manager of the travelling company. It leads almost straight in to 'Clinkety Clink' which is another drinking song involving Wycombe again, two of the players in the company who will figure more later, Nancy and Dick, and the host. It is unexceptional, but has neat modulations to the mediant major, a brightening effect that Quilter uses also in 'A Ribbon Here'.

'On a Morning in June' is sung by Julia, backed by the chorus, and marks her first meeting with Wycombe. The manuscript is marked 'Orchestration by Howard Carr'. It is a simple and undistinguished verse and refrain waltz and is immediately followed by the sprightly Chorus and Dance, the 'Polka' which provides an excuse for a set piece. The scoring, for small orchestra, is by Ernest Irving, and there is similarly no clue as to why Quilter did not orchestrate it himself. If it is the original, as used in 1936, then this was probably through lack of time; otherwise, it may have been a reorchestration, for again an unknown reason. It is a pretty piece; a short introduction on open strings makes the country setting clear and paves the way for the main polka theme, the chorus enters for the central section, supported by a sweeping countermelody on upper strings, and as the chorus exit, the polka theme returns on woodwind and the whole fades into the distance. It is attractive but not especially remarkable.

'Little Moth' is the third song in the first act for Julia; Walter Legge, reviewing in *The Manchester Guardian*, thought this was too much, and was probably right in terms of the amount that Julia has to sing. However, it is a delightful waltz about the dangers, as of a moth too near a flame, of seeking love. It has a key signature of one flat, but it is four bars before it settles down to a perfect cadence in F major. The melody is harmonised with a standard harmonic sequence, ii^7–V^7–I, so that for the melody as well as the introduction, the establishment of the key is delayed, and a three note chromatic motif, ♫ ♩, repeated across a hemiola, moves with balletic lightness to the central section. The melodic line is reminiscent of the last line of 'A Last Year's Rose': not perhaps a direct link, but certainly contributing to the character of the song. Quilter's setting matches the simple, direct words.

Ex. 11.5a, Quilter, 'A Last Year's Rose', bars 13–14
Ⓒ Copyright 1910 by Boosey & Co. Ltd.

Ex. 11.5b, Quilter, *Love at the Inn*, 'Little Moth'
Ⓒ Copyright 1946 Ascherberg, Hopwood & Crew Ltd., London W6 8BS. All Rights Reserved

The felicitous word-setting of the song with dance 'A Ribbon Here, A Ribbon There' is pure Sullivan. It opens Act 2 and shows Lucy decorating Julia's eighteenth-century costume, ready for the evening performance. The music, marked *Allegretto giocoso*, is in duple time with a polka motif that pervades the whole: ♪ | ♩♪ ♪♪ | ♪♩ . It was scored for a vocal quartet, renamed a duet for Julia and Lucy, and presumably therefore in *The Blue Boar*, the four parts remain intact and only a piano reduction is extant. Piquant harmonic clashes decorate the otherwise normal chord sequences; the modulations from the tonic D major to F♯ major and a lyrical F major are treated lightly and delicately, while the well-balanced extension of the phrase in the chorus comes as a beautifully judged surprise. In the chorus too, the delay of the tonic chord until the second bar, coupled with an anacrusis of three quavers, keeps the listener in suspense, and the feet in suspense too, waiting to come in with the dance. It remains unpublished and Quilter must surely have been disappointed not to have been able to include it in *Love at the Inn*; it is one of the most infectiously foot-tapping pieces he ever wrote, simple, unpretentious and an utter delight.

Ex. 11.6a, Quilter, *Julia*, 'A Ribbon Here, A Ribbon There', beginning of verse

The 'Cat Duet' is not included in the libretto, and it is unclear where it might have fitted. It was sung by 'two young ladies who are not countesses', evidently the actresses, Kate and Jane,[20] and a contretemps between them arising from their discussion of their admirers, Lord Baldoyle and Sir John Pepperley, shortly after the start of Act 2, seems to provide a suitable placing. It seems rather forcibly included in *Love at the Inn*, however. Despite that, it is an amusing piece, with dissonances representing hissing cats.

Julia contains an opera-within-an-opera, and Wycombe now rehearses part of it. Julia, Nancy, Dick, Kate and a solo voice taken from the male chorus sing 'The Patch', an eighteenth-century pastiche quintet – Grainger particularly liked it and wrote to Quilter to ask for a copy. It has a light touch with some deft part-writing; each verse starts with a short solo (the second phrase extended by a bar) in G minor, followed by a brief comment by the quintet over a dominant pedal. In the first verse there follow then ten bars of trio, and in the second, fourteen for quintet, in both cases in G major. This is an understated piece, making its points unobtrusively and concisely. There are some niceties in the words, which describe how much loveliness owes to small details, undetected by the casual eye: a comment equally applicable to Quilter's music. 'How much the rose, though passing fair of hue, her beauty owes to you small pearl of dew!' The song opens with a whisper of a quote from 'Go, Lovely Rose' (appropriately enough, given the lyrics) but the instrumental interlude between the two verses is slightly more overt in its brief glance at the 1922 song.

[20] Review, *The Times*, 4 December 1936.

Ex. 11.6b, Quilter, *Julia*, 'A Ribbon Here, A Ribbon There', beginning of chorus

Ex. 11.7a, Quilter, 'Go Lovely Rose', opening

Ex. 11.7b, Quilter, *Love at the Inn*, 'The Patch', introduction to second verse

According to the libretto for *Julia*, 'The Serenade' is a duet for Julia and David, who still does not know Julia's true identity. On the score, however, *The Blue Boar* is crossed out and *Love at the Inn* shown, with 'not used' in brackets and 'Act II, Scene 2' shown, and it is a solo, marked for Robert to sing, the footman in both *The Blue Boar* and *Julia*. The words are incomplete, but what few there are, are not incompatible with the situation that Julia and David are in. It is probable therefore that it is the same song, and that it was rearranged as a duet for *Julia*. The scoring, in Quilter's hand, is light and clear, the whole, a waltz alternating between E♭ major and E♭ minor.

It is not categorically certain that the music for the Minuet was the chorus 'What Can Compare?', but it is such a stately, graceful minuet and so well-written that it seems highly probable. It is marked *marcato, pomposo*, its repeated triplets on brass martial, and it is played on the inner stage, that is, as part of the opera-within-an-opera, its gracious manner thus suited to the celebratory occasion. Following his early experience in writing partsongs, Quilter continues to disregard parallel fifths, albeit rarely. Pedal notes, climbing bass lines, rhythmic variety for the singers, five-bar phrases: this is so attractive, so inventive and so carefully worked that if it did not appear in *Julia*, then it surely came originally from *The Blue Boar*. The lyrics do not lend themselves to an obvious rhythmic treatment, yet it seems impossible to imagine anything other than that which Quilter does.

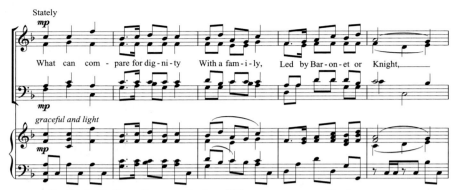

Ex. 11.8, Quilter, *Love at the Inn*, 'What can compare?', chorus entry

Given his family background, Quilter was no doubt fully cognisant of, and amused by, the irony of the words:

> What can compare for dignity
> With a family
>   Led by Baronet or Knight?
> Failing a Marquis or a Lord,
> Nature can afford
>   No more elevating sight.

The choral numbers are generally bright and breezy: the Country Dance chorus 'Oh Come and Dance Your Cares Away' for example, which opens Act 3, though disappointing on the whole, has a vigour (but mild) that is indicative of the energy that so appealed to Grainger. Overall, the variety of pace is thus usually provided by the principals' solos: 'Little Moth' and 'If Love Should Pass Me By', for example, are slower paced. The host's 'The Jolly Blue Boar', extolling the virtues of his inn, is similarly undistinguished, though competent.

'Youth and Beauty' is a sextet for SSATTB, graceful, with an elegant accompaniment; the lyrics are not Bennett's best, but are right for the occasion, where Broscius and Sir John Pepperley drink a toast – to youth and beauty – towards the end of Act 3. As an octet, it was also planned for inclusion in *Love and the Countess*, and the published music claims it for *Rosmé*.

With a lyrical triple-metre verse in D minor and a scherzo-like duple-metre chorus in D major, Wycombe's song railing at love, 'Laugh at Love', is brittle, unusually cynical and extremely effective.

The following are in *Love at the Inn* but not in *Julia*. The first song for principals in Act 1 – the polka Trio for Robert, Lucy and Emma, 'Mademoiselles and English Maids' – has close affinities with Sullivan's style of word-setting, with an appoggiatura at the end of a line on the word 'perfection'; Lucy and Emma are treated as a chorus.

Ex. 11.9, Quilter, *Love at the Inn*, 'Mademoiselles and English Maids'

In 'When Love is Ended', a standard verse and chorus duet, the short melismas to 'ah' – a common enough device – are again closely allied with Rosamund's song from *Where the Rainbow Ends*; Rosamund's wistful, longing nature is reflected here in the similar nature of the song, regretting love that is gone.

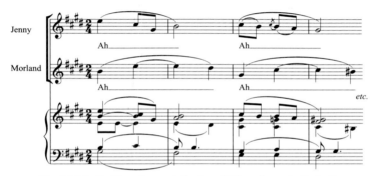

Ex. 11.10, Quilter, *Love at the Inn*, 'When Love is Ended'

The duet for John and Emma, 'The Same in the End', in Act 1 of *Love at the Inn* is light, with a similar lightness to 'It was a Lover and His Lass'.

Quilter uses flattened sevenths to establish period, the modal sound denoting an older time. It can be heard many times, but especially in the ballet with chorus, 'All is bustle, all is haste', a bright, sparkling curtain raiser to Act 2 of *Love at the Inn*.

The 'Gipsy Dance' would happily grace a summer seaside pier concert programme by a spa orchestra. The introduction to the solo song, marked *Poco andante quasi recitativo*, has an improvisatory mood aided by Quilter's harmonic shifts that constantly slip sideways chromatically to avoid the tonic. Heavy-handed rhymes ('Fools who from tomorrow borrow sorrow') are beyond Quilter's powers to improve, however, and the words are matched by equally heavy-handed suspensions.

The Act 2 Interlude takes the form of an elegant 'Gavotte'; it appears twice in *Love at the Inn*, harks back to 'It was a Lover and His Lass' and owes something to Grieg's *Holberg Suite*, particularly when comparing the central Musette section of Grieg's 'Gavotte', with Quilter's middle section; phrase extension is used in both places and the drone characteristic, too, is similar. The evocation of an earlier time is common to both, even though Holberg's time was a century and a half before the setting for *Julia*, and a century before that for *Love at the Inn*.

'Bread, Cheese and Beer' was introduced in the Overture to *Love at the Inn*. It moves sequentially through keys a major third apart – A major, Db major, F major – then back to A major, and cadencing on to the tonic D major. It is a hearty men's chorus with which to open Act 3, bright and unsubtle.

'Emma, Oh Emma' is less notable for its musical content than its dependence upon its singer, Emma; the song succeeds as long as she treats it as being in rather a music-hall style.

The Chorus with Dance 'Sailor Man, Soldier Man' is disappointing, a laboured and unnecessary interpolation that brings the action to a halt. As a single item, it is a little more effective once Quilter finishes with the conversational aspects, where men and women alternate in singing their parts, and settles down to a few bars of more conventional partsong writing, though the harmonies are unimaginative.

The unrelieved four-bar phrases of the Trio 'Are Men So Simple?' make for a dull song. This did not appear in *Julia*, and though it is not known whether it was used in *The Blue Boar*, its paucity of invention suggests that it was a late addition: on the whole, the best songs are those which used first in *Julia* or *The Blue Boar*.

The Finales for all three acts follow the usual pattern of reiteration of material already heard, leading to rousing climaxes; a hint of Wagner's *Tristan* in the short Finale of Act 2 of *Love at the Inn*, where Morland is angry at Anne's deception, neatly suggests the pain as well as the joy of love.

Ex. 11.11a, Quilter, *Love at the Inn*, Act 2 Finale

Ex. 11.11b, Wagner, *Tristan*, from the 'Prelude'

Other songs remain outside the main canon, intended for inclusion some-where, though where is not always known: 'Here's a Chapter Almost Ended' is a six-part (ternary form, for SSATBB) unaccompanied madrigal, as indicated by the recurrent 'fa-la's', but none the less for that. Reminiscent of the madrigal from Gilbert and Sullivan's *Mikado*, this is typically unpretentious, singing of the joys of leaving yesterday behind, and also how fleeting the minutes are; it itself is short and sweet. This is claimed for *Love at the Inn* but does not appear in the published vocal score; it could have been fitted in almost anywhere, but stands alone well enough. Quilter writes of a madrigal in *The Blue Boar* which may have been this one.[21]

Another song, in neither *Julia* nor *Love at the Inn*, is marked '*The Blue Boar*, Act 1, no. 10, TTBB Gentlemen off stage', in Quilter's hand; in a letter of 31 January 1930, Quilter told Bennett that he had invited some men round to sing various things including 'Here's to the Ladies' and the 'Aubade'. The Aubade was also intended for the *Beggar Prince* and was to be sung by the suitors for the hand of the princess. The writing, for accompanied men's chorus, is broadly chordal, with interest for all parts.

Another song from *The Blue Boar* was also earmarked for *Love and the Countess*, the Introduction to Act 2 Scene 1 and song 'They Leave It to Me'; Robert the footman tells his life-story in tuneful fashion. One song that exists in full score, but was only used in *The Blue Boar*, was the lilting song 'Lavender Bride', sung by Lucy the maid; the first chorus sung by sopranos and altos, the second by tenors and basses and the last by all. Many of these completely unknown songs are excellently written, fully scored and ready for performance; Quilter was very sure of himself in them. They stand well even out of context.

The content of *Julia*'s Overture is not known, but some indication of the Overture to *The Blue Boar* is given in Ralph Hill's article in the *Radio Times*, which prefaced the broadcast of the Overture on 31 August 1933, performed by the BBC Orchestra and conducted by Alfred Reynolds.[22] It opens 'in a brisk tempo', leading into the Gavotte (which reappears in Act 3) and is followed by the music of a chorus used in an inn scene – perhaps 'Here's to the Ladies' – and the music for a duet between hero and heroine: surely the waltz. The Coda uses material from the Finale to Act 2, at which point the hero and heroine have been matched up although much confusion amongst the other couples reigns. The confusion continues in considering which material might have been used from that for the Act 2 Finale, or whether indeed the Act 2 Finale music was entirely different from anything that now remains.

When Mark Raphael used to speak about *Julia* in after years, he would express bitter disappointment with what Quilter had written, even though he himself had sung in *The Blue Boar*: he thought Quilter had let himself down.[23] But this was Quilter's other side; he loved simple melody and the *joie de vivre* of

---

[21] Quilter to Bennett, 31 January 1930.
[22] Ralph Hill, 'Exquisite Miniaturist', *Radio Times*, 25 August 1933.
[23] As reported by his son Roger, in interview with the author, 29 June 1997.

the genre. Whatever Quilter's faults, being pompous or highbrow was not one of them, even though others might look disparagingly down upon mortals deemed the lesser for writing light music.

The songs have a simplicity and directness that is not usually found in his 'serious' songs, though 'An Old Carol' and 'The Fuchsia Tree' come close, partway along a continuum from the simple and direct to more coloured and refined, and Quilter's response to light words and a light genre. These are not trite songs, for all their light touch, as some of his other songs are: Quilter put as much effort into the composition of these numbers as into any others.

In neither *Julia* nor *Love at the Inn* does there appear to be anything of great significance in the choice of keys, and given the way in which the one was cannibalised to provide material for the other, this is hardly surprising. The choruses tend to use sharp keys, which favours the string section of the band, and the more melancholy solo songs tend to favour F major or its relative, D minor. Both use a conventional mixture of solos, small ensembles and choruses, and introductions commonly take their material from the start or end of the main song, with a few bars of vamp. Most of the time signatures are in Quilter's usual simple time, but he and Bennett discussed a passage in Act 1 of *The Blue Boar*, in a duet between the Countess and Lucy (no equivalent seems to have survived in *Love at the Inn*), where he suggested that a 6/8 time would be appropriate: 'If you have time to think of the Countess & Lucy in their duet in Act 1, how about a 6/8 time: we have not got any in Act 1? (except a few bars for the footman at the beginning).'[24]

Quilter invested enormous effort in the various versions, constantly trying to make them more attractive and commercially viable; but *Love at the Inn* is much less consistent than *Julia* and may have been felt to be too long: in an amateur production of *Love at the Inn*, performed by the John Lewis Partnership Music Society in April 1977, the whole of the Gipsy Dance and Gavotte Interlude was omitted and replaced with an instrumental version of 'If Love Should Pass Me By'; the shortening serves to keep the dramatic action moving, and indeed there were numerous small cuts throughout.

The Reviews of *Julia*

While *Julia* was not a success, neither was it a failure. Reviews did not bubble over with enthusiasm, but on the whole they appreciated its virtues, and that perception remained.[25] However, the reviewer in *The Musical Times*, commenting upon the company in its opening performances of the season, felt 'the actors did not enter into it with any natural aptitude or creative spirit of their own'[26] –

[24] Quilter to Bennett, 31 October [1929].
[25] H. C. Colles, 'Roger Quilter', Grove's *Dictionary of Music and Musicians*, 5th edn, ed. Eric Blom (London, 1954).
[26] 'British Music Drama Opera Company', *The Musical Times* (December 1936), p. 1132.

this was a description applied to the performances of *Boris Godounov* and *Madame Butterfly*, but if applied to *Julia* explains some of the lethargy that afflicted it subsequently; it may not have helped that Henry Wendon had a double set of rehearsals and performances, since he sang not only the lead tenor rôle in *Julia*, but also sang Pinkerton in the company's production of *Madame Butterfly*. The theatre was too big and grand for what was essentially a chamber opera, and some of the voices were too small to fill it readily.

Had Nigel Playfair taken it on, he might have made a success of it, with his ability to blend 'eighteenth-century comedy and twentieth-century satire' in a way that was 'perfectly adapted to the taste of the time',[27] but it followed too closely upon the heels of *Tantivy Towers*. The final nail in its coffin was that this was abdication year (the official announcement of which was eventually made just eight days after *Julia*'s première), and theatres were extremely reluctant to take any risks at all. And so, with each succeeding variant, the strengths of *The Blue Boar* and *Julia* were watered down, and the songs squeezed into their new surroundings like feet into ill-fitting shoes. With the few songs that perhaps were best left to sink quietly, were left others that were worthy of retention (published but unknown), in particular 'If Love Should Pass Me By' and 'Little Moth'. 'Love Calls through the Summer Night' has retained some small popularity, though unjustifiably little.

On 6 December 1936, the reviewer in *The Sunday Times* (probably Hubert Foss) commented on the kinship of the operetta with those at the Gaiety Theatre thirty-five or forty years previously, and claimed that:

> Roger Quilter's 'Julia' is, in essence, musical comedy; and very charming musical comedy. The type does not lend itself to musical characterisation; instead of attempting anything of the kind the composer had produced number after number fresh, melodious, and 'popular' in the best sense, daintily scored and eminently singable – alas that so few of them were 'sung'!

Foss's regrets over the quality of the singing were echoed, in varying terms, by some of the other reviewers, though not by any means all: in the *Daily Telegraph*, Ferruccio Bonavia approved of Margaret Bannerman's gentle voice, as did Stephen Williams in *The Evening Standard*.[28] But substantially common views were held on the music: it was light, pretty, lyrical, attractive and altogether charming. W. J. Turner, in a generally supercilious review, described it as *opéra comique* and felt 'the chief defect of the operetta [to be] its lack of musical variety; there is very little that can be called comic'.[29]

Turner gave an indication of the nature of the libretto in describing the operetta as 'spoken dialogue, interspersed with music numbers and ensembles' supporting Bonavia's contention that the dialogue was in need of pruning. Francis Toye, in *The Morning Post*, also commented adversely on the length and

[27] Geoffrey Whitworth, 'Sir Nigel Playfair', *Dictionary of National Biography* (Oxford, 1949).
[28] Reviews, *Daily Telegraph* and *Evening Standard*, both 4 December 1936.
[29] Review, *Illustrated London News*, 12 December 1936.

slowness of the libretto, but realised too what a handicap it was to stage the work at Covent Garden.

Bonavia was very taken with the quartet 'Hurry, Scurry' and the tenor's song in Act 1; both he and Williams acknowledged – with pleasure, unlike some of the others – the affinities with Edward German, and Williams also heard connections with Messager. Walter Legge, in *The Manchester Guardian*, thought that *Julia*'s production at Covent Garden meant it should be judged as an opera, and in doing so, found it wanting; he too complained of the quantity of spoken word, accusing it of being a musical play and not light opera, and, most heinous of all, describing the singing as 'West End show class' rather than operatic.[30] Quilter's normal melodic gifts had apparently deserted him, and the numbers lacked freshness. But Legge's agenda was an operatic one; he came looking for a grand opera version of Quilter songs and was bound to be disappointed.

The reviewers were at least of one accord in admiring Hamish Wilson's sets, Albert Coates's conducting of the London Symphony Orchestra and in approving the waltz-tune: it had after all appeared frequently throughout the evening (sending 'everyone humming contentedly to bed'[31]) and thus had more opportunity to ingratiate itself than the other songs.

More performances would of course have given more chance for the other songs and choruses to work their way into the audience's mind. Neither Offenbach's *Orphée aux Enfers* (1858) nor Cellier's *Dorothy* (1886) for example were immediate successes; *Orphée* benefited from a complaint by the critic Jules Janin, which gave some usefully lurid publicity, and it has remained in the repertory ever since. *Dorothy* was taken off and the production sold in its entirety after only a few weeks; following changes (of leading lady, and the insertion of a new song) it made enough money to build the Lyric Theatre in London's theatreland.[32] (Like *Julia* and the other variants, it too was set in the eighteenth century.) Operettas such as these normally had enough performances to give a chance for the production to be adjusted and fine-tuned, for songs to be removed or inserted, and the libretto to be sharpened. *Julia* was part of a short season and never had that chance.

It may well have been written too late in the theatrical day to succeed, but it was in any case stifled at birth. At several decades' distance, some of the problems of being too much out of its time fade; the music remains wonderfully fresh, and far too good to be kept hidden away.

---

[30] W[alter] L[egge], Review, *Manchester Guardian*, 5 December 1936.
[31] Stephen Williams, *Evening Standard*.
[32] Richard Traubner, *Operetta, A Theatrical History* (Oxford, 1983).

Appendix A The Quilter Family

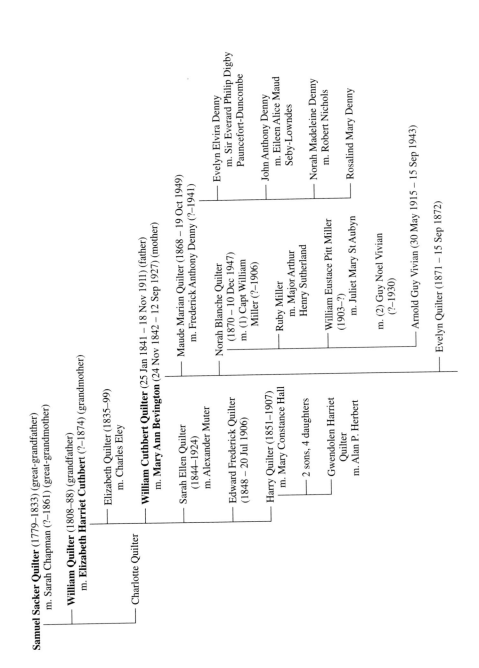

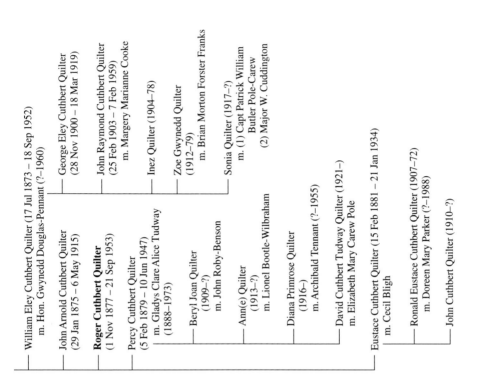

William Eley Cuthbert Quilter (17 Jul 1873 – 18 Sep 1952)
m. Hon. Gwynedd Douglas-Pennant (?–1960)

George Eley Cuthbert Quilter
(28 Nov 1900 – 18 Mar 1919)

John Raymond Cuthbert Quilter
(25 Feb 1903 – 7 Feb 1959)
m. Margery Marianne Cooke

Inez Quilter (1904–78)

Zoe Gwynedd Quilter
(1912–79)
m. Brian Morton Forster Franks

Sonia Quilter (1917–?)
m. (1) Capt Patrick William
Butler Pole-Carew
(2) Major W. Cuddington

John Arnold Cuthbert Quilter
(29 Jan 1875 – 6 May 1915)

Roger Cuthbert Quilter
(1 Nov 1877 – 21 Sep 1953)

Percy Cuthbert Quilter
(5 Feb 1879 – 10 Jun 1947)
m. Gladys Clare Alice Tudway
(1888–1973)

Beryl Joan Quilter
(1909–?)
m. John Roby-Benson

Ann(e) Quilter
(1913–?)
m. Lionel Bootle-Wilbraham

Diana Primrose Quilter
(1916–)
m. Archibald Tennant (?–1955)

David Cuthbert Tudway Quilter (1921–)
m. Elizabeth Mary Carew Pole

Eustace Cuthbert Quilter (15 Feb 1881 – 21 Jan 1934)
m. Cecil Bligh

Ronald Eustace Cuthbert Quilter (1907–72)
m. Doreen Mary Parker (?–1988)

John Cuthbert Quilter (1910–?)

Appendix B Professional Performances of *Where the Rainbow Ends*

Theatres are in London unless otherwise stated; the numbers in brackets are the numbers of performances in that season, where known. *The London Stage* as a source is the invaluable series of volumes of London theatrical productions, compiled by J. P. Wearing.

Year	Opening	Theatre	Source of information	Presented by	Comments
1911	21/12–3/2 (69)	Savoy	*London Stage*; *Times*, 1 Jan 1912, p. 8, c. 5	Charles Hawtrey	'A Romantic Fairy Play'
1912	11/12–1/2 (84)	Garrick	*London Stage*; *Times*, 1 Jan 1913, p. 6, c. 6	Charles Hawtrey	Quilter and Mills not mentioned
1913	26/12–31/1 (32)	Garrick	*London Stage*; *Times*, 1 Jan 1914, p. 8, c. 6	–	Matinées only
1914		King's, Hammersmith	*Times*, 31 Dec 1914, p. 8, c. 6	Tom B. Davis's Company, Garrick Production	Also 2 weeks at the Wimbledon Theatre, from 11 Jan 1915, Tom B. Davis's production
1915	27/12–22/1 (37)	Garrick	*London Stage*; *Times*, 1 Jan 1916	–	Mavis Yorke the only name mentioned
1916	26/12–20/1 (23)	Globe	*London Stage*; *Times*, 1 Jan 1917	–	Matinées only; no names
1917				No entry in *Times*	
1918		Victoria Palace	*Times*, 1 Jan 1919, p. 8, c. 6	–	
1919		Victoria Palace	*Times*, 1 Jan 1920, p. 10, c. 5	–	
1920	23/12–22/1 (26)	Apollo	*London Stage*; *Times*, 1 Jan 1921, p. 8, c. 3	–	Matinées
1921	22/12–28/1 (36)	Apollo	*London Stage*; *Times*, 1 Jan 1922, p. 8, c. 5	–	Matinées
1922	26/12	Holborn Empire	*Times*, 1 Jan 1923, p. 8, c. 6	Charles Gulliver and Italia Conti	By arrangement with G. & J. Kirby
1923		Holborn Empire	*Times* 1 Jan 1924, p. 10, c. 5	Charles Gulliver and Italia Conti	'Star cast with 50 of Italia Conti's wonderful children dancing to Roger Quilter's Delightful Music'
1924		Holborn Empire	*Times*, 2 Jan 1925	Charles Gulliver and Italia Conti	

Year	Opening	Theatre	Source of information	Presented by	Comments
1925		Holborn Empire	Times, 1 Jan 1926	Charles Gulliver and Italia Conti	billed as 16th year
1926		Holborn Empire	Times, 1 Jan 1927	Italia Conti	billed as 17th year
1927		Holborn Empire	Times, 1 Jan 1928	Italia Conti	
1928		Holborn Empire	Who's Who; Times, 1 Jan 1929, p. 10, c. 5	Italia Conti production	
1929		Holborn Empire	Who's Who; Times, 1 Jan 1930, p. 10, c. 6	Italia Conti production	
1930		Holborn Empire	Who's Who; Times, 1 Jan 1931, p. 10, c. 6	Italia Conti production	
1931		Holborn Empire	Who's Who; Times, 1 Jan 1932, p. 8, c. 6	Italia Conti production	
1932	22/12	Holborn Empire	London Stage; Times, 2 Jan 1933, p. 10, c. 6	Italia Conti production	
1933		Holborn Empire	Times, 20 Jan 1934, p. 8, c. 5	Italia Conti production	
1934		Holborn Empire	Times, 1 Jan 1935, p. 12, c. 6	Italia Conti production	
1935		Holborn Empire	Newspaper cutting (unidentified); Times, 24 Jan 1936, p. 10, c. 6	Italia Conti production	
1936		Holborn Empire	Newspaper cutting (unidentified); Times, 1 Jan 1937, p. 10, c. 6	Italia Conti production	billed as 26th year
1937		Holborn Empire	Times, 1 Jan 1938, p. 10, c. 5	Italia Conti production	billed as 27th year
1938		Holborn Empire	Times 2 Jan 1939, p. 12, c. 6	Italia Conti production	billed as 28th year
1939		Holborn Empire	Times, 15 Jan 1940	Italia Conti production	billed as 29th year. Ruth Conti records that Rainbow was performed in Bournemouth in 1939; Quilter conducted it in February 1940, and indeed Rainbow would usually go on tour after the main London production.
1940	21/12–11/1 (24)	New	London Stage; Times, 1 Jan 1941, p. 8, c. 6	–	

Year	Dates	Venue	Source	*Times*	Notes
1941	W/b 8/3/41	Theatre Royal, Norwich	*East Anglian Daily Times*, 8 March 1941	No entry in *Times*	Company led by Italia Conti (playing Mrs Carey)
1942				No entry in *Times*	
1943	27/12–29/1 (46)	Winter Garden	*London Stage*; *Times*, 4 Jan 1944, p. 6, c. 7	—	
1944				No entry in *Times*	
1945	October 29 (1 week)	Empire, Dewsbury On tour	Theatre Museum – flier	No other entry in *Times*	Billed as 34th year
1946			Score (BL Add. MS 54208)	No entry in *Times*	
1947		Princes', Croydon	Personal recollection, cast member	No entry in *Times*	May be one year out.
1948	22/12–22/1 (27)	Cambridge	*London Stage*; score; *Times*, 1 Jan 1949, p. 10, c. 1	—	
1949	24/12–21/1 (38)	Comedy	*London Stage*; score; *Times*, 2 Jan 1950, p. 4, c. 7	—	Anton Dolin billed
1950	23/12–20/1 (31)	Stoll	*London Stage*; score; *Times*, 1 Jan 1951, p. 2, c. 7	—	Anton Dolin billed
1951	24/12–19/1 (31)	Winter Garden	*London Stage*; score; *Times*, 1 Jan 1952, p. 12, c. 2	—	Donald Houston billed
1952	20/12–17/1 (33)	Prince's	*London Stage*; score; *Times*, 1 Jan 1953, p. 2, c. 1	—	
1953	26/12–16/1 (38)	Stoll	*London Stage*; score; *Times*, 1 Jan 1954, p. 2, c. 1	—	Anton Dolin played St George
1954		Royal Festival Hall	*Who was Who in the Theatre*; Markova; *Times*, 1 Jan 1955, p. 2, c. 1	—	Markova & Dolin with Claude Hulbert and Winifred Shetter
1955		Royal Festival Hall	*Who was Who in the Theatre*; Dolin; *Times*, 1 Jan 1956, p. 2, c. 1	—	Anton Dolin, Violetta Elvin, Alfred Marks, Valentine Dyall, London Philharmonic Orchestra Ballet
1956	24/12–12/1 (17)	Coliseum	*London Stage*; *Times*, 1 Jan 1957, p. 2, c. 1	—	Markova and Dolin
1957				No entry in *Times*	
1958	26/12–17/1 (24)	New Victoria	Programme (theatre now called the Apollo); *Times*, 1 Jan 1959, p. 2, c. 1	—	Markova and Dolin
1959	22/12–2/1	Granada, Sutton	Programme	—	

Appendix C Personalia

The amount of detail given in this highly selective list is often in inverse proportion to what is available elsewhere.

Marian Anderson (1897–1993) was a contralto, the best known black American female singer of her day, with a sumptuously warm voice. She came to England in October 1927 where she had support not just from Quilter, but also from other black musicians in London.[1]

Frederic Austin (1872–1952) was a singer and composer, most famous now for his arrangement of music for Nigel Playfair's production of *The Beggar's Opera*, at the Lyric Theatre, Hammersmith.[2]

Rodney Bennett was born in 1890 in Frimley, Surrey and died in 1948 in Devon. He was an author, writing children's stories and children's poetry; a modern eye would probably find his work rather twee, but it was popular in its day, and at the very least has the merit of innocence. He collaborated with Quilter on *The Blue Boar*, and also wrote the words to some of Quilter's later songs; he was a fine writer of words for songs, and wrote lyrics for Eric Coates under the name Roydon Barrie. His wife Joan was a pianist and they had three children, Anne, Margaret (poet and one of Quilter's god-children) and Richard, the composer.

Anthony Bernard (1895–1963) was a conductor, teacher, organist, choirmaster and all-round musician, founder of the London Chamber Orchestra in 1921, and champion of French music, so much so that in 1948 he was appointed an 'Officier d'Académie' by the French Government. He was the kind of person who knows everyone; his elder daughter was one of Quilter's god-daughters.

Hilda Blake was a singer to whom Quilter dedicated 'Fairy Lullaby' in 1921; she premièred 'Morning Song' in 1922.

The Reverend Fabian Brackenbury was born in 1853; he and his wife Edith (who taught music there) ran Pinewood School, Farnborough, the preparatory school that Quilter attended. Several of Brackenbury's children were educationalists; his son Cecil was father both of Tony, the first headmaster of the Yehudi Menuhin School in Cobham, Surrey, and also of John, who ultimately became Warden of Impington Village College, Cambridge; Fabian's daughter Biddy ran a school in Budleigh Salterton. He moved eventually to Monkton Thanet.

Lawrence Brown was a black accompanist who worked with many singers, especially Roland Hayes and later Paul Robeson.

---

[1] See Allan Keiler, *Marian Anderson, A Singer's Journey* (New York, 2000).
[2] See Martin Lee-Browne, *Nothing so Charming as Musick!, The Life and Times of Frederic Austin* (London, 1999).

Theodore Byard was an actor and singer, sometimes a travelling companion of Quilter's. In 1900 he was a director of Heinemann's, the publisher; later he went to study in Paris with Jean de Reske.

Charles B. Cochran (1872–1951), impresario, knighted in 1948, produced and directed numerous shows and revues in the 1920s and 1930s. He worked in partnership with Noël Coward; the partnership was often tempestuous.

Sibyl Colefax (1874–1950) was rather a collector of artists and musicians; the Sitwells nicknamed her Sibyl Coalbox. She kept a book, a kind of large birthday book, and acquired autographs from countless artistic figures of the period, the entries made on the appropriate birthday pages. Quilter's entry on 1 November shows his signature and a brief quote from 'To Daisies', the third song from *To Julia*.[3]

Italia Conti was born in about 1873 (not, as she usually claimed, the late 1870s) allegedly within the sound of Bow Bells;[4] she was educated at home and was 'compelled to pass the Oxford Local Exam before being allowed to go on the stage'. Armed with a letter of introduction from Ellen Terry, she made her first stage appearance at the Lyceum in 1891 when she was about eighteen, walking on in *The Last Word*, and the following year joined the Benson company, playing pages and small parts in their wide-ranging repertory. In 1894 she toured with Forbes-Robertson and Kate Rorke in *Diplomacy* and then with the Robert Brough Comedy Company in Australia, though it is not recorded whether or not she was able to meet her brother Ferdinand, who had emigrated there some years earlier. The high point of her acting career came in 1903, when she played Rosalind at the Royalty. She was a highly respected figure, and because of that, and her unique experience with the stage school she founded, she was able to make a major contribution to the legislature in 1918 – she sat on the advisory committee – that drastically changed the rules concerning the education and licensing of child actors.[5] She died in 1946.

Walter Creighton (1878–1958) was a son of Mandell Creighton, Bishop of London, and Louise Creighton, who was one of Robert von Glehn's daughters. He gave up training to be a doctor to train as a singer; he gave the first performance of Vaughan Williams's *Songs of Travel* in 1904 and also had a minor career as an actor. After various personal crises, he served with distinction in the First World War, and was awarded the Military Cross. He developed into an excellent organiser, and in 1924 organised the Pageant of Empire at Wembley Stadium; in 1934, he devised and organised the Pageant of Parliament at the Royal Albert Hall. In after years, he moved to Antibes.

Hubert Eisdell (1882–1948) was a well-known singer and as far as things Quilterian are concerned, most notable for recording *To Julia* in its piano quintet form during the 1920s. He married a piano pupil of Grainger's, Katherine Parker, who had come to England from Australia; she wrote some very pleasing songs, including *Love in Summer* and *As a Star* which were performed by Eisdell and Frederick Kiddle at the Wigmore Hall on 28 April 1919.

Gervase Elwes (1866–1921) was one of the finest tenors of his generation. He came of a

---

[3] The autograph book is in the Bodleian Library, Oxford.
[4] Family recollection claims Pimlico as the birthplace and that she was cradled in a drawer from a chest of drawers, having arrived unexpectedly early. To be born 'within the sound of Bow Bells' is the traditional definition of a London Cockney; Bow is an area in east London.
[5] *Times* obituary, 9 February 1946.

Lincolnshire county family, but felt his greater calling was to music, and he championed British composers and their songs.

Nora Forman (1886–1974) was the daughter of a Scottish engineer; she had four brothers scattered around the world. She was very wealthy and was an extremely knowledgeable and generous patron of the arts. Her home, a flat on two floors, was well known for its welcoming atmosphere, and she often held soirées after Mark Raphael's recitals.

Muriel Foster was a contralto; she sang in the première of Elgar's *The Apostles* in 1903, but retired from singing in 1906 when she married, though she did continue to give occasional performances, as when she premièred Quilter's Blake songs in 1917.

Luigino Franchetti was the son of the Baron and Baroness Franchetti who lived in the Palazzo Franchetti, Venice; his uncle Alberto Franchetti (born in 1860) was a composer, 'one of the most renowned contemporary composers both in operatic and instrumental fields'.[6] He was born in about 1891 and went to Eton and New College, Oxford.

Arthur Frith (1891–1961) was a baritone who met Quilter just before the First World War, in Suffolk. He was appointed choral vicar at St Paul's Cathedral, London, but became an alcoholic largely as a result of his war experiences, and had to resign, though the choir officials treated him sympathetically. He made a very few recordings and wrote some very fine war poetry, unfortunately unpublished. He had one son, Roger, a godson of Quilter, who is a poet and playwright.

Dinah de Glehn married Louis de Glehn in 1920 and moved into his house, Byron's Lodge, a rather attractive house with a thatched roof, in Grantchester, near Cambridge. She became a strong element in the de Glehn–Marsh–Creighton circle. In 1928 Louis and Dinah had another house built, Manor Field, again in Grantchester, in which they lived until Louis's death on 19 October 1951. Dinah was Scottish; she was a nurse in the First World War, and met Jane and Wilfrid de Glehn when they were all serving in France; they introduced her to Quilter and to Wilfrid's brother. Dinah's real name was Marion, but she never used it: when Jane de Glehn wrote to Quilter during the First World War, she only ever referred to 'Dinah', and Dinah reminded Quilter not to use her real name when she wrote to thank him for dedicating two songs to her and Louis.[7] She moved to Edinburgh after Louis's death; she herself died in the late 1960s.

Jane de Glehn (1873–1961) was American, née Emmet, of a New York family, many members of which were highly artistic, as was she; she was related to the playwright Robert Sherwood and to Henry James. Her portraits show great sensitivity but she seems to have been rather overshadowed by her husband, Wilfrid de Glehn.

Louis de Glehn (*c.*1868–1951) taught French at the Perse School in Cambridge according to the *Cours français* principles of learning through speaking, with a strong emphasis on excellent pronunciation and thorough knowledge of the grammar; this was an innovative approach for the time. His nickname there was Vonny, retained even after the change of family name from 'von Glehn' to 'de Glehn'. All his friends and family had given up on him ever marrying, until he met Dinah Cassels.

Wilfrid de Glehn (1870–1951), English impressionist painter and Louis's brother, met

[6] Eaglefield-Hull, *Dictionary of Modern Music and Musicians* (London, 1924). I am also indebted to Caroline Dalton, Archivist, New College, Oxford for most of the information about Franchetti.

[7] Dinah de Glehn to Quilter, 21 July 1922, BL Add. MS 70603, f. 140.

his wife Jane Emmet in 1903 while accompanying the artist John Singer Sargent who had returned to Boston to oversee the installation of his mural *Christianity*. De Glehn and Sargent regularly travelled together on painting tours abroad.

Herbert Golden was a fellow student at Frankfurt; his son Geoffrey was a godson of Quilter.

Harry Plunket Greene (1865–1936), singer, wrote a well-known book of the day, *Interpretation in Song*, and a biography of C. V. Stanford as well as children's books. His father-in-law was Sir Hubert Parry.

Charles Hawtrey was noted for his superb sense of comic timing, and for his large-scale gambling on horses. He was born in 1858, knighted in 1922, and died in 1923. George Hartree, of the Carry On films, later appropriated his name; there is an alleged filial connection.

Roland Hayes (1887–1976) was a black tenor, one of the earlier (but not the earliest) black American musicians to come to Europe and make a name for himself. He returned to the United States and his name is all but forgotten. His daughter is a pianist, and his grand-daughter a ballet-dancer.[8]

A. P. Herbert (1890–1971), writer and Member of Parliament, married Gwendolen, one of Harry Quilter's daughters, and was thus Quilter's cousin by marriage. Quilter later commented on the difficulty of setting his words to music.[9]

Robin Hollway, one of Quilter's young Oxford friends, was born in 1894 and educated at Eton and Balliol College, Oxford. He was a gifted scholar, intense and highly strung. He committed suicide in March 1921.

Frederick Kiddle was for a time resident accompanist at the Proms, and known best as Gervase Elwes's regular accompanist. He studied the organ at the Royal College of Music, under Sir Walter Parratt.

Willie King (1894–1963) was another of Quilter's Oxford friends, but survived longer than Hollway. Educated at Eton and Balliol College, Oxford, he saw active service with the Third Royal Sussex Regiment and in the Intelligence Corps. In later years he became a ceramics expert, and held an appointment at the British Museum. He was married to Viva, who, as Viva Booth, had had an affair with Peter Warlock.

Lucian Swift Kirtland (1881–1965) was a travel writer, one of the Oxford circle; he did not figure large in Quilter's life but was referred to in correspondence.

Edward Knoblock (1874–1945), the American playwright, was at Harvard with Henry James's nephews, and was taught by James's brother William. He was born Edward Knoblauch and achieved fame for his play *Kismet* which was later turned into a musical of the same name.

Florence Koehler (1861–1944) specialised in creating *pâte de verre* jewellery. Roger Fry wrote a long article on her which was reproduced in a brochure about her, published after her death.[10] She was rather opinionated and sometimes tried to dictate to her friends with whom they should or should not consort.

Albert Clinton Landsberg (Bertie) was born in 1889, the son of a Jewish Brazilian

---

[8] See MacKinley Helm, *Angel Mo' and Her Son, Roland Hayes* (Boston, 1943).
[9] Quilter to Bennett, 26 February, probably 1932, Bennett archive.
[10] Laurie Eglington Kaldis, ed., *Portrait of an Artist, The Paintings and Jewelry of Florence Koehler 1861–1944* (Rhode Island School of Design, 1947).

banker, educated at Harrow and Cambridge, and domiciled largely in Paris. Just before the beginning of the First World War, Bertie's family returned to Brazil, but he remained in Neuilly throughout, not succumbing to family pressures to return until after the war. An aesthete, he was extremely knowledgeable about art, and figures in Barr's work on Matisse; the Matisse and Landsberg families were well acquainted and Matisse painted a portrait of Yvonne Landsberg, Bertie's sister. Bertie wrote a short biography of Florence Koehler, and in 1925 bought and gradually restored one of Palladio's Italian palaces, Malcontenta, near Venice. He married Dorothea in about 1940.

Robin Legge was music editor and critic for the *Daily Telegraph*, after fifteen years as assistant music critic for *The Times*. He was born in 1866, and studied at Frankfurt, a generation ahead of the Frankfurt five.

Madame Louise Kirkby Lunn (1873–1930), often known simply as Kirkby Lunn, was a contralto, one of the more significant ones of the day.

Clifford Mills was the pen-name of Emlie Clifford, née Bennet, a writer of short stories and plays. She married Harold Mills Clifford in 1889 and they had one child, Evelyn. Harold Clifford spent a considerable time in India, as a captain in the Indian army, and Evelyn went to school in England, her mother returning to England periodically to escape the Indian heat; Evelyn retained the Indian connection by later marrying a colonel in the Indian Army, Rex Shillington. Clifford Mills was an opinionated and strong-willed woman.[11] She had considerable success with some of her plays, especially *The Basker* and *The Luck of the Navy*.

Norah Nichols was the daughter of Quilter's elder sister Maude Denny. In 1922, Norah married the poet Robert Nichols (1893–1944), and went with him to Tokyo where he was Professor of English from 1921–4; later they went to Hollywood. She wrote a very small amount of music, lived in Suffolk and was a supporter of the Aldeburgh Festival; she died in about 1963.

Leo Ornstein is a Russian-American Jewish pianist-composer, born in 1892 or thereabouts, noted for his virtuoso technique and for his extraordinary compositions, which are now beginning to attract serious critical attention.

Reginald Owen (1887–1972) trained at Herbert Tree's Academy of Dramatic Art, in London, from 1905 to 1908, and made his US debut in 1923. He appeared in Sondheim's *A Funny Thing Happened on the Way to the Forum* in 1972–3, and played in films for over thirty-five years: these films included *Mary Poppins* (Admiral Boom), *Mrs Miniver* (Foley), and the 1950 Errol Flynn version of *Kim* (Father Victor).

Nigel Playfair (1874–1934) was a noted director of the period, later to become Sir Nigel; in 1931 he produced *Tantivy Towers*, the opera by Thomas Dunhill, to a libretto by A. P. Herbert.

Sir Raymond Quilter (1902–59) was Roger Quilter's nephew, the surviving son of William Eley Cuthbert Quilter. He was a fine golfer and shot, but his real love was aviation. He lived mostly in Woking, Surrey, and from the 1920s was heavily involved in the development and manufacture of parachutes, including testing them himself, and often freefall parachuting: at one time he held the record for a delayed jump. His hobby

---

[11] Mrs J. Wall (Clifford Mills's great-niece) to Langfield, 5 August 1998. Other aspects of family history are provided either in the same letter, or from details supplied by Ruth Conti in a number of letters over the period January 1998 to July 2000. Harold Clifford's middle name 'Mills' was his maternal grandmother's maiden name, common practice for the time.

was bomb disposal. His wife Margery was very stoical (and retains a wonderful sense of humour). He died in 1959, only seven years after his father; his son Sir Anthony lives in the area today.

Mark Raphael (1900–88) was a Jewish baritone, from the East End of London, who became Quilter's primary singer after Gervase Elwes died. Quilter took him under his wing and gave him financial help and introductions to some of the musical families of Vienna when he toured Germany and Austria in the 1920s. He became a cantor in one of the north London synagogues, and he remained a loyal friend.

Alfred Reynolds (1884–1969) was a composer and conductor, and at one time, honorary secretary of the Conductors' Association, which later was absorbed into the Musicians' Union. He was an excellent musician, best known for the ballad opera *Love in a Village* of 1923 for which he arranged some of the music, and wrote the rest. He knew Quilter well and respected him greatly, though it was mutual: Quilter equally greatly admired Reynolds' ability as an orchestrator. Like Quilter, Reynolds was a member of the Savile Club, and Quilter came to know his family well.

Winthrop L. Rogers was an American publisher; after his early death in December 1921, his wife took over the business. Their daughter Calista, a singer, sold the business to Hawkes and Son in late 1924 or early 1925.

The Stern family. Dr Rudolf Stern was a Jewish scientist from Vienna; Quilter had known him and his wife for many years and gave them substantial financial and moral support, including giving them a Brinsmead grand piano in July 1951. Their daughter Harriet married a French Catholic with an American mother, the Count de Gebhard. Quilter was very fond of them, and jokingly suggested that he adopt Dr Stern, so that when Harriet had her children, Quilter would become a great-grandfather without any fuss. Harriet named her elder son Roger.

Constance Wathen was probably related to Katherine Wathen, known as Kitty, who was an old friend of Quilter's mother.

Herbert Withers, cellist, was a long-standing friend of Quilter; they played in the war-time concerts that Quilter organised.

Leslie Woodgate (1902–61) was one of a large family of musicians, actors and artists of one kind or another. Many of his generation were in *Rainbow*. He is known for his connection with the BBC, as Chorusmaster, and with Quilter, as his musical secretary during the 1920s. He studied at the Royal College of Music from 1921 to 1925, holding the George Carter Scholarship for the last three years, and he studied composition with Armstrong Gibbs and organ with Walter Alcock. Although composition was his primary study, he came away from one visit to Wood Hall rather despondent after Lady Quilter told him what she thought of his work.[12] A Memorial Service to him was held at the Church of St Sepulchre, Holborn Viaduct, on 15 June 1961.

---

[12] Quilter to Mark Raphael, 1 August 1924, BL Add. MS 70607, f. 21.

Appendix D Catalogue of Works

Manuscript source abbreviations:

BH	Boosey & Hawkes Archive, London
BL	British Library, London
GM	Grainger Museum Collection, University of Melbourne
LE	Archives held by Leslie East
RCM	Royal College of Music, London
RR	Collection of Roger Raphael
VL	Collection of Valerie Langfield

Manuscripts are in Quilter's autograph unless otherwise stated.

Keys given are the original keys, as best they can be determined; details of alternative keys, and the sources of the poems, are not usually given here; they are to be found (for those songs with opus numbers) in Michael Pilkington's excellent and thorough *English Solo Song Guides to the Repertoire: Gurney, Ireland, Quilter and Warlock* (Duckworth, London, 1989).

Music is listed in order of composition, as far as it can be established.

Songs with piano (solo voice unless otherwise stated)

Two Songs
1. 'Come Spring! Sweet Spring!' *Key* G major
2. 'The Reign of the Stars' *Key* A minor
Text Quilter *Published* Weeks & Co. 1897 under the pseudonym Ronald Quinton. *Dedicated* To my mother
Quilter's copy marked: 'on no account to be reprinted in any form or under my name: Roger Quilter: 1916'

Should One of Us Remember
Text Christina Rossetti *Composed* August 1897 *Unpublished, manuscript* sold at Sotheby's May 1968

Mond, du bist glücklicher als ich
Text Anon. *Key* A♭ major *Unpublished, dedicated* To Cyril Meir Scott from the composer *Manuscript* GM

Two Songs
1. 'Come Back!' *Key* C minor
2. 'A Secret' *Key* E♭ major *Completed* 6 May 1898
Text Quilter *Published* Elkin 1903 *Manuscript* BL Add. MS 72089; another manuscript of 'Secret' sold at Sotheby's May 1968

Four Songs of the Sea, Op. 1
1. 'I Have a Friend' *Key* C major
2. 'The Sea-Bird' *Key* E minor
3. 'Moonlight' *Key* D major
4. 'By the Sea' *Key* D minor
Text Quilter *Composed c.*1900 *Published* Forsyth Bros. 1901; revised as *Three Songs of the Sea*, 1911, omitting first song ('The Sea-Bird' dated 9 May 1911, and 'By the Sea' dated 10 May 1911), and later still reissued in the original four-song set *Dedicated* To my mother *Manuscript* of 1911 versions of 'The Sea-Bird' and 'By the Sea': LE

Four Songs of Mirza Schaffy, Op. 2
1. 'Neig' schöne Knospe dich zu mir' *Key* G major
2. 'Und was die Sonne glüht' *Key* G minor
3. 'Ich fühle deinen Odem' *Key* Db major *Published* 1906
4. 'Die helle Sonne leuchtet' *Key* F major
Text Friedrich Bodenstedt *Published* Elkin 1903 (translation by W. Creighton); *revised and published* 1911 (translation by R. H. Elkin) *Dedicated* 1903, In remembrance of Frankfort days; 1911, To J. Walter and Marie English *First performance* Walter Creighton, 9 June 1903, Bechstein Hall, with cello obbligato (Herbert Withers) *Manuscript* BL Add. MS 72089
No 3 published separately in 1911 as 'The Magic of thy Presence', R. H. Elkin translation

At Close of Day
Text Laurence Binyon *Key* C minor *Published* Boosey 1904 *Manuscript* BH

The Answer
Text Laurence Binyon *Key* Eb major *Published* Boosey 1904 *Manuscript* BH

A London Spring
Text Julian Sturgis *Keys* D, F major (original is not identified) *Published* Boosey 1928 under the pseudonym Claude Romney *First performance* Alys Bateman, accompanied by Quilter, Bechstein Hall, 21 November 1904, as 'A London Spring Song'

Three Songs, Op. 3
1. 'Love's Philosophy' *Text* Shelley *Key* F major *Published* Boosey 1905 *Dedicated* To Gervase Elwes *Manuscript* BH
2. 'Now Sleeps the Crimson Petal' *Text* Tennyson *Key* Eb major *Completed* 31 March 1897 *Published* Boosey 1904, revised 1946 *Dedicated* To Mrs E. P. Balmain *Manuscript* 1897, BL Add. MS 54227; 1946 Boosey and Hawkes
3. 'Fill a Glass with Golden Wine' *Text* W. E. Henley *Key* C major *Published* Boosey 1905 *Dedicated* To William Higley *Manuscript* BH

June
Text Nora Hopper *Key* D major *Published* Boosey 1905 *Dedicated* To Miss Ada Crossley *Manuscript* BH

Four Child Songs, Op. 5
1. 'A Good Child' *Key* F major
2. 'The Lamplighter' *Key* Eb major
3. 'Where Go the Boats?' *Key* A major
4. 'Foreign Children' *Key* E minor
Text R. L. Stevenson *Published* Chappell 1914 *Dedicated* To my sister Norah
Nos. 1 and 3 revised and republished Chappell 1945

Three Shakespeare Songs, Op. 6 (First set)
1. 'Come Away, Death' *Key* C minor *Manuscript* BH
2. 'O Mistress Mine' *Key* E♭ major *Published* 1906 *Manuscript* BH, Eton College
3. 'Blow, Blow, Thou Winter Wind' *Key* C minor *Manuscript* BH
No. 3 also published in the 1919 set 'Songs from *As You Like It*'
Text Shakespeare *Composed* 1905 *The set published* Boosey 1905 *Dedicated* To Walter Creighton *Manuscript* BH

To Julia, Op. 8
Prelude
1. 'The Bracelet' *Key* D minor
2. 'The Maiden Blush' *Key* F major
3. 'To Daisies' *Key* D♭ major
4. 'The Night Piece' *Key* C♯ minor/D♭ major
5. 'Julia's Hair' *Key* A♭ major
Interlude
6. 'Cherry Ripe' *Key* F major
Text Herrick *Composed* 1905 *Published* Boosey 1906 *Dedicated* To Gervase Elwes *First performance* Gervase Elwes and Quilter, Aeolian Hall, 31 October 1905 *Manuscript* BH
Nos. 2, 3 and 4 published separately

Songs of Sorrow, Op. 10
1. 'A Coronal' *Key* B♭ major *Composed* June 1907
2. 'Passing Dreams' *Key* E♭ minor *Composed* c.1904; later MS marked: 'altered and finished June 1907' *First performance* Mrs Duncan Gregory (Gwendolen Maud) and Quilter, 15 December 1904 at 37 Cheyne Walk
3. 'A Land of Silence' *Key* D♭ major *Composed* June 1907
4. 'In Spring' *Key* E major *Composed* June 1907
Text Ernest Dowson *Published* Boosey 1908 *Dedicated* To my friends Wilfrid, and Jane von Glehn
First performance as a set Edith Miller and Quilter, Bechstein Hall, 16 November 1907 *Manuscript* LE, BH
No. 3 published separately

Seven Elizabethan Lyrics, Op. 12
1. 'Weep You No More' *Text* Anon. *Key* F minor *Composed* July 1907 *Manuscript* LE (C minor), RR (E♭ minor)
2. 'My Life's Delight' *Text* Campian *Key* G major *Composed* December 1907 *Manuscript* LE
3. 'Damask Roses' *Text* Anon. *Key* D major *Composed* July 1907 *Manuscript* LE
4. 'The Faithless Shepherdess' *Text* Anon. *Key* B♭ minor
5. 'Brown is My Love' *Text* Anon. *Key* B♭ major *Composed* December 1907 *Manuscript* LE
6. 'By a Fountainside' *Text* Ben Jonson *Key* C♯ minor *Composed* November 1907 *Manuscript* LE
7. 'Fair House of Joy' *Text* Anon. attrib. Tobias Hume *Key* D♭ major *Composed* November 1907 *Manuscript* LE, BH (2 copies, in D♭ major and in A♭ major)
The set published Boosey 1908 *Dedicated* To the memory of my friend Mrs Cary Elwes *First performance* probably by Gervase Elwes and Quilter, 17 November 1908, Bechstein Hall *Complete set in manuscript* BH
No. 1, 'Weep You No More', published separately in 1914, and arranged as a duet in

1938; no. 2, 'My Life's Delight', published separately; no. 6, 'By a Fountainside', published separately in 1923; no. 7, 'Fair House of Joy', published separately in 1916

Four Songs, Op. 14

1. 'Autumn Evening' *Text* Arthur Maquarie *Key* G minor *Manuscript* LE
2. 'April' *Text* William Watson *Key* A♭ major *Manuscript* LE, BH
3. 'A Last Year's Rose' *Text* W. E. Henley *Key* D♭ major *Published* 1910 *Manuscript* BH
4. 'Song of the Blackbird' *Text* W. E. Henley *Key* B♭ major *Published* 1911 *Manuscript* BH (non-autograph, but shows that the song was originally entitled 'The Blackbird') *Composed* 1909–10 *Published* Boosey 1910 *Dedicated* To Robin and Aimée Legge

Slumber Song

Text Clifford Mills *Key* *Composed* 1911 *Published* Elkin 1911 *Manuscript* BL Add. MS 72089

Three Songs, Op. 15

1. 'Cuckoo Song' *Text* Alfred Williams *Key* D major *Completed* 26 July 1913 *Published* Boosey 1913 *Dedicated* 'dedicated to and sung by Madame Melba' *Manuscript* LE, BH
2. 'Amaryllis at the Fountain' *Text* Anon. 16th Century *Key* G major *Composed* 1914 *Published* Boosey 1914 *Dedicated* To Rose Grainger *First performance* Mrs Duncan Gregory (Gwendolen Maud) and Quilter, 15 December 1904 at 37 Cheyne Walk, London *Manuscript* LE, BH
3. 'Blossom-Time' *Text* Nora Hopper *Key* G major *Composed* 1914 *Published* Boosey 1914 *Dedicated* To F. B. Kiddle *Manuscript* BH

Six Songs, Op. 18

1. 'To Wine and Beauty' *Text* Earl of Rochester *Key* E♭ major *Composed* 1913 *Published* Elkin 1914 *Dedicated* To Theodore Byard *Manuscript* BL Add. MS 72089; LE (an alternative title 'Bacchus' Song' crossed out)
2. 'Where be You Going?' *Text* Keats *Key* D major *Composed* 1913 *Published* Elkin 1914 *Dedicated* To H. Plunket Greene *Manuscript* BL Add. MS 72089
3. 'The Jocund Dance' *Text* Blake *Key* G major *Composed* 1913 *Published* Elkin 1914 *Dedicated* To Frederic Austin *Manuscript* BL Add. MS 72089
4. 'Spring is at the Door' *Text* Nora Hopper *Key* D major *Composed* April 1914 *Published* Elkin 1914 *Dedicated* To Madame Kirkby Lunn *Manuscript* LE
Two September Songs:
5. 'Through the Sunny Garden' *Key* E major
6. 'The Valley and the Hill' *Key* D minor
Text Mary Coleridge *Composed* January 1916 *Published* Elkin 1916 *Dedicated* To Miss Muriel Foster *Manuscript* BL Add. MS 72089
Nos. 1–4 were published separately; nos. 1–3 were republished in 1920 as *Three Songs for Baritone or Tenor*; nos. 5 and 6 were published as a pair

Three Songs of William Blake, Op. 20

1. 'Dream Valley' *Key* D major *Completed* 18 September 1916 *Manuscript* RR (E major) with German translation by Ida Goldschmidt-Livingston, the song not finally included in Schott's publication
2. 'The Wild Flower's Song' *Key* G major *Completed* (marked 'finished') 3 March 1917
3. 'Daybreak' *Key* E♭ minor *Completed* 4 March 1917
Text William Blake *Published* Winthrop Rogers 1917 *First performance* Muriel Foster, 14 December 1917, Wigmore Hall *Manuscript* LE

Three Pastoral Songs, Op. 22

1. 'I Will Go with My Father A-Ploughing' *Key* Ab major *Manuscript* LE
2. 'Cherry Valley' *Key* E major *Manuscript* LE
3. 'I Wish and I Wish' *Key* C minor
Text Joseph Campbell *Composed* 1920 *Published* Elkin 1921 *Dedicated* To Monica Harrison
Originally scored for piano trio accompaniment; published with and without string parts. No. 1 published separately

Five Shakespeare Songs, Op. 23 (Second set)

1. 'Fear No More the Heat of the Sun' *Key* F minor *Composed* 1921 *Dedicated* To the memory of Robin Hollway *Manuscript* LE, BH in copyist's hand with some markings added by Quilter
2. 'Under the Greenwood Tree' *Key* D major *Composed* 1919 *Published* Boosey 1919 *Dedicated* To Walter Creighton *Manuscript* BH (Eb major; a second manuscript in D major in copyist's hand with some markings added by Quilter)
First published in the set 'Songs from *As You Like It*'
3. 'It was a Lover and His Lass' *Key* duet G major, solo E major *Composed* duet 1919, solo 1921 *Published* Boosey duet 1919, solo 1921 *Dedicated* (both duet and solo) To Walter Creighton *Manuscript* BH (duet and solo copies)
First published in the set 'Songs from *As You Like It*' (duet form)
4. 'Take, O Take Those Lips Away' *Key* Db major *Composed* 1921 *Dedicated* To A. C. Landsberg
Manuscript BH in copyist's hand with some markings added by Quilter
5. 'Hey, Ho, the Wind and the Rain' *Text* Shakespeare *Key* C major *Composed* 1919 *Published* Boosey 1919 *Dedicated* To Walter Creighton
The set published Boosey 1921
Published separately: 'It was a Lover and His Lass' 1922 (duet and solo)

Old English Popular Songs

'Three Poor Mariners'
Text Words and Air From Freeman's Songs in *Deuteromelia 1609 Dedicated* For Guy Vivian
'Drink to Me Only'
Text Ben Jonson *Key* Eb major *Melody* Air by Colonel Mellish *Dedicated* For Arthur Frith *Manuscript* LE
'Over the Mountains'
Text Words from Percy's *Reliques Melody* Air from *Musick's Recreation on the Lyra Viol 1652 Dedicated* For Theodore Byard
'The Jolly Miller'
Text Words from *Love in a Village 1762 Composed* 1921 *Dedicated* For Joseph Farrington *Manuscript* RR in Leslie Woodgate's writing, showing composition date
'Barbara Allen'
Text Words and air traditional *Dedicated* For Frederick Ranalow
The songs published separately Winthrop Rogers 1921
'Drink to Me Only' also published in D minor in 1921, with a French translation by Lilian Fearn

Fairy Lullaby

Text Quilter *Keys* F, Ab, Bb major (original key is unidentified) *Composed* 1921 *Published* Chappell 1921 *Dedicated* To Miss Hilda Blake

Five English Love Lyrics, Op. 24
1. 'There be None of Beauty's Daughters' *Text* Byron *Key* E♭ major *Composed* 1922 *Published* Chappell 1922 *Dedicated* To Roland Hayes *First performance* 22 August 1922, Queen's Hall
2. 'Morning Song' *Text* Thomas Heywood *Key* E major *Composed* May 1922 *Published* Chappell 1922 *Dedicated* John Coates *First performance* 4 October 1922 Queen's Hall
3. 'Go, Lovely Rose' *Text* Edmund Waller *Key* G♭ major *Composed* 1922 *Published* Chappell 1923 *Dedicated* To Hubert Eisdell *First performance* Hubert Eisdell, 17 August 1923, Promenade Concert, Queen's Hall
4. 'O, the Month of May' *Text* Thomas Dekker *Key* D major *Composed* 1926 *Published* Chappell 1927 *Dedicated* To Maude Valérie White
5. 'The Time of Roses' *Text* Thomas Hood *Key* D minor *Composed* 1928 *Published* Chappell 1928 *Dedicated* To my sister Maude

Six Songs, Op. 25
1. 'Song of the Stream' *Text* Alfred Williams *Key* E major *Completed* 6 November 1921 *Published* Winthrop Rogers 1922 *Dedicated* To Pauline Hill *Manuscript* LE (in key F major)
2. 'The Fuchsia Tree' *Text* Manx ballad, attrib. Charles Dalmon *Key* B minor *Completed* 18 February 1923 *Published* Winthrop Rogers 1923 *Dedicated* To Leslie Woodgate *Manuscript* LE
3. 'An Old Carol' *Text* Anon. 15th Century *Key* D major *Composed* 1923 *Published* Winthrop Rogers 1924 *Dedicated* To Constance Wathen *First performance* Mark Raphael and Quilter, 8 December 1923, Wigmore Hall *Manuscript* LE, RR (E major)
4. 'Arab Love Song' *Text* Shelley *Key* C minor *Published* Winthrop Rogers 1927 *Dedicated* To Mary Kinsley Rogers *Manuscript* RR, LE
5. 'Music, When Soft Voices Die' *Text* Shelley *Key* A♭ major *Composed* Christmas 1926 *Published* Winthrop Rogers 1927 *Dedicated* To Norah Nichols *Manuscript* LE (in G♭ major); RR (in A♭ major); BH in copyist's hand with some markings added by Quilter
6. 'In the Bud of the Morning-O' *Text* James Stephens *Key* D major *Composed* 1926 *Published* Winthrop Rogers 1927 *Dedicated* To Evelyn Marthèze Conti *Manuscript* BH in copyist's hand with some markings added by Quilter and originally entitled 'A Field of Daisies'

Two Songs, Op. 26
1. 'In the Highlands' *Key* E♭ major *Composed* June 1922 *Dedicated* To Louis and Dinah de Glehn
2. 'Over the Land is April' *Key* C major *Composed* June 1922 *Dedicated* To Louis and Dinah de Glehn
Text R. L. Stevenson *Published separately* Elkin 1922 *Manuscript* LE (in B♭ major)

Five Jacobean Lyrics, Op. 28
1. 'The Jealous Lover' *Text* Earl of Rochester *Key* D major *Composed* 1923 *Published* Boosey 1923 *Manuscript* RR in Leslie Woodgate's hand with some markings added by Quilter
2. 'Why So Pale and Wan?' *Text* Suckling *Key* C♯ minor *Composed* 1925 *Manuscript* RR in Leslie Woodgate's hand with some markings added by Quilter
3. 'I Dare Not Ask a Kiss' *Text* Herrick *Key* D♭ major *Composed* December 1925 *Manuscript* RR (this copy entitled 'To Electra')

4. 'To Althea, from Prison' *Text* Lovelace *Key* E♭ major *Composed* 1925 *Manuscript* RR in Leslie Woodgate's hand with some markings added by Quilter
5. 'The Constant Lover' *Text* Suckling *Key* D major *Composed* 1925 *Manuscript* RR in Leslie Woodgate's hand with some markings added by Quilter
The set dedicated To Mark Raphael *Published* Boosey 1926

Drei Shakespeare-Lieder
1. 'Come Away Death/ Komm herbei, Tod!' (German translation by Schlegel)
2. 'O Mistress Mine/ O Liebste mein' (German translation by Ida Goldschmidt-Livingston)
3. 'Blow, Blow, Thou Winter Wind/ Stürm, stürm, du Winterwind' (German translation by Schlegel)
Published Schott

Englische Lyrik, Fünf Lieder mit Klavierbegleitung
1. 'Now Sleeps the Crimson Petal/ Nacht-Gesang'
2. 'Love's Philosophy/ Liebes-Philosophie'
3. 'To Daisies/ An die Massliebchen'
4. 'Weep You No More/ Wein' nicht mehr'
5. 'It was a Lover and His Lass/ Es war ein Knabe und sein Liebe'
German translations by Ida Goldschmidt-Livingston
Published Schott 1924

I Arise from Dreams of Thee, Serenade, Op. 29
Text Shelley *Key* E♭ minor *Composed* 1928 *Published* Boosey 1931 *Dedicated* To Robert Allerton
Manuscript RR, C♯ minor, in Leslie Woodgate's hand, but with some markings added by Quilter and marked at the end 'R.Q. 1928' in Woodgate's hand; a second manuscript in the same archive is in RQ's autograph, again in C♯ minor, without a date, but showing cue letters.

Four Shakespeare Songs, Op. 30 (Third set)
1. 'Who is Silvia?' *Key* unknown *Composed* 1926 *Published* Boosey 1927 *Dedicated* To Nora Forman *Manuscript* RR, E♭ major, in Leslie Woodgate's writing but with some markings added by Quilter
2. 'When Daffodils Begin to Peer' *Key* unknown *Composed* 1933 *Dedicated* To Mark Raphael *Manuscript* RR (in B♭ major)
3. 'How Should I Your True Love Know?' *Key* unknown *Composed* 1933 *Dedicated* To Eva Raphael
4. 'Sigh No More, Ladies' *Key* unknown *Composed* 1933 *Dedicated* To Arnold Vivian *Manuscript* RR (in D♭ major)
Text Shakespeare *The set published* Boosey 1933

The Passing Bell
Duet for soprano and alto
Text Winnifred Tasker *Key* A♭ major *Completed* 1934 *Unpublished, manuscript* BH

Blossom-Time
Duet for soprano and alto
Text Nora Hopper *Key* E major *Published* Boosey 1934 *Manuscript* LE
Arrangement of the solo song, Op. 15, no. 3

Music and Moonlight
Text Shelley *Key* E♭ major *Composed* January 1935 *Published* Curwen 1935 *Manuscript* private archive; also RR

Spring Voices
Text Romney Marsh (pseudonym for Quilter) *Key* F major *Composed* 1936 *Published* Ascherberg, Hopwood and Crew 1936 *Dedicated* [Miss Grace Moore]
Grace Moore wrote to Quilter in June 1936 to thank him for his dedication, but it is not clear to which song she was referring. 'Wind from the South' is a possible alternative, but neither song in fact shows a dedication.

Wind from the South
Text John Irvine *Key* E♭ major *Published* Ascherberg, Hopwood and Crew 1936 *Manuscript* RR
See 'Spring Voices'

If Love Should Pass Me By, from *Love at the Inn* [and *Julia*]
Text Rodney Bennett *Key* F major *Published* Ascherberg, Hopwood and Crew 1948

Island of Dreams, Venetian Serenade, from *Love and the Countess*
Text Quilter *Key* E♭ major *Published* Ascherberg, Hopwood and Crew 1946 *Dedicated* To Jeffrey Lambourne

Love Calls through the Summer Night, from *Rosmé*
Solo, duet
Text Rodney Bennett *Published* Ascherberg, Hopwood and Crew 1940

Come Lady-Day
Text May Pemberton *Key* G major *Composed* 1938 *Published* Ascherberg, Hopwood and Crew 1938

Summer Sunset
Duet for soprano and alto
Text Romney Marsh *Key* F major *Composed* 1938 *Published* Ascherberg, Hopwood and Crew 1938

Wild Cherry
Text Olive Mary Denson *Key* E♭ major *Composed* 21 July 1938 *Published* Ascherberg, Hopwood and Crew 1938 *Manuscript* LE

Windy Nights
Duet for soprano and alto
Text R. L. Stevenson *Key* E minor *Published* Ascherberg, Hopwood and Crew 1949

Two Shakespeare Songs, Op. 32
1. 'Orpheus with his Lute' *Key* C major
2. 'When Icicles Hang by the Wall' *Key* C major/minor *Manuscript* LE, BH
Text Shakespeare *Composed* 1938 *Published* Boosey 1939

Weep You No More, Op. 12, no. 1
Duet for soprano and alto, arranged from the solo song
Text Anon. *Key* F minor *Composed* 1938 *Published* Boosey 1939 *Manuscript* BH

Trollie Lollie Laughter
Text Victor B. Neuberg *Key* C minor *Composed* 1939 *Published* Ascherberg, Hopwood and Crew 1939
Manuscript LE

Freedom
Text Rodney Bennett *Key* E♭ major *Composed* 1941 *Published* 1941 *Manuscript* BH
Originally called 'A Song of Freedom'

The Rose of Tralee
Text E. Mordaunt Spencer *Key* B♭ major *Composed* May 1941 *Published* Ascherberg, Hopwood and Crew *Manuscript* LE, RR
Arranged from melody of Charles Glover

Drooping Wings
Text Edith Sterling-Levis *Key* G minor *Composed* 1944 *Published* Chappell 1945

Hymn for Victory
Text A. P. Herbert *Key* D major *Published* Curwen 1945 For solo, or unison voices

Four Child Songs, Op. 5
1. 'A Good Child' *Key* F major
3. 'Where Go the Boats?' *Key* A major
Text R. L. Stevenson *Revised and republished* Chappell 1945; first published in 1914

The Cradle in Bethlehem
Text Rodney Bennett *Key* D major *Composed* 1945 *Published* Michael Joseph 1945 in *Voices on the Green*

Hark, Hark, the Lark!
Text Shakespeare *Key* D major *Published* Boosey and Hawkes 1946 *Manuscript* RR

The Arnold Book of Old Songs
1. 'Drink to Me Only with Thine Eyes' *Text* Ben Jonson *Key* E♭ major *Melody* English Melody 18th Century
2. 'Over the Mountains' *Text* from Percy's 'Reliques' *Key* G major *Melody* Old English Melody
3. 'My Lady Greensleeves' *Text* John Irvine *Key* F minor *Melody* Old English Melody *Composed* June 1942 *Manuscript* LE; a second manuscript in the archive sets the original words by Ben Jonson; a third manuscript in the archive is in E minor, marked 'For Arnold', showing both Jonson's and Irvine's texts
4. 'Beleive Me, If All Those' *Text* Thomas Moore *Key* E♭ major *Melody* Old Irish Melody *Manuscript* LE (G major and E♭ major)
5. 'Oh! 'tis Sweet to Think' *Text* Thomas Moore *Key* G major *Melody* Old Irish Melody *Manuscript* LE
6. 'Ye Banks and Braes' *Text* Robert Burns *Key* G♭ major *Melody* Old Scottish Melody *Manuscript* LE
7. 'Charlie is My Darling' *Text* Anon. *Key* C minor *Melody* Scottish Jacobite marching tune (1775) *Manuscript* LE
8. 'Ca' the Yowes to the Knowes' *Text* Robert Burns *Key* A minor *Melody* Old Scottish Melody *Manuscript* LE (G♯ minor)
9. 'The Man behind the Plough (Le Pauvre Laboureur)' *Text* Rodney Bennett *Key* G major *Composed* 1926 *Melody* Old French Melody *Manuscript* LE; RR, in Leslie Woodgate's writing, gives the composition date. It was performed on 15 May 1934 at the Dorchester Hotel by Mark Raphael, Quilter accompanying.
10. 'My Lady's Garden (L'Amour de Moy)' *Text* Rodney Bennett *Key* D♭ major *Melody* Old French Melody *Manuscript* LE (in D♭ major and C major); John Turner collection (this undated version, also in D♭ major, differs from the published one)

11. 'Pretty Month of May (Joli Moi de Mai)' *Text* Anon. *Key* E♭ major *Melody* Old French Melody *Manuscript* LE

12. 'The Jolly Miller' *Text* Anon. *Key* G minor *Melody* Old English Melody

13. 'Barbara Allen' *Text* Trad. *Key* D major *Melody* Old English Melody

14. 'Three Poor Mariners' *Text* Anon. *Key* E♭ major *Melody* Old English Melody

15. 'Since First I Saw Your Face' *Text* Anon. *Key* E major *Melody* by Ford 17th century

16. 'The Ash Grove' *Text* Rodney Bennett *Key* A♭ major *Melody* Old Welsh Melody *Manuscript* LE

Published singly Boosey and Hawkes 1947 *and as a set* Boosey and Hawkes 1951
Each one dedicated To the memory of Arnold Guy Vivian

One Word is Too Often Profaned

Text Shelley *Key* G♭ major *Composed* 1946 *Published* Curwen 1947

Tulips

Text Herrick *Key* E♭ major *Composed* 1947 *Published* Ascherberg, Hopwood and Crew 1947
Arranged from the partsong of 1946

Music

Text Shelley *Key* D major *Composed* 1947 *Published* Curwen 1948 *Manuscript* Private archive

Come unto These Yellow Sands

Text Shakespeare *Key* E♭ major *Composed* 1946 *Published* Boosey and Hawkes 1951 *Manuscript* BH

Tell Me where is Fancy Bred

Text Shakespeare *Key* D major *Composed* 1946 *Published* Boosey and Hawkes 1951 *Manuscript* BH

Daisies after Rain

Text Judith Bickle *Key* G major *Composed* 1951 *Published* Ascherberg, Hopwood and Crew 1951

The Walled-in Garden

Text Arthur Heald *Key* D major *Composed* June 1952 *Published* Chappell 1952 *Manuscript* LE

April Love

Text Quilter *Key* A minor *Published* Ascherberg, Hopwood and Crew 1952 *Dedicated* For my friend Newton Goodson

A Song at Parting

Text Christina Rossetti *Key* B♭ or D major (original key is unidentified) *Published* Elkin 1952 *Manuscript* sold at Sotheby's May 1968, under first line 'When I am Dead, My Dearest'. Presumed to be the same song

My Heart Adorned with Thee

Solo version:
Text trans. from German of [Mirza Schaffy] by Quilter *Key* E♭ major *Completed* Autumn 1951 *Published* Elkin 1953 *Manuscript* Private archive
Duet version (mezzo and baritone):
Text trans. from German of [Mirza Schaffy] by Quilter *Key* E♭ major *Published* Elkin 1953

I Got a Robe
Text Anon. *Key* A major *Composed* 1928 *Unpublished, first performance* Marian Anderson, 15 June 1928, Wigmore Hall *Manuscript* RR
Arrangement of Negro Spiritual, originally called 'Heav'n, Heav'n' and arranged by Harry Burleigh

What Will You Do, Love?
Text Samuel Lover *Key* E♭ major *Composed* June 1942 *Unpublished, dedicated* For Arnold *Manuscript* LE

Full Fathom Five
Text Shakespeare *Unpublished, manuscript* lost

If Thou Would'st Ease Thine Heart
Text Beddoes *Unpublished, manuscript* lost

Love is a Bable
Text Anon. *Unpublished, manuscript* lost

Where the Bee Sucks
Text Shakespeare *Unpublished, manuscript* lost

Songs with instrumental groups

O Mistress Mine, Op. 6, no. 2, arranged from the solo song
Scoring piano quartet *Key* E♭ major *Text* Shakespeare *Unpublished, manuscript* BH

To Julia, Op. 8, arranged from the solo song cycle
Scoring piano quintet *Text* Herrick *Composed* probably 1923 *Unpublished, manuscript* BH

Dream Valley, Op. 20, no. 1
Scoring cello, piano *Text* Blake *Key* D♭ major *Composed* September 1917 *Unpublished, dedicated* Monica Harrison *manuscript* RCM

Good Morrow, 'tis St Valentine's Day
Scoring Piano conductor score for string quartet and harp; reduction for piano or harp *Text* D'Urfey *Key* A major *Composed* 1917, revised 1919 *Unpublished, manuscript* (both versions) BL Add. MS 72089

Three Pastoral Songs, Op. 22
1. 'I Will Go with My Father A-Ploughing' *Key* A♭ major
2. 'Cherry Valley' *Key* E major
3. 'I Wish and I Wish' *Key* C minor
Scoring violin, cello, piano *Text* Joseph Campbell *Composed* 1920 *Published* Elkin 1921 *Dedicated* To Monica Harrison *Manuscript* LE

Hey, Ho, the Wind and the Rain, Op. 23, no. 5.
Scoring Low voice, two violins, cello, piano *Text* Shakespeare *Key* C major *Unpublished, manuscript* BH
Arranged from the solo song by Quilter and Leslie Woodgate

An Old Carol, Op. 25, no. 3
Scoring String quartet (part marked for piano, although piano part has not been added) *Text* Anon. 15th Century *Key* E major *Unpublished, manuscript* BH
Arranged from the solo song

Songs with orchestra

Now Sleeps the Crimson Petal, Op. 3, no. 2, arranged from the solo song
Scoring voice and string orchestra, harp or piano ad lib *Text* Tennyson *Key* E♭ major *Composed* post-1946 *Unpublished, manuscript* BH
Scoring small orchestra 1111 – harp strgs *Text* Tennyson *Key* G♭ major *Composed* post-1946 *Unpublished, manuscript* BH

Fill a Glass, Op. 3, no. 3, arranged from the solo song
Scoring orchestra 2121 223 – timp perc harp strgs piano ad lib *Text* W. E. Henley *Key* F major *Unpublished, manuscript* BH

Come Away, Death, Op. 6, no. 2, arranged from the solo song
Scoring small orchestra 2122 22(cornets) – *Text* Shakespeare *Key* C minor *Unpublished, manuscript* BH
Scoring Small orchestra 2121 22 – timp harp/piano *Text* Shakespeare *Key* E♭ minor *Unpublished, manuscript* BH

O Mistress Mine, Op. 6, no. 2, arranged from the solo song
Scoring string orchestra, piano ad lib *Text* Shakespeare *Key* E♭ major *Published* Boosey 1944
Scoring string orchestra *Text* Shakespeare *Key* E♭ major *Unpublished, manuscript* BH
Scoring string orchestra *Text* Shakespeare *Key* G♭ major *Unpublished, manuscript* BH
These two the same, but transposed
Scoring small orchestra 2122 2 – strgs *Text* Shakespeare *Key* E♭ major *Unpublished, manuscript* BH

Blow, Blow, Op. 6, no. 3, arranged from the solo song
Scoring string orchestra, piano ad lib *Text* Shakespeare *Key* C minor *Published* Boosey and Hawkes 1945 *Manuscript* BH
Scoring small orchestra 2122 22(cornets) – timp, trgl, strgs *Text* Shakespeare *Key* C minor *Unpublished, manuscript* BH

Weep You No More, Op. 12, no. 1, arranged from the solo song
Scoring soprano and alto duet, small orchestra 2121 22 – timp harp strgs *Text* Anon. *Key* F minor *Unpublished, manuscript* BH
Scoring string orchestra, piano ad lib *Text* Anon. *Key* D minor *Unpublished, manuscript* BH

The Faithless Shepherdess, Op. 12, no. 4, arranged from the solo song
Scoring Full (large) orchestra *Text* Anon. *Key* B♭ minor *Manuscript* LE
Arranged for the BBC

Fair House of Joy, Op. 12, no. 7
Scoring small orchestra 2121 222 – timp harp stgs *Text* Anon. attrib. Hume *Key* D♭ major *Unpublished, manuscript* BH

Under the Greenwood Tree, Op. 23, no. 2
Scoring small orchestra 1121 1 – strgs piano (if no orchestra) *Text* Shakespeare *Key* F major *Unpublished, manuscript* BH
Arranged from the solo song by Quilter and Leslie Woodgate

It was a Lover and His Lass, Op. 23, no. 3, arranged from the solo song
Scoring string orchestra, piano ad lib. *Text* Shakespeare *Key* E major *Unpublished, manuscript* BH

Scoring small orchestra 111–1 – timp trgl harp *Text* Shakespeare *Key* E major *Unpublished, manuscript* BH

Take, O Take Those Lips Away, Op. 23, no. 4, arranged from the solo song
Scoring string orchestra and harp ad lib. (harp part incomplete) *Text* Shakespeare *Key* D major *Unpublished, manuscript* BH

Hey, Ho, the Wind and the Rain, Op. 23, no. 5, arranged from the solo song
Scoring small orchestra 1121 22 – timp harp strgs *Text* Shakespeare *Key* E major *Unpublished, manuscript* BH

I Arise from Dreams of Thee, Serenade for voice and orchestra, Op. 29
Scoring Full orchestra *Text* Shelley *Key* E♭ minor *Unpublished, dedicated* To Robert Allerton *First performance* 24 July 1929, Harrogate Festival *Manuscript* BH

When Love is Ended, from *Love at the Inn*
Scoring duet, small orchestra *Text* Rodney Bennett *Key* G major *Published* Ascherberg, Hopwood and Crew, date unknown, *c.*1948

Choral music (piano accompaniment unless otherwise stated)

Verses from 'The Rubāïyat of Omar Khayām', Sketch for Chorus
Partsong for alto, tenor 1, tenor 2 (or baritone), bass 1, bass 2, unaccompanied
Text translated by E. A. Johnson *Key* C major *Composed* 1902 *Unpublished, manuscript* GM

Two Partsongs, for SATB
1. 'To Daffodils' *Key* D major *Manuscript* BH, LE
'Boosey's Choral Miscellany No. 262'
2. 'To the Virgins' *Key* E♭ major *Manuscript* BH
'The Choralist No. 350'
Unaccompanied
Text Herrick *Published* Boosey 1904

Five Lyrics of Robert Herrick, for SATB, Op. 7
1. 'Cupid' *Key* B♭ major
2. 'A Dirge' *Key* G minor
3. 'Morning Song' *Key* C minor
4. 'To Electra' *Key* F major *Manuscript* LE
5. 'To Violets' *Key* D major
Unaccompanied
Text Herrick *Composed c.*1905 *Published* Forsyth 1907 *Dedicated* To my dear friend Percy Grainger

It was a Lover and His Lass, Op. 23, no. 3
Partsong for two voices, accompanied
Text Shakespeare *Published* Boosey 1935

Lead Us, Heavenly Father for tenor, chorus [SATB] and orchestra
Text James Edmeston *Key* D♭ major *Completed* 22 July 1909 *Published* Stainer and Bell 1924 *Dedicated* For Ida Legge *Manuscript* LE

An Old Carol
Unison song, accompanied

Text Anon. 15th Century *Key* D major *Composed* 1923 *Published* Winthrop Rogers 1924 ('Festival Series of Choral Music')
Also marked 'This song is published in the December number of 'Our Own Gazette', the YWCA Magazine, 22 George Street, Hanover Square, W'.

What Shall He Have that Killed the Deer?
Partsong for men's voices, unaccompanied
Text Shakespeare *Key* D major *Published* Boosey 1924
'Boosey's Modern Festival Series No. 320'

Non Nobis, Domine
Partsong, SATB, accompanied
Text Rudyard Kipling *Key* E♭ *Composed* 1934 *Dedicated* Walter Creighton *First performance* Pageant of Parliament, July 1934, Royal Albert Hall, London *Manuscript* LE (full score)
The partsong was published for various choral voices with piano accompaniment. It was also scored for strings or full orchestra, parts being available for hire. All versions were published by Boosey.
SATB *Key* D major *Composed* 1934 *Published* 1934 'Boosey's Modern Festival Series, No. 461' *Manuscript* BH
Two-part for men's voices plus optional 2nd bass *Key* D major *Composed* 1934 *Published* 1934 'Boosey's Modern Festival Series, No. 348' *Manuscript* BH
Unison *Key* C major *Published* 1938 'Boosey's Modern Festival Series, No. 69'
SSC *Key* E♭ major *Published* 1951 'Boosey's Modern Festival Series, No. 224'
String orchestra *Key* D major *Published* 1937 *Manuscript* VL (score)

You've Money to Spend
Partsong, SATBarB, accompanied
Text Anon. *Key* D major *Composed* 1934 *Unpublished, printed copy* BL (vocal score) *First performance* Pageant of Parliament, July 1934, Royal Albert Hall, London
An orchestral arrangement was made by Cyril James Clarke *Manuscript* BBC Library

To A Harebell by a Graveside
Partsong for soprano and alto voices, accompanied
Text George Darley *Key* E major *Composed* 1938 *Published* Ascherberg, Hopwood and Crew 1938

Come Lady-Day
Partsong for women's voices, soprano and alto, accompanied
Text May Pemberton *Key* F major *Composed* 1938 *Published* Ascherberg, Hopwood and Crew 1938
'Mortimer Series of Modern Part Songs, no. 43'

The Starlings
Partsong for women's voices, SA
Text Charles Kingsley *Key* E minor *Composed* 1938 *Published* Ascherberg, Hopwood and Crew 1938
Performed 15 December 1904 by Mrs Duncan Gregory (Gwendolen Maud) at 37 Cheyne Walk, accompanied by Quilter
'Mortimer Series of Modern Part Songs, no. 44'

Weep You No More, Op. 12, no. 1
Partsong for women's voices, arranged from the solo song, accompanied

Text Anon. *Key* F minor *Composed* 1938 *Published* Boosey and Hawkes 1939 *Manuscript* BH
'Boosey's Modern Festival Series, no. 146'

Summer Sunset
Partsong for soprano and alto voices, accompanied
Text Romney Marsh *Key* F major *Composed* 1938 *Published* Ascherberg, Hopwood and Crew 1949
'Mortimer Series of Modern Part Songs, no. 228'

Madrigal in Satin
Partsong for men's voices TTBB, unaccompanied
Text Rodney Bennett *Key* B♭ major *Composed* 1939 *Published* Ascherberg, Hopwood and Crew 1939
'Mortimer Series of Modern Part Songs no. 71'

Fairy Lullaby
Partsong for women's voices in three parts, accompanied
Text Quilter *Key* F, A♭ or B♭ major (original not clear) *Published* Chappell 1939

Freedom
Text Rodney Bennett *Key* E♭ major *Composed* 1941 *Unpublished, first performance* 10 July 1941 *Manuscript* BBC Library (full score)
Originally called 'A Song of Freedom', and commissioned by the BBC
The partsong was published for various choral voices with piano accompaniment. It was also scored for strings and for full orchestra. All versions were published by Boosey
Unison voices, with accompanying chorus ad lib, and piano accompaniment *Key* E♭ major *Published* 1941 'Choral Miscellany No. 203' *Manuscript* LE
Partsong for SSC *Published* 1942
Piano-conductor and string parts *Published* 1942

Youth and Beauty, from *Rosmé*
Partsong for SSATTB, accompanied
Text Rodney Bennett *Key* G major *Published* Ascherberg, Hopwood and Crew 1941
'Mortimer Series of Modern Part Songs, no. 116'

Here's a Chapter Almost Ended [from *The Blue Boar*]
Partsong for six voices
Text Rodney Bennett *Key* F major *Published* Ascherberg, Hopwood and Crew 1946
The score claims it is from *Love at the Inn* though it is not in the vocal score and may have been used in *The Blue Boar*

Love Calls through the Summer Night, from *Julia, Love at the Inn, Rosmé* etc.
Partsong SATB, accompanied
Text Rodney Bennett *Key* E minor/E major *Published* Ascherberg, Hopwood and Crew 1954
Arranged by Leslie Woodgate
'Mortimer Series of Modern Part Songs, no. 382'

Here's to the Ladies, from *Julia, Love at the Inn* etc.
Scoring chorus, small orchestra *Text* Rodney Bennett *Key* C major *Published* Ascherberg, Hopwood and Crew, date unknown, *c.*1948

The Rose of Tralee
SATB, accompanied

Text E. Mordaunt Spencer *Key* D♭ major *Composed* 1941 *Published* Ascherberg, Hopwood and Crew 1951
Arranged from melody of Charles Glover
'Mortimer Series of Modern Part Songs, no. 313'

My Lady Greensleeves
Partsong for soprano and alto voices, accompanied
Text John Irvine *Key* G minor *Composed* 1942 *Published* Boosey and Hawkes 1942 *Manuscript* BH

The Sailor and His Lass
Soprano, baritone solo, SCTB, orchestra
Text Rodney Bennett *Composed* 1943 *Published* (Vocal Score) Curwen 1948 *First performance* near Leicester in 1945/early 1946
Read and rejected by the BBC in January 1944

Where Go the Boats?
Partsong for women's voices, SA, accompanied
Text R. L. Stevenson *Key* G major *Published* Chappell 1945
Arranged from the solo song, no. 3 of *Four Child Songs*, Op. 5

Hymn for Victory
Partsong for four voices, unaccompanied
Text A. P. Herbert *Key* C major *Published* Curwen 1945

The Pretty Birds Do Sing
SATB, unaccompanied
Text Thomas Nashe *Key* G major *Composed* 1945 *Published* Ascherberg, Hopwood and Crew 1946
'Mortimer Series of Modern Part Songs, no. 180'

The Cradle in Bethlehem
Unison song, accompanied
Text Rodney Bennett *Key* E major *Composed* 1945 *Published* Curwen 1949
Also partsong for two (unspecified) voices, accompanied *Key* F major *Published* Curwen 1950
Arranged from the solo song

Farewell to Shan-Avon, Song of the Forlorn Warriors, for men's voices
TTBB, unaccompanied
Text Darley *Key* F minor *Published* Ascherberg, Hopwood and Crew 1946 *Manuscript* LE
'Mortimer Series of Modern Part Songs, no. 166'

Tulips
SATB, unaccompanied
Text Herrick *Key* G♭ major *Composed* 1946 *Published* Ascherberg, Hopwood and Crew 1946
'Mortimer Series of Modern Part Songs, no. 167'

Windy Nights
Partsong for women's voices, SA, accompanied
Text R. L. Stevenson *Key* E minor *Published* Ascherberg, Hopwood and Crew 1949
'Mortimer Series of Modern Part Songs, no. 229'

Daisies after Rain
Partsong for two soprano voices, accompanied
Text Judith Bickle *Key* G major *Composed* 1952 *Published* Ascherberg, Hopwood and Crew 1952
'Mortimer Series of Modern Part Songs, no. 338'

Dancing on the Green
SCTB, unaccompanied
Text Quilter *Key* C major *Published* Ascherberg, Hopwood and Crew 1954
Edited by Leslie Woodgate
'Mortimer Series of Modern Part Songs, no. 389'

Drink to Me Only with Thine Eyes
TTBB, unaccompanied
Arranged 1939 *Text* Ben Jonson *Key* G major *Published* Boosey 1955

Piano music (piano solo, unless otherwise stated)

Theme
Composed 1899 *Unpublished, manuscript* John Turner collection. The score is marked 'For Pianoforte or Organ'

Three Studies for Piano, Op. 4
1. *Composed* 1901 *First performance* earlier than 8 June 1903, when Evelyn Suart played it in a recital at the Wigmore Hall *Manuscript* National Library of Scotland; LE
2. *Composed* April 1909 *Manuscript* LE
3. *Composed* 1909 *Manuscript* LE
The set published Winthrop Rogers 1910, reissued Cary and Co., *c.*1915, and again in 1921, Winthrop Rogers; no. 1 also published separately *Dedicated* To Madame Pura Heierhoff-de Castelaro

Three English Dances, Op. 11
Piano solo, piano duet
Both: published Boosey 1910 *Dedicated* To my friend Percy Grainger *Manuscript* BH
Both forms arranged from the orchestral original

Slumber Song, from *Where the Rainbow Ends*
Published Elkin 1912
Arranged from the solo song

Suite from Where the Rainbow Ends
1. 'Rosamund and Will-o'-the-Wisp'
2. 'Goblin Forest'
3. 'Moonlight on the Lake'
4. 'Fairy Revels'
Published Elkin 1912

Music from Where the Rainbow Ends
Published Elkin 1919

Two Dances from Where the Rainbow Ends
1. 'Fairy Ballet'
2. 'Fairy Frolic'
Published Elkin 1919

Four Dances from Where the Rainbow Ends
1. 'Fairy Ballet'
2. 'Will-o'-the-Wisp'
3. 'Dance of the Spirit of the Lake'
4. 'Fairy Frolic'
Published Elkin 1919

Three Pieces for Piano, Op. 16
1. 'Dance in the Twilight' *Composed* sketched 1909, completed 1915 *Dedicated* To Luigino Franchetti
Manuscript LE (MS has alternative opus nos: Op. 14 no 2 and Op. 15 no. 1 crossed out; this was evidently begun before the Op. 14 Songs)
2. 'Summer Evening' *Composed* pencil sketch, May 5 1915 *Dedicated* To the memory of Charlotte Emelia Bellot *Manuscript* LE
3. 'At a Country Fair' *Composed* May 1916 *Dedicated* To Leo Ornstein *Manuscript* LE
Published as a set and each piece separately Winthrop Rogers 1916

Two Impressions for Piano, Op. 19
1. 'In a Gondola' *Composed* 5 May 1914. Originally called 'Barcarole'
2. 'Lanterns' *Composed* 1919. Originally called 'Carnival'
Published separately Winthrop Rogers 1920 *Dedicated* To my friend Percy Grainger
Manuscript LE

A Children's Overture, Op. 17
Piano solo
Arranged from the orchestral original by Quilter
Piano duet
Arranged from the orchestral original by Anthony Bernard
Both published Winthrop Rogers 1920 *Dedicated* To my brother Percy

Suite from As You Like It, Op. 21
Arranged for piano solo
1. 'Shepherd's Holiday'
2. 'Evening in the Forest'
3. 'Merry Pranks'
4. 'Country Dance'
Completed 1920 *Published* Boosey 1920 *Dedicated* To H. Balfour Gardiner *Manuscript* BH

Country Pieces for Piano, Op. 27
1. 'Shepherd Song'
2. 'Goblins'
3. 'Forest Lullaby'
4. 'Pipe and Tabor'
Composed 1923 *Published* Winthrop Rogers 1923 *Dedicated* To Mrs Fabian Bracken-bury

The Rake, a ballet
1. 'Dance at the Feast'
2. 'The Light-hearted Lady'
3. 'The Frolicsome Friend'
4. 'Allurement'
5. 'Midnight Revels'

Composed 1925 *Published* Ascherberg, Hopwood and Crew 1925

Drink to Me Only
Composed 1927 *Published* Winthrop Rogers 1927

Chamber and instrumental music

To Daisies, Op. 8, no. 2
Scoring cello, piano *Completed* 1918 *Unpublished, manuscript* BH

Julia's Hair, Op. 8, no. 5
Scoring violin, piano *Published* Boosey 1919
Scoring cello, piano *Published* Boosey 1919

Love Song to Julia (Cherry Ripe), Op. 8, no. 6
Scoring violin, piano *Completed* 1918 *Published* Boosey 1919 *First performed* (under the title 'Cherry Ripe') May Harrison and Quilter, 5 June 1917, Wigmore Hall *Manuscript* BH

Rosamund: Interlude from the Fairy Play [from *Where the Rainbow Ends*]
Scoring violin, piano *Published* Elkin 1918 *First performance* Margaret Harrison and Hamilton Harty, 4 December 1918, Wigmore Hall *Manuscript* LE

Slumber Song [from *Where the Rainbow Ends*]
Scoring violin, piano *Published* Elkin 1912
Scoring cello, piano *Published* Elkin 1912

Intermezzo: Moonlight on the Lake [from *Where the Rainbow Ends*]
Scoring 2 violins, cello, bass ad lib, piano *Published* Elkin 1922

Two Pieces for Piano and Strings [from *Where the Rainbow Ends*]
Scoring two violins, viola, cello, bass ad lib, piano, with optional part for a third violin in place of the viola
1. 'Moonlight on the Lake'
2. 'Water Nymph'
Published Elkin 1937

Fairy Frolic for piano trio [from *Where the Rainbow Ends*]
Scoring violin, cello, piano *Published* Elkin 1929

Two Old English Tunes
1. 'Drink to Me Only'
2. 'Three Poor Mariners'
Scoring violin, cello, piano *Published* Winthrop Rogers 1917
Scoring violin, piano *Published* Winthrop Rogers 1917

Dream Valley
Scoring violin, piano *Published* Winthrop Rogers 1917 *Dedicated* for May Harrison *First performance* May Harrison and Quilter, 5 June 1917, Wigmore Hall *Manuscript* RCM

L'Amour de Moy (My Lady's Garden)
Scoring cello, piano *Unpublished, manuscript* RCM
Undated, but possibly from the same time as the voice, cello and piano arrangement of 'Dream Valley', 1917
Scoring cello, piano *Unpublished, manuscript* RCM
Undated, but a reduction of an orchestral version probably dating from 1933.

Gipsy Life, **fantasy quintet**
Scoring two violins, viola, cello, bass, piano, with optional part for a third violin in place of the viola *Published* Goodwin and Tabb 1935 *Dedicated* To Leslie Bridgewater

Orchestral works

Serenade for Orchestra, **Op. 9**
Scoring small orchestra *Composed* May 1907 *Unpublished, dedicated* To Professor Ivan Knorr in gratitude and admiration *First performance* Promenade Concert, Queen's Hall, London 27 August 1907 *Manuscript* LE
Marked 'I intend rewriting and rescoring this composition (as Op. 9): R. Q. 1919 otherwise it must *on no account* be published' and 'to be reorchestrated & 3rd movt. lengthened: October 1952 Roger Quilter'

Three English Dances, **for small orchestra, Op. 11**
Scoring full orchestra *Published* Boosey 1910 *First performance* Promenade concert, Queen's Hall 30 June 1910 *Manuscript* LE (full score)
Scoring (by Percy Fletcher) small band *Published* Boosey 1912

Suite from the Fairy Play, **Where the Rainbow Ends**
Scoring full orchestra
1. 'Rainbow Land', 'Will-o'-the-Wisp'
2. 'Rosamund'
3. 'Fairy Frolic'
4. 'Goblin Forest'

Two Pieces [**from Where the Rainbow Ends**]
Scoring small orchestra
1. 'Moonlight on the Lake' BL Add. MS 72089 (copyright dated 1936 and 1952)
2. 'Water Nymph[s]' *Manuscript* BL Add. MS 72089 (copyright dated 1951)
Published Elkin 1937

Fairy Ballet [**from Where the Rainbow Ends**]
Scoring full orchestra *Unpublished, manuscript* BBC Library
Score marked 'from Beginning to letter T Rescored by Roger Quilter letter T to end rescored by Leslie Woodgate'; the writing style in fact changes just after cue letter J

A Children's Overture for Orchestra, **Op. 17**
Scoring full orchestra *Composed* 'sketched 1911: finished 1919' *Unpublished, dedicated* To my brother Percy *First performance* Promenade concert, Queen's Hall, 18 September 1919 *Manuscript* LE
Arranged for small orchestra by Quilter *Published* Chappell's, by arrangement with Winthrop Rogers 1921 'Chappell & Co.'s Popular Orchestral Edition' *Manuscript* LE
Originally intended as the overture to *Where the Rainbow Ends*

Suite from As You Like It **for small orchestra, Op. 21**
1. 'Shepherd's Holiday'
2. 'Evening in the Forest'
3. 'Merry Pranks'
4. 'Country Dance'
Composed 1920 *Published* Boosey 1921 *Dedicated* To H. Balfour Gardiner *Manuscript* LE *First performed* September 1920 (London Ballad Concert at the Royal Albert Hall;

London Symphony Orchestra). Arranged from the incidental music to the Old Vic production of *As You Like It*

Fanfare for Children
Scoring 4 trumpets, 4 trombones, timpani, cymbals *Composed c.*1930, 1931 *Unpublished, first performance* Annual Dinner of Musicians' Benevolent Fund (written for the occasion) *Manuscript* in copyist's hand, Royal Military School of Music, Kneller Hall
Derived from *A Children's Overture*

L'Amour de Moy (My Lady's Garden)
Scoring Small orchestra *Unpublished, manuscript* RCM
Undated, but probably dating from 1933. Some in Quilter's hand, though most is in a copyist's hand

Titania, a little dream ballet for orchestra, Op. 31
Unpublished, manuscript lost

Concert Waltz, from *Rosmé*
Scoring small orchestra, full orchestra *Published* Ascherberg, Hopwood and Crew 1941
A concert version of the waltz theme from *Julia*

In Georgian Days, from *Rosmé*
Scoring strings, piano *Published* Ascherberg, Hopwood and Crew 1941
The Gavotte from *Love at the Inn*

Ding Dong Bell, Suite for strings from *Nursery Rhyme Tunes*
Scoring string orchestra *Composed* 1951 *Unpublished, manuscript* LE

Valse
Scoring orchestra *Manuscript* LE (parts only)

Theatre music

Where the Rainbow Ends, fairy play for children
Text Clifford Mills & John Ramsay *Composed* 1911 *Unpublished in its entirety First performance* Savoy Theatre, London, 21 December 1911 *Manuscript* various versions BL Add. MSS 54208, 72086, 72087, 72088

As You Like It, incidental music
Incidental music to the production of *As You Like It. First performance* Old Vic 17 October 1921 *Manuscript* lost, but arranged as a Suite (see 'Orchestral works')

The Rake, a ballet
1. 'Dance at the Feast'
2. 'The Light-hearted Lady'
3. 'The Frolicsome Friend'
4. 'Allurement'
5. 'Midnight Revels'
Scoring Small orchestra *Composed* 1925 *Published* Ascherberg, Hopwood and Crew 1925 *Manuscript* LE
Manuscript score marked 'arranged from the original score by Sydney Baynes'
First performance in the original ballet 17 March 1925, Palace Theatre, Manchester, an item in C. B. Cochran's revue *On with the Dance*

The Blue Boar/Julia/Rosmé/Love and the Countess/Love at the Inn, a light opera
The only complete version is *Love at the Inn*, published in vocal score with separate libretto, by Ascherberg, Hopwood and Crew 1940, 1948, 1949
Several songs were published separately, from one or other version of the opera:
'Youth & Beauty', 1941 (partsong)
'In Georgian Days', Gavotte, from *Rosmé*, 1941 (instrumental)
'Island of Dreams', Venetian Serenade, 1946 (solo song)
'Here's a Chapter Almost Ended', 1946 (partsong)
'If Love Should Pass Me By', 1948 (solo song)
'Love Calls through the Summer Night', 1954 (partsong)
'Here's to the Ladies', from *Julia*, *Love at the Inn* etc. (partsong) date unknown, *c.*1948
'When Love is Ended', from *Love at the Inn* (duet with orchestra) date unknown, *c.*1948
These are listed elsewhere in the catalogue, under the relevant section
Composed 1929–1936 *Manuscript* lost as a single entity
The Blue Boar: Lyrics and libretto Rodney Bennett *First performance* 23 October 1933 in a one-act concert version, BBC
Julia: Libretto Stanley Grey (and/or Vladimir Rosing) and Caswell Garth *Lyrics* Rodney Bennett *First performance* 3 December 1936, Royal Opera House, Covent Garden
Love at the Inn: Book Jeffrey Lambourne *Lyrics* Rodney Bennett

Appendix E Discography

My information is from, and my deepest thanks are due to, 78 Record Exchange, Stockport, UK, in whose Aladdin's cave I have spent many happy hours; Frank Andrews of the City of London Phonograph & Gramophone Society; and Timothy Day of the National Sound Archive of the British Library.

The details available vary greatly. Record labels and numbers are given where known and where I am reasonably certain of their accuracy; sometimes I have been able to establish merely that a recording by particular artists took place. Matrix numbers are given where known and where I can find no other information.

I have listed all published songs and partsongs (and manuscripts where they are known to exist and are worthy of attention), even if not recorded, since this highlights those that await recording; songs are generally listed under the individual title. Exceptions are those sets that have often been recorded in their entirety: *Three Shakespeare Songs*; *Four Shakespeare Songs*; *Five Shakespeare Songs*; *Seven Elizabethan Lyrics*; *To Julia*. Those who have recorded the entire set are listed first, followed by singers of individual songs. Several singers have recorded LPs or CDs devoted to, or with a substantial content of, Quilter songs: John Mark Ainsley, Jeffrey Benton, David Johnston, Paul Austin Kelly, Christopher Keyte, Benjamin Luxon, Lisa Milne, Anthony Rolfe Johnson, David Wilson-Johnson and Alexander Young.

Songs shown in brackets have not, to my knowledge, been recorded; of the piano music, only *Three Country Dances* appear to have been recorded, and it is not clear exactly what these are (probably *Three English Dances*). The only music for chamber combinations that appears to have been recorded is the occasional arrangement of a song; such arrangements are shown under the song.

Record labels and abbreviations

Ae	Aeolian
AmCol	USA Columbia records
BH	Boosey and Hawkes
Cantil	Cantilena
CC	Collins Classics
Ch	Chandos
Col	Columbia
D	Decca
Del	Delos
Ecl	Eclipse
G	The Gramophone Co.
GAC	Georgina Colwell
GM	GM Recordings
HM	Harmonia Mundi

HMV	His Master's Voice
Hy	Hyperion
IMP	Innovative Music
Lon	London
MP	Marco Polo
Od	Odeon
Oi	Oiselet
OL	L'Oiseau-Lyre
P	Parlophone
Pe	Pearl
Ph	Philips
Picc	Piccadilly
Re	Regal
RO	Private recording; in this discography only applicable to the Quilter–Raphael recordings
Sym	Symposium
ToES	HMV Treasury of English Song
UA	United Artists
Vic	Victor
VirgC	Virgin Classics
Voc	Vocalion

CD	compact disc
iss.	issued
LP	33 rpm
rec.	recorded
rev.	reviewed (useful if no other dates are available)
TC	cassette recording

There is one CD under the Collins Classics label: the Duke Quartet is heard in many of the tracks and its members are: Louisa Fuller, Rick Koster (violins), John Metcalfe (viola), Ivan McCready (cello).

Songs, and arrangements of songs for instrumental combinations

Amaryllis at the Fountain, **Three Songs, Op. 15, no. 2**
Sarah Leonard (soprano), Malcolm Martineau (piano) (rec. 15–16 Nov 1999 at St Philip's Church, London SW16) SOMM.SOMMCD 224 (CD)
Lisa Milne (soprano), Graham Johnson (piano) CC.15122 (CD)

L'Amour de Moy, **The Arnold Book of Old Songs** – see under *My Lady's Garden*

(The Answer)

April, **Four Songs, Op. 14, no. 2**
Benjamin Luxon (baritone), David Willison (piano) (rec. 3–4 May 1989 at the Maltings, Snape, iss. 1989, rev. Mar 1990) Ch.CHAN8782 (CD) ABTD 1417 (TC)

(April Love)

Arab Love Song, **Six Songs, Op. 25, no. 4**
John Mark Ainsley (tenor), Malcolm Martineau (piano) (rec. 18–20 Feb 1996) Hy.CDA66878 (CD)

Sarah Leonard (soprano), Malcolm Martineau (piano) (rec. 15–16 Nov 1999 at St Philip's Church, London SW16) SOMM.SOMMCD 224 (CD)

Benjamin Luxon (baritone), David Willison (piano) (rec. 3–4 May 1989 at the Maltings, Snape, iss. 1989) Ch.CHAN8782 (CD) ABTD 1417 (TC)

Anthony Roden (tenor), Geoffrey Parsons (piano) BBC recording, broadcast Radio 3, 18 Jan 1989

Alexander Young (tenor), Gordon Watson (piano) (rev. Apr 1955) Argo.RG36 (LP)

The Arnold Book of Old Songs – see under individual songs

The Ash Grove, The Arnold Book of Old Songs
Jeffrey Benton (baritone), Rona Lowe (piano) (iss. 1993) Sym.1159 (CD)
Robert Ivan Foster (baritone), Mary Earl (piano) (rec. in Apr 1966) Onslow

At Close of Day
Benjamin Luxon (baritone), David Willison (piano) (rec. 3–4 May 1989 at the Maltings, Snape, iss. 1989) Ch.CHAN8782 (CD) ABTD 1417 (TC)

Autumn Evening, Four Songs, Op. 14, no. 1
John Mark Ainsley (tenor), Malcolm Martineau (piano) (rec. 18–20 Feb 1996) Hy.CDA66878 (CD)
Sarah Leonard (soprano), Malcolm Martineau (piano) (rec. 16–18 Oct 1991 in St Michael's Church, Highgate, London, UK, iss. 1992) IMP Classics (Pickwick Group) PCD 1029 (CD)
Benjamin Luxon (baritone), David Willison (piano) (rec. 3–4 May 1989 at the Maltings, Snape, iss. 1989, rev. Mar 1990) Ch.CHAN8782 (CD) ABTD 1417 (TC)
Lisa Milne (soprano), Graham Johnson (piano) CC.15122 (CD)
Derek Oldham (tenor), Madame Adami (piano) (rec. 18 Dec 1925) HMV.E426 (78)
Jonathan Veira (baritone), Malcolm Martineau (piano) (rec. 15–16 Nov 1999 at St Philip's Church, London SW16) SOMM.SOMMCD 224 (CD)
David Wilson-Johnson (baritone), David Owen Norris (piano) (rec. 1–2 Apr 1986, rev. Mar 1987) Hy.A66208 (LP)

Barbara Allen, The Arnold Book of Old Songs
John Mark Ainsley (tenor), Malcolm Martineau (piano) (rec. 18–20 Feb 1996) Hy.CDA66878 (CD)
Thomas Allen (baritone), Roger Vignoles (piano) (rec. 28 Aug 1990 at the Queen's Hall, Edinburgh, Scotland, at the Edinburgh International Festival)
Jeffrey Benton (baritone), Rona Lowe (piano) (iss. 1993) Sym.1159 (CD)
Robert Ivan Foster (baritone), Mary Earl (piano) (rec. in Apr 1966) Onslow
Susan Kessler (mezzo-soprano), Geoffrey Parsons (piano) (iss. Sep 1984) Meridian.E77074 (stereo LP)
David Wilson-Johnson (baritone), David Owen Norris (piano) Hy.A66208 (LP)

Believe Me, If All Those Endearing Young Charms, The Arnold Book of Old Songs
Jeffrey Benton (baritone), Rona Lowe (piano) (iss. 1993) Sym.1159 (CD)
Robert Ivan Foster (baritone), Mary Earl (piano) (rec. in Apr 1966) Onslow
Cesare Valletti (tenor), L. Taubman (piano)

(Blossom-Time), Three Songs, Op. 15, no. 3

Blow, Blow, Thou Winter Wind – see under *Three Shakespeare Songs*, Op. 6

The Bracelet – see under *To Julia*, Op. 8

Brown is My Love – see under *Seven Elizabethan Lyrics*, Op. 12

By a Fountainside – see under *Seven Elizabethan Lyrics*, Op. 12

(By the Sea), Four Songs of the Sea, Op. 1, no. 4

Ca' the Yowes to the Knowes, The Arnold Book of Old Songs
Jeffrey Benton (baritone), Rona Lowe (piano) (iss. 1993) Sym.1159 (CD)
Robert Ivan Foster (baritone), Mary Earl (piano) (rec. in Apr 1966) Onslow
Lisa Milne (soprano), Graham Johnson (piano) CC.15122 (CD)

Charlie is My Darling, The Arnold Book of Old Songs
Jeffrey Benton (baritone), Rona Lowe (piano) (iss. 1993) Sym.1159 (CD)
Robert Ivan Foster (baritone), Mary Earl (piano) (rec. in Apr 1966) Onslow
Benjamin Luxon (baritone), David Willison (piano) (rec. 13–14 Sep 1990 at the
    Maltings, Snape, Suffolk, UK) Ch. (CD)
Lisa Milne (soprano), Graham Johnson (piano) CC.15122 (CD)

Cherry Ripe – see under *To Julia*, Op. 8

Cherry Valley, Three Pastoral Songs, Op. 22, no. 2
Lisa Milne (soprano), Louisa Fuller (violin), Ivan McCready (cello), Graham Johnson
    (piano) CC.15122 (CD)
Mark Raphael (baritone), Frederick Grinke (violin), Herbert Withers (cello), Roger
    Quilter (piano) (rec. 29 Nov 1934, CA14804–3, iss. 1 Aug 1936) RO78; Col.DB1648
    (78)
Sarah Walker (mezzo-soprano), Marcia Crayford (violin), Christopher van Kampen
    (cello), Ian Brown (piano) (rec. live)

Come Away, Death – see under *Three Shakespeare Songs*, Op. 6

(Come Back!), Two Songs

(Come Lady-Day) (partsong and solo versions)

(Come Spring! Sweet Spring!), Two Songs

Come unto These Yellow Sands
Paul Wade (tenor), Geoffrey Hamilton (piano) (rev. Sep 1977) LK/LP.6125 (LP)

The Constant Lover, Five Jacobean Lyrics, Op. 28, no. 5
David Wilson-Johnson (baritone), David Owen Norris (piano) (rev. Mar
    1987) Hy.A66208 (LP)

(A Coronal), Songs of Sorrow, Op. 10, no. 1

(The Cradle in Bethlehem) (partsong and solo versions)

Cuckoo Song, Three Songs, Op. 15, no. 1
Gervase Elwes (tenor), [Frederick Kiddle (piano)] (iss. Oct 1916) Col.L1074 (78)
    reissued on Op.OPAL 9844 (rev. 1982) (CD)

Cupid, Five Lyrics of Robert Herrick, Op. 7, no. 1 (partsong)
Kasschau's Solo Chorus (4 men, 4 women) (rec. 14 Sep 1925) AmCol.77111M (78)

(Daisies after Rain)

Damask Roses – see under *Seven Elizabethan Lyrics*, Op. 12

(Dancing on the Green) (partsong)

Daybreak, Three Songs of William Blake, Op. 20, no 3
Benjamin Luxon (baritone), David Willison (piano) (rec. 3–4 May 1989 at the Maltings, Snape, iss. 1989, rev. Mar 1990) Ch.CHAN8782 (CD) ABTD 1417 (TC)
Alexander Young (tenor), Gordon Watson (piano) (iss. 1955) Argo.RG36 (LP)

The Dazzling Sun is Glistening – see under 'Die helle Sonne leuchtet'

A Dirge, Five Lyrics of Robert Herrick, Op. 7, no. 2
Kasschau's Solo Chorus AmCol.77111M

Dream Valley, Three Songs of William Blake, Op. 20, no. 1
Jeffrey Benton (baritone), Rona Lowe (piano) (iss. 1993) Sym.1159 (CD)
David Johnston (tenor), Daphne Ibbott (piano)
 Pe.SHE531 (iss. and rev. Sep 1976); Lilac LIL300 (iss. 1972) (LP)
Sarah Leonard (soprano), Malcolm Martineau (piano) (rec. 15–16 Nov 1999 at St Philip's Church, London SW16) SOMM.SOMMCD 224 (CD)
Benjamin Luxon (baritone), David Willison (piano) (rec. 3–4 May 1989 at the Maltings, Snape, iss. 1989, rev. Mar 1990) Ch.CHAN8782 (CD) ABTD 1417 (TC)
Walter Midgley (tenor), Gerald Moore (piano) (rec. 8 Apr 1952, iss. May 1953) HMV.DA2036 (78)
Alexander Young (tenor), Gordon Watson (piano) (rev. 1955) Argo.RG36 (LP)

Drink to Me Only, The Arnold Book of Old Songs
John Mark Ainsley (tenor), Malcolm Martineau (piano) (rec. 18–20 Feb 1996) Hy.CDA66878 (CD)
Thomas Allen (baritone), Malcolm Martineau (piano) Hy.CDA67290 (CD)
Thomas Allen (baritone), Roger Vignoles (piano) (rec. 28 Aug 1990 at the Queen's Hall, Edinburgh, Scotland, at the Edinburgh International Festival)
Jeffrey Benton (baritone), Rona Lowe (piano) (iss. 1993) Sym.1159 (CD)
Delmé Bryn-Jones (baritone), Richard Nunn (piano) (rec. 22 June 1981, rev. Sep 1982) Hy.A66029 (stereo LP)
Victor Carne (tenor), Stanley Chapple (piano) (iss. Feb 1926) Voc.X9710 (78)
Kathleen Ferrier (contralto), Phyllis Spurr (piano) (rec. 10–12 Dec 1951) D.M679 (78); D.LX3098 (78) reissued as D.70135; Reader's Digest (details unknown); D.ACL309 (LP) and D.KACL309 (TC) (both iss. Oct 1968)
Robert Ivan Foster (baritone), Mary Earl (piano) (rec. in Apr 1966) Onslow
Lois Marshall (soprano) with Weldon Kilburn (piano) (iss. Apr 1959) HMV.ALP1671 (mono LP)
Henry Millidge (tenor), with string quartet (rec. 11 Feb 1929) Re.G9269 (78)
Elisabeth Schwarzkopf (soprano), Gerald Moore (piano) Col. SE1589 (iss. Jan 1959); Col.CX1404 (iss. Feb 1959); Col.SAX2265 (iss. Mar 1959); Col.ES16225 (iss. Dec 1959)
Cesare Valletti (tenor), L. Taubman (piano)
Robert White (tenor), Stephen Hough (piano) Hy.CDA66818 (CD)
David Wilson-Johnson (baritone), David Owen Norris (piano) (rev. Mar 1987) Hy.A66208 (LP)
A. Woodrow (tenor), T. Hammond (piano) Equitaine.MS90381
Arranged for violin and piano:
A. Spalding (violin) with piano (iss. 1935) Vic.1703

H. White (violin) and P. Lastain [?]
Arranged for orchestra:
Murray, New Light Symphony Orchestra (rec. 20 Feb 1935, iss. Sep 1935) HMV.B8347 (78)
Paul Robeson (bass), Ronnie Munro (conductor) with orchestra (rec. 20 Nov 1938) HMV.B8231 (78)
Arranged for band:
Band of HM Grenadier Guards (iss. summer 1934) D.F3961 (78)

Drooping Wings
David Wilson-Johnson (baritone), David Owen Norris (piano) Hy.A66208 (LP)

Fair House of Joy – see under *Seven Elizabethan Lyrics*, Op. 12

Fairy Lullaby
Jeffrey Benton (baritone), Rona Lowe (piano) (iss. 1993) Sym.1159 (CD)
Rosina Buckman (soprano), Mrs Baker (piano) (rec. 17 Mar 1922, iss. Aug 1922) HMV.E259 (78)

The Faithless Shepherdess – see under *Seven Elizabethan Lyrics*, Op. 12

(Farewell to Shan-Avon) (partsong)

Fear No More the Heat o' the Sun – see under *Five Shakespeare Songs*

Fill a Glass with Golden Wine, Three Songs, Op. 3, no. 3
George Baker (baritone), Madame Adami (piano) (rec. 15 Apr 1924, iss. April 1925) HMV.B2123 (78)
Hubert Eisdell (tenor), W. T. Best (piano) (rec. 14 May 1930, iss. Jan 1932) Col.DB693 (78)
Gervase Elwes (tenor), [Frederick Kiddle (piano)] (iss. Nov 1916) Col.L1101 (78) reissued on Op.OPAL 9844 (rev. 1982) (CD)
Stewart Gardner (baritone), with piano (iss. Mar 1924) Ae.Voc.X9396 (78)
Julien Henry (iss. Jun 1913) Edison Bell Velvet Face Record 1301
A. Pengelly (tenor), A. M. Whipp (piano) Pengelly AJP2
Frank Titterton (tenor) with piano (rec. 1930, iss. mid-Feb 1931) Decca (78)

(Foreign Children), Four Child Songs, Op. 5, no. 4

(Freedom), partsong

The Fuchsia Tree, Six Songs, Op. 25, No. 2
Jeffrey Benton (baritone), Rona Lowe (piano) (iss. 1993) Sym.1159 (CD)
Elizabeth Harwood (soprano), John Constable (piano) (iss. 1984) Conifer.CFRA120
Carmen Hill (mezzo-soprano), Madame Adami (piano) (rec. 19 Dec 1923 in Hayes, Middx. UK) HMV.E322 (78) reissued HMV ToES.EX2909113 (LP) and EX2909115 (TC)
Arranged for piano (Hough):
Stephen Hough (piano) (rec. Oct 1987 at the Abbey Road Studios, London, UK) VirgC.VC 7 59509 2 (CD; also LP and TC); reissued on the MusicMasters label; reissued on EMI Virgin Classics 7243 5 61498 2 3

Go, Lovely Rose, Five English Love Lyrics, Op. 24, no. 3
John Mark Ainsley (tenor), Malcolm Martineau (piano) (rec. 18–20 Feb 1996, rev. Sep 1982) Hy.CDA66878 (CD)
Jeffrey Benton (baritone), Rona Lowe (piano) (iss. 1993) Sym.1159 (CD)
Delmé Bryn-Jones (baritone), Richard Nunn (piano) (rec. 22 June 1981) Hy.A66029

Frederick Harvey (baritone), Roger Quilter (piano) BBC Transcription recording (32069), 14 August 1945

Frederick Harvey (baritone), Jack Byfield (piano) (iss. Oct 1965) HMV.CLP1901 (mono LP); HMV.CSD1621 (stereo LP)

Robert Irwin (baritone), Gerald Moore (piano) Pearl

David Johnston (tenor), Daphne Ibbott (piano) Pe.SHE531 (iss. Sep 1976); Lilac LIL300 (iss. and rev. 1972) (LP)

J. Lawrenson (baritone), Jack Byfield (piano)

Benjamin Luxon (baritone), David Willison (piano) (rec. 3–4 May 1989 at the Maltings, Snape, iss. 1989, rev. Mar 1990) Ch.CHAN8782 (CD) ABTD 1417 (TC)

Glenda Maurice (rec. 11 Jan 1988 at the Wigmore Hall, London) Etcetera.KTC1099 (TC)

Walter Midgley (tenor), Gerald Moore (piano) (rec. 8 Apr 1952) HMV.DA2014 (78)

Ian Partridge (tenor), Jennifer Partridge (piano) (iss. 1977) Enigma.K53539/VAR 1027

Peter Pears (tenor), Roger Vignoles (piano) (rec. live from the Jubilee Hall, Aldeburgh) BBC transcription 141971-S

Mark Raphael (baritone), Roger Quilter (piano) (rec. 3 Dec 1934, CA14802–3) RO77; Col.DB1583 (78)

Anthony Rolfe Johnson (tenor), Graham Johnson (piano) CC.15122 (CD)

David Wilson-Johnson (baritone), David Owen Norris (piano) (rev. Mar 1987) Hy.A66208 (LP)

A Good Child, Four Child Songs, Op. 5, no. 1
John Mark Ainsley (tenor), Malcolm Martineau (piano) (rec. 18–20 Feb 1996) Hy.CDA66878 (CD)

Hark, Hark, the Lark!
Frederick Harvey (baritone), Roger Quilter (piano) BBC Transcription recording (32065), 14 August 1945

Anthony Rolfe Johnson (tenor), Graham Johnson (piano) CC.15122 (CD)

Graham Trew (baritone), Roger Vignoles (piano) (rec. 18 Dec 1980) Hy.A66026

Die helle Sonne leuchtet, Four Songs of Mirza Schaffy, Op. 2, no. 4
John Mark Ainsley (tenor), Malcolm Martineau (piano) (rec. 18–20 Feb 1996) Hy.CDA66878 (CD)

Angela Beale (soprano), John King (baritone), Elaine Hugh-Jones (piano) BBC recording broadcast Radio 3, 3 Nov 1977

Hey, Ho, the Wind and the Rain – see under *Five Shakespeare Songs,* Op. 23

How should I your true love know – see under *Four Shakespeare Songs,* Op. 30

(Hymn for Victory), unison and partsong

I Arise from Dreams of Thee, Op. 29
Georgina Anne Colwell (soprano), Nigel Foster (piano) (rec. Dec 1993 at Walton-on-Thames, Surrey, UK) GAC

Benjamin Luxon (baritone), David Willison (piano) (rec. 3–4 May 1989 at the Maltings, Snape, iss. 1989, rev. Mar 1990) Ch.CHAN8782 (CD) ABTD 1417 (TC)

Anthony Rolfe Johnson (tenor), Graham Johnson (piano) CC.15122 (CD)

I Dare Not Ask a Kiss, Five Jacobean Lyrics, Op. 28, no. 3
Anthony Rolfe Johnson (tenor), Graham Johnson (piano) CC.15122 (CD)

David Wilson-Johnson (baritone), David Owen Norris (piano) (rev. Mar 1987) Hy.A66208 (LP)
Arranged for voice and piano quartet:
Mark Raphael (baritone), Frederick Grinke (violin), Max Gilbert (viola), Herbert Withers (cello), Roger Quilter (piano) (rec. 13 Dec 1934, CA14796–4, iss. Feb 1936) RO75; Col.DB1602 (78)

I Feel Thy Soul's Dear Presence – see under *Ich fühle deinen Odem*

(I Got a Robe), in manuscript only

(I Have a Friend), Four Songs of the Sea, Op. 1, no. 1

I Will Go with My Father A-Ploughing, Three Pastoral Songs, Op. 22, no. 1
Lisa Milne (soprano), Louisa Fuller (violin), Ivan McCready (cello), Graham Johnson (piano) CC.15122 (CD)
Sarah Walker (mezzo-soprano), Marcia Crayford (violin), Christopher van Kampen (cello), Ian Brown (piano) (rec. live)

I Wish and I Wish, Three Pastoral Songs, Op. 22, no. 3
Lisa Milne (soprano), Louisa Fuller (violin), Ivan McCready (cello), Graham Johnson (piano) CC.15122 (CD)
Sarah Walker (mezzo-soprano), Marcia Crayford (violin), Christopher van Kampen (cello), Ian Brown (piano) (rec. live)

Ich fühle deinen Odem, Four Songs of Mirza Schaffy, Op. 2, no. 3
John Mark Ainsley (tenor), Malcolm Martineau (piano) (rec. 18–20 Feb 1996) Hy.CDA66878 (CD)
Angela Beale (soprano), John King (baritone), Elaine Hugh-Jones (piano) BBC recording broadcast Radio 3, 3 Nov 1977

(In Spring), Songs of Sorrow, Op. 10, no. 4

In the Bud of the Morning-O, Six Songs, Op. 25, no. 6
Olga Haley (mezzo-soprano), Ivor Newton(piano) (iss. Aug 1927) Voc.K05308 (78)
Benjamin Luxon (baritone), David Willison (piano) (rec. 3–4 May 1989 at the Maltings, Snape, iss. 1989, rev. Mar 1990) Ch.CHAN8782 (CD) ABTD 1417 (TC)

(In the Highlands), Two Songs, Op. 26, no. 1

It was a Lover and His Lass – see under Five Shakespeare Songs, Op. 23

The Jealous Lover, Five Jacobean Lyrics, Op. 28, no. 1
Derek Oldham (tenor), Miss M. Swale (piano) (rec. 26 Aug 1926) G. mx Bb8880–1,–2,–3 (unissued)
Mark Raphael (baritone), Roger Quilter (piano) (rec. 13 Dec 1934, CA14796–4, iss. Feb 1936) RO75; Col.DB1602 (78)
David Wilson-Johnson (baritone), David Owen Norris (piano) (rev. Mar 1987) Hy.A66208 (LP)

The Jocund Dance, Six Songs, Op. 18, no. 3
Anthony Roden (tenor), Geoffrey Parsons (piano) BBC recording, broadcast Radio 3, 18 Jan 1989

The Jolly Miller, The Arnold Book of Old Songs
Jeffrey Benton (baritone), Rona Lowe (piano) (iss. 1993) Sym.1159 (CD)
Robert Ivan Foster (baritone), Mary Earl (piano) ['The Miller of Dee'] (rec. Apr 1966) Onslow

David Wilson-Johnson (baritone), David Owen Norris (piano) Hy.A66208 (LP)

June

John Mark Ainsley (tenor), Malcolm Martineau (piano) (rec. 18–20 Feb 1996) Hy.CDA66878 (CD)

Valerie Baulard (contralto), Simon Wright (piano) MaxSound.4 MSCB12, 4 MSCB13 (double TC)

The Lamplighter, **Four Child Songs, Op. 5, no. 2**

John Mark Ainsley (tenor), Malcolm Martineau (piano) (rec. 18–20 Feb 1996) Hy.CDA66878 (CD)

A Land of Silence, **Songs of Sorrow, Op. 10, no. 3**

Derek Oldham (tenor), Madame Adami (piano) (rec. 18 Dec 1925, iss. June 1926) HMV.E426

Jonathan Veira (baritone), Malcolm Martineau (piano) (rec. 15–16 Nov 1999 at St Philip's Church, London SW16) SOMM.SOMMCD 224 (CD)

A Last Year's Rose, **Four Songs, Op. 14, no. 3**

John Mark Ainsley (tenor), Malcolm Martineau (piano) (rec. 18–20 Feb 1996) Hy.CDA66878 (CD)

Benjamin Luxon (baritone), David Willison (piano) (rec. 3–4 May 1989 at the Maltings, Snape, iss. 1989, rev. Mar 1990) Ch.CHAN8782 (CD) ABTD 1417 (TC)

Lisa Milne (soprano), Graham Johnson (piano) CC.15122 (CD)

(Lead Us, Heavenly Father) **(partsong)**

Lean, Opening Blossom – see under *Neig' schön' Knospe dich zu mir*

(A London Spring)

Love Calls through the Summer Night, **from** *Julia/Love at the Inn*

Lisa Milne (soprano), Anthony Rolfe Johnson (tenor), Graham Johnson (piano) CC.15122 (CD)

Love's Philosophy, **Three Songs, Op. 3, no. 1**

John Aler (tenor), Grant Gershon (piano) (rec. 1–12 June 1995 at First Congregational Church) Delos DE 3181 (CD)

John Mark Ainsley (tenor), Malcolm Martineau (piano) (rec. 18–20 Feb 1996) Hy.CDA66878 (CD)

Arleen Auger (soprano), Dalton Baldwin (piano) (rec. 7–8 March 1988) Del.DE3712/ DE3029 (CD)

Janet Baker (mezzo-soprano), Gerald Moore (piano) (rec. 9 Feb 1967 at Abbey Road Studios, London, UK) HMV.HQS1091 (iss. and rev. July 1967) (stereo LP); HMV.LP.SLS5275 (stereo LP) and HMV.4TC-SLS5725 (TC); HMV Greensleeves LP.ESD100642–1 (stereo LP) and 4TC-ESD100642–4 (TC)

Valerie Baulard (contralto), Simon Wright (piano) MaxSound.4 MSCB12, 4 MSCB13 (double TC)

Jeffrey Benton (baritone), Ro..a Lowe (piano) (iss. 1993) Sym.1159 (CD)

Miriam Bowen (soprano), Michael Pollock (piano) BBC lunchtime concert, broadcast on Radio 3 on 13 Jan 1997, Sain SCD 2099 (CD)

Georgina Anne Colwell (soprano), Nigel Foster (piano) (rec. Dec 1993 at Walton-on-Thames, Surrey, UK) GAC

Astra Desmond (alto), Gerald Moore (piano) D.DM524 (78)

Wendy Eathorne (soprano), G. Pratley (piano) Hassell.HASLP2058

Gervase Elwes (tenor), Frederick Kiddle (piano) (iss. Sep 1916) Col.L1055 (78) reissued on Op.OPAL 9844 (rev. 1982) (CD)

Linda Finnie (mezzo-soprano), Anthony Legge (piano) (rec. 14–16 Feb 1989 at the Maltings, Snape, Suffolk, UK) (rev. Apr 1990) Ch.4 ABTD1388 (TC); Ch.CHAN8749 (CD)

Stewart Gardner (baritone), with piano (iss. Mar 1924) Ae.Voc.X9396 (78)

Joan Hammond (soprano), Ivor Newton (piano) (iss. Feb 1965) HMV.ALP2068 (mono)/ASD616 (stereo) (LP)

Frederick Harvey (baritone), Roger Quilter (piano) BBC Transcription recording (32064), 14 August 1945

Elizabeth Harwood (soprano), John Constable (piano) (iss. 1984) Conifer.CFRA120

W. Herbert (tenor), Jack Byfield (piano) BBC recording, date unknown 13452

Peter Jeffes (tenor), David Woodcock (piano) (iss. 1995) Sym.1183 (CD)

David Johnston (tenor), Daphne Ibbott (piano) Pe.SHE531 (iss. Sep 1976); Lilac LIL300 (iss. and rev. 1972) (LP)

Sarah Leonard (soprano), Malcolm Martineau (piano) (rec. 16–18 Oct 1991 at St Michael's Church, Highgate, London, UK) IMP PCD 1029 (CD)

Sarah Leonard (soprano), Malcolm Martineau (piano) (rec. 15–16 Nov 1999 at St Philip's Church, London SW16) SOMM.SOMMCD 224 (CD)

Felicity Lott (soprano), Graham Johnson (piano) (rec. 24–26 Oct 1988 at the Maltings, Snape, Suffolk, UK) Ch.

Benjamin Luxon (baritone), David Willison (piano) (rec. 3–4 May 1989 at the Maltings, Snape, iss. 1989, rev. Mar 1990) Ch.CHAN8782 (CD) ABTD 1417 (TC)

John McCormack (tenor), [Charles Marshall (piano)] (rec. 1908) Odeon recording LX2965 (78)

Peter Pears (tenor), Viola Tunnard (piano) BBC recording broadcast Third Network, 5 Jan 1966

Mark Raphael (baritone), Roger Quilter (piano) (rec. 13 Dec 1934 at the Abbey Road Studios, Studio 2, London, UK, CA14795–5, iss. Feb 1936) RO75; Col.DB1602 (78) reissued HMV ToES.EX290911–3 (LP) and EX290911–5 (TC)

J. Reddy (soprano), D. Harper (piano) Cabaletta.CVA008

Elizabeth Ritchie (soprano), Jennifer Purvis (piano) (rec. 3–4 May 1989 at St Paul's, New Southgate, London, UK) IMP

Forbes Robinson (bass), Robin Stapleton (piano) (iss. Oct 1976) Argo. ZDA174

Anthony Roden (tenor), Geoffrey Parsons (piano) BBC recording, broadcast Radio 3, 18 Jan 1989

Anthony Rolfe Johnson (tenor), Graham Johnson (piano) CC.15122 (CD)

Joan Sutherland (soprano), Richard Bonynge (piano) (rec. 1973) A.N.N.A. Recording Company ANNA1029A/B

Maggie Teyte (soprano), R. Mackay (piano) broadcast performance 1937 D.LXT6126 (LP); Lon.5839; Ecl.ECM830 (mono LP, iss. 1971)

Jennifer Vyvyan (soprano), Ernest Lush (piano) D.LXT2797 (LP, rev. Sep 1953); Belart; Ecl.ECS589 (stereo LP, reissued 1971)

David Wilson-Johnson (baritone), David Owen Norris (piano) (rev. Mar 1987) Hy.A66208 (LP)

F. Yeend (soprano), J. Benner (piano) Da Vinci 203

Alexander Young (tenor), Gordon Watson (piano) (iss. 1955) Argo.RG36 (LP)

Arranged for voice and orchestra:

Kenneth McKellar (tenor) and orchestra SKL4156 (LP)

Rosa Ponselle (soprano) with orchestra, conducted by Rosario Bourdon (rec. 11 Apr 1924) Romophone Victor 1057A

Arranged by Goff Richards:
King's Singers Vocal Ensemble (rec. June 1992 at SARM East Studios London) RCA Victor 09026–6 1427-A (TC)

(Madrigal in Satin), partsong

The Maiden Blush – see under *To Julia*, Op. 8

The Man behind the Plough, The Arnold Book of Old Songs
Jeffrey Benton (baritone), Rona Lowe (piano) (iss. 1993) Sym.1159 (CD)

Moonlight, Four Songs of the Sea, Op. 1, no. 3
Frederick Harvey (baritone), Roger Quilter (piano) BBC Transcription recording (32068), 14 August 1945 (1911 version)

(Morning Song), Five Lyrics of Robert Herrick, Op. 7, no. 3

Morning Song, Five English Love Lyrics, Op. 24, no. 2
Jeffrey Benton (baritone), Rona Lowe (piano) (iss. 1993) Sym.1159 (CD)
Hubert Eisdell (tenor) with piano (iss. July 1923) Col.D1453 (78)

Music
Anthony Roden (tenor), Geoffrey Parsons (piano) BBC recording, broadcast Radio 3, 11 Jan 1989

Music and Moonlight
Georgina Anne Colwell (soprano), Nigel Foster (piano) (rec. Dec 1993 at Walton-on-Thames, Surrey, UK) GAC
Anthony Roden (tenor), Geoffrey Parsons (piano) BBC recording, broadcast Radio 3, 11 Jan 1989

Music, When Soft Voices Die, Six Songs, Op. 25, no. 5
John Mark Ainsley (tenor), Malcolm Martineau (piano) (rec. 18–20 Feb 1996) Hy.CDA66878 (CD)
Arleen Auger (soprano), Dalton Baldwin (piano) (rec. 7–8 March 1988) Del.DE3712/ DE3029 (CD)
Georgina Anne Colwell (soprano), Nigel Foster (piano) (rec. Dec 1993 at Walton-on-Thames) GAC
Olga Haley (mezzo-soprano), Ivor Newton(piano) (iss. Aug 1927) Voc.K05308 (78)
Benjamin Luxon (baritone), David Willison (piano) (rec. 3–4 May 1989 at the Maltings, Snape, iss. 1989) Ch.CHAN8782 (CD) ABTD 1417 (TC)
Lisa Milne (soprano), Graham Johnson (piano) CC.15122 (CD)
Mark Raphael (baritone), Roger Quilter (piano) (rec. 13 Dec 1934 at Abbey Road, Studio 2, CA14795–5, iss. Feb 1936) RO75; Col.DB1602 (78) reissued HMV ToES.EX290911–3 (LP) and EX290911–5 (TC)
Elizabeth Ritchie (soprano), Jennifer Purvis (piano) (rec. 24/25 Nov 1992 at St George's Hall, Bristol) IMP
Alexander Young (tenor), Gordon Watson (piano) (iss. 1955, rev. Apr 1955) Argo.RG36 (LP)

(My Heart Adorned with Thee), solo and duet versions

My Lady Greensleeves, The Arnold Book of Old Songs
Jeffrey Benton (baritone), Rona Lowe (piano) (iss. 1993) Sym.1159 (CD)
Robert Ivan Foster (baritone), Mary Earl (piano) (rec. in Apr 1966) Onslow

My Lady's Garden (L'Amour de Moy), The Arnold Book of Old Songs
Jeffrey Benton (baritone), Rona Lowe (piano) (iss. 1993) Sym.1159 (CD)

My Life's Delight – see under *Seven Elizabethan Lyrics*, Op. 12

Neig' schöne Knospe dich zu mir, Four Songs of Mirza Schaffy, Op. 2, no. 1
John Mark Ainsley (tenor), Malcolm Martineau (piano) (rec. 18–20 Feb 1996) Hy.CDA66878 (CD)

The Night Piece – see under *To Julia*, Op. 8

Non Nobis, Domine, partsong
Finchley Choral Society and Barnet and District Choral Society, with the Central Band of the Royal Air Force, J. L. Wallace (conductor) (arranged by [Norman] Richardson) (iss. Sep 1965) HMV.CLP1892 (mono LP); HMV.CSD1615 (stereo LP)
Hamilton Academy Youth Choir, Peter Mooney (organ) Herald
Holloway Royal Hospital Church Choir (Davies) Woodwind MW917
The Morriston Orpheus Choir (rec. 7 Mar 1993) Grasmere
Mousehole Male Voice Choir, Eric Dale (conductor), Ann Pomeroy (piano) Sentinel
Sheffield Schools Choir, H. Edward Hall (conductor), Enid Longden (piano) HMV.B10310 (78)
The Treorchy Male Choir and the Cory Band (H. A. Kenney or John Cynan Jones) (rec. 2 Dec 1973 at the Brangwyn Hall, Swansea) EMI.TWOX1014
Treverne [?] Male Voice Choir DG.2L60226
A. Fredrik Boys Choir, Hillerud (conductor) SS.SLT33269

Now Sleeps the Crimson Petal, Three Songs, Op. 3, no. 2
John Mark Ainsley (tenor), Malcolm Martineau (piano) (rec. 18–20 Feb 1996) Hy.CDA66878 (CD)
Thomas Allen (baritone), Geoffrey Parsons (piano) (rec. July 1989 at St Martin's, East Woodhay, UK) VirgC.
Thomas Allen (baritone), Roger Vignoles (piano) (rec. 28 Aug 1990 at the Queen's Hall, Edinburgh, Scotland, at the Edinburgh International Festival)
Valerie Baulard (contralto), Simon Wright (piano) MaxSound.4 MSCB12, 4 MSCB13 (double TC)
Jeffrey Benton (baritone), Rona Lowe (piano) (iss. 1993) Sym.1159 (CD)
Ian Bostridge (tenor), Julius Drake (piano) EMI CDC5 568302 (CD)
William Brownlow (baritone), Hilda Mostyn (piano) (rec. 21 May 1930, iss. Sep 1930) Col.DB179 (78)
Brian Rayner Cook (baritone), Antony Saunders (piano)
Gervase Elwes (tenor), [Frederick Kiddle (piano)] (iss. Sep 1916) Col.L1055 (78) reissued on Op.OPAL 9844 (rev. 1982) (CD)
Kathleen Ferrier (contralto), Phyllis Spurr (piano) (rec. 10–12 Dec 1951) D.M680 (78); D.LX3098 (78); D.45–71139 (45)(rev. Aug 1956); D.AKF1–7 (mono LP); D.BR3052 (iss. Jul 1960) (LP); D.cep726 (iss. Mar 1962) (45); ACL309 (LP) and KACL309 (TC) (iss. Oct 1968); D.DECC417 (iss. Jun 1988) (CD) [Reader's Digest]
Linda Finnie (mezzo-soprano), Anthony Legge (piano) (rec. 14–16 Feb 1989 at the Maltings, Snape, Suffolk, UK) (rev. Apr 1990) Ch.CHAN8749 (CD)
Louis Graveure (tenor), W. Sanfor Schlussel (piano) (rec. 8 Apr 1930) AmCol.2425-D (78)
Peter Jeffes (tenor), David Woodcock (piano) (iss. 1995) Sym.1183 (CD)

David Johnston (tenor), Daphne Ibbott (piano) Pe.SHE531 (iss. Sep 1976); Lilac LIL300 (iss. and rev. 1972) (LP)

Sarah Leonard (soprano), Malcolm Martineau (piano) (rec. 16–18 Oct 1991 in St Michael's Church, Highgate, London, UK) IMP 1029 (CD)

Sarah Leonard (soprano), Malcolm Martineau (piano) (rec. 15–16 Nov 1999 at St Philip's Church, London SW16) SOMM.SOMMCD 224 (CD)

Richard Lewis (tenor), Ernest Lush (piano) (rec. June 1966) BBC recording, broadcast on Radio 3 on 15 Nov 1991

Sinclair Logan (baritone, self-accompanied on piano) (rec. July 1948) Leech

Ernest Lough (baritone), Gerald Moore (piano) (rec. 7 Sep 1938, iss. Oct 1938) HMV.B8792 (78)

Louise Kirkby Lunn (Madame Kirkby Lunn) (contralto), Percy Pitt (piano) (rec. 26 Sep 1918 in London, UK) HMV single-side 2–2311 (iss. Dec 1918); HMV.DA434 (iss. Mar 1924)

Benjamin Luxon (baritone), David Willison (piano) D.Argo.ZFB95–6 (iss. Oct 1976); Ch.CHAN8782 (CD) ABTD 1417 (TC) (rec. 3–4 May 1989 at the Maltings, Snape, iss. 1989)

John McCormack (tenor), Edwin Schneider (piano) (rec. 2 Sep 1927) HMV.DA1111 (78); Vic1307; HMV Great Records of the Century COLH124 (iss. Jun 1965); HMV.EX29000563 (LP) 4EX29000565 (TC) (both iss. Jun 1984); EMI Great Records RCA.LP.RL84997 (LP) and 4RK.84997 (TC) (rev. Jul 1984)

Valerie Masterson (soprano), John Constable (piano) (rec. 11 Mar 1989 at the Henry Wood Hall, London) Novello NVLCD107; Gamut Classics

Lisa Milne (soprano), Graham Johnson (piano) CC.15122 (CD)

Browning Mummery (tenor), Anne Williams (piano) (rec. 20 Jul 1926, iss. Nov 1926) HMV.B2355 (78)

M. O'Higgins HMV.IM970 (78)

Derek Oldham (tenor), Miss Swale (piano) (rec. 24 Sep 1928 at the Queen's Hall (small hall), London, UK) HMV.B2870 (78) reissued HMV ToES.EX290911–3 (LP) and EX290911–5 (TC); Rubini GV51

Peter Pears (tenor), Viola Tunnard (piano) BBC recording broadcast Third Network, 5 Jan 1966

Peter Pears (tenor), Roger Vignoles (piano) (rec. live from the Jubilee Hall, Aldeburgh) BBC transcription 141971-S

Paul Robeson (bass), Lawrence Brown (piano) (rec. 29 Sep 1939, iss. Aug 1942) HMV.B9281 (78)

Paul Robeson (bass), Harriet Wingreen (piano) (rec. live in 1958 at Carnegie Hall) Fontana.TFL6063 (LP); Golden Hour; Vanguard.VSD79193 (stereo LP, iss. Jul 1972); Pye

Paul Robeson (bass), Alan Booth (piano) (rev. Sep 1960) Topic.TOP32; Supraphon.-SUA10062 (iss. Sep 1960)

Thomas Round (tenor), Clive Timms (piano) Pe. SHE528

Maggie Teyte (soprano), Rita MacKay (piano) (broadcast performance) (iss. Oct 1964) D.LP.TXT6126 LP)

Maggie Teyte (soprano), Gerald Moore (piano) (rec. 6 Jan 1942) HMV.DA1807 (78); HMV.7er5101 (rev. Nov 1959) (45)

Frank Titterton (tenor) with piano (rec. 1930, iss. Feb 1931) D.F2187

Betty Trump (contralto), Muriel Rabley (piano) (rec. at Rosskerry Hotel, Bideford, England) Sentinel.SENS1027

Sarah Walker (mezzo-soprano), Roger Vignoles (piano) (rec. 30 July 1990 at St Paul's, New Southgate, London, UK) CRD3473

Robert White (tenor), Stephen Hough (piano) (rec. 6–8 June 1995) Hy.CDA66818 (CD)

David Wilson-Johnson (baritone), David Owen Norris (piano) (rev. Mar 1987) Hy.A66208 (LP)

Arranged for voice and organ:
Simon Roberts (vocals), Tim Rishton (piano, organ) (rec. 1991) Sain.C461

Arranged for piano (Hough) and called 'The Crimson Petal':
Stephen Hough (piano) (rec. Nov 1986 at Theresa L. Kaufmann Concert Hall, New York) VirgC.VC 7 59509 2 (CD; also LP and TC); reissued on the MusicMasters label; reissued on EMI Virgin Classics 7243 5 61498 2 3

Arranged for voice and orchestra:
Richard Crooks (tenor) with orchestra from Victor (78): Rubini.GV700

Ivor Foster (baritone) with orchestra (iss. Jun 1912) Odeon Record 0769, reissued X-57692 (Jul 1922) (78)

Kenneth McKellar (tenor), Bob Sharples (conductor) with orchestra D.SKL4150 (LP)

Arranged for voice, piano and violin:
Henry Millidge (tenor), Clarence Raybould (piano), violin obbligato (rec. 7 Jun 1928) Re.G9170 (78)

O Mistress Mine – see under **Three Shakespeare Songs, Op. 6**

O, the Month of May, Five English Love Lyrics, Op. 24, no. 4
Jeffrey Benton (baritone), Rona Lowe (piano) (iss. 1993) Sym.1159 (CD)

Mark Raphael (baritone), Roger Quilter (piano) (rec. 29 Nov 1934, CA14801–2) RO77; Col.DB1583 (78)

Jonathan Veira (baritone), Malcolm Martineau (piano) (rec. 15–16 Nov 1999 at St Philip's Church, London SW16) SOMM.SOMMCD 224 (CD)

Oh! 'tis Sweet to Think, The Arnold Book of Old Songs
Jeffrey Benton (baritone), Rona Lowe (piano) (iss. 1993) Sym.1159 (CD)

An Old Carol, Six Songs, Op. 25, no. 3
Sarah Leonard (soprano), Malcolm Martineau (piano) (rec. 15–16 Nov 1999 at St Philip's Church, London SW16) SOMM.SOMMCD 224 (CD)

Anthony Rolfe Johnson (tenor), Graham Johnson (piano) CC.15122 (CD)

David Wilson-Johnson (baritone), David Owen Norris (piano) (rev. Mar 1987) Hy.A66208 (LP)

(One word is too often profan'd)

Orpheus with his Lute, Two Shakespeare songs, Op. 32, no.1
Jeffrey Benton (baritone), Graham Kirkland (piano) (iss. 1995) Sym.1184 (CD)

Ian Partridge (tenor), Jennifer Partridge (piano) (rec. 8–9 June 1998 in St George's Church, Bristol, UK) Upbeat.URCD143 (CD)

Anthony Rolfe Johnson (tenor), Graham Johnson (piano) CC.15122 (CD)

Over the Land is April, Two Songs, Op. 26, no. 2
Brian Rayner Cook (baritone), Antony Saunders (piano)

Eric Astor David Marshall (baritone), Maurice Jaconson (piano) (rec. 18 Nov 1925, iss. Mar 1928) HMV.E490 (78)

Mark Raphael (baritone), Roger Quilter (piano) (rec. 29 Nov 1934, CA14803–2) RO78; Col.DB1648 (78)

Over the Mountains, The Arnold Book of Old Songs
John Mark Ainsley (tenor), Malcolm Martineau (piano) (rec. 18–20 Feb 1996) Hy.CDA66878 (CD)
Marian Anderson (contralto), Franz Rupp (piano) (rec. 20 Dec 1955) (78)
Jeffrey Benton (baritone), Rona Lowe (piano) (iss. 1993) Sym.1159 (CD)
Kathleen Ferrier (contralto), Phyllis Spurr (piano) D.LX3098 (78); 45–71139 (rev. Aug 1956); D.AFK1–7 (LP); cep726 (rev. Mar 1962) (45); ACL309 (LP) and KACL309 (TC) (iss. Oct 1968); D.DECC417 (rev. Jun 1988) (CD)
Robert Ivan Foster (baritone), Mary Earl (piano) (rec. in Apr 1966) Onslow
Susan Kessler (mezzo-soprano), Geoffrey Parsons (piano) (iss. Sep 1984) Meridian.E77074 (stereo LP)
Edna Thornton (contralto), Madame Adami (piano) (rec. 6 Jun 1924, iss. Jan 1925) HMV.E365 (78)
Graham Trew (baritone), Roger Vignoles (piano) (rec. 24 June 1981, iss. 1984) Hy.A66026 (stereo LP)
David Wilson-Johnson (baritone), David Owen Norris (piano) (rev. Mar 1987) Hy.A66208 (LP)

Passing Dreams, Songs of Sorrow, Op. 10, no. 2
Anthony Rolfe Johnson (tenor), Graham Johnson (piano) CC.15122 (CD)
Graham Trew (baritone), Roger Vignoles (piano) (rec. 24 June 1981, iss. 1984, rev. Oct 1984) Hy.A66026 (stereo LP)

The Pretty Birds Do Sing, partsong
Broadland Singers, Angela Dugdale (conductor) BBC recording, broadcast Radio 3, 6 May 1987

Pretty Month of May, The Arnold Book of Old Songs
Jeffrey Benton (baritone), Rona Lowe (piano) (iss. 1993) Sym.1159 (CD)
Robert Ivan Foster (baritone), Mary Earl (piano) (rec. Apr 1966) Onslow
Michael Leighton-Jones (baritone), Howard Blake (piano) BBC recording, broadcast on Radio 4, 24 July 1981

(The Reign of the Stars), Two Songs

(The Rose of Tralee), partsong and solo versions

(The Sailor and His Lass), choral work

(A Secret), Two Songs

(The Sea-Bird), Four Songs of the Sea, Op. 1, no. 2

Seven Elizabethan Lyrics, Op. 12
John Mark Ainsley (tenor), Malcolm Martineau (piano) (rec. 18–20 Feb 1996) Hy.CDA66878 (CD)
Jeffrey Benton (baritone), Rona Lowe (piano) (iss. 1995) Sym.1184 (CD)
Martin Hirambush (?), Alan Cuckston (piano) SWIN.4FEW116 (TC)
David Johnston (tenor), Daphne Ibbott (piano) Pe.SHE531 (iss. 1976, rev. July 1976); Lilac LIL300 (iss. 1972) (LP)
Paul Austin Kelly (tenor), Michael Recchiuti (piano) GM.2022CD (CD)
Benjamin Luxon (baritone), David Willison (piano) (rec. 3–4 May 1989 at the Maltings, Snape, iss. 1989, rev. Mar 1990) Ch.CHAN8782 (CD) ABTD 1417 (TC)
Robert Tear (tenor), J. Barker (piano) Cabaletta.CDN5006
Graham Trew (baritone), Roger Vignoles (piano) Hy.A66085

Alexander Young (tenor), Gordon Watson (piano) (iss. 1955, rev. Apr 1955) Argo.RG36 (LP)

1. *Weep You No More*

Elly Ameling (soprano), Rudolf Jansen (piano) (rec. Oct 1983 in Haarlem, Netherlands, rev. May 1985) Phi.412

Linda Finnie (mezzo-soprano), Anthony Legge (piano) (rec. 14–16 Feb 1989 at the Maltings, Snape, Suffolk, UK, rev. Apr 1990) Ch.4 ABTD1388 (TC); Ch.CHAN8749 (CD)

William Brownlow (baritone), Hilda Mostyn (piano) (rec. 11 Mar 1930) Col.DB 179 (78)

Sarah Leonard (soprano), Malcolm Martineau (piano) (rec. 16–18 Oct 1991 in St Michael's Church, Highgate, London, UK) IMP PCD 1029 (CD)

Mark Raphael (baritone), Roger Quilter (piano) (rec. 27 Nov 1934, CA14793–2) RO76; Col.DB1643 (78)

Paul Spindler (treble), Charles Thompson (piano) (rec. 28–29 Apr 1990) Alpha CAPS 403 (CD)

Graham Trew (baritone), Roger Vignoles (piano) (rec. 24 June 1981) Hy.A66026

Arranged for piano (Hough):

Stephen Hough (piano) (rec. March 1991 at BBC Studio 7, Manchester) VirgC.VC 7 59304 2 (CD); reissued on EMI Virgin Classics 7243 5 61498 2 3

2. *My Life's Delight*

George Baker (baritone), Madame Adami (piano) (rec. 15 Apr 1924, iss. Apr 1925) HMV.B2123 (78)

Lynne Dawson (soprano), Malcolm Martineau (piano), Hy.CDA67227 (CD)

Olga Haley (mezzo-soprano), Ivor Newton(piano) (iss. Aug 1927) Voc.K05308 (78)

3. *Damask Roses*

George Baker (baritone), Madame Adami (piano) (rec. 15 Apr 1924, iss. Apr 1925) HMV.B2123 (78)

Astra Desmond (alto), Gerald Moore (piano) (rec. 8 Oct 1941, iss. Jan 1943) D.M524 (78)

Frank Titterton (tenor), Stanley Chapple (piano) (rec. 1926) Voc. K0525 (78)

4. *The Faithless Shepherdess*

5. *Brown is My Love*

Frank Titterton (tenor), Stanley Chapple (piano) (rec. 1926) Voc. K0525 (78)

Stefania Woytowicz (soprano), Wanda Klimowicz (piano) (rec. 19 Jan 1959 at the British Council Warsaw)

6. *By a Fountainside*

Angela Beale (soprano), John King (baritone), Elaine Hugh-Jones (piano) BBC recording, broadcast Radio 3, 3 Nov 1977

Stefania Woytowicz (soprano), Wanda Klimowicz (piano) (rec. 19 Jan 1959 at the British Council Warsaw)

7. *Fair House of Joy*

Valerie Baulard (contralto), Simon Wright (piano) MaxSound.4 MSCB12, 4 MSCB13 (double TC)

Lynne Dawson (soprano), Malcolm Martineau (piano), Hy.CDA67227 (CD)

Gervase Elwes (tenor), [Frederick Kiddle (piano)] (rec. 1916) Col.L1119 (78) reissued on Op.OPAL 9844 (rev. 1982) (CD)

L. Evans-Williams (soprano), D. Kelly (piano) D.F7477 (78)

Kathleen Ferrier (contralto), Phyllis Spurr (piano)(rec. 10–12 Dec 1951) D.LX3098 (78); D.45–71139 (rev. Aug 1956) (45); D.AKF1–7 (mono LP); ACL309 (LP) and KACL309 (TC) (both iss. Oct 1968); D.DECC417 (rev. Jun 1988) (CD)

Linda Finnie (mezzo-soprano), Anthony Legge (piano) (rec. 14–16 Feb 1989 at the Maltings, Snape, Suffolk, UK) (rev. Apr 1990) Ch.4 ABTD1388 (TC); Ch.CHAN8749 (CD)

Olga Haley (mezzo-soprano), Ivor Newton(piano) (iss. Aug 1927) Voc.K05308 (78)

Joan Hammond (soprano), Ivor Newton (piano) HMV.ALP2068 (mono)/ASD616 (stereo) (LP, both iss. Feb 1965)

Sarah Leonard (soprano), Malcolm Martineau (piano) (rec. 16–18 Oct 1991 in St Michael's Church, Highgate, London, UK) IMP PCD 1029 (CD)

Derek Oldham (tenor), Madame Adami (piano) (rec. 24 Jul 1924, iss. Jun 1925) HMV.E385 (78)

A. Pengelly (tenor), A. M. Whipp (piano) Pengelly.AJP2

J. Reddy (soprano), D. Harper (piano) Cabaletta.CVA003

Elizabeth Ritchie (soprano), Jennifer Purvis (piano) (rec. 24/25 Nov 1992 at St George's Hall, Bristol) IMP

Anthony Roden (tenor), Geoffrey Parsons (piano) BBC recording, broadcast Radio 3, 18 Jan 1989

Graham Trew (baritone), Roger Vignoles (piano) (rec. 18 Dec 1980) Hy.A66085

Northern Convent School Chorus HMV.C3524 (78)

Three Shakespeare Songs, Op. 6

John Mark Ainsley (tenor), Malcolm Martineau (piano) (rec. 18–20 Feb 1996) Hy.CDA66878 (CD)

George Baker (baritone), Gerald Moore (piano) (no. 1 rec. 9 Nov 1925; nos 2 and 3 rec. 19 Aug 1926, iss. Sep 1927) HMV.B2500 (78); reissued HMV.HMQ1200 (LP)

Jeffrey Benton (baritone), Rona Lowe (piano) (iss. 1995) Sym.1184 (CD)

Brian Rayner Cook (baritone), Antony Saunders (piano)

Christopher Keyte (baritone), Rae de Lisle (piano) (rev. Nov 1976) Pe.SHE531

Benjamin Luxon (baritone), David Willison (piano) (rec. 3–4 May 1989 at the Maltings, Snape, iss. 1989, rev. Mar 1990) Ch.CHAN8782 (CD) ABTD 1417 (TC)

Graham Trew (baritone), Roger Vignoles (piano) (rec. 18 Dec 1980, rev. Oct/Dec 1981) Hy.A66026

Paul Wade (tenor), Geoffrey Hamilton (piano) (rev. Sep 1977) LK/LP.6125 (LP)

David Wilson-Johnson (baritone), David Owen Norris (piano) (rev. Mar 1987) Hy.A66208 (LP)

The set arranged for voice and piano trio:

Derek Oldham (tenor) with unnamed violinist, cellist and pianist (rec. 4 Oct 1932 at Abbey Road Studios, Studio 3, London, UK, iss. Jun 1933) HMV.B4379 (78)

The set arranged for voice and orchestra:

Stephen Varcoe (baritone), Richard Hickox (conductor), City Of London Sinfonia (rec. 13–14 Mar 1989 at St Jude's, Central Square, London, UK) Ch.ABRD1382 (LP) 4ABRT1382 (TC) Ch.8743 (CD) (all rev. Jan 1990)

1. *Come Away, Death*

Georgina Anne Colwell (soprano), Margaret Bruce (piano) (rec. Nov 1994 at the Riverside Arts Centre, UK) GAC

George Baker (baritone), Madame Adami (piano) (rec. 13 Nov 1923) HMV.B1731 (78)

Ian Bostridge (tenor), Julius Drake (piano) EMI CDC5 56830 2 (CD)

John Heddle Nash (baritone), Ernest Lush (piano) (rec. 10 Feb 1954, iss. Sep 1954) HMV.C4255; reissued HM.CDLX7104

Derek Oldham (tenor) with unnamed violinist, cellist and pianist (rec. 4 Oct 1932 at Abbey Road Studios, Studio 3, London, UK, iss. Jun 1933) this song reissued HMV ToES.EX290911–3 (LP) and EX290911–5 (TC)

Anthony Rolfe Johnson (tenor), Graham Johnson (piano) (rec. 6–8 Feb 1991) Hy.CDA66480 (CD)

Anthony Rolfe Johnson (tenor), Catherine Edwards (piano) (rec. live Jan 1992 in Glasgow, Scotland)

Alistair Smith (treble), Charles Thompson (piano) (rec. 28–29 Apr 1990 at Bruern Abbey, Oxfordshire) Alpha CAPS 403 (CD)

Frank Titterton (tenor), Stanley Chapple (piano) (rec. 1926)   Voc. K0525 (78)

Henry Wendon (tenor) with piano (may have been rec. but not iss.) Decca

Arranged for voice and piano quartet:

Mark Raphael (baritone), Frederick Grinke (violin), Max Gilbert (viola), Herbert Withers (cello), Roger Quilter (piano) (rec. 8 Nov 1934 at Abbey Road Studios, Studio 2, London, UK, CA14797–2) RO73; Col.DB1598 (78)

2. O Mistress Mine

Gwynne Davies (tenor) [with piano] (iss. May 1915) Pathé Discs 5604

Gervase Elwes (tenor), [Frederick Kiddle (piano)] (rec. 1916) Col.L1119 (78) reissued on Op.OPAL 9844 (rev. 1982) (CD)

Frederick Harvey (baritone), Gerald Moore (piano) (iss. Jan 1961) HMV.CLP3587 and CSD3587 (LP)

Frederick Harvey (baritone), [Jack Byfield (piano)] (iss. Oct 1965) HMV.CLP1901 (mono LP); HMV.CSD1621 (stereo LP)

Frederick Harvey (baritone), Roger Quilter (piano) BBC Transcription recording (32067), 14 August 1945

Richard Lewis (tenor), Ernest Lush (piano) (rec. June 1966) BBC recording, broadcast on Radio 3 on 15 Nov 1991

Walter Midgley (tenor), Gerald Moore (piano) (rec. 8 Apr 1952, iss. May 1953) HMV.DA2036

Henry Millidge (tenor), Clarence Raybould (piano) (rec. 7 Jun 1928) Re.G9208 (78)

Frank Mullings (tenor) with piano (rec. 13 Jan 1926) Col.D1537, transferred to Col.4817 (78)

John Heddle Nash (baritone), Ernest Lush (piano) HMV.C4255; reissued HM.CDLX7104

Derek Oldham (tenor), Madame Adami (piano) (rec. 24 Jul 1924, iss. Jun 1925) HMV.E385 (78)

Derek Oldham (tenor) with unnamed violinist, cellist and pianist (rec. 4 Oct 1932 at Abbey Road Studios, Studio 3, London, UK, iss. Jun 1933) this song reissued HMV ToES.EX290911–3 (LP) and EX290911–5 (TC)

Ian Partridge (tenor), Jennifer Partridge (piano) (iss. 1977) Enigma.K53539/VAR1027

Ian Partridge (tenor), Jennifer Partridge (piano) (rec. 8–9 June 1998 in St George's Church, Bristol, UK) Upbeat.URCD143

Peter Pears (tenor), Benjamin Britten (piano) (rec. 4 June 1972 at the Maltings, Snape, England, UK) BBC transcription 131071; BBC Legends BBCB.8015–2

Mark Raphael (baritone), Roger Quilter (piano) (rec. 13 Dec 1934, CA14800–4, iss. Apr 1936) RO74; Col.DB1629 (78)

Paul Robeson (bass), A. Booth (piano) Monitor.MC581

Anthony Rolfe Johnson (tenor), Graham Johnson (piano) CC.15122 (CD)

Frank Titterton (tenor), Stanley Chapple (piano) (rec. 1926) Voc. K0525 (78)

Henry Wendon (tenor) with piano (iss. Jan 1931) D.F2062 (78)

Arranged for voice and orchestra:

Charles Bryan (tenor) with orchestra (rec. 1930) Picc.5046, repressed as Octacros.471A

3. Blow, Blow, Thou Winter Wind

Marian Anderson (contralto), Franz Rupp (piano) (rec. 20 Dec 1955) (78)

George Baker (baritone), Madame Adami (piano) (rec. 13 Nov 1923) HMV.B1731 (78)

John Coates (tenor), Berkeley Mason (piano) (iss. Aug 1917) Ae.Voc.2056 (78)

Georgina Anne Colwell (soprano), Margaret Bruce (piano) (rec. Nov 1994 at the Riverside Arts Centre, UK) GAC

Gwynne Davies (tenor) [with piano] (iss. May 1915) Pathé Disc 5604

Gervase Elwes (tenor), [Frederick Kiddle (piano)] (iss. Sep 1916) Col.L1055 (78), reissued on Op.OPAL 9844 (rev. 1982) (CD)

Frederick Harvey (baritone), Roger Quilter (piano) BBC Transcription recording (32066), 14 August 1945

Frank Mullings (tenor) with piano (rec. 13 Jan 1926, iss. Apr 1926) Col.D1537, transferred (in Feb 1928) to Col.4817 (78)

Jan Peerce (tenor) (concert at Carnegie Hall, rec. c.1964) UA.UAL3412

Cesare Valletti (tenor), L. Taubman (piano)

Henry Wendon (tenor) with piano (iss. Jan 1931) D.F2062 (78)

Catherine Wyn-Rogers (soprano), Malcolm Martineau (piano) (BBC recording, live broadcast 13 Jan 1997 from St John's, Smith Square, London)

Northern Convent School Chorus (rec. 6 Apr 1946, iss. Dec 1946) HMV.C3524 (78)

Arranged for voice and orchestra

Ivor Foster (baritone) wth orchestra Odeon Record 0517 (iss. Jun 1909); reissued as Odeon X-66484 (iss. Jun 1922)

Four Shakespeare Songs, Op. 30

John Mark Ainsley (tenor), Malcolm Martineau (piano) (rec. 18–20 Feb 1996) Hy.CDA66878 (CD)

Jeffrey Benton (baritone), Rona Lowe (piano) (iss. 1995) Sym.1184 (CD)

Paul Wade (tenor), Geoffrey Hamilton (piano) (rev. Sep 1977) LK/LP.6125 (LP)

Arranged for vocals (by the McLynns):

The McLynns CBS

1. Who is Silvia?

2. When Daffodils Begin to Peer

3. How Should I Your True Love Know?

Lisa Milne (soprano), Graham Johnson (piano) CC.15122 (CD)

4. Sigh No More, Ladies

Five Shakespeare Songs, Op. 23

John Mark Ainsley (tenor), Malcolm Martineau (piano) (rec. 18–20 Feb 1996) Hy.CDA66878 (CD)

Jeffrey Benton (baritone), Graham Kirkland (piano) (iss. 1995) Sym.1184 (CD)

Christopher Keyte (baritone), Rae de Lisle (piano) Pe.SHE531

Paul Wade (tenor), Geoffrey Hamilton (piano) (rev. Sep 1977) LK/LP.6125 (LP)

1. *Fear No More the Heat o' the Sun*

Paul Dutton (treble), Donald Hunt (piano) (recorded at Leeds Parish Church) (iss. 1970) Abbey

Richard Lewis (tenor), Ernest Lush (piano) (rec. June 1966) BBC recording, broadcast on Radio 3 on 15 Nov 1991

Peter Pears (tenor), Benjamin Britten (piano) (rec. 4 June 1972 at the Maltings, Snape, England, UK) BBC transcription 131071, BBC Legends BBCB.8015–2

Mark Raphael (baritone), Roger Quilter (piano) (rec. 6 Dec 1934, CA14799–3, iss. Apr 1936) RO74; Col.DB1629 (78)

Anthony Rolfe Johnson (tenor), Graham Johnson (piano) (rec. 6–8 Feb 1991) Hy.CDA66480 (CD)

Anthony Rolfe Johnson (tenor), Catherine Edwards (piano) (rec. live Jan 1992 in Glasgow, Scotland)

2. *Under the Greenwood Tree*

Georgina Anne Colwell (soprano), Margaret Bruce (piano) (rec. Nov 1994 at the Riverside Arts Centre, UK) GAC

3. *It was a Lover and His Lass*

Duet:

Felicity Lott (soprano), Anne Murray (mezzo-soprano) Graham Johnson (piano) (rec. 20–22 June 1991 at the Maltings, Snape, Suffolk, UK) Ch. (CD)

Lisa Milne (soprano), Anthony Rolfe Johnson (tenor), Graham Johnson (piano) CC.15122 (CD)

Solo:

Janet Baker (mezzo-soprano), Gerald Moore (piano) (rec. 1973) HMV.ASD2929, TCASD2929 (TC) (both iss. Nov 1973); HMV Greensleeves ESD10244391 (LP), HMV.ASD4TC102434 (TC)

Roland Hayes (tenor), Reginald Boardman (piano) (iss. by 1945) AmCol.17177D, in album M393 (78)

Heddle Nash (tenor), Gerald Moore (piano) (rec. 5 Mar 1952) HMV.B10265 (78); Dutton

John Heddle Nash (baritone), Ernest Lush (piano) HMV.C4255 (78); reissued HM.CDLX7104

Ian Partridge (tenor), Beryl Korman (soprano), Jennifer Partridge (piano) (rec. 8–9 June 1998 in St George's Church, Bristol, UK) Upbeat.URCD143

Mark Raphael (baritone), Roger Quilter (piano) (rec. 6 Dec 1934 at the Abbey Road Studios, Studio 2, London, UK, CA14798–4) RO73; Col.DB1598 (78) reissued HMV ToES.EX290911–3 (LP) and EX290911–5 (TC)

Anthony Rolfe Johnson (tenor), Graham Johnson (piano) (rec. 6–8 Feb 1991) Hy.CDA66480 (CD)

Alistair Smith (treble), Charles Thompson (piano) (rec. 28–29 Apr 1990 at Bruern Abbey, Oxfordshire) Alpha CAPS 403 (CD)

G. Stratton (baritone), A. Byram (piano) Cantil.6 237

Arranged for chorus and orchestra:

The Keynotes, Harry Rabinowitz (conductor), BBC Revue Orchestra BBC Radio Collection

4. *Take, O Take Those Lips Away*
Hubert Eisdell (tenor), W. T. Best (piano) (rec. 14 May 1930, iss. Jan 1931) Col.DB334 (78)
Peter Jeffes (tenor), David Woodcock (piano) (iss. 1995) Sym.1183 (CD)
Elizabeth Ritchie (soprano), Jennifer Purvis (piano) (rec. 24/25 Nov 1992 at St George's Hall, Bristol) IMP
Anthony Rolfe Johnson (tenor), Graham Johnson (piano) (rec. 6–8 Feb 1991) Hy.CDA66480 (CD)
Anthony Rolfe Johnson (tenor), Graham Johnson (piano) CC.15122 (CD)
Arranged for voice and piano quartet:
Mark Raphael (baritone), Frederick Grinke (violin), Max Gilbert (viola), Herbert Withers (cello), Roger Quilter (piano) (rec. 13 Dec 1934, CA14800–4, iss. Apr 1936) RO74; Col.DB1629 (78)

5. *Hey, Ho, the Wind and the Rain*
Paul Dutton (treble), Donald Hunt (piano) (recorded at Leeds Parish Church) (iss. 1970) Abbey
Hubert Eisdell (tenor) with piano Col.DB334 (78)
John Heddle Nash (baritone), Ernest Lush (piano) HMV.C4255; reissued HM.CDLX7104
Paul Spindler (treble), Charles Thompson (piano) (rec. 28–29 Apr 1990 at Bruern Abbey, Oxfordshire, UK) Alpha CAPS 403 (CD)
Graham Trew (baritone), Roger Vignoles (piano) (rec. 18–19 Dec 1980) Hy.A66026

Sigh No More, Ladies – see under **Four Shakespeare Songs, Op. 30**

***Since First I Saw Your Face*, The Arnold Book of Old Songs**
Jeffrey Benton (baritone), Rona Lowe (piano) (iss. 1993) Sym.1159 (CD)

Slumber Song*, from *Where the Rainbow Ends
David Wilson-Johnson (baritone), David Owen Norris (piano) (rev. Mar 1987) Hy.A66208 (LP)
Arranged for cello and piano:
Julian Lloyd Webber (cello), John Lenehan (piano) (rec. Oct 1993 at Henry Wood Hall, UK) Ph. 442 426–PH

***Song of the Blackbird*, Four Songs, Op. 14, no. 4**
Gervase Elwes (tenor), [Frederick Kiddle (piano)] (rec. 17 Oct 1911, iss. Mar 1912) HMV single-side 4–2195 coupled with 'To Daisies' in Sep 1915 as HMV.B321 (78)
Benjamin Luxon (baritone), David Willison (piano) (rec. 3–4 May 1989 at the Maltings, Snape, iss. 1989, rev. Mar 1990) Ch.CHAN8782 (CD) ABTD 1417 (TC)
Mark Raphael (baritone), Roger Quilter (piano) (rec. 6 Dec 1934, CA14794–4) RO76; Col.DB1643 (78)

A Song at Parting
David Wilson-Johnson (baritone), David Owen Norris (piano) (rev. Mar 1987) Hy.A66208 (LP)

***(Song of the Stream)*, Six Songs, Op. 25, no. 1**

***Spring is at the Door*, Six Songs, Op. 18, no. 4**
Lisa Milne (soprano), Graham Johnson (piano) CC.15122 (CD)

Spring Voices
David Johnston (tenor), Daphne Ibbott (piano) (iss. 1972) Lilac LIL300 (LP) (this song was not on the Pearl reissue)

(The Starlings), partsong

(Summer Sunset), partsong

Take, O Take Those Lips Away – see under *Five Shakespeare Songs*, Op. 23

Tell Me Where Is Fancy Bred
Paul Wade (tenor), Geoffrey Hamilton (piano) (rev. Sep 1977) LK/LP.6125 (LP)

(There be None of Beauty's Daughters), Five English Love Lyrics, Op. 24, no. 1
Derek Oldham (tenor), Miss M. Swale (piano) (rec. 26 Aug 1926) HMV matrix Bb8880, takes -1,-2,-3 (unissued)

Three Poor Mariners, The Arnold Book of Old Songs
Jeffrey Benton (baritone), Rona Lowe (piano) (iss. 1993) Sym.1159 (CD)
Robert Ivan Foster (baritone), Mary Earl (piano) (rec. in Apr 1966) Onslow
David Wilson-Johnson (baritone), David Owen Norris (piano) (rev. Mar 1987) Hy.A66208 (LP)

Through the Sunny Garden, Two September Songs, Op. 18, no. 5
John Mark Ainsley (tenor), Malcolm Martineau (piano) (rec. 18–20 Feb 1996) Hy.CDA66878 (CD)
John King (baritone), Elaine Hugh-Jones (piano) BBC recording broadcast on Radio 3, 3 Nov 1977

(The Time of Roses), Five English Love Lyrics, Op. 24, no. 5

To Althea from Prison, Five Jacobean Lyrics, Op. 28, no. 4
Brian Rayner Cook (baritone), Antony Saunders (piano)
David Wilson-Johnson (baritone), David Owen Norris (piano) (rev. Mar 1987) Hy.A66208 (LP)

To Daffodils, Two Partsongs for SATB, Op. 13, no. 2
Leslie Woodgate, BBC Chorus (rec. 24 June 1936) D.K832 (78)

To Daisies – see under *To Julia*, Op. 8

(To Electra), Five Lyrics of Robert Herrick, Op. 7, no. 4

(To a Harebell by a Graveside)

To Julia, Op. 8
Jeffrey Benton (baritone), Graham Kirkland (piano) (iss. 1995) Sym.1184 (CD)
Stuart Burrows (tenor), John Constable (piano) (rev. Sep 1971) OL.SOL323
Wynford Evans (tenor), Stephen Rose (piano) BBC broadcast
Paul Austin Kelly (tenor), Michael Recchiuti (piano) GM.2022CD (CD)
Benjamin Luxon (baritone), David Willison (piano) (rec. 3–4 May 1989 at the Maltings, Snape, iss. 1989, rev. Mar 1990) Ch.CHAN8782 (CD) ABTD 1417 (TC)
Ian Partridge (tenor), Jennifer Partridge (piano) BBC recording 4 Apr 1966, broadcast 6 Apr 1966
David Wilson-Johnson (baritone), David Owen Norris (piano) (rev. Mar 1987) Hy.A66208 (LP)
Alexander Young (tenor), Gordon Watson (piano) (iss. 1955, rev. Apr 1955) Argo.RG36 (LP)

Arranged by Quilter for voice and piano quintet:
Hubert Eisdell (tenor), string quartet, directed by Roger Quilter [piano] (iss. November 1923) Col.D1460–2 (78)
Anthony Rolfe Johnson (tenor), The Duke Quartet, Graham Johnson (piano) CC.15122 (CD)

1. *The Bracelet*

2. *The Maiden Blush*
Peter Jeffes (tenor), David Woodcock (piano) (iss. 1995) Sym.1183 (CD)

3. *To Daisies*
Isobel Baillie (soprano), Gerald Moore (piano) (rec. 27 Jan 1944, iss. Jun 1947) Col.DB 2303 (78)
Gervase Elwes (tenor), Frederick Kiddle (piano) (rec. 17 Oct 1911, iss. Mar 1912) HMV single-side 4–2195 coupled with 'Song of the Blackbird' in Sep 1915 as HMV.B321 (78)
Kathleen Ferrier (contralto), Phyllis Spurr (piano) (rec. 10–12 Dec 1951 at Decca Studios, Broadhurst Gardens, London, UK) D.M680 (78); 45–71139 (rev. Aug 1956) (45); D.AKF1–7 (mono LP); ACL309 (LP) and KACL309 (TC) (both iss. Oct 1968); D.DECC417 (CD)
Brabazon Lowther (voice), Daniel Kelly (piano) Playback
Walter Midgley (tenor), Gerald Moore (piano) (rec. 8 Apr 1952, iss. Oct 1952) HMV.DA2014
Mark Raphael (baritone), Roger Quilter (piano) (rec. 6 Dec 1934, CA14794–4) RO76; Col.DB1643 (78)
Frank Titterton (tenor) with piano (rec. 1924) Ae.Voc.X9476 (78)

4. *The Night Piece*

5. *Julia's Hair*

6. *Cherry Ripe*

(To Violets), Five Lyrics of Robert Herrick, Op. 7, no. 5

To the Virgins, Two Partsongs for SATB, Op. 13, no. 1
Leslie Woodgate, BBC Chorus (rec. 24 June 1936) D.K832 (78)

To Wine and Beauty, Six Songs, Op. 18, no. 1
David Wilson-Johnson (baritone), David Owen Norris (piano) (rev. Mar 1987) Hy.A66208 (LP)

(Trollie Lollie Laughter)

Tulips, partsong
Simon Joly (conductor), Antony Saunders (piano), BBC Singers , BBC recording broadcast Radio 3, 12 Dec 1980

Und was die Sonne glüht, Four Songs of Mirza Schaffy, Op. 2, no. 2
John Mark Ainsley (tenor), Malcolm Martineau (piano) (rec. 18–20 Feb 1996) Hy.CDA66878 (CD)

Under the Greenwood Tree – see under *Five Shakespeare Songs*, Op. 23

The Valley and the Hill, Two September Songs, Op. 18, no. 6
John Mark Ainsley (tenor), Malcolm Martineau (piano) (rec. 18–20 Feb 1996) Hy.CDA66878 (CD)
Jeffrey Benton (baritone), Rona Lowe (piano) (iss. 1993) Sym.1159 (CD)

John King (baritone), Elaine Hugh-Jones (piano) BBC recording broadcast on Radio 3, 3 Nov 1977

The Walled-in Garden
David Wilson-Johnson (baritone), David Owen Norris (piano) (rev. Mar 1987) Hy.A66208 (LP)

Weep You No More – see under *Seven Elizabethan Lyrics*, Op. 12

(What Shall He Have that Killed the Deer), partsong

When Daffodils Begin to Peer – see under *Four Shakespeare Songs*, Op. 30

When Icicles Hang by the Wall, Two Shakespeare Songs, Op. 32, no. 2
Jeffrey Benton (baritone), Graham Kirkland (piano) (iss. 1995) Sym.1184 (CD)

Where be You Going?, Six Songs, Op. 18, no. 2
Mark Raphael (baritone), Roger Quilter (piano) (rec. 29 Nov 1934, CA14803–2) RO78; Col.DB1648 (78)

Where Go the Boats?, Four Child Songs, Op. 5, no. 3
John Mark Ainsley (tenor), Malcolm Martineau (piano) (rec. 18–20 Feb 1996) Hy.CDA66878 (CD)
Arranged for cello and piano:
Julian Lloyd Webber (cello), John Lenehan (piano) (rec. Oct 1993 at Henry Wood Hall, UK) Ph. 442 426–2 PH

Where'er the Sun Doth Glow – see under *Und was die Sonne glüht*

Who is Silvia? – see under *Four Shakespeare Songs*, Op. 30

Why So Pale and Wan?, Five Jacobean Lyrics, Op. 28, no. 2
Brian Rayner Cook (baritone), Antony Saunders (piano)
David Wilson-Johnson (baritone), David Owen Norris (piano) (rev. Mar 1987) Hy.A66208 (LP)

(Wild Cherry)

The Wild Flower's Song, Three Songs of William Blake, Op. 20, no. 2
Benjamin Luxon (baritone), David Willison (piano)(rec. 3–4 May 1989 at the Maltings, Snape, iss. 1989, rev. Mar 1990) Ch.CHAN8782 (CD) ABTD 1417 (TC)
Alexander Young (tenor), Gordon Watson (piano) (iss. 1955, rev. Apr 1955) Argo.RG36 (LP)

Wind from the South
Jeffrey Benton (baritone), Rona Lowe (piano) (iss. 1993) Sym.1159 (CD)

(Windy Nights), partsong

Ye Banks and Braes, The Arnold Book of Old Songs
Jeffrey Benton (baritone), Rona Lowe (piano) (iss. 1993) Sym.1159 (CD)
Kathleen Ferrier (alto), P. Spurr (piano) (rec. 10–12 Dec 1951) D.M679 (78); D.LX3098 (78); D.AKF1–7 (mono LP); D.cep726 (45); D.BR3052; D.cep518; D.45–71053 (these last 3 rev. Jul 1960); Reader's Digest, details unknown
Robert Ivan Foster (baritone), Mary Earl (piano) (rec. in Apr 1966) Onslow
Susan Kessler (mezzo-soprano), Geoffrey Parsons (piano) (iss. Sep 1984) Meridian.E77074 (stereo LP)
Lisa Milne (soprano), Graham Johnson (piano) CC.15122 (CD)

(Youth and Beauty), partsong

A reissue of some or all of the Quilter-Raphael recordings was made, but the items have not been identified. The record (LP) was of Mark Raphael singing 'Two English composers: Samuel Alman: Roger Quilter', on the Chicago: Musique Internationale label, 1984. Cat. No. M7381.

Orchestral and other works

As You Like It, Suite, Op. 21

1. *Shepherd's Holiday*

2. *Evening in the Forest*

3. *Merry Pranks*

4. *Country Dance*

Ashley Lawrence, BBC Concert Orchestra BBC recording broadcast Radio 3, 31 Oct 1977

Adrian Leaper, Czecho-Slovak Radio Symphony Orchestra MP.8.223444 (CD)

Country Dance (only)

Rae Jenkins, New Concert Orchestra BH.OT2030

A Children's Overture, Op. 17

Sir John Barbirolli, London Philharmonic Orchestra (rec. 21 July 1933) HMV.C2603)78); Vic.36370 (78); EMI.EX29107–3 and 4EX290107–5 (TC) (both iss. Jul 1984)

Otto Dobrindt, Grand Symphony Orchestra [the German Parlophone Orchestter, Berlin Studios] (rec. 12 Jun 1929, iss. Nov 1929) P.E10912 (78)

Sir Vivian Dunn, Light Music Society Orchestra (rec. 3 Dec 1969 at Abbey Road, Studio 1) Col.TWO295 (LP) reissued on EMI Arabesque 3037 (CD)

Adrian Leaper, Czecho-Slovak Radio Symphony Orchestra MP.8.223444 (CD)

Alick Maclean, New Queen's Hall Light Orchestra (rec. 20 Dec 1922) Col.L1471–2 (78)

Stanford Robinson, BBC Concert Orchestra (rec. live and broadcast on 19 Dec 1959 from the Dome, Brighton, UK, as part of the Saturday 'Pop' Concert)

Ger de Roos (conductor), Helen van Capellen (vocal), The Parrakeets and Ger de Roos and his orchestra without a name D.

Royal Opera House Covent Garden Orchestra (rec. in 1994 at All Saint's Church, Petersham) Royal Opera House

Sir Malcolm Sargent, New Light Symphony Orchestra (parts 1&2 rerec. 15 Oct 1928, parts 3&4 rec. 21 Sep 1928) HMV.B2860/1 (78); matrices sent to Camden, New Jersey, for production of Vic.22098/9 (iss. 18 Feb 1930) (78)

Sidney Torch and his Orchestra (rec. 28 Nov 1949, iss. Sep 1950) P.E11469 (78)

H.-J. Walther, Hamburg Philharmonia MSB.78022

George Weldon, London Symphony Orchestra (rec. 5 Dec 1952) Col.DX1869 (78); Col.DOX1013 (78); SCD2107 (45)

Sir Henry Wood, London Philharmonic Orchestra (rec. 3 Oct 1932) Col.DB951/2 (78); Oi.DO 988/9

Arranged for band:

Band of H.M. Grenadier Guards, Capt. George Miller (conductor) (rec. 18 Oct 1933) D.T206; renumbered K998 (78)

Arranged for Brass Band

Black Dyke Mills Band, Roy Newsome (conductor) (rec. at St George's Hall, Bradford, UK) Pye; Golden Hour

Fairey Band, Kenneth Dennison (conductor) (arranged by Wright) (iss. Jul 1975) D.SB318

Royal Corps of Signals (Bowling) Indigo.GOLP7003

Arranged for organ:

William A. Davies (organ) (Wurlitzer organ originally built in 1930, U.S.A.) (rec. 15 Nov 1960 at Elephant and Castle, London)

Concert Waltz, from Rosmé

Adrian Leaper, Czecho-Slovak Radio Symphony Orchestra MP.8.223444 (CD)

Country Pieces for piano, Op. 23:

1. *Shepherd Song*

2. *Goblins*

3. *Forest Lullaby*

4. *Pipe and Tabor*
Arranged for orchestra (by Ernest Tomlinson):
Adrian Leaper, Czecho-Slovak Radio Symphony Orchestra MP.8.223444 (CD)

Fanfare for Fun *(Fanfare for Children)*
Capt. H. E. Adkins, Kneller Hall Musicians (rec. 17 Jun 1932, iss. Sep 1932) HMV.C2445 (78)

The Rake, Suite:

1. *Dance at the Feast*

2. *The Light-hearted Lady*

3. *The Frolicsome Friend*

4. *Allurement*

5. *Midnight Revels*
Ashley Lawrence, BBC Concert Orchestra BBC recording broadcast Radio 3, 31 Oct 1977
Adrian Leaper, Czecho-Slovak Radio Symphony Orchestra MP.8.223444 (CD)

Three English Dances, Op. 11
Richard Hickox, Northern Sinfonia (rec. 14–15 May 1989 at All Saints, Newcastle, UK, iss. Sep 1991) EMI.CDC7 49933–2; CDM5 66542–2
Rae Jenkins, New Concert Orchestra (probably Fletcher's orchestration) BH.OT2030
Ashley Lawrence, BBC Concert Orchestra
Adrian Leaper, Czecho-Slovak Radio Symphony Orchestra (certainly Fletcher's orchestration) MP.8.223444 (CD)
J. A. Murray, New Light Symphony Orchestra (probably Fletcher's orchestration) (rec. 16 Jan 1935, iss. Sep 1935) HMV.B8346/7 (78)
Arranged for piano:
Alan Cuckston (piano) SWIN.4FEW111 (TC)

Where the Rainbow Ends, Suite:

1. *Rainbow Land*
2. *Will-o'-the-Wisp*
3. *Rosamund*
4. *Fairy Frolic*
5. *Goblin Forest*

Sir Vivian F. Dunn, Bournemouth Symphony Orchestra (rec. 1974 at the Guildhall, Southampton) Ch.CBR1002 (LP)

Richard Hickox, Northern Sinfonia (rec. 14–15 May 1989 at All Saints, Newcastle, UK, iss. Sep 1991) EMI.CDC7 49933–2; CDM5 66542–2 (CD)

Adrian Leaper, Czecho-Slovak Radio Symphony Orchestra MP.8.223444 (CD)

Brian Wright, BBC Concert Orchestra

6. *Selection*

Frederic Bayco (Wurlitzer organ, Gaumont State Cinema, Kilburn, London) (Rosamund, Fairy Frolic) HMV.CLP3505 and ASD3505 (stereo LP) (both iss. Mar 1966)

Sir Vivian F. Dunn (Rosamund) (rev. Sep 1971) Polydor.CBR1002 (LP) 4CBT1002 (TC)

Quilter, Salon Orchestra [Victor Olof Orchestra] (Dragon King/Will-o'-the-Wisp, Rosamund, Fairy Frolic, Fairy Ballet, Slumber Song, St George) (rec. 1930 on Odeon (London) matrices, iss. Dec 1931) P.E11175 (78)

Sidney Torch (Christie Unit Organ, Regal Cinema, Edmonton, London) (rec. 26 Oct 1934) (Part 1: St George, Land Where the Rainbow Ends, Will-o'-the-Wisp, Dragon Forest, Dance of the Mischievous Elves; Part 2: Fairy Frolic, Magic Carpet, Rosamund, Fairy Ballet, St George) Col.DX647 (78)

Alick Maclean, New Queen's Light Orchestra (Rosamund, Fairy Frolic) (78) (rec. 20 Dec 1922, iss. May 1923) Col.L1472 (78)

George Weldon, Pro Arte Orchestra (1963) (Rosamund) Col.DX1869; HMV.CLP1662 (LP); CSD1503 (LP); HMV.SXLP30123; CFP

Appendix F CD Contents

This CD has been possible because of the generosity of Robert Clarke, Lewis Foreman and Steven Plunkett in loaning records from their collections.

Tracks 1–25 and 32–37 have been re-mastered from much played 78s (the only or best copies available) by Dave Le Good. Tracks 26–31 have been re-mastered by Will Prentice of the British Library National Sound Archive from the near perfect archive copies held by them on behalf of the BBC. My grateful thanks to both engineers. Tracks 26–31 are released by arrangement with BBC Music.

Mark Raphael (baritone), **Roger Quilter** (piano)
Private recording for the Roger Quilter Society, in a presentation set signed by Quilter; reissued on Columbia at bi-monthly intervals. The RO number refers to the private recording, the DB number to the Columbia recording.

1. *Love's Philosophy*, Three Songs, Op. 3, no. 1
Matrix CA14795–5, RO75, DB1602, recorded 13 Dec 1934 at the Abbey Road Studios, Studio 2, London, UK, issued Feb 1936

2. *Come Away, Death*, Three Shakespeare Songs, Op. 6, no. 1
With Frederick Grinke (violin), Max Gilbert (viola), Herbert Withers (cello). Matrix CA14797–2, RO73, DB1598, recorded 8 Nov 1934 at Abbey Road Studios, Studio 2, London

3. *O Mistress Mine*, Three Shakespeare Songs, Op. 6, no. 2
Matrix CA14800–4, RO74, DB1629, recorded 13 Dec 1934, issued Apr 1936

4. *To Daisies*, To Julia, Op. 8, no. 3
Matrix CA14794–4, RO76, DB1643, recorded 6 Dec 1934

5. *Weep You No More*, Seven Elizabethan Lyrics, Op. 12, no. 1
Matrix CA14793–2, RO76, DB1643, recorded 27 Nov 1934

6. *Song of the Blackbird*, Four Songs, Op. 14, no. 4
Matrix CA14794–4, RO76, DB1643, recorded 6 Dec 1934

7. *Where be You Going?*, Six Songs, Op. 18, no. 2
Matrix CA14803–2, RO78, DB1648, recorded 29 Nov 1934

8. *Cherry Valley*, Three Pastoral Songs, Op. 22, no. 2
With Frederick Grinke (violin), Herbert Withers (cello). Matrix CA14804–3, RO78, DB1648, recorded 29 Nov 1934, issued 1 Aug 1936

9. *Fear No More the Heat o' the Sun*, Five Shakespeare Songs, Op. 23, no. 1
Matrix CA14799–3, RO74, DB1629, recorded 6 Dec 1934, issued Apr 1936

10. *It was a Lover and His Lass*, Five Shakespeare Songs, Op. 23, no. 3

Matrix CA14798–4, RO73, DB1598, recorded 6 Dec 1934 at the Abbey Road Studios, Studio 2, London, UK

11. *Take, O Take Those Lips Away,* Five Shakespeare Songs, Op. 23, no. 4
With Frederick Grinke (violin), Max Gilbert (viola), Herbert Withers (cello). Matrix CA14800–4, RO74, DB1629, recorded 13 Dec 1934, issued Apr 1936

12. *Go, Lovely Rose,* Five English Love Lyrics, Op. 24, no. 3
Matrix CA14802–3, RO77, DB1583, recorded 3 Dec 1934

13. *O, the Month of May,* Five English Love Lyrics, Op. 24, no. 4
Matrix CA14801–2, RO77, DB1583, recorded 29 Nov 1934

14. *Music, When Soft Voices Die,* Six Songs, Op. 25, no. 5
Matrix CA14795–5, RO75, DB1602, recorded 13 Dec 1934 at Abbey Road, Studio 2, London, UK, issued Feb 1936

15. *Over the Land is April,* Two Songs, Op. 26, no. 2
Matrix CA14803–2, RO78, DB1648, recorded 29 Nov 1934

16. *The Jealous Lover,* Five Jacobean Lyrics, Op. 28, no. 1
Matrix CA14796–4, RO75, DB1602, recorded 13 Dec 1934, issued Feb 1936

17. *I Dare Not Ask a Kiss,* Five Jacobean Lyrics, Op. 28, no. 3
With Frederick Grinke (violin), Max Gilbert (viola), Herbert Withers (cello). Matrix CA14796–4, RO75, DB1602, recorded 13 Dec 1934, issued Feb 1936

Hubert Eisdell (tenor), with string quartet, directed by **Roger Quilter** [piano]
Issued November 1923 on Columbia, D1460–2
To Julia, Op. 8:

18. *Prelude,* matrix A76, D1460

19. *The Bracelet,* matrix A76, D1460

20. *The Maiden Blush,* matrix A77, D1460

21. *To Daisies,* matrix A78, D1461

22. *The Night Piece,* matrix A79, D1461

23. *Julia's Hair,* matrix A77, D1460

24. *Interlude,* matrix A80, D1462

25. *Cherry Ripe,* matrix A80, D1462

Frederick Harvey (baritone), **Roger Quilter** (piano)
Recorded by BBC Transcription Services on 14 August 1945

26. *Moonlight,* Four Songs of the Sea, Op. 1, no. 3, 1911 version (32068)

27. *Love's Philosophy,* Three Songs, Op. 3, no. 1 (32064)

28. *O Mistress Mine,* Three Shakespeare Songs, Op. 6, no. 2 (32067)

29. *Blow, Blow, Thou Winter Wind,* Three Shakespeare Songs, Op. 6, no. 3 (32066)

30. *Go, Lovely Rose,* Five English Love Lyrics, Op. 24, no. 3 (32069)

31. *Hark, Hark, the Lark!* (32065)

Salon Orchestra [Victor Olof Orchestra] conducted by **Roger Quilter**
Where the Rainbow Ends, selection

Recorded 1930 on Odeon (London) matrices, issued Dec 1931, Parlophone E11175

Matrix XXL-3706–1

32. *Dragon King and Will-o'-the-Wisp*

33. *Rosamund*

34. *Fairy Frolic*

Matrix XXL3707–1

35. *Fairy Ballet*

36. *Slumber Song*

37. *St George*

Bibliography

Occasional comments in square brackets after a title indicate its area of relevance, where it might not otherwise be obvious.

Unpublished sources

These are numerous, and only the major repositories are shown here, either of letters, or of other significant material. Absence of an institution merely means that its contribution, though valuable, was not especially large.

Archives of American Art, Smithsonian Institution, Washington, D.C., USA (Emmet family papers)

BBC Written Archives Centre, Caversham Park, Reading

The British Library

Archives held by Leslie East

Grainger Museum, University of Melbourne, Australia

Rare Book & Manuscript Library, University of Pennsylvania (Marian Anderson archives)

Royal Academy of Music, London

Articles and booklets, including dictionary entries

Allégret, Marc, 'Notes prises en courant sur le voyage en Angleterre', ed. Daniel Durosay, *Bulletin des amis d'André Gide*, no. 125, vol. XXVIII (Janvier 2000), pp. 87–131.

Ampersand, 'Song Composers of the Day: Roger Quilter', *Musical Opinion and Music Trade Review*, February 1924, pp. 535–7.

Armstrong, Thomas, 'The Frankfort Group', *Proceedings of the Royal Musical Association*, vol. LXXXV (1958–9), pp. 1–16.

Banfield, Stephen, 'Roger Quilter: A Centenary Note', *The Musical Times*, vol. CXVIII (1977), pp. 903–6.

Banfield, Stephen, 'Roger Quilter', *New Grove Dictionary of Music and Musicians*, ed. Stanley Sadie (London, 1980), vol. 15, pp. 906–7.

B[eechey[, G[wilym] E., 'Robert Herrick (1591–1674), and Some Settings of His Poems', *The Consort: Annual Journal of the Dolmetsch Foundation*, vol. XLVII (1991), pp. 1–4.

Bennett, Rodney, 'Song-Writers of the Day: II: Roger Quilter', *The Music Teacher*, vol. V (July 1926), pp. 409–11.

Bennett, Rodney, 'Roger Quilter's Songs', *Radio Times* (29 June 1934), p. 973.

Boase, F., 'William Quilter', *Modern English Biography* (1892), p. 1690.

'British Music Drama Company', *The Musical Times* (December 1936), p. 1132.

Cahn, Peter, 'Percy Grainger's Frankfurt Years', *Studies in Music* (University of Western Australia), vol. 12 (1978), pp. 101–13.

Chislett, W. A., 'Centenary note' *Gramophone*, vol. 55 (November 1977), p. 809.

Colles, H. C., 'Roger Quilter', *Grove's Dictionary of Music and Musicians*, ed. Eric Blom (London, 1954), vol. 6, pp. 1034–5.

Doyle, Brian, 'Remembering the Rainbow', *Story Paper Collectors' Digest* (December 1993), pp. 30–3, and (January 1994), pp. 16–20.

East, Leslie, 'Roger Quilter (1877–1953)', *Music and Musicians*, vol. 26 (November 1977), pp. 28–30.

Goddard, Scott, 'The Art of Roger Quilter', *The Chesterian*, vol. VI, no. 47 (June 1925), pp. 213–17.

Green, Jeffrey P., 'Roland Hayes in London, 1921', *The Black Perspective in Music*, vol. 10, no. 1 (Spring 1982), pp. 29–42.

Greenwood, George A., 'A Composer of Quality', *Great Thoughts* (December 1936), pp. 122–3.

Havergal, Henry, 'Roger Cuthbert Quilter', *Dictionary of National Biography* (1951–60), pp. 830–1.

Hill, Sir Quintin, 'Roger Quilter: 1877–1953', *Music and Letters*, vol. XXXV (1954), pp. 15–16.

Hill, Ralph, 'Exquisite Miniaturist', *Radio Times* (25 August 1933), p. 999.

Hogarth, Basil, 'Our Modern Music Makers, VII: Roger Quilter', *The Musical Progress and Mail* (December 1931), pp. 94–5.

Holdin, Roger, 'Roger Quilter', *The Musical Mirror and Fanfare* (May 1931), pp. 158–9.

Kaye, Ernest, 'Hermann Baron, An Appreciation', *Peter Warlock Society Newsletter*, no. 44 (April 1990), p. 8.

Lloyd, Stephen, 'Grainger and the "Frankfurt Group" Letter', *Studies in Music* (University of Western Australia), vol. 16 (1982), pp. 111–18.

Lowe, George, 'The Music of Roger Quilter', *Musical Opinion and Music Trade Review*, vol. 496 (January 1919), pp. 210–11.

Miller, Major Eustace, 'Those were the Days My Friend, We Thought They'd Never End', *Suffolk Fair* (October 1981), pp. 57–61, p. 103 and (January 1982), pp. 51–5.

'Women who Have Made Good, VI: A Woman Playwright: Mrs Clifford Mills', *Lady's Pictorial* (13 March 1920), p. 338.

Milnes, Rodney, 'Love at the Inn' (Review), *Opera*, vol. 28 (June 1977), p. 608.

Obituary, *Illustrated London News* (26 Sep 1953), p. 467.

Obituary, *Monthly Musical Record*, vol. 83 (Nov 1953), p. 246.

Obituary, *Musical America*, vol. 73 (Oct 1953), p. 26.

Obituary, *Musical Courier*, vol. 148 (1 Oct 1953), p. 31.

Obituary, *Musical Opinion*, vol. 77 (Nov 1953), p. 79.

Obituary, *New York Times* (22 Sep 1953).

Obituary, *The Times* (22 Sep 1953).

Ould, Herman, 'Two English Song-Writers: Roger Quilter and Cyril Scott', *English Review*, vol. XLVIII (April 1929), pp. 478–82.

Palmer, Christopher, 'Cyril Scott: Centenary Reflections', *The Musical Times*, vol. CXX (September 1979), pp. 738–41.

'Sir Cuthbert Quilter', *Suffolk County Handbook* (1912), p. 462.

Ranson, F. Lingard, *Lavenham, Suffolk*, 1988.

Raphael, Mark, 'Roger Quilter: 1877–1953, the Man and His Songs', *Tempo*, vol. 30 (1953–4), p. 20.

Robert, William, 'Harry Quilter 1851–1907', *Dictionary of National Biography* (1912).

Robert, William, 'Sir William Cuthbert Quilter 1841–1911', *Dictionary of National Biography* (1912).

Rye, Howard, and Jeffrey Green, 'Black Musical Internationalism in England in the 1920s', *Black Music Research Journal*, vol. 15, no. 1 (Spring 1995), pp. 93–108.

Scott, Cyril, 'Iwan Knorr 1853–1916', *The Monthly Musical Record*, vol. 46 (1 September 1916), pp. 240–2.

Scott, Cyril, trans. G. Marbach, 'Die "Frankforter Gruppe"': Erinnerungen von Cyril Scott', *Neue Leipziger Zeitschrift für Musik*, vol. 119 (3 Feb 1958), pp. 81–3.

Sutcliffe, B. C., 'Roger Quilter and the Rainbow Children' *Sussex Life* (November 1977), p. 33.

Woodgate, Leslie, 'Roger Quilter', *The Musical Times*, vol. XCIV (November 1953), pp. 503–5.

Books

These are divided into two sections: of direct relevance; and of broader contextual interest.

A. Direct relevance

Amory, Martin, *Lord Berners, The Last Eccentric* (London, 1998) [La Casati].

Anderson, Garrett, *Hang Your Halo in the Hall* (London, 1993) [history of the Savile Club].

Anderson, Marian, *My Lord, What a Morning* (New York, 1956).

Anderson, Robert, *Elgar* (London, 1993).

Banfield, Stephen, *Sensibility and English Song* (Cambridge, 1985).

Barr Jr., Alfred H., *Matisse, His Art and his Public* (New York, 1951) [Bertie Landsberg].

Bird, John, *Percy Grainger*, 3rd edn (Oxford, 1999).

Bonham Carter, Violet, *Winston Churchill as I Knew Him* (London, 1966).

Brook, Donald, *Composers' Gallery: Biographical Sketches of Contemporary Composers* (London, 1946).

Brooke, Rupert, *The Collected Poems of Rupert Brooke: With a Memoir* (London, 1918) [Col. Arnold Quilter].

Cahn, Peter, *Das Hoch'sche Konservatorium 1878–1978* (Frankfurt-am-Main, 1979).

Campbell, Marguerite, *Dolmetsch, the Man and His Work* (London, 1975).

Cardus, Neville, ed., *Kathleen Ferrier, 1912–1953* (London, 1954).

Carley, Lionel, ed., *Delius, A Life in Letters 1862–1908* (London, 1983).

Carpenter, Humphrey, with research by Jennifer Doctor, *The Envy of the World: Fifty Years of the BBC Third Programme and Radio 3, 1946–1996* (London, 1997).

Coates, Eric, *Suite in Four Movements* (London, 1986).

Cochran, Charles B., *Showman Looks On* (London, 1945).

Colville, John, *The Fringes of Power: Downing Street Diaries 1939–1955* (London, 1985) [Benton Fletcher].

Covert, James, *A Victorian Marriage: Mandell and Louise Creighton* (London, 2000).

Covert, James Thayne, ed., *Memoir of a Victorian Woman: Reflections of Louise Creighton, 1850–1936* (Bloomington, 1994).

Covert, James Thayne, ed., *A Victorian Family, as Seen through the Letters of Louise Creighton to her Mother 1872–1880* (New York, 1998).

Coward, Noël, *Present Indicative* (London, 1937).

Cox, David, *The Henry Wood Proms* (London, 1980).

Cranmer-Byng, L., ed., *A Lute of Jade* (New York, 1909).

Cust, Lionel, *A History of Eton College* (London, 1899).

Dibble, Jeremy, *C. Hubert H. Parry* (Oxford, 1992).

Duberman, Martin Bauml, *Paul Robeson* (London, 1989).

Edel, Leon, and Lyall H. Powers, eds., *The Complete Notebooks of Henry James* (Oxford, 1987).

Ehrlich, Cyril, *The Piano, A History*, revised edn (Oxford, 1990).

Elliott, Sir Ivo, Bart. (ICS retd), ed., *Balliol College Register, 1900–1950*, 2nd edn, volume printed for private circulation by Charles Batey at the University Press (Oxford, 1953) [Robin Hollway].

Elwes, Lady Winefride and Richard, *Gervase Elwes* (London, 1935).

Fisher, Clive, *Noel Coward* (London, 1992).

Goossens, Eugène, *Overture and Beginners: A Musical Autobiography* (London, 1951) [Quilter's *Fanfare*].

Grainger, Percy, *The Farthest North of Humanness: Letters of Percy Grainger 1901–14*, ed. Kay Dreyfus (Melbourne, 1985).

Graves, Charles L., *Hubert Parry, His Life and Works* (London, 1926) [the von Glehns].

Green, Jeffrey P., 'The Negro Renaissance and England', Chapter 10 in *Black Music in the Harlem Renaissance*, ed. Samuel A. Floyd, Jr. (Knoxville, 1993), pp. 151–71.

Harding, James, *Cochran, A Biography* (London, 1988).

Harrison, Beatrice, ed. Patricia Cleveland-Peck, *The Cello and the Nightingales: the Autobiography of Beatrice Harrison* (London., 1985).

Hassall, Christopher, *Rupert Brooke, A Biography* (London, 1964) [Col Arnold Quilter].

Hawtrey, Charles, *The Truth at Last* (London, 1924).

Hawtrey, Florence Molesworth, *The History of the Hawtrey Family, Vols. 1 & 2* (London, 1903).

Helm, MacKinley, *Angel Mo' and Her Son, Roland Hayes* (Boston, 1943).

Herbert, A. P., *A.P.H., His Life and Times* (London, 1970).

Hoare, Philip, *Noël Coward, A Biography* (London, 1996).

Holbrooke, Joseph, *Contemporary British Composers* (London, 1925).

Hold, Trevor, *The Walled-in Garden: A Study of the Songs of Roger Quilter*, 2nd edn (London, 1996).

Howes, Frank, *The English Musical Renaissance* (London, 1966).

Hudson, Derek, *Norman O'Neill, A Life of Music* (London, 1945).

Jobson, Allan, *In Suffolk Borders* (London, 1967) [Bawdsey Manor].

Jobson, Allan, *Suffolk Villages* (London, 1971) [Bawdsey Manor].

Jones, R. V., *Most Secret War: British Scientific Intelligence 1939–1945* (London, 1978) [Bawdsey Manor].

Junge, Ewald, *Anthony Bernard: A Life in Music* (London, 1992) (private publication; limited edition).

Keiler, Allan, *Marian Anderson: A Singer's Journey* (New York, 2000).

Knoblock, Edward, *Round the Room: An Autobiography* (London, 1939).

Lambert, Herbert, *Modern British Composers, Seventeen Portraits* (London, 1923).

Laver, James, *Whistler*, 2nd edn (London, 1976).

Lee-Browne, Martin, *Nothing So Charming as Musick! The Life and Times of Frederic Austin* (London, 1999).

Lees-Milne, James, *Diaries 1942–1945: Ancestral Voices & Prophesying Peace* (London, 1975) [Benton Fletcher].

Lloyd, Stephen, *H. Balfour Gardiner* (Cambridge, 1984).

Lloyd, Stephen, *Sir Dan Godfrey, Champion of British Composers* (London, 1995).

Martens, Frederick H., *Leo Ornstein, the Man – His Ideas – His Work* (New York, 1918).

Mitchell, S. J. D., *Perse, A History of the Perse School 1615–1976* (Cambridge, 1976) [Louis de Glehn].

Moore, Jerrold Northrop, ed., *Edward Elgar: Letters of a Lifetime* (Oxford, 1990) [Walter Creighton].

Mosse, Werner E., ed., *Second Chance, Two Centuries of German-Speaking Jews in the United Kingdom* (Tübingen, 1991).

Pilkington, Michael, *Gurney, Ireland, Quilter, Warlock* (London, 1989).

Pottle, Mark, ed., *Champion Redoubtable, The Diaries and Letters of Violet Bonham Carter 1914–1945* (London, 1998).

Scott, Cyril, *My Years of Indiscretion* (London, 1924).

Scott, Cyril, *Bone of Contention, Life Story and Confessions* (London, 1969).

Smith, Barry, *Peter Warlock, The Life of Philip Heseltine* (Oxford, 1994).

Sutherland, David, *He Who Dares. Recollections of Service in the SAS, SBS and MI5* (Barnsley, 1998) [Norah Quilter].

Warlock, Peter (Philip Heseltine), rev. Hubert Foss, *Frederick Delius* (London, 1952).

Warlock, Peter, *Cursory Rhymes, Limericks and Other Poems in the Best Interests of Morality* (London, 2000) (limited edition).

White, Maude Valérie, *Friends and Memories* (London, 1914).

Wortley, Laura, *Wilfrid de Glehn RA, John Singer Sargent's Painting Companion* (Marlow, n.d.).

Young, Percy M., *George Grove 1820–1900, A Biography* (London, 1980) [the von Glehns].

B. Broader contextual interest

Bax, Arnold, *Farewell, My Youth* (London, 1943).

Beecham, Sir Thomas, *Frederick Delius* (London, 1959).

Bennett, Mary, *Artists of the Pre-Raphaelite Circle, the First Generation, Catalogue of Works in the Walker Art Gallery, Lady Lever Art Gallery and Sudley Art Gallery* (London, 1988) [Sir Cuthbert Quilter's art collection].

Bettelheim, Bruno, *The Uses of Enchantment: The Meaning and Importance of Fairy Tales* (London, 1976).

Blom, Eric, *Music in England*, revised edn (West Drayton, 1947).

Bushaway, Bob, 'Name upon Name: The Great War and Remembrance', *Myths of the English*, ed. Roy Porter (Cambridge, 1992), pp. 136–67.

Cannadine, David, 'Gilbert and Sullivan: The Making and Un-making of a British "Tradition"', *Myths of the English*, ed. Roy Porter (Cambridge, 1992), pp. 12–32.

Carpenter, Humphrey, *Benjamin Britten, A Biography* (London, 1992).

Clinton-Baddeley, V. C., ed., *Words for Music* (Cambridge, 1941).

Copley, I. A., *The Music of Peter Warlock, A Critical Survey* (London, 1979).

Dorum, Eileen, *Percy Grainger, The Man behind the Music* (Hawthorn, Australia, 1986).

Elkin, Robert, *Queen's Hall 1893–1941* (London, 1944).

Ellmann, Richard, *Oscar Wilde* (London, 1987).

Emmerson, George S., *Arthur Darling, the Romance of Arthur Sullivan and Rachel Scott Russell (from Her Love Letters)* (Ontario, 1980).

Fellowes, E. H., ed., *English Madrigal Verse*, 3rd edn, ed. Frederick W. Sternfeld, David Greer (Oxford, 1967).

Fletcher, Benton, *Royal Homes near London* (London, 1930).

Foreman, Lewis, ed., *The Percy Grainger Companion* (London, 1981).

Foreman, Lewis, *From Parry to Britten, A Chronological Anthology* (London, 1987).

Foss, Hubert, *Ralph Vaughan Willliams, A Study* (London, 1950).

Fuller Maitland, J. A., *English Music in the XIXth Century* (London, 1902).

Godfrey, Sir Dan, *Memories and Music, Thirty-five Years of Conducting* (London, 1924).

Grainger, Percy, *The All-Round Man: Selected Letters of Percy Grainger*, ed. M. Gillies and D. Pear (Oxford, 1994).

Graves, Charles L., *The Life and Letters of Sir George Grove, CB* (London, 1903) [the von Glehns].

Greene, H. Plunket, *Interpretation in Song* (London, 1912).

Greene, H. Plunket, *Charles Villiers Stanford* (London, 1935) [the von Glehns].

Greer, David, ed., *The English Lute-Songs*, series 2, vol. 21 (London, 1969).

Hanson, Bruce K., *The Peter Pan Chronicles: The Nearly 100 Year History of "The Boy Who Wouldn't Grow Up"* (New York, 1993).

Hibberd, Dominic, ed., *Poetry of the First World War, A Casebook* (London, 1981).

Hibberd, Dominic, and John Onions, eds., *Poetry of the Great War, An Anthology* (London, 1986).

Hinton, Alastair, 'Kaikhosru Shapurji Sorabji: An Introduction', *Sorabji: A Critical Celebration*, ed. Paul Rapoport (London, 1992).

Hurd, Michael, *Vincent Novello – and Company* (London, 1981) [the von Glehns].

Hyde, H. Montgomery, *The Other Love, An Historical and Contemporary Survey of Homosexuality in Britain* (London, 1970).

Jacobs, Arthur, *Arthur Sullivan, A Victorian Musician* (Oxford, 1986) [the von Glehns].

King, W. A. H., *English Porcelain Figures of the Eighteenth Century* (London, 1925).

Lamont, Corliss, and Lansing Lamont, eds., *Letters of John Masefield to Florence Lamont* (London, 1979).

Lancelyn Green, Roger, *Fifty Years of Peter Pan* (London, 1954).

Langham, Mike, and Colin Wells, *Buxton, A Pictorial History* (Chichester, 1993).

Lawrence, Arthur, *Sir Arthur Sullivan, Life-Story, Letters, and Reminiscences* (London, 1899) [the von Glehns].

Lehmann, R. C., MP, *Memories of Half a Century, A Record of Friendships* (London, 1908) [the von Glehns].

Mackerness, E. D., *A Social History of English Music* (London, 1964).

Mander, Raymond, and Joe Mitchenson, *The Theatres of London*, 2nd, revised edn (London, 1975).

Mitchell, W. R., *Mr Elgar and Dr. Buck, A Musical Friendship* (Giggleswick, 1991).

Moore, Gerald, *Singer and Accompanist* (London, 1982).

Musgrave, Michael, *The Musical Life of the Crystal Palace* (Cambridge, 1995).

Nicholas, Jeremy, *Godowsky, the Pianists' Pianist* (Hexham, 1989) [Leo Ornstein].

Northcote, Sydney, *Byrd to Britten* (London, 1966).

Palmer, Christopher, *Portrait of a Cosmopolitan* (London, 1976).

Philip, Robert, *Early Recordings and Musical Style: Changing Tastes in Instrumental Performance, 1900–1950* (Cambridge, 1992).

Pratt, A. T. C., *People of the Period* (1897) [Sir Cuthbert Quilter].

Reid, Charles, *Malcolm Sargent, A Biography* (London, 1968).

Rohrer, Katherine T., 'Interactions of Phonology and Music in Purcell's Two Settings of "Thy genius, lo"', *Studies in the History of Music*, vol. 1, Music and Language (New York, 1983).

Rosen, Carole, *The Goossens, A Musical Century* (London, 1993).

Scott, Derek B., *The Singing Bourgeois: Songs of the Victorian Drawing Room and Parlour*, 2nd edn (Aldershot, 2001).

Scowcroft, Philip L., *British Light Music: A Personal Gallery of 20th-Century Composers* (London, 1997).

Shorter, Edward, *A History of Psychiatry: from the Era of the Asylum to the Age of Prozac* (New York, 1997) [mental health treatments].

Smith, Barry, ed., *The Occasional Writings of Philip Heseltine (Peter Warlock)*, Vol. 1 (London, 1997).

Smith, Constance Babington, *John Masefield, A Life* (Oxford, 1978) [Jane and Wilfrid de Glehn].

Stanford, Sir Charles Villiers, *Pages from an Unwritten Diary* (London, 1914) [the von Glehns].

Stephen, Leslie, ed., *Letters of John Richard Green* (London, 1901) [the von Glehns].

Stevens, Denis, ed., *A History of Song* (London, 1960).

Taruskin, Richard, '"Entoiling the Falconet": Russian Musical Orientalism in Context', *The Exotic in Western Music*, ed. Jonathan Bellman (Boston, 1998).

Tertis, Lionel, *My Viola and I, A Complete Autobiography* (London, 1974).

Traubner, Richard, *Operetta, A Theatrical History* (Oxford, 1983).

Trend, Michael, *The Music Makers, Heirs and Rebels of the English Musical Renaissance* (London, 1985).

Tunley, David, *Salons, Singers and Songs, A Background to Nineteenth Century French Song* (Aldershot, 2002).

Van Wyk Smith, Malvern, *Drummer Hodge, The Poetry of the Anglo-Boer War (1899–1902)* (Oxford, 1978).

Walker, Ernest, *A History of Music in England*, revised and enlarged by J. A. Westrup, 3rd edn (Oxford, 1952).

Warlock, Peter, *The English Ayre* (Oxford, 1926).

Warwick, Peter, ed., *The South African War: The Anglo-Boer War 1899–1902* (Harlow, 1980).

Watkins, Michael, *An East Anglian Journey – Landscape with Figures* (Ipswich, 1983) [Bawdsey Manor].

Weeks, Jeffrey, and Kevin Porter, eds., *Between the Acts: Lives of Homosexual Men 1885–1967*, 2nd edn (London, 1998).

Weininger, Otto, *Sex and Character*, 2nd edn (London, 1906).

Weinreb, Ben, and Christopher Hibbert, eds., *The London Encyclopaedia* (London, 1983).

Williams, Harcourt, *Old Vic Saga* (London, 1949) [*As You Like It*].

Wolfson, John, *Sullivan and the Scott Russells, A Victorian Love Affair Told through the Letters of Rachel and Louise Scott Russell to Arthur Sullivan 1864–1870* (Chichester, 1984) [the von Glehns].

Wood, Henry J., *My Life of Music* (London, 1938).

Wyndham, H. Saxe, *Arthur Seymour Sullivan (1842–1900)* (London, 1926).

Wyndham, H. Saxe, *August Manns and the Saturday Concerts* (London, 1909).

Young, Kenneth, *Music's Great Days in the Spas and Watering-Places* (London, 1968).

Young, Percy M., *Pageant of England's Music* (Cambridge, 1939).

Zipes, Jack, *Fairy Tale as Myth, Myth as Fairy Tale* (Lexington, 1994).

General Index

Index of Works

First lines of texts, where they differ from the title of the song

Works